Far From The Madding Crowd:

The Study Guide Edition

Thomas Hardy

Francis Gilbert

This edition first published in 2015 by FGI publishing:
www.francisgilbert.co.uk;
fgipublishing.com
Copyright © 2015 Francis Gilbert
FGI Publishing, London UK, sir@francisgilbert.co.uk
British Library Cataloguing-in-Publications Data
A catalogue record for this book is available from the British Library.
ISBN-13: 978-1519759139

ISBN-10: 1519759134

Dedication
For Jennifer Logan.

Acknowledgments
First, huge thanks must go to my wife, Erica Wagner, for always supporting me with my writing and teaching. Second, I'm very grateful to all the students, teachers, lecturers and other lively people who have helped me write this book.
Also by Francis Gilbert:
I'm A Teacher, Get Me Out Of Here (2004)
Teacher On The Run (2005)
Yob Nation (2006)
Parent Power (2007)
Working The System: How To Get The Very State Education For Your Child (2011)
The Last Day Of Term (2012)
Gilbert's Study Guides on: *Frankenstein, Far From The Madding Crowd, The Hound of the Baskervilles, Pride and Prejudice, The Strange Case of Dr Jekyll and Mr Hyde, The Turn of the Screw, Wuthering Heights* (2013)
Dr Jekyll & Mr Hyde: The Study Guide Edition (2014)
Romeo and Juliet: The Study Guide Edition (2014)
Charlotte Brontë's Jane Eyre: The Study Guide Edition (2015)
Austen's Pride and Prejudice: The Study Guide Edition (2015)
Mary Shelley's Frankenstein: The Study Guide Edition (2015)
The Turn of the Screw: The Study Guide Edition (2015)
The Hound of the Baskervilles: The Study Guide Edition

Contents

Introduction

This study guide takes a different approach from most other similar texts. It does not seek to tell you about the story and characters in a boring, useless fashion, but attempts to show how it is the author's techniques and interests that inform every single facet of this classic novel. Most study guides simply tell you *what* is going on, and tack on bits at the end which tell you *how* the writer created suspense and drama at certain points in the book, informing you a little about *why* the writer might have done this.

This study guide starts with the *how* and the *why*, showing you right from the start *how* and *why* the writer shaped the key elements of the book.

Definition:
The context of a book is both the *world* the book creates in the reader's mind (contexts of reading), and the *world* it came out from (contexts of writing).

How to use this Study Guide Edition

This study guide is deliberately interactive; it is full of questions, tasks and links to other sources of information. You will learn about *Far From The Madding Crowd* much more effectively if you have a go at the questions and tasks set, rather than just copying out notes.

Contexts

Understanding Contexts

In order to fully appreciate a text, you need to appreciate the contexts in which it was written – known as its contexts of writing – and the contexts in which you read the book, or the contexts of reading.

This is potentially a huge area to explore because 'contexts' essentially means the 'worlds' from which the book has arisen. For the best books, these are many and various. The most obvious starting point is the writer's own life: it is worth thinking about how and why the events in a writer's life might have influenced his or her fiction. However, you do have to be careful not to assume too much. For example, some critics have suggested that Bathsheba, the feisty, beautiful heroine of the novel, is based on Hardy's cousin, Tryphena Sparks, but you must remember that Bathsheba is a character in her own right in the novel – a vital cog in the narrative wheel, a literary construct and not a real person!

As a result, it is particularly fruitful to explore other contexts of writing.

We can look at the broader world from which Thomas Hardy arose (the rural Dorset society he grew up in, the respectable Victorian world he came to know as an adult), and consider carefully how, in his writing, he both adopted and rejected the morals of his time. Other contexts might be the influence of the literary world that [the author] inhabited (what other authors were writing at the time), how religion shaped his views, and so on.

Just as important as the contexts of *writing* are the contexts of *reading*: how we read the novel today. Most of us, before we read a classic novel by Thomas Hardy, have a lot of preconceived ideas about it. Many of us will have seen one or more of the many film versions of the book, and/or been influenced by what we have already heard about Hardy. Your own personal context is very important too. A feminist will view Bathsheba's search for independence in a very different light from a person who believes a woman's place is in the home. In order for you to fully consider the contexts of reading rather than my telling you what to think, I have posed open-ended questions that seem to me to be important when considering this issue.

Questions

What do we mean by context? Why do you need to understand the idea of context in order to write well about *Far From The Madding Crowd*?

Useful links

This BBC Bitesize webpage refers to poetry, but is relevant for all literature, providing a good visual organizer of the relevant things to think about when talking about context:
http://www.bbc.co.uk/education/guides/z8kyg82/revision

Contexts of Writing: Thomas Hardy's Life

Thomas Hardy was both on 2nd June 1840 in a picturesque thatched cottage in a tiny hamlet called Higher Bockhampton. Set amidst a wood, it was surrounded by a huge heath, Egdon or Puddletown Heath. The cottage remains as it was in Hardy's day and is now a museum devoted to the writer.

There's no doubt that the formative person in his early life was his mother whose maiden name was Jemima Hand. She'd been a cook and had grown up in extreme poverty, being orphaned at an early age. Her one escape into another world was books – a love of which she passed onto her son. Her husband, the 'second' Thomas Hardy – the first TH being reputedly a smuggler – was a skilled violinist and building contractor who employed about a dozen men.

Hardy nearly died at birth, having had a difficult birth. Three more children followed: Mary, Henry and Katherine. None of them married and there were no Hardys in the next generation. Hardy throughout his life had a sense there was something wrong with his family. He wrote once: "The decline and fall of the Hardys much in evidence hereabout...So we go down, down, down." His father, although initially successful as a business man failed to expand his empire, refusing to move from the tiny hamlet of Higher Bockhampton. While the Hardys were amongst the upper class of the village, once they stepped outside it, they were insignificant. It's perhaps no surprise that a deep sense of class consciousness permeates all of Hardy's novels as a consequence. This is particularly the case with *Far From The Madding Crowd*; in order to appreciate the novel fully you have to understand the nuances of class which run throughout the book.

As a child Hardy was very precocious, reading before he could walk, learning the violin quickly and immersing himself in the mysteries of the local church at Stinsford. A sickly child, he seems to have stayed home much of the time under the protection of his mother. At the age of eight, he attended Isaac Last's Academy in Dorchester. He walked the three miles there and back through the country lanes every day. He became an outstanding pupil, winning the Latin prize and excelling in maths and French. Leaving school in 1856, at the age of sixteen, he was apprenticed to an architect in Dorchester, John Hicks. In the large, bustling town of Dorchester, which Hardy would later immortalise as Casterbridge, he met Horace Moule, a young man eight years older than Hardy, who was a freelance writer: it was Moule would become a guiding light, encouraging Hardy to read widely and take up writing poetry.

In 1862, he "started alone for London, to pursue the art and science of architecture on the more advanced lines". There he completed his education, developing his skill as an architectural draughtsman: he became a student at King's College, London and won prizes for his work at the Royal Institute of British Architects and the Architectural Association.

Although unhappy in London, he investigated the city intensively. At this point, he was determined to be a poet – but never assumed he would become famous. However, while he gained a deeper professional knowledge as an architect in London and developed his poetry, he was lonely and ill. In 1867, he returned to the country on leave, becoming much better. In Dorchester, he fell in love with his cousin, Tryphena Sparks, who was a teacher at a local school in Puddletown, becoming engaged to her. On returning to London, his friendship with his cousin Tryphena Sparks developed further: she too was in London at a training college. For some unknown reason, the engagement was broken off and Tryphena lost her job at the Puddletown school. Some biographers have speculated this was because she was pregnant, claiming she gave birth to Hardy's son, who died in childhood. None of this is definitely proven, but we do know she later married another man, having four children by him, before dying at the age of 38.

In the late 1860s, Hardy began writing, penning one of the first socialist novels – which was never published – and then pursuing more commercial fiction. Publishers were interested in his fascinating portraits of country life, something that middle class readers of the time loved to read about. In March 1870, having finished another novel, Hardy went down to Cornwall to restore the parish church of St. Juliot, where he met and fell in love with Emma Gifford. This time in Cornwall would have a profound effect upon him. After Emma's death, in 1912, he would write some of the finest love poems in the language about his memories of falling in love with her amidst the beauty of the coast. While later on Emma would become ashamed of Hardy's writing, there is no doubt she encouraged him to pursue a career as a novelist. Having suffered from a relative lack of success, she insisted he carried on writing. Her encouragement would pay off because he was contracted to write for the *Cornhill Magazine*, writing novels in serial form, and publishing chapters in a weekly or monthly form. Writing in serial form meant Hardy had to write to a deadline and pack his chapters with action and drama because otherwise no one would want to buy the next edition. Furthermore, because the magazines were aimed a respectable middle-class audience, he had to make sure he did not offend any sensibilities. In such a way, he wrote *A Pair Of Blue Eyes*, a romantic comedy, and then began work on *Far From The Madding Crowd*.

He had now given up his architectural work and working full-time as a writer in Dorset, enjoying the solitude of the countryside, which helped him to do good work. The novel is, in many ways, shaped by the serial form in which it came out: virtually every chapter contains some kind of cliff-hanger, and there are definite moments when Hardy leaves his reader begging for more. The book did offend some people: the seduction of Fanny Robin prompted some complaints. But overall, the novel was a triumphant success – and to this day remains the popular favourite among Hardy's novels because of its happy ending, which again was there because of the way it was published. The story was so successful that Hardy felt he could get married to Emma. On 17th September 1874 he and Emma had a quiet wedding in London.

In many ways, *Far From The Madding Crowd* launched Hardy's literary career because it was so successful. It was the novel that his Victorian public wanted him to write again and again, but in his biography he notes that "he had not the slightest intention of writing for ever about sheep-farming, as the reading public was apparently expecting him to do, and as, in fact, they resented his not doing."

When the book was published in book form, Hardy was surprised to see so many people carrying copying. The book was warmly received on both sides of the Atlantic. The novelist, Henry James, wrote one of the most interesting reviews, saying: "The most genuine thing in his book, to our sense, is a certain aroma of the meadows and lanes – a natural relish for harvesting and sheep-washings. He has laid his scene in the agricultural county, and his characters are the children of the soil – unsophisticated country folk." The review is important because it characterises what many people thought of Hardy's work at the time: that it was rather brilliant at describing country ways, but that it was essential unsophisticated.

This was a straight-jacket that Hardy spent the rest of his career as a novelist trying to escape. The rest of his novel writing career is really about him experimenting. While he has his share of novels that don't quite succeed, he writes a number of masterpieces. In *The Return Of The Native* (1878), he evoked the great heath of his childhood, telling the story about a teacher who returns to his rural home to try and change the world but like Oak becomes enraptured by a difficult, beautiful woman. In 1885, he published *The Mayor Of Casterbridge* which is about a drunk who sells his wife only to repent his sin and become a very important member of the community, but finding his past crime comes back to haunt him. Switching scene, Hardy describes the life of his childhood's village in *The Woodlanders* (1887), depicting a local woodlander finding his lover leaves him for an educated doctor. His last two novels are overwhelming tragic in tone. With *Tess of the D'Urbervilles* (1891), he describes how a dairy maid murders her husband and has to be executed for the crime. While with *Jude the Obscure* (1895), he uncovers the life of a stone mason who dreams of becoming a scholar but can't because of his lowly social position, taking up with the wife of a school teacher, he has a child with her – and is ostracized as a result.

Jude the Obscure provoked a furious reaction amongst the reading public who were disgusted at its sympathetic portrayal of an unmarried couple having sex and children. The Bishop of Wakefield publicly burnt the book. Hardy was so depressed by the reaction to the novel that he gave up writing novels and turned his attention to poetry. He wrote a huge amount of poetry, but nothing was as successful as the poems he wrote after the death of his first wife in 1912. After her death, he made a trip to Cornwall and re-visited the places they spent time together.

He married his secretary, Florence Emily Dugdale, in 1914. She was 39 years his junior. However, he remained pre-occupied with his first wife until the day he died, revisiting the themes of love and loss again and again in his best poetry. By the end of his life, Hardy became an establishment figure, receiving the Order of Merit in 1910, gaining honorary degrees from Oxford and Cambridge, and being buried in Poet's Corner in Westminster Abbey after his death as a very old man in 1928.

Questions

Why do you think the book might be called *Far From The Madding Crowd*?

What events, people and ideas in Hardy's life and the wider society may have influenced the writing of the story?

Useful links

For more on Hardy's life look here:

http://www.victorianweb.org/authors/hardy/bio.html
https://en.wikipedia.org/wiki/Thomas_Hardy
http://www.britannica.com/biography/Thomas-Hardy

This British Library article contains some fascinating contextual points about the novel:

http://www.bl.uk/romantics-and-victorians/articles/writing-publishing-and-revising-far-from-the-madding-crowd

Selected Reading on Thomas Hardy's Life

Claire Tomalin: *Thomas Hardy: The Time-torn Man* (Penguin: 2007)

Tomalin is our foremost literary biographer, writing classic biographies of Pepys, Austen, Dickens. Her account of Hardy puts his poems about his wife at the centre of all his work, the defining moment of his literary career. Tomalin rejects the notion that Hardy had a child by Tryphena Sparks as somewhat fanciful, but considers all the evidence. Above all, she evokes the times Hardy lived in and the people he knew. It is the most readable of all the biographies.

Ralph Pite: Thomas Hardy: *The Guarded Life* (Picador: 2007)

An exhaustive biography which details all the links between the life and the work.

Thomas and Florence Hardy: *The Life of Thomas Hardy* (Wordsworth Literary Lives: 2007) This book was originally attributed to Hardy's second wife, but now is generally believed to be Hardy's own work. It skips over the more difficult episodes in his life – his engagement with Tryphena Sparks is glossed over – but is remarkable because of the way it talks about the influences upon his work: the ballads, the poems, and the country life.

Contexts of Reading

We read *Far From The Madding Crowd* now very differently from the way Hardy's Victorian readership read the book. But before we explore those differences, it is worth exploring some similarities. Above all, it is worth bearing in mind that the rural life that Hardy describes would have been just as foreign to most of his readers as it is to us. Most of his readers were middle-class urban Victorians who had virtually no contact with agricultural workers and very little knowledge of the lives they led. Moreover, in the novel, Hardy is describing the lost world of his childhood, certain rituals such as the tossing of the hymn-book, the sheep-washing, the hay-making, the drinking of the cider in the malt-house were vanishing rapidly as Hardy wrote the book as the farms became more mechanised and dispensed with farm labourers. His readership were just as remote from these things as we are, perhaps more so because, unlike us, they had very little access to pictures, photographs, information about farming. It's worth bearing this in mind because much of the pleasure that can be gained from reading the book is enjoying the richness of detail about this lost world: certainly this is how Hardy's readers enjoy his novels now, losing themselves in the rural worlds he evokes.

At the root of our differences in the way we perceive the novel are our perceptions of the main protagonist, Bathsheba. Certainly, nearly all of Hardy's readers would have read the novel as an essentially moral fable about how Bathsheba is tamed by events and Oak: they would have viewed this as a good thing. Her behaviour for them at the beginning of the novel – her rejection of Oak, her determination to run the farm, her sending of the Valentine to Boldwood, her rejection of him, her marriage to Troy – would have been viewed as outrageous behaviour for a proper lady. Thus, when she finally marries Oak and has obviously been humbled by the experience, the Victorian readers would have viewed that as a good thing.

Modern readers may view the 'taming' of the wild Bathsheba very differently. From our perspective now, we could view this novel as an essentially feminist novel about one woman's struggle for independence in a man's world. The novel is about her attempt to find her own path in life: to find the work she wants to do, to find the partner she most wants to be with, to live the life she wants to lead. But the society that she lives in and fate thwarts her: she is forced to give up being bailiff of the farm because she has not the technical know-how to do the job – she hasn't been educated that way – and she finds that her husband has had a child with another woman. Eventually, by the end of the novel, she has to concede that she can't make her way without a steady man by her side. In such a way, a feminist might view her marriage to Oak at the end as an admission of defeat; an acceptance that she needs him to sustain her life. She has clearly been deeply traumatized and crushed by the events that have happened to her: she is no longer the vivacious girl of a few years before.

Furthermore, the modern reader might see more clearly than the

Victorian readership that this novel is about desire and sexual awakenings. It is Bathsheba's sexual awakening which creates the most memorable scene in the book when she is mesmerised by Troy's sword exercise. Freudian critics have viewed Troy's sword as a phallic symbol, an embodiment of his sexual prowess, and Bathsheba's hypnotised, guilty pleasure in being kissed as evidence of her sexual awakening. Finally, with Troy she has found what she believes is a sexually compatible partner, a man who she desires physically. However, she learns during the marriage that he has lost interest in her – that his lust for her was in the chase, not in being with her. This and the discovery of his affair and child by Fanny Robin prompt a breakdown from which she never fully recovers. She realises that her friendship with Oak is the stuff on which marriages are built – the way they talk to each other, the way they work together – not her sexual infatuation with Troy.

Bathsheba is a truly complex characterisation, living beyond the realm of stereotype: Hardy takes great care to present her as someone whose emotions and thoughts are constantly changing, constantly re-evaluating events and people. The same could not be said of Troy, who rarely goes beyond the stereotype of the seductive soldier. He has stepped out of a country ballad: the glittering soldier who ruins women. It is clear that his motivations are in hunting women, not being with them. He never comes to understand the nature of his desire because he is not a fully-rounded character, although there are a few moments when he is looking at the dead Fanny and child when we see him as a more complex, tragic figure, trapped by his desire to chase and never settle – and realising this.

William Boldwood is another character who has an alarming sexual awakening: the sending of the Valentine triggers an obsession which eventually causes him to murder Troy. Again, the modern reader interprets him very differently from the Victorian one. His obsession with Bathsheba is definitely voyeuristic: he has to watch her from afar, preferring not to talk to her but simply view her. He has actually little interest in her personality, but is obsessive about her appearance and about possessing her. In such a way, we could say that Hardy's characterisation of him is very modern: there is a fetishism revealed about Boldwood at the end of the novel. His buying of clothes for Bathsheba which suggests he gains sexual gratification from them. He is like a character you might now find in a thriller, someone who intent upon spying upon a woman obsessively. The Victorians would have viewed him very differently: he is the one respectable character in the book, the local landowner and gentry. His fall from grace would have been less shocking for them because they wouldn't have interpreted sexual motives: they would have believed that Bathsheba was foolish to reject him.

Finally, Oak could be viewed differently now. Whereas in Victorian times, Oak would have definitely been a character who embodied the Victorian virtues of stability, of upright morals, of loving fidelity, now we could interpret him as a more troubling figure. Feminists might say that he crushes Bathsheba: he frequently spies upon her, criticises her, and, at the end of the novel, makes sure that she keeps to his bidding. It is clear at the end of the novel that he is the one who is in charge. Perhaps though this is an uncharitable way of looking at him. Most saliently, Oak, being a child of nature and a farmer, does not undergo any kind of sexual awakening: it is clear that he treats sex as a natural phenomena and, unlike Boldwood, is not lacking in knowledge about the nature of his desire. This is obvious at the beginning of the novel, when he proposes to Bathsheba, promising to give her plenty of babies because he is very attracted to her. As his name suggests, Oak is both of the earth and angelic; he is both like the angel Gabriel, constantly watching over Bathsheba, and rooted in the earth like an oak tree. He embodies true rural English qualities: he is natural, strong, faithful. These still virtues people value now, but perhaps we value them less than the Victorians did because we are a society which is more materialistic than the Victorian world. Ultimately, Oak is the one character who is truly 'far from the madding crowd' because he is not interested in worldly approbation but strives to be loyal and true.

Questions

It is worth doing some work on contexts before starting the actual book. I would suggest you write a *Far From The Madding Crowd* **learning journal** that records all your thoughts and feelings about the book. Records the truth! After reading the book once, we will then look at academic responses but on the first reading we will really focus upon your thoughts about it.

There are two major questions to consider when thinking about contexts: where is the book coming from and where am I coming from?

The first question is best answered while reading the book; what sorts of values and ideas are enshrined in this book? What is its historical context? What is its literary context? What is its philosophical context? How does the book relate to the life of the author?

It is worth you trying to analyse where you are coming from. Everyone holds a set of assumptions and ideas that profoundly affects how he or she sees the world. Try and answer these questions:

What are your attitudes towards stories set in the country and about love and betrayal? What are your favourite love stories and why? Who are your favourite heroes and heroines in romantic stories and why?

What is the position of women in these stories?

What are your attitudes towards strong women?

What do the concepts of love and betrayal mean to you? Why do you think love and betrayal are often closely linked?

Now onto the text

What are the vital ingredients of a story? Why is that we are able to believe that a "whole load of words" contain a new world?

Now jot down your expectations about *Far From The Madding Crowd*. What kind of book do you expect it to be?

Write/sketch/spider-diagram what you think the story will be. Write out how you think it will be structured. What will be the main events of the story? Who will be the main characters and why?

While reading the novel, look back over the notes you have made for this section and constantly ask yourself; how does my context affect the way I read the novel and feel/think about the characters/situations/themes? I have already suggested that you write a **learning journal** as you read it through, jotting down these thoughts as you go along. Then once you have finished reading, think about the novel's overall effects and how it speaks to you personally.

Why do you think *Far From The Madding Crowd* is such a popular novel today? Why have so many films/plays/operas etc. been made of it?

Useful links

This *Guardian* article compares the book a modern film version: **http://www.theguardian.com/books/2015/apr/24/far-from-the-madding-crowd-hardys-novel**

This Wikipedia entry discusses the most famous film version made in the 1960s:
https://en.wikipedia.org/wiki/Far_from_the_Madding_Crowd_(1967_film)

This webpage gives details on a modern version:
http://www.imdb.com/title/tt2935476/

This article discusses the relevance of the novel now:
http://interestingliterature.com/2015/04/19/interesting-facts-about-far-from-the-madding-crowd/

A modern day best-selling author discusses the feminist aspects of the book here:
http://www.harpersbazaar.co.uk/culture-news/news/david-nicholls-on-feminism-in-far-from-the-madding-crowd

Structure and Theme

There are a few different ways of looking at this novel. Its two most obvious themes are love and fate. If we were to examine how Hardy structures the novel around the theme of love we could take either Oak or Bathsheba see that he cleverly shapes the narrative around their search for love. In some senses, this novel is about Oak's quest for Bathsheba's love and we could break it down accordingly into some distinct stages. Oak sees, meets and is rescued from death by Bathsheba in the Norcombe farm area of Wessex. His love for her develops quickly and he proposes to her, only to be rejected. Having all his fortune and livelihood when his sheep die, he meets her again and spends much time trying to look after her while she is pursued by Boldwood and then pursues and marries Troy. After the death of Troy and the incarceration of Boldwood, he remains with her but decides to leave because he feels he can't have her: she then proposes to him in a very indirect way. He achieves his goal: to marry Bathsheba. If we were to view the novel as being shaped around Bathsheba's quest for love, it would be more complex because her emotional life is much more turbulent than Oak's. After her initial rejection of Oak, she is enticed by Boldwood's lack of interest in her and sends him a Valentine. However, she is not enamoured by his approaches to her at the sheep-washing and rejects his offer of marriage, feeling considerably confused about her troubling behaviour towards him. She falls in love with Troy because it is clear to us – though not to her --- that she is sexually enraptured by him. The marriage fails because the two of them are not compatible: she is too clever and independent for Troy, he is too irresponsible and uninterested for her. The discovery of the dead Fanny and child prompt a crisis and breakdown in Bathsheba. Troy disappears. Now that he is gone, Bathsheba is beaten down by Boldwood's obsessive insistence that he must marry her: she agrees to do so in six years' time. When Troy returns and is killed by Boldwood, both of the difficult men in her life are removed in one fell swoop. She comes to realise that she actually needs Oak more than anybody: it is clear though that her attraction for him is borne of practical need and friendship, more than strident desire. She has learnt what true love is.

While love is the dominant theme of the book, fate plays a huge role too. Indeed, most the events in the novel happen because of fate. Oak's life is only saved by Bathsheba when she hears his dog barking by chance. The loss of Oak's sheep prompts him fatefully to find work at Bathsheba's farm, which, by coincidence, happens to be on fire as he is passing. His putting out of the fire leads him to gain work at the farm, which he realises now is owned by Bathsheba. Fate plays the dominant role in the sending of the Valentine which triggers Boldwood's obsession with Bathsheba. Likewise, it is only fate which brings Troy and Bathsheba together when they are tangled up together in the fir plantation. Bathsheba might not have learnt about Fanny and the child if Joseph Poorgrass had got the coffin to the cemetery on time. Fate brings Troy back to Bathsheba when he sees her by chance at the fayre: it is this sighting which leads to the tragic climax of the novel.

However, even though love and fate are undoubtedly the dominant themes of the novel, I think it is most fruitful to see the novel as being structured around Bathsheba's quest for independence: this is what makes the novel so modern, if not in atmosphere, but in theme. It is a proto-type feminist novel in this sense.

We could break down the novel into the following structure:

Opening
Bathsheba rejects Oak's proposal because she needs to be tamed, she is too independent;
Bathsheba fatefully inherits Weatherbury farm after the death of her uncle and becomes mistress of her own destiny.

Complications
Bathsheba tries to assert her independence by making herself bailiff of the farm: she is in charge of the day-to-day running of the farm;
Bathsheba sends the Valentine but rejects Boldwood's offer of marriage because she wants to find someone she truly loves;
She meets Troy, becomes infatuated by him, pursues him, and marries him abruptly and secretly.

Crisis
Bathsheba is troubled by her husband's reluctance to help running the farm, his resentment of her independence;
She discovers the truth about Troy's affair with Fanny.

Climax
Troy disappears and she struggles to remain independent from Boldwood, accepting his proposal of marriage, albeit in a very reluctant fashion;
Boldwood shoots Troy, leaving her independent once again.

Resolution
Bathsheba realises that she can't be an independent woman: she is clearly a broken woman, much of her old wild spirit having vanished;
She encourages Oak to marry her.

Useful links to help you get to know the novel better

You can find detailed summaries on these websites:
http://www.cliffsnotes.com/literature/f/far-from-the-madding-crowd/book-summary
http://www.sparknotes.com/lit/maddingcrowd/summary.html

You can find a very **simple version** of the story here:
http://www.penguinreaders.com/pdf/downloads/pr/teachers-notes/9781405879569.pdf

For quizzes on the story, look here:
http://www.cliffsnotes.com/literature/f/far-from-the-madding-crowd/study-help/quiz
http://www.sparknotes.com/lit/maddingcrowd/quiz.html
http://www.shmoop.com/far-from-the-madding-crowd/symbols-quiz.html

Questions/tasks

Once you have read the book, ask yourself this question: to what extent is the novel a successful story? What are its exciting moments and why? Are there moments when the story feels less successful? Give reasons for your answers.

Compare one or two filmed versions with the novel; what events/characters/ideas do the film-makers use and what do they leave out, and why?

The Influence of Genre: the pastoral

Far from the madding crowd's ignoble strife,
Their sober wishes never learn'd to stray;
Along the cool sequester'd vale of life
They kept the noiseless tenour of their way.
From Thomas Gray's 'Elegy Written in a Country Grave-
yard'.

The genre of the 'pastoral idyll' pervades the whole of *Far From The Madding Crowd*. The fact that the title is taken from Thomas Gray's famous long poem which celebrates the unknown heroes who have lived 'far from the madding crowd' in the country, away from the 'ignoble strife' – or shameful fighting – of the city indicates Hardy's love of the genre. On every page of the book, you'll find lovingly described details of rural Dorset life. The novel is, above all, a celebration of the ways of the country: the rhythms of the seasons, the times of the day, the rituals and songs of country-folk, the honest toil of farming. By the end of the novel, the reader has not only read an entertaining narrative but is also much better informed about the tending of sheep, farmer's markets, hay-making, hiving of bees, the making and drinking of cider, country fayres, storms, blazing hot days and cool, mysterious nights. In this sense, Hardy's portrait of the country is influenced by the pastoral idyll of the countryside which chiefly has been written about by poets, not novelists. In his lush, loving descriptions, you can see the influence of Shakespeare (As You Like It and a Midsummer Night's Dream) of Christopher Marlowe (The Passionate Shepherd to his Love), of Wordsworth (The Prelude), of Keats (To Autumn), William Blake (The Songs of Innocence). What is fascinating about Hardy is that he manages to take these poetic influences and help them paint a backdrop to his novel.

The narrative too is very much influenced by the pastoral: the fact that the primary theme is about love means that Hardy has taken a central theme of the pastoral idyll and structured it into a dynamic story. Moreover, there are elements of the country ballad in the story; particularly with the narrative of Fanny Robin and Troy. A very familiar country ballad is the story of the fair maiden who is ruined by a dashing soldier.

For all the romanticism that Hardy shows, this is not purely an 'idyllic' portrait of the countryside in the way that many poets have painted with their words. Hardy reveals the countryside to be far from perfect. This is perhaps most chillingly illustrated in the treatment of Fanny, who pregnant and without work, starves to death being forced to find refuge in the evil workhouse. While Bathsheba is keen to protect her workers, it is clear that she is very much the exception: Fanny does not find help elsewhere. Furthermore, the narrative itself is by no means a light comedy. Most strikingly, Boldwood's psychotic, jealous fury is not what one would expect from a squire in a pastoral idyll.

There are though plenty of other genres that influenced Hardy in the writing of the book. The fact that it was written for serial meant that Hardy had to have a very eventful narrative to keep his readers hooked: he did this by taking elements of the domestic melodrama. In this sense, Trollope's *Barchester Towers* could be said to be a formative influence, not in its subject matter – it's about the world of the church – but in the way it depicts the lives of small-town people, showing them in minute, psychological detail. Unlike Trollope, Hardy is not overwhelmingly comic, though there are often moments of comedy, particularly with the locals. The end of the novel, perhaps one of the weakest elements of the book, is pure Victorian theatre: the shooting of Troy is the stuff that would have been found on the London stage at the time Hardy was living there.

Most importantly though, Hardy is forging his own genre here: the Wessex novel. The world he conjures in the book is one which he will return to again and again in his fiction and poetry, using the fictional place names to evoke a community which is both realistic and romantic. No writer before Hardy had been so accurate in writing about ordinary country folk, so precise with in their description of nature, so ambitious in their ability to embrace the great cosmic themes of love, fate and frustration, so subtle in their charting of human psychology. For all his interest in the tiny world of Weatherbury farm, Hardy's ambitions are huge: he is determined to explore huge issues, the nature of human desire, the meaning of life, the true moral path to travel down.

Questions for Genre

How was Hardy influenced by other writers and genres in the writing of the story? Where did he get his ideas for his characters from?

Useful links

Shmoop website discusses genre here:
http://www.shmoop.com/far-from-the-madding-crowd/genre.html
This British Library website contains a wealth of information about the novel:
http://www.bl.uk/works/far-from-the-madding-crowd

Critical Perspectives

Is this novel really about sex?

Many critics have argued that it is! The most famous of these is the novelist D.H. Lawrence who asserts that Troy is the only person who understands Bathsheba because he understands her sexual nature. Meanwhile, other critics assert that Bathsheba is one in a long line of women that Hardy created that he, himself, was sexually enthralled by and thus we see how she uses the sexual fascination that men have in her to manipulate them to do her bidding. Moreover, most critics now accept that the underlying them of the novel is sexual desire in all its manifest forms: every main character is sexually motivated. Oak's desire for Bathsheba means he never leaves her and when he does finally marry her, he insists that she wears her hair in the same way that she did when he most desired her when they first met. Boldwood, as we have seen, is so obsessed with her that he keeps her imaginary clothes close to him. Troy spends his happiest moments with her pursuing her, attempting to seduce her.

Feminists insist that for all her sexual fascination, Bathsheba is a victim of male desire. Some have argued that Oak's criticism of Bathsheba's vanity is an 'insidious form of subjugation' – in other words, for his protestations of love, Oak's main motivation is to control Bathsheba, not love her. For them, they see the novel's success created by society's increasing unease about the role of women. Fascinatingly the novel became very popular again during the 1960s when Julie Christie played Bathsheba in a filmed version of the book: it struck a chord because Christie played Bathsheba as a proto-feminist – and Oak was like a hippy, living off the land, a child of nature. Boldwood represented the old guard, the establishment, who the youth of Bathsheba and Troy reject and humiliate.

Other critics have focused upon the way Hardy depicts the country folk in the novel, noticing that they are very much victims of an iniquitous system. Hardy reveals them to be intelligent, hard-working and keen, but essentially dispensable, the playthings of their masters. It is a theme which Hardy will develop in his other works: there is very much a socialist sensibility implicit in the novel though because there is a deep sense of the inequality and injustice in the novel. The way Hardy juxtaposes the fate of Fanny Robin with Bathsheba is the best example of this: Fanny and her child die because she is poor.

Selected Reading & weblinks on Hardy's writing and *Far From The Madding Crowd*

Geoffrey Harvey: *The Complete Critical Guide to Thomas Hardy* (Routledge; 2003) An excellent, well-written, modern guide to Thomas Hardy which deals extensively with the novel, talking about how Hardy's life influenced the novel, the influence of the pastoral, and different critics' views of the novel.

Merryn Williams *A Preface to Hardy* (Longman; 1976) The Longman Guides remain unsurpassed in their ability to discuss the contexts of Hardy's life and his literary influences.

Ian Gregor: *The Great Web – The Form of Hardy's Major Fiction* (Faber and Faber; 1974) There is an excellent, detailed chapter on the novel in this lively exploration of Hardy's work.

There is a discussion of the novel here:
http://www.online-literature.com/hardy/madding/

Questions

What differing views do literary critics have of the novel? Which critics do you most agree with and why? Which ones do you agree with the least and why?

Part 2: Complete text & tasks

How to read and study the novel

What follows is the complete text of *Far From The Madding Crowd* interspersed with commentaries and questions on the text. The text is broken up with analysis and points for discussion. I have deliberately provided a variety of different question types at the ends of chapters; I have started with "simple" comprehension questions and then moved onto more analytical and creative questions, which not only require you to understand the plot but also arrive at your own personal responses, using evidence from the text to back up your points. The answers to the comprehension questions can be found in the **Answers to the questions** section. The GCSE/A Level questions that follow the comprehension ones are more difficult and don't usually have "right and wrong" answers. The GCSE style questions are the sorts of questions you might typically get in a GCSE exam; the same is true for the A Level questions, which usually invite students to show they have read more and are able to compare and contrast texts in depth. Please interpret the categories of GCSE/A Level in a relaxed fashion: have a go at the exercises which will help you rather than rigidly sticking to the exercises that are "your level". The categories are only rough guidelines. Devising a visual organiser to represent ideas/characters/plot-lines in the novel can be very helpful rather than answering the questions in sentences etc.; this means doing a spider-diagram/chart/flow diagram etc. depending upon what you feel is most relevant. To find out more (sometimes known as graphic organisers) look here:
https://www.teachingenglish.org.uk/article/graphic-organisers
Remember if you are uncertain about the plot, you can also refer to the websites listed in the section **Structure and Theme**. These websites are good at helping you understand the plot but they won't help you get the higher marks because you really need to think for yourself if you are going to get the top grades.

As I have suggested, you could, while reading the book, put all your answers, notes, creative responses together into a *Far From The Madding Crowd* file or **learning journal**. You could be creative with this file: draw scenes of the important incidents; include spider-diagrams/visual organisers of significant characters and situations; storyboards of the key scenes; copies of articles/literary criticism which you have annotated; creative pieces etc.

Helpful vocabulary to learn before you start reading

While reading the book, **you should keep a vocabulary list**, writing down the difficult words and learning their meanings/spellings, and possibly using the vocabulary in your own writing. The complex vocabulary and sentence structures in the story can be off-putting at first but you should not be put off by the language; embrace it, love it! You will become much better educated when you learn the vocabulary. This is why reading pre-20th century writing is so useful: it makes you more intelligent because you widen your vocabulary and ability to understand difficult passages.

There are some words, I would strongly advise you looking up the meanings of and learning their spellings/meanings before reading; the websites listed below are helpful in this regard.

The eBook on Kindle (free with the paperback) is great because you can automatically look up difficult words. Remember, you learn more effectively when you look them up for yourself; it's for this reason, I have avoided providing detailed definitions, which could potentially be very long!

Weblink to help you learn difficult vocabulary

You can test yourself on the difficult vocabulary here:
http://www.verbalworkout.com/b/b1063.htm

Far From The Madding Crowd

Thomas Hardy

PREFACE

In reprinting this story for a new edition I am reminded that it was in the chapters of "Far from the Madding Crowd," as they appeared month by month in a popular magazine, that I first ventured to adopt the word "Wessex" from the pages of early English history, and give it a fictitious significance as the existing name of the district once included in that extinct kingdom. The series of novels I projected being mainly of the kind called local, they seemed to require a territorial definition of some sort to lend unity to their scene. Finding that the area of a single county did not afford a canvas large enough for this purpose, and that there were objections to an invented name, I disinterred the old one. The press and the public were kind enough to welcome the fanciful plan, and willingly joined me in the anachronism of imagining a Wessex population living under Queen Victoria;—a modern Wessex of railways, the penny post, mowing and reaping machines, union workhouses, lucifer matches, labourers who could read and write, and National school children. But I believe I am correct in stating that, until the existence of this contemporaneous Wessex was announced in the present story, in 1874, it had never been heard of, and that the expression, "a Wessex peasant," or "a Wessex custom," would theretofore have been taken to refer to nothing later in date than the Norman Conquest.

I did not anticipate that this application of the word to a modern use would extend outside the chapters of my own chronicles. But the name was soon taken up elsewhere as a local designation. The first to do so was the now defunct Examiner, which, in the impression bearing date July 15, 1876, entitled one of its articles "The Wessex Labourer," the article turning out to be no dissertation on farming during the Heptarchy, but on the modern peasant of the south-west counties, and his presentation in these stories.

Since then the appellation which I had thought to reserve to the horizons and landscapes of a merely realistic dream-country, has become more and more popular as a practical definition; and the dream-country has, by degrees, solidified into a utilitarian region which people can go to, take a house in, and write to the papers from. But I ask all good and gentle readers to be so kind as to forget this, and to refuse steadfastly to believe that there are any inhabitants of a Victorian Wessex outside the pages of this and the companion volumes in which they were first discovered.

Moreover, the village called Weatherbury, wherein the scenes of the present story of the series are for the most part laid, would perhaps be hardly discernible by the explorer, without help, in any existing place nowadays; though at the time, comparatively recent, at which the tale was written, a sufficient reality to meet the descriptions, both of backgrounds and personages, might have been traced easily enough. The church remains, by great good fortune, unrestored and intact, and a few of the old houses; but the ancient malt-house, which was formerly so characteristic of the parish, has been pulled down these twenty years; also most of the thatched and dormered cottages that were once lifeholds. The game of prisoner's base, which not so long ago seemed to enjoy a perennial vitality in front of the worn-out stocks, may, so far as I can say, be entirely unknown to the rising generation of schoolboys there. The practice of divination by Bible and key, the regarding of valentines as things of serious import, the shearing-supper, and the harvest-home, have, too, nearly disappeared in the wake of the old houses; and with them have gone, it is said, much of that love of fuddling to which the village at one time was notoriously prone. The change at the root of this has been the recent supplanting of the class of stationary cottagers, who carried on the local traditions and humours, by a population of more or less migratory labourers, which has led to a break of continuity in local history, more fatal than any other thing to the preservation of legend, folk-lore, close inter-social relations, and eccentric individualities. For these the indispensable conditions of existence are attachment to the soil of one particular spot by generation after generation.

T. H.

February 1895

Questions

What are the main points Hardy makes here?
Why do you think Hardy wrote this preface?

CHAPTER I
DESCRIPTION OF FARMER OAK –
AN INCIDENT

When Farmer Oak smiled, the corners of his mouth spread till they were within an unimportant distance of his ears, his eyes were reduced to chinks, and diverging wrinkles appeared round them, extending upon his countenance like the rays in a rudimentary sketch of the rising sun.

His Christian name was Gabriel, and on working days he was a young man of sound judgment, easy motions, proper dress, and general good character. On Sundays he was a man of misty views, rather given to postponing, and hampered by his best clothes and umbrella: upon the whole, one who felt himself to occupy morally that vast middle space of Laodicean neutrality which lay between the Communion people of the parish and the drunken section,—that is, he went to church, but yawned privately by the time the congregation reached the Nicene creed, and thought of what there would be for dinner when he meant to be listening to the sermon. Or, to state his character as it stood in the scale of public opinion, when his friends and critics were in tantrums, he was considered rather a bad man; when they were pleased, he was rather a good man; when they were neither, he was a man whose moral colour was a kind of pepper-and-salt mixture.

Since he lived six times as many working-days as Sundays, Oak's appearance in his old clothes was most peculiarly his own—the mental picture formed by his neighbours in imagining him being always dressed in that way. He wore a low-crowned felt hat, spread out at the base by tight jamming upon the head for security in high winds, and a coat like Dr. Johnson's; his lower extremities being encased in ordinary leather leggings and boots emphatically large, affording to each foot a roomy apartment so constructed that any wearer might stand in a river all day long and know nothing of damp—their maker being a conscientious man who endeavoured to compensate for any weakness in his cut by unstinted dimension and solidity.

Mr. Oak carried about him, by way of watch, what may be called a small silver clock; in other words, it was a watch as to shape and intention, and a small clock as to size. This instrument being several years older than Oak's grandfather, had the peculiarity of going either too fast or not at all. The smaller of its hands, too, occasionally slipped round on the pivot, and thus, though the minutes were told with precision, nobody could be quite certain of the hour they belonged to. The stopping peculiarity of his watch Oak remedied by thumps and shakes, and he escaped any evil consequences from the other two defects by constant comparisons with and observations of the sun and stars, and by pressing his face close to the glass of his neighbours' windows, till he could discern the hour marked by the green-faced timekeepers within. It may be mentioned that Oak's fob being difficult of access, by reason of its somewhat high situation in the waistband of his trousers (which also lay at a remote height under his waistcoat), the watch was as a necessity pulled out by throwing the body to one side, compressing the mouth and face to a mere mass of ruddy flesh on account of the exertion required, and drawing up the watch by its chain, like a bucket from a well.

But some thoughtful persons, who had seen him walking across one of his fields on a certain December morning—sunny and exceedingly mild— might have regarded Gabriel Oak in other aspects than these. In his face one might notice that many of the hues and curves of youth had tarried on to manhood: there even remained in his remoter crannies some relics of the boy. His height and breadth would have been sufficient to make his presence imposing, had they been exhibited with due consideration. But there is a way some men have, rural and urban alike, for which the mind is more responsible than flesh and sinew: it is a way of curtailing their dimensions by their manner of showing them. And from a quiet modesty that would have become a vestal, which seemed continually to impress upon him that he had no great claim on the world's room, Oak walked unassumingly and with a faintly perceptible bend, yet distinct from a bowing of the shoulders. This may be said to be a defect in an individual if he depends for his valuation more upon his appearance than upon his capacity to wear well, which Oak did not.

He had just reached the time of life at which "young" is ceasing to be the prefix of "man" in speaking of one. He was at the brightest period of masculine growth, for his intellect and his emotions were clearly separated: he had passed the time during which the influence of youth indiscriminately mingles them in the character of impulse, and he had not yet arrived at the stage wherein they become united again, in the character of prejudice, by the influence of a wife and family. In short, he was twenty-eight, and a bachelor.

Analysis: Hardy is at pains to present Oak as a happy, kind-hearted man who has a smile "like the rays in a rudimentary sketch of the rising sun". For most of the time, he wears the clothes of a hard-working farmer, but dresses up on Sunday; however, it's clear that he is not particularly religious. Being twenty-eight and a bachelor, it's clear that he needs to find a wife, although unlike an author like Jane Austen Hardy does not state this explicitly. The tone here is lightly humorous but not ironic as a rule: Hardy, like the great late Victorian novelists, is primarily a realist, intent upon describing in minute details the dress, manners, and physical characteristics of his characters, he is only ironic at important moments in the text. Reading the first chapter, the reader might be forgiven into thinking that Oak is a simpleton: we are told he has an ancient watch, the size of a clock, which he keeps down his trousers and has to pull out with great effort to tell the time. He seems a little dozy, a little stupid. Of course, subsequent events in the novel will prove Oak to be anything but stupid. However, Hardy is keen to disarm his readership at the beginning of the novel, to make his readers laugh and enjoy his character without being threatened by his intellectual powers. Later on in the novel, Oak will become a very astute character, supervising two huge farms and owning a stake in one of them, using new machinery to cultivate the land. How different he is here! A simple, down-to-earth comic farmer struggling to make something of himself. His spiritual and intellectual journey in the novel is vast.

Discussion point: How successful is this as an opening to a novel? What do you think of the way Hardy presents Oak here?

The field he was in this morning sloped to a ridge called Norcombe Hill. Through a spur of this hill ran the highway between Emminster and Chalk-Newton. Casually glancing over the hedge, Oak saw coming down the incline before him an ornamental spring waggon, painted yellow and gaily marked, drawn by two horses, a waggoner walking alongside bearing a whip perpendicularly. The waggon was laden with household goods and window plants, and on the apex of the whole sat a woman, young and attractive. Gabriel had not beheld the sight for more than half a minute, when the vehicle was brought to a standstill just beneath his eyes.

"The tailboard of the waggon is gone, Miss," said the waggoner.

"Then I heard it fall," said the girl, in a soft, though not particularly low voice. "I heard a noise I could not account for when we were coming up the hill."

"I'll run back."

"Do," she answered.

The sensible horses stood—perfectly still, and the waggoner's steps sank fainter and fainter in the distance.

The girl on the summit of the load sat motionless, surrounded by tables and chairs with their legs upwards, backed by an oak settle, and ornamented in front by pots of geraniums, myrtles, and cactuses, together with a caged canary—all probably from the windows of the house just vacated. There was also a cat in a willow basket, from the partly-opened lid of which she gazed with half-closed eyes, and affectionately surveyed the small birds around.

The handsome girl waited for some time idly in her place, and the only sound heard in the stillness was the hopping of the canary up and down the perches of its prison. Then she looked attentively downwards. It was not at the bird, nor at the cat; it was at an oblong package tied in paper, and lying between them. She turned her head to learn if the waggoner were coming. He was not yet in sight; and her eyes crept back to the package, her thoughts seeming to run upon what was inside it. At length she drew the article into her lap, and untied the paper covering; a small swing looking-glass was disclosed, in which she proceeded to survey herself attentively. She parted her lips and smiled.

Analysis: Our first glimpse of Bathsheba is of her smiling at her reflection in the mirror. As with Hardy's presentation of Oak, her first appearance is somewhat misleading. As the events of the novel unfold we realise that she does not understand the power of her beauty at all; this scene can be interpreted very differently on a second reading. On first reading we could be forgiven for thinking that Bathsheba is very aware of the power of her beauty, smiling Salome-like at her power. However, on second reading we perceive

her more like a beautiful bird admiring her plumage. In the way, that she deals with Boldwood and Troy, we realise that she is not able to comprehend the way she intoxicates men. She secretly admires herself her; not fully aware of whom she is. Notice here how Hardy deploys a real variety of sentences to convey his message: a number of complex sentences are followed by the short compound sentence "She parted her lips and smiled." The effect is striking; the reader thinks hard about her lips and her smiling. The overall atmosphere is mysterious and sensual: we are drawn in by her exotic beauty, her strange situation, the remote setting.

Discussion point: What do you think of the way Bathsheba is presented here?

It was a fine morning, and the sun lighted up to a scarlet glow the crimson jacket she wore, and painted a soft lustre upon her bright face and dark hair. The myrtles, geraniums, and cactuses packed around her were fresh and green, and at such a leafless season they invested the whole concern of horses, waggon, furniture, and girl with a peculiar vernal charm. What possessed her to indulge in such a performance in the sight of the sparrows, blackbirds, and unperceived farmer who were alone its spectators,—whether the smile began as a factitious one, to test her capacity in that art,—nobody knows; it ended certainly in a real smile. She blushed at herself, and seeing her reflection blush, blushed the more.

The change from the customary spot and necessary occasion of such an act—from the dressing hour in a bedroom to a time of travelling out of doors—lent to the idle deed a novelty it did not intrinsically possess. The picture was a delicate one. Woman's prescriptive infirmity had stalked into the sunlight, which had clothed it in the freshness of an originality. A cynical inference was irresistible by Gabriel Oak as he regarded the scene, generous though he fain would have been. There was no necessity whatever for her looking in the glass. She did not adjust her hat, or pat her hair, or press a dimple into shape, or do one thing to signify that any such intention had been her motive in taking up the glass. She simply observed herself as a fair product of Nature in the feminine kind, her thoughts seeming to glide into far-off though likely dramas in which men would play a part—vistas of probable triumphs—the smiles being of a phase suggesting that hearts were imagined as lost and won. Still, this was but conjecture, and the whole series of actions was so idly put forth as to make it rash to assert that intention had any part in them at all.

The waggoner's steps were heard returning. She put the glass in the paper, and the whole again into its place.

When the waggon had passed on, Gabriel withdrew from his point of espial, and descending into the road, followed the vehicle to the turnpike-gate some way beyond the bottom of the hill, where the object of his contemplation now halted for the payment of toll. About twenty steps still remained between him and the gate, when he heard a dispute. It was a difference concerning twopence between the persons with the waggon and the man at the toll-bar.

"Mis'ess's niece is upon the top of the things, and she says that's enough that I've offered ye, you great miser, and she won't pay any more." These were the waggoner's words.

"Very well; then mis'ess's niece can't pass," said the turnpike-keeper, closing the gate.

Oak looked from one to the other of the disputants, and fell into a reverie. There was something in the tone of twopence remarkably insignificant. Threepence had a definite value as money—it was an appreciable infringement on a day's wages, and, as such, a higgling matter; but twopence—"Here," he said, stepping forward and handing twopence to the gatekeeper; "let the young woman pass." He looked up at her then; she heard his words, and looked down.

Gabriel's features adhered throughout their form so exactly to the middle line between the beauty of St. John and the ugliness of Judas Iscariot, as represented in a window of the church he attended, that not a single lineament could be selected and called worthy either of distinction or notoriety. The red-jacketed and dark-haired maiden seemed to think so too, for she carelessly glanced over him, and told her man to drive on. She might have looked her thanks to Gabriel on a minute scale, but she did not speak them; more probably she felt none, for in gaining her a passage he had lost her her point, and we know how women take a favour of that kind.

The gatekeeper surveyed the retreating vehicle. "That's a handsome maid," he said to Oak.

"But she has her faults," said Gabriel.

"True, farmer."

"And the greatest of them is—well, what it is always."

"Beating people down? ay, 'tis so."

"O no."

"What, then?"

Gabriel, perhaps a little piqued by the comely traveller's indifference, glanced back to where he had witnessed her performance over the hedge, and said, "Vanity."

Analysis:
Once more the tone is lightly humorous: having not been thanked for giving Bathsheba money to pass through the toll-gate, Gabriel comments upon her acidly that she is vain. This is certainly our judgement upon her at this point, although again a second reading makes us aware that Bathsheba is not vain, she merely wants to be independent. Perhaps the most important theme of the book for a modern audience is her desire to be independent of men: we see here how she resents being dependent upon Oak to pass through the toll-gate. Thus the scene works both on a realistic and symbolic level: her resentment is the resentment of all intelligent Victorian women who have to depend upon men for their passage through life.

Notice also, how Bathsheba is being spied upon here. Even though she is 'far from the madding crowd' she is being watched more closely than she ever would in the city. Hardy introduces a theme which important throughout the whole novel: spying and voyeurism. Constantly, Bathsheba is watched by Oak, by Boldwood, by Troy, and by the country-folk.

Discussion point: What is vanity in your view and does Bathsheba exhibit it here?

Questions

How old Gabriel Oak?

What time of year is it and what is the weather like?

Who and what does Oak see in the wagon?

What is the young woman doing when she thinks no one is looking?

What does Oak do to help the young woman and wagoner at the tollgate?

What thanks does he get from the young woman?

What does Oak think her problem is?

GCSE style question: how effective is this as an opening chapter to a novel?

A Level style question: compare and contrast this opening with another opening in a similar text of your choice.

Creative response: write a poem/story called 'Vanity' where you describe in clear detail someone who is vain and show them being vain.

CHAPTER II
NIGHT—THE FLOCK—AN INTERIOR—ANOTHER INTERIOR

It was nearly midnight on the eve of St. Thomas's, the shortest day in the year. A desolating wind wandered from the north over the hill whereon Oak had watched the yellow waggon and its occupant in the sunshine of a few days earlier.

Norcombe Hill—not far from lonely Toller-Down—was one of the spots which suggest to a passer-by that he is in the presence of a shape approaching the indestructible as nearly as any to be found on earth. It was a featureless convexity of chalk and soil—an ordinary specimen of those smoothly-outlined protuberances of the globe which may remain undisturbed on some great day of confusion, when far grander heights and dizzy granite precipices topple down.

The hill was covered on its northern side by an ancient and decaying plantation of beeches, whose upper verge formed a line over the crest, fringing its arched curve against the sky, like a mane. To-night these trees sheltered the southern slope from the keenest blasts, which smote the wood and floundered through it with a sound as of grumbling, or gushed over its crowning boughs in a weakened moan. The dry leaves in the ditch simmered and boiled in the same breezes, a tongue of air occasionally ferreting out a few, and sending them spinning across the grass. A group or two of the latest in date amongst the dead multitude had remained till this very mid-winter time on the twigs which bore them and in falling rattled against the trunks with smart taps.

Between this half-wooded half-naked hill, and the vague still horizon that its summit indistinctly commanded, was a mysterious sheet of fathomless shade—the sounds from which suggested that what it concealed bore some reduced resemblance to features here. The thin grasses, more or less coating the hill, were touched by the wind in breezes of differing powers, and almost of differing natures—one rubbing the blades heavily, another raking them piercingly, another brushing them like a soft broom. The instinctive act of humankind was to stand and listen, and learn how the trees on the right and the trees on the left wailed or chaunted to each other in the regular antiphonies of a cathedral choir; how hedges and other shapes to leeward then caught the note, lowering it to the tenderest sob; and how the hurrying gust then plunged into the south, to be heard no more.

The sky was clear—remarkably clear—and the twinkling of all the stars seemed to be but throbs of one body, timed by a common pulse. The North Star was directly in the wind's eye, and since evening the Bear had swung round it outwardly to the east, till he was now at a right angle with the meridian. A difference of colour in the stars—oftener read of than seen in England—was really perceptible here. The sovereign brilliancy of Sirius pierced the eye with a steely glitter, the star called Capella was yellow, Aldebaran and Betelgueux shone with a fiery red.

To persons standing alone on a hill during a clear midnight such as this, the roll of the world eastward is almost a palpable movement. The sensation may be caused by the panoramic glide of the stars past earthly objects, which is perceptible in a few minutes of stillness, or by the better outlook upon space that a hill affords, or by the wind, or by the solitude; but whatever be its origin, the impression of riding along is vivid and abiding. The poetry of motion is a phrase much in use, and to enjoy the epic form of that gratification it is necessary to stand on a hill at a small hour of the night, and, having first expanded with a sense of difference from the mass of civilised mankind, who are dreamwrapt and disregardful of all such proceedings at this time, long and quietly watch your stately progress through the stars. After such a nocturnal reconnoitre it is hard to get back to earth, and to believe that the consciousness of such majestic speeding is derived from a tiny human frame.

Suddenly an unexpected series of sounds began to be heard in this place up against the sky. They had a clearness which was to be found nowhere in the wind, and a sequence which was to be found nowhere in nature. They were the notes of Farmer Oak's flute.

The tune was not floating unhindered into the open air: it seemed muffled in some way, and was altogether too curtailed in power to spread high or wide. It came from the direction of a small dark object under the plantation hedge—a shepherd's hut—now presenting an outline to which an uninitiated person might have been puzzled to attach either meaning or use.

The image as a whole was that of a small Noah's Ark on a small Ararat, allowing the traditionary outlines and general form of the Ark which are followed by toy-makers—and by these means are established in men's imaginations among their firmest, because earliest impressions—to pass as an approximate pattern. The hut stood on little wheels, which raised its floor about a foot from the ground. Such shepherds' huts are dragged into the fields when the lambing season comes on, to shelter the shepherd in his enforced nightly attendance.

It was only latterly that people had begun to call Gabriel "Farmer" Oak. During the twelvemonth preceding this time he had been enabled by sustained efforts of industry and chronic good spirits to lease the small sheep-farm of which Norcombe Hill was a portion, and stock it with two hundred sheep. Previously he had been a bailiff for a short time, and earlier still a shepherd only, having from his childhood assisted his father in tending the flocks of large proprietors, till old Gabriel sank to rest.

This venture, unaided and alone, into the paths of farming as master and not as man, with an advance of sheep not yet paid for, was a critical juncture with Gabriel Oak, and he recognised his position clearly. The first movement in his new progress was the lambing of his ewes, and sheep having been his speciality from his youth, he wisely refrained from deputing the task of tending them at this season to a hireling or a novice.

The wind continued to beat about the corners of the hut, but the flute-playing ceased. A rectangular space of light appeared in the side of the hut, and in the opening the outline of Farmer Oak's figure. He carried a lantern in his hand, and closing the door behind him, came forward and busied himself about this nook of the field for nearly twenty minutes, the lantern light appearing and disappearing here and there, and brightening him or darkening him as he stood before or behind it.

Oak's motions, though they had a quiet-energy, were slow, and their deliberateness accorded well with his occupation. Fitness being the basis of beauty, nobody could have denied that his steady swings and turns in and about the flock had elements of grace. Yet, although if occasion demanded he could do or think a thing with as mercurial a dash as can the men of towns who are more to the manner born, his special power, morally, physically, and mentally, was static, owing little or nothing to momentum as a rule.

A close examination of the ground hereabout, even by the wan starlight only, revealed how a portion of what would have been casually called a wild slope had been appropriated by Farmer Oak for his great purpose this winter. Detached hurdles thatched with straw were stuck into the ground at various scattered points, amid and under which the whitish forms of his meek ewes moved and rustled. The ring of the sheep-bell, which had been silent during his absence, recommenced, in tones that had more mellowness than clearness, owing to an increasing growth of surrounding wool. This continued till Oak withdrew again from the flock. He returned to the hut, bringing in his arms a new-born lamb, consisting of four legs large enough for a full-grown sheep, united by a seemingly inconsiderable membrane about half the substance of the legs collectively, which constituted the animal's entire body just at present.

Analysis: Hardy is very careful in the way he presents Oak early on in the novel. He is, above all, the loving shepherd who nurtures life itself. This is never more vividly presented than here where he holds a "new-born lamb" in his arms. Being a "Gabriel" we find that there is an angelic quality about him; he is man who nurtures and saves lives, guiding them by example. He is also an "Oak". There is an earthy, stout, inimitably English quality about him. We see this here as well: he is familiar with natures' processes in a very hard-headed fashion. Indeed, his matter-of-fact approach to issues like sex and reproduction will shock the closeted Bathsheba later on. Notice also, the pictorial qualities of Hardy's writing: the scene he is describing her with Oak, the lantern, and the lamb is like a Pre-Raphaelite painting that were so fashionable at the time of writing.

Discussion point: What are the qualities of a shepherd? Are they qualities that God has? In what ways is Hardy's writing like a painting?

The little speck of life he placed on a wisp of hay before the small stove, where a can of milk was simmering. Oak extinguished the lantern by blowing into it and then pinching the snuff, the cot being lighted by a candle suspended by a twisted wire. A rather hard couch, formed of a few corn sacks thrown carelessly down, covered half the floor of this little habitation, and here the young man stretched himself along, loosened his woollen cravat, and closed his eyes. In about the time a person unaccustomed to bodily labour would have decided upon which side to lie, Farmer Oak was asleep.

The inside of the hut, as it now presented itself, was cosy and alluring, and the scarlet handful of fire in addition to the candle, reflecting its own genial colour upon whatever it could reach, flung associations of enjoyment even over utensils and tools. In the corner stood the sheep-crook, and along a shelf at one side were ranged bottles and canisters of the simple preparations pertaining to ovine surgery and physic; spirits of wine, turpentine, tar, magnesia, ginger, and castor-oil being the chief. On a triangular shelf across the corner stood bread, bacon, cheese, and a cup for ale or cider, which was supplied from a flagon beneath. Beside the provisions lay the flute, whose notes had lately been called forth by the lonely watcher to beguile a tedious hour. The house was ventilated by two round holes, like the lights of a ship's cabin, with wood slides.

The lamb, revived by the warmth began to bleat, and the sound entered

Gabriel's ears and brain with an instant meaning, as expected sounds will. Passing from the profoundest sleep to the most alert wakefulness with the same ease that had accompanied the reverse operation, he looked at his watch, found that the hour-hand had shifted again, put on his hat, took the lamb in his arms, and carried it into the darkness. After placing the little creature with its mother, he stood and carefully examined the sky, to ascertain the time of night from the altitudes of the stars.

The Dog-star and Aldebaran, pointing to the restless Pleiades, were half-way up the Southern sky, and between them hung Orion, which gorgeous constellation never burnt more vividly than now, as it soared forth above the rim of the landscape. Castor and Pollux with their quiet shine were almost on the meridian: the barren and gloomy Square of Pegasus was creeping round to the north-west; far away through the plantation Vega sparkled like a lamp suspended amid the leafless trees, and Cassiopeia's chair stood daintily poised on the uppermost boughs.

"One o'clock," said Gabriel.

Being a man not without a frequent consciousness that there was some charm in this life he led, he stood still after looking at the sky as a useful instrument, and regarded it in an appreciative spirit, as a work of art superlatively beautiful. For a moment he seemed impressed with the speaking loneliness of the scene, or rather with the complete abstraction from all its compass of the sights and sounds of man. Human shapes, interferences, troubles, and joys were all as if they were not, and there seemed to be on the shaded hemisphere of the globe no sentient being save himself; he could fancy them all gone round to the sunny side.

Occupied thus, with eyes stretched afar, Oak gradually perceived that what he had previously taken to be a star low down behind the outskirts of the plantation was in reality no such thing. It was an artificial light, almost close at hand.

To find themselves utterly alone at night where company is desirable and expected makes some people fearful; but a case more trying by far to the nerves is to discover some mysterious companionship when intuition, sensation, memory, analogy, testimony, probability, induction—every kind of evidence in the logician's list—have united to persuade consciousness that it is quite in isolation.

Farmer Oak went towards the plantation and pushed through its lower boughs to the windy side. A dim mass under the slope reminded him that a shed occupied a place here, the site being a cutting into the slope of the hill, so that at its back part the roof was almost level with the ground. In front it was formed of board nailed to posts and covered with tar as a preservative. Through crevices in the roof and side spread streaks and dots of light, a combination of which made the radiance that had attracted him. Oak stepped up behind, where, leaning down upon the roof and putting his eye close to a hole, he could see into the interior clearly.

The place contained two women and two cows. By the side of the latter a steaming bran-mash stood in a bucket. One of the women was past middle age. Her companion was apparently young and graceful; he could form no decided opinion upon her looks, her position being almost beneath his eye, so that he saw her in a bird's-eye view, as Milton's Satan first saw Paradise. She wore no bonnet or hat, but had enveloped herself in a large cloak, which was carelessly flung over her head as a covering.

"There, now we'll go home," said the elder of the two, resting her knuckles upon her hips, and looking at their goings-on as a whole. "I do hope Daisy will fetch round again now. I have never been more frightened in my life, but I don't mind breaking my rest if she recovers."

The young woman, whose eyelids were apparently inclined to fall together on the smallest provocation of silence, yawned without parting her lips to any inconvenient extent, whereupon Gabriel caught the infection and slightly yawned in sympathy.

"I wish we were rich enough to pay a man to do these things," she said.

"As we are not, we must do them ourselves," said the other; "for you must help me if you stay."

"Well, my hat is gone, however," continued the younger. "It went over the hedge, I think. The idea of such a slight wind catching it."

> Analysis: Once again, we see Bathsheba's resentment about not being a man; she wishes she could pay a man to do the rough and ready business of reviving Daisy the cow. Hardy once again makes the scene tenser and suspenseful because Oak is spying upon Bathsheba here. There is a sense of mystery about their mundane task because of this. Oak is so intently watching them that he even starts imitates their yawn. Hardy also sets up the issue of the missing hat which will become important later on.

> Discussion point: How does Hardy create suspense out of such a mundane scene?

The cow standing erect was of the Devon breed, and was encased in a tight warm hide of rich Indian red, as absolutely uniform from eyes to tail as if the animal had been dipped in a dye of that colour, her long back being mathematically level. The other was spotted, grey and white. Beside her Oak now noticed a little calf about a day old, looking idiotically at the two women, which showed that it had not long been accustomed to the phenomenon of eyesight, and often turning to the lantern, which it apparently mistook for the moon, inherited instinct having as yet had little time for correction by experience. Between the sheep and the cows Lucina had been busy on Norcombe Hill lately.

"I think we had better send for some oatmeal," said the elder woman; "there's no more bran."

"Yes, aunt; and I'll ride over for it as soon as it is light."

"But there's no side-saddle."

"I can ride on the other: trust me."

Oak, upon hearing these remarks, became more curious to observe her features, but this prospect being denied him by the hooding effect of the cloak, and by his aerial position, he felt himself drawing upon his fancy for their details. In making even horizontal and clear inspections we colour and mould according to the wants within us whatever our eyes bring in. Had Gabriel been able from the first to get a distinct view of her countenance, his estimate of it as very handsome or slightly so would have been as his soul required a divinity at the moment or was ready supplied with one. Having for some time known the want of a satisfactory form to fill an increasing void within him, his position moreover affording the widest scope for his fancy, he painted her a beauty.

By one of those whimsical coincidences in which Nature, like a busy mother, seems to spare a moment from her unremitting labours to turn and make her children smile, the girl now dropped the cloak, and forth tumbled ropes of black hair over a red jacket. Oak knew her instantly as the heroine of the yellow waggon, myrtles, and looking-glass: prosily, as the woman who owed him twopence.

They placed the calf beside its mother again, took up the lantern, and went out, the light sinking down the hill till it was no more than a nebula. Gabriel Oak returned to his flock.

Questions

What instrument is Oak playing?
What is he caring for?
Where does Oak live?
What do the stars tell Oak about his watch?
What does Oak spy through the roof of the farm?
What does the young woman complain about?
Who is this young woman?
GCSE style question: how does Hardy create sympathy for Oak in this chapter?
A Level style question: compare and contrast Hardy's representations of the night-time in the country with another similar scene in a text of your choice.
Creative response: write a description/poem about the night-time.

CHAPTER III A GIRL ON HORSEBACK—CONVERSATION

The sluggish day began to break. Even its position terrestrially is one of the elements of a new interest, and for no particular reason save that the incident of the night had occurred there Oak went again into the plantation. Lingering and musing here, he heard the steps of a horse at the foot of the hill, and soon there appeared in view an auburn pony with a girl on its back, ascending by the path leading past the cattle-shed. She was the young woman of the night before. Gabriel instantly thought of the hat she had mentioned as having lost in the wind; possibly she had come to look for it. He hastily scanned the ditch and after walking about ten yards along it found the hat among the leaves. Gabriel took it in his hand and returned to his hut. Here he ensconced himself, and peeped through the loophole in the direction of the rider's approach.

She came up and looked around—then on the other side of the hedge. Gabriel was about to advance and restore the missing article when an unexpected performance induced him to suspend the action for the present. The path, after passing the cowshed, bisected the plantation. It was not a bridle-path—merely a pedestrian's track, and the boughs spread horizontally at a height not greater than seven feet above the ground, which made it impossible to ride erect beneath them. The girl, who wore no riding-habit, looked around for a moment, as if to assure herself that all humanity was out of view, then dexterously dropped backwards flat upon the pony's back, her head over its tail, her feet against its shoulders, and her eyes to the sky. The rapidity of her glide into this position was that of a kingfisher—its noiselessness that of a hawk. Gabriel's eyes had scarcely been able to follow her. The tall lank pony seemed used to such doings, and ambled along unconcerned. Thus she passed under the level boughs.

Analysis: Again Bathsheba is being spied upon. This time, unlike the scenes with the mirror and the cow, she performs an incredible and suggestive act: leaning back with her legs spread on the shoulders of a horse. Notice how Hardy generates not only sexual tension here in his suggestive description of the girl lying on the horse's back, but also a sense of her beautiful movements. She glides like a "kingfisher" and moves as noiselessly as a "hawk". There is something miraculous about her movements here because even the keen Oak is "scarcely able to follow her". She passes under the level boughs without any difficulty. Here we see a different side to Bathsheba: we see how she is a creature of nature, as natural in nature as a kingfisher and a hawk. We deepen our appreciation and admiration for her here. Hardy builds tension by having Oak watch these astonishing acrobatic feats and thereby making us think about his thoughts and feelings.

Discussion point: What do you think of the way Bathsheba and Oak are presented here?

The performer seemed quite at home anywhere between a horse's head and its tail, and the necessity for this abnormal attitude having ceased with the passage of the plantation, she began to adopt another, even more obviously convenient than the first. She had no side-saddle, and it was very apparent that a firm seat upon the smooth leather beneath her was unattainable sideways. Springing to her accustomed perpendicular like a bowed sapling, and satisfying herself that nobody was in sight, she seated herself in the manner demanded by the saddle, though hardly expected of the woman, and trotted off in the direction of Tewnell Mill.

Oak was amused, perhaps a little astonished, and hanging up the hat in his hut, went again among his ewes. An hour passed, the girl returned, properly seated now, with a bag of bran in front of her. On nearing the cattle-shed she was met by a boy bringing a milking-pail, who held the reins of the pony whilst she slid off. The boy led away the horse, leaving the pail with the young woman.

Soon soft spirts alternating with loud spirts came in regular succession from within the shed, the obvious sounds of a person milking a cow. Gabriel took the lost hat in his hand, and waited beside the path she would follow in leaving the hill.

She came, the pail in one hand, hanging against her knee. The left arm was extended as a balance, enough of it being shown bare to make Oak wish that the event had happened in the summer, when the whole would have been revealed. There was a bright air and manner about her now, by which she seemed to imply that the desirability of her existence could not be questioned; and this rather saucy assumption failed in being offensive because a beholder felt it to be, upon the whole, true. Like exceptional emphasis in the tone of a genius, that which would have made mediocrity ridiculous was an addition to recognised power. It was with some surprise that she saw Gabriel's face rising like the moon behind the hedge.

The adjustment of the farmer's hazy conceptions of her charms to the portrait of herself she now presented him with was less a diminution than a difference. The starting-point selected by the judgment was her height. She seemed tall, but the pail was a small one, and the hedge diminutive; hence, making allowance for error by comparison with these, she could have been not above the height to be chosen by women as best. All features of consequence were severe and regular. It may have been observed by persons who go about the shires with eyes for beauty, that in Englishwoman a classically-formed face is seldom found to be united with a figure of the same pattern, the highly-finished features being generally too large for the remainder of the frame; that a graceful and proportionate figure of eight heads usually goes off into random facial curves. Without throwing a Nymphean tissue over a milkmaid, let it be said that here criticism checked itself as out of place, and looked at her proportions with a long consciousness of pleasure. From the contours of her figure in its upper part, she must have had a beautiful neck and shoulders; but since her infancy nobody had ever seen them. Had she been put into a low dress she would have run and thrust her head into a bush. Yet she was not a shy girl by any means; it was merely her instinct to draw the line dividing the seen from the unseen higher than they do it in towns.

That the girl's thoughts hovered about her face and form as soon as she caught Oak's eyes conning the same page was natural, and almost certain. The self-consciousness shown would have been vanity if a little more pronounced, dignity if a little less. Rays of male vision seem to have a tickling effect upon virgin faces in rural districts; she brushed hers with her hand, as if Gabriel had been irritating its pink surface by actual touch, and the free air of her previous movements was reduced at the same time to a chastened phase of itself. Yet it was the man who blushed, the maid not at all.

"I found a hat," said Oak.

"It is mine," said she, and, from a sense of proportion, kept down to a small smile an inclination to laugh distinctly: "it flew away last night."

"One o'clock this morning?"

"Well—it was." She was surprised. "How did you know?" she said.

"I was here."

"You are Farmer Oak, are you not?"

"That or thereabouts. I'm lately come to this place."

"A large farm?" she inquired, casting her eyes round, and swinging back her hair, which was black in the shaded hollows of its mass; but it being now an hour past sunrise the rays touched its prominent curves with a colour of their own.

"No; not large. About a hundred." (In speaking of farms the word "acres" is omitted by the natives, by analogy to such old expressions as "a stag of ten.")

"I wanted my hat this morning," she went on. "I had to ride to Tewnell Mill."

"Yes you had."

"How do you know?"

"I saw you."

"Where?" she inquired, a misgiving bringing every muscle of her lineaments and frame to a standstill.

"Here—going through the plantation, and all down the hill," said Farmer Oak, with an aspect excessively knowing with regard to some matter in his mind, as he gazed at a remote point in the direction named, and then turned back to meet his colloquist's eyes.

A perception caused him to withdraw his own eyes from hers as suddenly as if he had been caught in a theft. Recollection of the strange antics she had indulged in when passing through the trees was succeeded in the girl by a nettled palpitation, and that by a hot face. It was a time to see a woman redden who was not given to reddening as a rule; not a point in the milkmaid but was of the deepest rose-colour. From the Maiden's Blush, through all varieties of the Provence down to the Crimson Tuscany, the countenance of Oak's acquaintance quickly graduated; whereupon he, in considerateness, turned away his head.

The sympathetic man still looked the other way, and wondered when she would recover coolness sufficient to justify him in facing her again. He heard what seemed to be the flitting of a dead leaf upon the breeze, and looked. She had gone away.

Analysis: The mystery of Bathsheba grows while Hardy develops Oak's comedic presentation. He rather haplessly gives her the hat, suddenly appearing from behind a hedge. Bathsheba is obviously very put out now that she realises that Oak was observing her on the horse. Hardy describes her as having a "nettled palpitation" and a "hot face". She's clearly embarrassed, but Oak is sympathetic: we see him acquiring sensitivity before our very eyes. She regains her mystery by vanishing in the "flitting of a dead leave on the breeze". The imagery here is fascinating: the "dead leaf" contrasting with the vibrancy and flush of Bathsheba's youth and beauty. Notice again, how Hardy emphasizes Bathsheba's power by following some complex sentences with a short simple one: "She had gone away".

Discussion point: This is an awkward social situation. What makes it so awkward? Can you think of having similarly awkward social encounters when you have tried to help someone but just embarrassed them instead?

With an air between that of Tragedy and Comedy Gabriel returned to his work.

Five mornings and evenings passed. The young woman came regularly to milk the healthy cow or to attend to the sick one, but never allowed her vision to stray in the direction of Oak's person. His want of tact had deeply offended her— not by seeing what he could not help, but by letting her know that he had seen it. For, as without law there is no sin, without eyes there is no indecorum; and she appeared to feel that Gabriel's espial had made her an indecorous woman without her own connivance. It was food for great regret with him; it was also a contretemps which touched into life a latent heat he had experienced in that direction.

The acquaintanceship might, however, have ended in a slow forgetting, but for an incident which occurred at the end of the same week. One afternoon it began to freeze, and the frost increased with evening, which drew on like a stealthy tightening of bonds. It was a time when in cottages the breath of the sleepers freezes to the sheets; when round the drawing-room fire of a thick-walled mansion the sitters' backs are cold, even whilst their faces are all aglow. Many a small bird went to bed supperless that night among the bare boughs.

As the milking-hour drew near, Oak kept his usual watch upon the cowshed. At last he felt cold, and shaking an extra quantity of bedding round the yearling ewes he entered the hut and heaped more fuel upon the stove. The wind came in at the bottom of the door, and to prevent it Oak laid a sack there and wheeled the cot round a little more to the south. Then the wind spouted in at a ventilating hole—of which there was one on each side of the hut.

Gabriel had always known that when the fire was lighted and the door closed one of these must be kept open—that chosen being always on the side away from the wind. Closing the slide to windward, he turned to open the other; on second thoughts the farmer considered that he would first sit down leaving both closed for a minute or two, till the temperature of the hut was a little raised. He sat down.

His head began to ache in an unwonted manner, and, fancying himself weary by reason of the broken rests of the preceding nights, Oak decided to get up, open the slide, and then allow himself to fall asleep. He fell asleep, however, without having performed the necessary preliminary.

How long he remained unconscious Gabriel never knew. During the first stages of his return to perception peculiar deeds seemed to be in course of enactment. His dog was howling, his head was aching fearfully—somebody was pulling him about, hands were loosening his neckerchief.

On opening his eyes he found that evening had sunk to dusk in a strange manner of unexpectedness. The young girl with the remarkably pleasant lips and white teeth was beside him. More than this—astonishingly more—his head was upon her lap, his face and neck were disagreeably wet, and her fingers were unbuttoning his collar.

Analysis:
We have had a couple of scenes where Oak has 'rescued' Bathsheba in the broadest sense of the word: rescued her from being turned away at the toll-gate, rescued her hat. Now Bathsheba rescues him from certain death, from being suffocated in his hut. Oak's confusion is wonderfully evoked: Oak's hurting head, the dog howling, Bathsheba's lips, her teeth, his head upon her lap, her unbuttoning him. It is the stuff of male fantasy. There is real sexual tension here. The scene recalls a similarly famous scene when a heroine rescues a hero: Jane Eyre's rescue of Rochester from his horse. The tone here though much more sensual. Hardy, writes nearly fifty years after Charlotte Bronte, is much more modern in his emphasis upon the bodies of his two protagonists.

Discussion point:
How does Hardy generate tension and drama in this extract?

"Whatever is the matter?" said Oak, vacantly.

She seemed to experience mirth, but of too insignificant a kind to start enjoyment.

"Nothing now," she answered, "since you are not dead. It is a wonder you were not suffocated in this hut of yours."

"Ah, the hut!" murmured Gabriel. "I gave ten pounds for that hut. But I'll sell it, and sit under thatched hurdles as they did in old times, and curl up to sleep in a lock of straw! It played me nearly the same trick the other day!" Gabriel, by way of emphasis, brought down his fist upon the floor.

"It was not exactly the fault of the hut," she observed in a tone which showed her to be that novelty among women—one who finished a thought before beginning the sentence which was to convey it. "You should, I think, have considered, and not have been so foolish as to leave the slides closed."

"Yes I suppose I should," said Oak, absently. He was endeavouring to catch and appreciate the sensation of being thus with her, his head upon her dress, before the event passed on into the heap of bygone things. He wished she knew his impressions; but he would as soon have thought of carrying an odour in a net as of attempting to convey the intangibilities of his feeling in the coarse meshes of language. So he remained silent.

She made him sit up, and then Oak began wiping his face and shaking himself like a Samson. "How can I thank 'ee?" he said at last, gratefully, some of the natural rusty red having returned to his face.

"Oh, never mind that," said the girl, smiling, and allowing her smile to hold good for Gabriel's next remark, whatever that might prove to be.

"How did you find me?"

"I heard your dog howling and scratching at the door of the hut when I came to the milking (it was so lucky, Daisy's milking is almost over for the season, and I shall not come here after this week or the next). The dog saw me, and jumped over to me, and laid hold of my skirt. I came across and looked round the hut the very first thing to see if the slides were closed. My uncle has a hut like this one, and I have heard him tell his shepherd not to go to sleep without leaving a slide open. I opened the door, and there you were like dead. I threw the milk over you, as there was no water, forgetting it was warm, and no use."

"I wonder if I should have died?" Gabriel said, in a low voice, which was rather meant to travel back to himself than to her.

"Oh no!" the girl replied. She seemed to prefer a less tragic probability; to have saved a man from death involved talk that should harmonise with the dignity of such a deed—and she shunned it.

"I believe you saved my life, Miss—I don't know your name. I know your aunt's, but not yours."

"I would just as soon not tell it—rather not. There is no reason either why I should, as you probably will never have much to do with me."

"Still, I should like to know."

"You can inquire at my aunt's—she will tell you."

"My name is Gabriel Oak."

"And mine isn't. You seem fond of yours in speaking it so decisively, Gabriel Oak."

"You see, it is the only one I shall ever have, and I must make the most of it."

"I always think mine sounds odd and disagreeable."

"I should think you might soon get a new one."

"Mercy!—how many opinions you keep about you concerning other people, Gabriel Oak."

"Well, Miss—excuse the words—I thought you would like them. But I can't match you, I know, in mapping out my mind upon my tongue. I never was very clever in my inside. But I thank you. Come, give me your hand."

She hesitated, somewhat disconcerted at Oak's old-fashioned earnest conclusion to a dialogue lightly carried on. "Very well," she said, and gave him her hand, compressing her lips to a demure impassivity. He held it but an instant, and in his fear of being too demonstrative, swerved to the opposite extreme, touching her fingers with the lightness of a small-hearted person.

"I am sorry," he said the instant after.

"What for?"

"Letting your hand go so quick."

"You may have it again if you like; there it is." She gave him her hand again.

Oak held it longer this time—indeed, curiously long. "How soft it is—being winter time, too—not chapped or rough or anything!" he said.

"There—that's long enough," said she, though without pulling it away.

"But I suppose you are thinking you would like to kiss it? You may if you want to."

"I wasn't thinking of any such thing," said Gabriel, simply; "but I will—"

"That you won't!" She snatched back her hand.

Gabriel felt himself guilty of another want of tact.

"Now find out my name," she said, teasingly; and withdrew.

Analysis: Here we see what Hardy excels in, and what makes him such a modern writer: his attention to the psychological subtleties of attraction. Oak's forwardness in asking to hold Bathsheba's hand and his response to her "demure impassivity" – which he finds difficult to read – leads to him thinking he is being too "demonstrative" and thus touching her "with the lightness of a small-hearted person". His apology is borne of these internal processes. Bathsheba plays with his desire, inviting him to kiss her hand, but being put out that he wasn't thinking of kissing it and, as a result, withdrawing it.

Discussion point: How does Hardy generate interest and tension in his description of the interaction with Bathsheba and Oak here?

Questions

What item of clothing does Gabriel get which belongs to the girl?

What does Gabriel spy the girl doing on the horse?

Why is the girl embarrassed when Gabriel gives her the hat?

What does the girl do for the next five days?

Why is Gabriel nearly killed?

Why and how does the girl rescue him?

What does she allow Gabriel to do and what will she not allow him to know?

GCSE style question: How does Hardy represent Bathsheba in this chapter?

A Level style question: How does Hardy explore the theme of spying in these first three chapters of the book?

Creative response: write a poem/short story called 'The Spy' about someone who enjoys spying on another person.

CHAPTER IV
GABRIEL'S RESOLVE—THE VISIT—THE MISTAKE

The only superiority in women that is tolerable to the rival sex is, as a rule, that of the unconscious kind; but a superiority which recognizes itself may sometimes please by suggesting possibilities of capture to the subordinated man.

This well-favoured and comely girl soon made appreciable inroads upon the emotional constitution of young Farmer Oak.

Love, being an extremely exacting usurer (a sense of exorbitant profit, spiritually, by an exchange of hearts, being at the bottom of pure passions, as that of exorbitant profit, bodily or materially, is at the bottom of those of lower atmosphere), every morning Oak's feelings were as sensitive as the money-market in calculations upon his chances. His dog waited for his meals in a way so like that in which Oak waited for the girl's presence, that the farmer was quite struck with the resemblance, felt it lowering, and would not look at the dog. However, he continued to watch through the hedge for her regular coming, and thus his sentiments towards her were deepened without any corresponding effect being produced upon herself. Oak had nothing finished and ready to say as yet, and not being able to frame love phrases which end where they begin; passionate tales—

—Full of sound and fury,
—Signifying nothing—

he said no word at all.

By making inquiries he found that the girl's name was Bathsheba Everdene, and that the cow would go dry in about seven days. He dreaded the eighth day.

At last the eighth day came. The cow had ceased to give milk for that year, and Bathsheba Everdene came up the hill no more. Gabriel had reached a pitch of existence he never could have anticipated a short time before. He liked saying "Bathsheba" as a private enjoyment instead of whistling; turned over his taste to black hair, though he had sworn by brown ever since he was a boy, isolated himself till the space he filled in the public eye was contemptibly small. Love is a possible strength in an actual weakness. Marriage transforms a distraction into a support, the power of which should be, and happily often is, in direct proportion to the degree of imbecility it supplants. Oak began now to see light in this direction, and said to himself, "I'll make her my wife, or upon my soul I shall be good for nothing!"

All this while he was perplexing himself about an errand on which he might consistently visit the cottage of Bathsheba's aunt.

He found his opportunity in the death of a ewe, mother of a living lamb. On a day which had a summer face and a winter constitution—a fine January morning, when there was just enough blue sky visible to make cheerfully-disposed people wish for more, and an occasional gleam of silvery sunshine, Oak put the lamb into a respectable Sunday basket, and stalked across the fields to the house of Mrs. Hurst, the aunt—George, the dog walking behind, with a countenance of great concern at the serious turn pastoral affairs seemed to be taking.

Gabriel had watched the blue wood-smoke curling from the chimney with strange meditation. At evening he had fancifully traced it down the chimney to the spot of its origin—seen the hearth and Bathsheba beside it—

beside it in her out-door dress; for the clothes she had worn on the hill were by association equally with her person included in the compass of his affection; they seemed at this early time of his love a necessary ingredient of the sweet mixture called Bathsheba Everdene.

He had made a toilet of a nicely-adjusted kind—of a nature between the carefully neat and the carelessly ornate—of a degree between fine-market-day and wet-Sunday selection. He thoroughly cleaned his silver watch-chain with whiting, put new lacing straps to his boots, looked to the brass eyelet-holes, went to the inmost heart of the plantation for a new walking-stick, and trimmed it vigorously on his way back; took a new handkerchief from the bottom of his clothes-box, put on the light waistcoat patterned all over with sprigs of an elegant flower uniting the beauties of both rose and lily without the defects of either, and used all the hair-oil he possessed upon his usually dry, sandy, and inextricably curly hair, till he had deepened it to a splendidly novel colour, between that of guano and Roman cement, making it stick to his head like mace round a nutmeg, or wet seaweed round a boulder after the ebb.

Nothing disturbed the stillness of the cottage save the chatter of a knot of sparrows on the eaves; one might fancy scandal and rumour to be no less the staple topic of these little coteries on roofs than of those under them. It seemed that the omen was an unpropitious one, for, as the rather untoward commencement of Oak's overtures, just as he arrived by the garden gate, he saw a cat inside, going into various arched shapes and fiendish convulsions at the sight of his dog George. The dog took no notice, for he had arrived at an age at which all superfluous barking was cynically avoided as a waste of breath—in fact, he never barked even at the sheep except to order, when it was done with an absolutely neutral countenance, as a sort of Commination-service, which, though offensive, had to be gone through once now and then to frighten the flock for their own good.

A voice came from behind some laurel-bushes into which the cat had run:

"Poor dear! Did a nasty brute of a dog want to kill it;—did he, poor dear!"

"I beg your pardon," said Oak to the voice, "but George was walking on behind me with a temper as mild as milk."

Almost before he had ceased speaking, Oak was seized with a misgiving as to whose ear was the recipient of his answer. Nobody appeared, and he heard the person retreat among the bushes.

Gabriel meditated, and so deeply that he brought small furrows into his forehead by sheer force of reverie. Where the issue of an interview is as likely to be a vast change for the worse as for the better, any initial difference from expectation causes nipping sensations of failure. Oak went up to the door a little abashed: his mental rehearsal and the reality had had no common grounds of opening.

Bathsheba's aunt was indoors. "Will you tell Miss Everdene that somebody would be glad to speak to her?" said Mr. Oak. (Calling one's self merely Somebody, without giving a name, is not to be taken as an example of the ill-breeding of the rural world: it springs from a refined modesty, of which townspeople, with their cards and announcements, have no notion whatever.)

Bathsheba was out. The voice had evidently been hers.

"Will you come in, Mr. Oak?"

"Oh, thank 'ee," said Gabriel, following her to the fireplace. "I've brought a lamb for Miss Everdene. I thought she might like one to rear; girls do."

"She might," said Mrs. Hurst, musingly; "though she's only a visitor here. If you will wait a minute, Bathsheba will be in."

"Yes, I will wait," said Gabriel, sitting down. "The lamb isn't really the business I came about, Mrs. Hurst. In short, I was going to ask her if she'd like to be married."

"And were you indeed?"

"Yes. Because if she would, I should be very glad to marry her. D'ye know if she's got any other young man hanging about her at all?"

"Let me think," said Mrs. Hurst, poking the fire superfluously... "Yes— bless you, ever so many young men. You see, Farmer Oak, she's so good-looking, and an excellent scholar besides—she was going to be a governess once, you know, only she was too wild. Not that her young men ever come here—but, Lord, in the nature of women, she must have a dozen!"

"That's unfortunate," said Farmer Oak, contemplating a crack in the stone floor with sorrow. "I'm only an every-day sort of man, and my only chance was in being the first comer ... Well, there's no use in my waiting, for that was all I came about: so I'll take myself off home-along, Mrs. Hurst."

Analysis: Hardy's portrayal of Oak is fascinating here: we see him giving her up immediately before having spoken to Bathsheba. He feels his attractions are limited: "my only chance was in being the first comer". His surrender before he's even started is deeply ironic because, of course, he is the person who never gives up loving Bathsheba in the book. Mrs Hurst's portrayal of Bathsheba tells us that the girl is very clever, having the skills to be a "governess", and is pursued. The mystery about Bathsheba deepens though, because we, like Oak, are prompted to think: who are all these admirers?

Discussion point: Why does Oak think he only has a chance if he is the "first comer"?

When Gabriel had gone about two hundred yards along the down, he heard a "hoi-hoi!" uttered behind him, in a piping note of more treble quality than that in which the exclamation usually embodies itself when shouted across a field. He looked round, and saw a girl racing after him, waving a white handkerchief.

Oak stood still—and the runner drew nearer. It was Bathsheba Everdene. Gabriel's colour deepened: hers was already deep, not, as it appeared, from emotion, but from running.

"Farmer Oak—I—" she said, pausing for want of breath pulling up in front of him with a slanted face and putting her hand to her side.

"I have just called to see you," said Gabriel, pending her further speech.

"Yes—I know that," she said panting like a robin, her face red and moist from her exertions, like a peony petal before the sun dries off the dew. "I didn't know you had come to ask to have me, or I should have come in from the garden instantly. I ran after you to say—that my aunt made a mistake in sending you away from courting me—"

Gabriel expanded. "I'm sorry to have made you run so fast, my dear," he said, with a grateful sense of favours to come. "Wait a bit till you've found your breath."

"—It was quite a mistake—aunt's telling you I had a young man already," Bathsheba went on. "I haven't a sweetheart at all—and I never had one, and I thought that, as times go with women, it was such a pity to send you away thinking that I had several."

"Really and truly I am glad to hear that!" said Farmer Oak, smiling one of his long special smiles, and blushing with gladness. He held out his hand to take hers, which, when she had eased her side by pressing it there, was prettily extended upon her bosom to still her loud-beating heart. Directly he seized it she put it behind her, so that it slipped through his fingers like an eel."

"I have a nice snug little farm," said Gabriel, with half a degree less assurance than when he had seized her hand.

"Yes; you have."

"A man has advanced me money to begin with, but still, it will soon be paid off, and though I am only an every-day sort of man, I have got on a little since I was a boy." Gabriel uttered "a little" in a tone to show her that it was the complacent form of "a great deal." He continued: "When we be married, I am quite sure I can work twice as hard as I do now."

He went forward and stretched out his arm again. Bathsheba had overtaken him at a point beside which stood a low stunted holly bush, now laden with red berries. Seeing his advance take the form of an attitude threatening a possible enclosure, if not compression, of her person, she edged off round the bush.

"Why, Farmer Oak," she said, over the top, looking at him with rounded eyes, "I never said I was going to marry you."

"Well—that is a tale!" said Oak, with dismay. "To run after anybody like this, and then say you don't want him!"

"What I meant to tell you was only this," she said eagerly, and yet half conscious of the absurdity of the position she had made for herself—"that nobody has got me yet as a sweetheart, instead of my having a dozen, as my aunt said; I hate to be thought men's property in that way, though possibly I shall be had some day. Why, if I'd wanted you I shouldn't have run after you like this; 'twould have been the forwardest thing! But there was no harm in hurrying to correct a piece of false news that had been told you."

"Oh, no—no harm at all." But there is such a thing as being too generous in expressing a judgment impulsively, and Oak added with a more appreciative sense of all the circumstances—"Well, I am not quite certain it was no harm."

"Indeed, I hadn't time to think before starting whether I wanted to marry or not, for you'd have been gone over the hill."

"Come," said Gabriel, freshening again; "think a minute or two. I'll wait a while, Miss Everdene. Will you marry me? Do, Bathsheba. I love you far more than common!"

"I'll try to think," she observed, rather more timorously; "if I can think out of doors; my mind spreads away so."

"But you can give a guess."

"Then give me time." Bathsheba looked thoughtfully into the distance, away from the direction in which Gabriel stood.

"I can make you happy," said he to the back of her head, across the bush. "You shall have a piano in a year or two—farmers' wives are getting to have pianos now—and I'll practise up the flute right well to play with you in the evenings."

"Yes; I should like that."

"And have one of those little ten-pound gigs for market—and nice flowers, and birds—cocks and hens I mean, because they be useful," continued Gabriel, feeling balanced between poetry and practicality.

"I should like it very much."

"And a frame for cucumbers—like a gentleman and lady."

"Yes."

"And when the wedding was over, we'd have it put in the newspaper list of marriages."

"Dearly I should like that!"

"And the babies in the births—every man jack of 'em! And at home by the fire, whenever you look up, there I shall be—and whenever I look up there will be you."

"Wait, wait, and don't be improper!"

Her countenance fell, and she was silent awhile. He regarded the red berries between them over and over again, to such an extent, that holly seemed in his after life to be a cypher signifying a proposal of marriage. Bathsheba decisively turned to him.

"No; 'tis no use," she said. "I don't want to marry you."

"Try."

"I have tried hard all the time I've been thinking; for a marriage would be very nice in one sense. People would talk about me, and think I had won my battle, and I should feel triumphant, and all that, But a husband—"

"Well!"

"Why, he'd always be there, as you say; whenever I looked up, there he'd be."

"Of course he would—I, that is."

"Well, what I mean is that I shouldn't mind being a bride at a wedding, if I could be one without having a husband. But since a woman can't show off in that way by herself, I shan't marry—at least yet."

"That's a terrible wooden story!"

At this criticism of her statement Bathsheba made an addition to her dignity by a slight sweep away from him.

"Upon my heart and soul, I don't know what a maid can say stupider than that," said Oak. "But dearest," he continued in a palliative voice, "don't be like it!" Oak sighed a deep honest sigh—none the less so in that, being like the sigh of a pine plantation, it was rather noticeable as a disturbance of the atmosphere. "Why won't you have me?" he appealed, creeping round the holly to reach her side.

"I cannot," she said, retreating.

"But why?" he persisted, standing still at last in despair of ever reaching her, and facing over the bush.

"Because I don't love you."

Analysis: This first proposal scene is worth looking at in depth because of what it tells about the characters and the society of the time. Notice how Hardy generates tension in this section by the way in which he reveals the changing emotions of the characters. Oak is like a chess player who doesn't quite know how to play the game but occasionally alights upon the right move, only to scupper himself with a stupid one. Notice how he draws in Bathsheba to his proposal by talking about all the things they will own as a couple: the piano, the gig, the cucumber frame. Bathsheba is clearly interested in having a high social status because she likes the thought of owning all of these things, and having her name in the paper when she is married. Again though, there is mystery about her character because we can tell she's not totally materialistic, she just wants to be thought of highly, to prized above all else by society. Oak, as an aspiring farmer, might be in a position to offer her a relatively good social position in a few years' time when he has established himself: at the moment though, we are aware he is dreaming. He only has a hut to live in.

He blunders when he talks about having lots of children. Oak, as a farmer, is blunt about reproduction: it is clear from his statement that he intends to have sex with Bathsheba a lot. She is horrified by his comment and upbraids him for being "improper". She is part of the Victorian society which is prudish about such things. In this sense, she echoes the sentiments of Hardy's readers here who would have been middle-class Victorians with strict morals about sex. After this comment, it is clear that Oak has lost Bathsheba, who admits that she does not love him.

Discussion point: What does this proposal reveal about Oak and Bathsheba? What does it reveal about the attitudes of middle-class Victorians of the day?

"Yes, but—"

She contracted a yawn to an inoffensive smallness, so that it was hardly ill-mannered at all. "I don't love you," she said.

"But I love you—and, as for myself, I am content to be liked."

"Oh Mr. Oak—that's very fine! You'd get to despise me."

"Never," said Mr Oak, so earnestly that he seemed to be coming, by the force of his words, straight through the bush and into her arms. "I shall do one thing in this life—one thing certain—that is, love you, and long for you, and keep wanting you till I die." His voice had a genuine pathos now, and his large brown hands perceptibly trembled.

"It seems dreadfully wrong not to have you when you feel so much!" she said with a little distress, and looking hopelessly around for some means of escape from her moral dilemma. "How I wish I hadn't run after you!" However she seemed to have a short cut for getting back to cheerfulness, and set her face to signify archness. "It wouldn't do, Mr Oak. I want somebody to tame me; I am too independent; and you would never be able to, I know."

Oak cast his eyes down the field in a way implying that it was useless to attempt argument.

"Mr. Oak," she said, with luminous distinctness and common sense, "you are better off than I. I have hardly a penny in the world—I am staying with my aunt for my bare sustenance. I am better educated than you—and I don't love you a bit: that's my side of the case. Now yours: you are a farmer just beginning; and you ought in common prudence, if you marry at all (which you should certainly not think of doing at present), to marry a woman with money, who would stock a larger farm for you than you have now."

Gabriel looked at her with a little surprise and much admiration.

"That's the very thing I had been thinking myself!" he naïvely said.

Farmer Oak had one-and-a-half Christian characteristics too many to succeed with Bathsheba: his humility, and a superfluous moiety of honesty. Bathsheba was decidedly disconcerted.

"Well, then, why did you come and disturb me?" she said, almost angrily, if not quite, an enlarging red spot rising in each cheek.

"I can't do what I think would be—would be—"

"Right?"

"No: wise."

"You have made an admission now, Mr. Oak," she exclaimed, with even more hauteur, and rocking her head disdainfully. "After that, do you think I could marry you? Not if I know it."

He broke in passionately. "But don't mistake me like that! Because I am open enough to own what every man in my shoes would have thought of, you make your colours come up your face, and get crabbed with me. That about your not being good enough for me is nonsense. You speak like a lady—all the parish notice it, and your uncle at Weatherbury is, I have heerd, a large farmer—much larger than ever I shall be. May I call in the evening, or will you walk along with me o' Sundays? I don't want you to make-up your mind at once, if you'd rather not."

"No—no—I cannot. Don't press me any more—don't. I don't love you—so 'twould be ridiculous," she said, with a laugh.

No man likes to see his emotions the sport of a merry-go-round of skittishness. "Very well," said Oak, firmly, with the bearing of one who was going to give his days and nights to Ecclesiastes for ever. "Then I'll ask you no more."

Analysis: As if to contradict the prudish response that Bathsheba gave before, she now confesses that Oak will never "tame" her. There is a wildness about her which is very un-Victorian, which she recognises is inside her. Her insistence upon being "independent" would have shocked the readers of the day, but now make this a very modern novel. In many ways, Bathsheba's search for independence shapes the narrative of the book and echoes the search for independence that many women in the West desire today. Bathsheba, in this sense, is a proto-feminist.

Discussion point: What are the reasons that Bathsheba gives for not wanting to marry Oak? What do you think of these reasons? Do you think she is right to refuse him?

Questions

Why is Gabriel upset that the cows have run dry?

What does he decide to do?

How does he prepare for his proposal?

What does the aunt say when he states he wants to marry the girl?

What does Bathsheba do when Gabriel leaves?

How does Gabriel try to tempt Bathsheba into marrying him?

What is Bathsheba's response?

What does Gabriel say he will do?

What does Bathsheba tell him to do? GCSE style question: How does Hardy make Gabriel's first proposal such a comic and touching moment?

A Level style question: compare and contrast this proposal scene with another one in a text of your choice.

Creative response: write a poem/story called 'The Proposal' which could be about a marriage proposal, or some other kind of proposal. Or write Bathsheba's diary for this chapter.

CHAPTER V
DEPARTURE OF BATHSHEBA—A PASTORAL TRAGEDY

The news which one day reached Gabriel, that Bathsheba Everdene had left the neighbourhood, had an influence upon him which might have surprised any who never suspected that the more emphatic the renunciation the less absolute its character.

It may have been observed that there is no regular path for getting out of love as there is for getting in. Some people look upon marriage as a short cut that way, but it has been known to fail. Separation, which was the means that chance offered to Gabriel Oak by Bathsheba's disappearance, though effectual with people of certain humours, is apt to idealize the removed object with others—notably those whose affection, placid and regular as it may be, flows deep and long. Oak belonged to the even-tempered order of humanity, and felt the secret fusion of himself in Bathsheba to be burning with a finer flame now that she was gone—that was all.

His incipient friendship with her aunt had been nipped by the failure of his suit, and all that Oak learnt of Bathsheba's movements was done indirectly. It appeared that she had gone to a place called Weatherbury, more than twenty miles off, but in what capacity—whether as a visitor, or permanently, he could not discover.

Gabriel had two dogs. George, the elder, exhibited an ebony-tipped nose, surrounded by a narrow margin of pink flesh, and a coat marked in random splotches approximating in colour to white and slaty grey; but the grey, after years of sun and rain, had been scorched and washed out of the more prominent locks, leaving them of a reddish-brown, as if the blue component of the grey had faded, like the indigo from the same kind of colour in Turner's pictures. In substance it had originally been hair, but long contact with sheep seemed to be turning it by degrees into wool of a poor quality and staple.

This dog had originally belonged to a shepherd of inferior morals and dreadful temper, and the result was that George knew the exact degrees of condemnation signified by cursing and swearing of all descriptions better than the wickedest old man in the neighbourhood. Long experience had so precisely taught the animal the difference between such exclamations as "Come in!" and "D———— ye, come in!" that he knew to a hair's breadth the rate of trotting back from the ewes' tails that each call involved, if a staggerer with the sheep crook was to be escaped. Though old, he was clever and trustworthy still.

The young dog, George's son, might possibly have been the image of his mother, for there was not much resemblance between him and George. He was learning the sheep-keeping business, so as to follow on at the flock when the other should die, but had got no further than the rudiments as yet—still finding an insuperable difficulty in distinguishing between doing a thing well enough and doing it too well. So earnest and yet so wrong-headed was this young dog (he had no name in particular, and answered with perfect readiness to any pleasant interjection), that if sent behind the flock to help them on, he did it so thoroughly that he would have chased them across the whole county with the greatest pleasure if not called off or reminded when to stop by the example of old George.

Thus much for the dogs. On the further side of Norcombe Hill was a chalk-pit, from which chalk had been drawn for generations, and spread over adjacent farms. Two hedges converged upon it in the form of a V, but without quite meeting. The narrow opening left, which was immediately over the brow of the pit, was protected by a rough railing.

One night, when Farmer Oak had returned to his house, believing there would be no further necessity for his attendance on the down, he called as usual to the dogs, previously to shutting them up in the outhouse till next morning. Only one responded—old George; the other could not be found, either in the house, lane, or garden. Gabriel then remembered that he had left the two dogs on the hill eating a dead lamb (a kind of meat he usually kept from them, except when other food ran short), and concluding that the young one had not finished his meal, he went indoors to the luxury of a bed, which latterly he had only enjoyed on Sundays.

It was a still, moist night. Just before dawn he was assisted in waking by the abnormal reverberation of familiar music. To the shepherd, the note of the sheep-bell, like the ticking of the clock to other people, is a chronic sound that only makes itself noticed by ceasing or altering in some unusual manner from the well-known idle twinkle which signifies to the accustomed ear, however distant, that all is well in the fold. In the solemn calm of the awakening morn that note was heard by Gabriel, beating with unusual violence and rapidity. This exceptional ringing may be caused in two ways—by the rapid feeding of the sheep bearing the bell, as when the flock breaks into new pasture, which gives it an intermittent rapidity, or by the sheep starting off in a run, when the sound has a regular palpitation. The experienced ear of Oak knew the sound he now heard to be caused by the running of the flock with great velocity.

He jumped out of bed, dressed, tore down the lane through a foggy dawn, and ascended the hill. The forward ewes were kept apart from those among which the fall of lambs would be later, there being two hundred of the latter class in Gabriel's flock. These two hundred seemed to have absolutely vanished from the hill. There were the fifty with their lambs, enclosed at the other end as he had left them, but the rest, forming the bulk of the flock, were nowhere. Gabriel called at the top of his voice the shepherd's call:

"Ovey, ovey, ovey!"

Not a single bleat. He went to the hedge; a gap had been broken through it, and in the gap were the footprints of the sheep. Rather surprised to find them break fence at this season, yet putting it down instantly to their great fondness for ivy in winter-time, of which a great deal grew in the plantation, he followed through the hedge. They were not in the plantation. He called again: the valleys and farthest hills resounded as when the sailors invoked the lost Hylas on the Mysian shore; but no sheep. He passed through the trees and along the ridge of the hill. On the extreme summit, where the ends of the two converging hedges of which we have spoken were stopped short by meeting the brow of the chalk-pit, he saw the younger dog standing against the sky—dark and motionless as Napoleon at St. Helena.

A horrible conviction darted through Oak. With a sensation of bodily faintness he advanced: at one point the rails were broken through, and there he saw the footprints of his ewes. The dog came up, licked his hand, and made signs implying that he expected some great reward for signal services rendered. Oak looked over the precipice. The ewes lay dead and dying at its foot—a heap of two hundred mangled carcasses, representing in their condition just now at least two hundred more.

Oak was an intensely humane man: indeed, his humanity often tore in pieces any politic intentions of his which bordered on strategy, and carried him on as by gravitation. A shadow in his life had always been that his flock ended in mutton—that a day came and found every shepherd an arrant traitor to his defenseless sheep. His first feeling now was one of pity for the untimely fate of these gentle ewes and their unborn lambs.

It was a second to remember another phase of the matter. The sheep were not insured. All the savings of a frugal life had been dispersed at a blow; his hopes of being an independent farmer were laid low—possibly for ever.

Analysis: The shocking death of Oak's sheep marks the end of the opening of the book. The sex comedy of the first chapters is now replaced by a darker tone: death and fate intrude. It's an important event in a narrative sense because Oak now has to go, cap in hand, in search of work and, of course, finds it at Bathsheba's farm. It is also important marker of Hardy's intentions with the narrative: the author is telling us that this is no light rural comedy but a serious book, which will deal with the most extreme issues. He is showing country life "red in tooth and claw" here; his depiction of the "two hundred mangled carcasses" is horrific and deals a savage blow to Oak. His social aspirations are ruined: he has no real chance of being "independent" now. Later on in the chapter, he comments how he is pleased he is not married to Bathsheba because he would have brought ruin to her. We see his true humanity of character here: when faced with the worst of circumstances, he remains a generous man.

Discussion point: How and why does Hardy darken the tone here?

Gabriel's energies, patience, and industry had been so severely taxed during the years of his life between eighteen and eight-and-twenty, to reach his present stage of progress that no more seemed to be left in him. He leant down upon a rail, and covered his face with his hands.

Stupors, however, do not last for ever, and Farmer Oak recovered from his. It was as remarkable as it was characteristic that the one sentence he uttered was in thankfulness:—

"Thank God I am not married: what would she have done in the poverty now coming upon me!"

Oak raised his head, and wondering what he could do, listlessly surveyed the scene. By the outer margin of the Pit was an oval pond, and over it hung the attenuated skeleton of a chrome-yellow moon which had only a few days to last—the morning star dogging her on the left hand. The pool glittered like a dead man's eye, and as the world awoke a breeze blew, shaking and elongating the reflection of the moon without breaking it, and turning the image of the star to a phosphoric streak upon the water. All this Oak saw and remembered.

As far as could be learnt it appeared that the poor young dog, still under the impression that since he was kept for running after sheep, the more he ran after them the better, had at the end of his meal off the dead lamb, which may have given him additional energy and spirits, collected all the ewes into a corner, driven the timid creatures through the hedge, across the upper field, and by main force of worrying had given them momentum enough to break down a portion of the rotten railing, and so hurled them over the edge.

George's son had done his work so thoroughly that he was considered too good a workman to live, and was, in fact, taken and tragically shot at twelve o'clock that same day—another instance of the untoward fate which so often attends dogs and other philosophers who follow out a train of reasoning to its logical conclusion, and attempt perfectly consistent conduct in a world made up so largely of compromise.

Gabriel's farm had been stocked by a dealer—on the strength of Oak's promising look and character—who was receiving a percentage from the farmer till such time as the advance should be cleared off. Oak found that the value of stock, plant, and implements which were really his own would be about sufficient to pay his debts, leaving himself a free man with the clothes he stood up in, and nothing more.

Questions

What wakes Gabriel?
What does he discover has happened to his pregnant ewes?
Why is this a disaster for Gabriel?
What does he do with his sheep dog?
 What is his financial situation after he sells off his stock and equipment?
GCSE style question: how does Hardy make the death of the sheep such a shocking moment in the novel?
A Level style question: compare and contrast this "disaster" scene with another representation of a disaster in a text of your choice.
Creative response: write a poem/story in which someone loses everything by an accident of fate.

CHAPTER VI
THE FAIR—THE JOURNEY—THE FIRE

Two months passed away. We are brought on to a day in February, on which was held the yearly statute or hiring fair in the county-town of Casterbridge.

At one end of the street stood from two to three hundred blithe and hearty labourers waiting upon Chance—all men of the stamp to whom labour suggests nothing worse than a wrestle with gravitation, and pleasure nothing better than a renunciation of the same. Among these, carters and waggoners were distinguished by having a piece of whip-cord twisted round their hats; thatchers wore a fragment of woven straw; shepherds held their sheep-crooks in their hands; and thus the situation required was known to the hirers at a glance.

In the crowd was an athletic young fellow of somewhat superior appearance to the rest—in fact, his superiority was marked enough to lead several ruddy peasants standing by to speak to him inquiringly, as to a farmer, and to use "Sir" as a finishing word. His answer always was,—

"I am looking for a place myself—a bailiff's. Do ye know of anybody who wants one?"

Gabriel was paler now. His eyes were more meditative, and his expression was more sad. He had passed through an ordeal of wretchedness which had given him more than it had taken away. He had sunk from his modest elevation as pastoral king into the very slime-pits of Siddim; but there was left to him a dignified calm he had never before known, and that indifference to fate which, though it often makes a villain of a man, is the basis of his sublimity when it does not. And thus the abasement had been exaltation, and the loss gain.

In the morning a regiment of cavalry had left the town, and a sergeant and his party had been beating up for recruits through the four streets. As the end of the day drew on, and he found himself not hired, Gabriel almost wished that he had joined them, and gone off to serve his country. Weary of standing in the market-place, and not much minding the kind of work he turned his hand to, he decided to offer himself in some other capacity than that of bailiff.

All the farmers seemed to be wanting shepherds. Sheep-tending was Gabriel's speciality. Turning down an obscure street and entering an obscurer lane, he went up to a smith's shop.

"How long would it take you to make a shepherd's crook?"

Analysis: Throughout all of his writing, Hardy is very sensitive to the issue of social position. Here we can see that Oak is suffering because he sees himself as a "bailiff" – a superintendent of a farm – and not a lowly shepherd. This is because he was once a proper farmer, a proud social position. However, he learns that he will never be accepted in the bailiff position precisely because he was a farmer: the other farmers mistrust him, thinking he will be too high and mighty. Oak swallows his pride and looks for the inferior social position.

Discussion point: What do we learn about Oak's character here? What do we learn about Victorian society here?

"Twenty minutes."

"How much?"

"Two shillings."

He sat on a bench and the crook was made, a stem being given him into the bargain.

He then went to a ready-made clothes' shop, the owner of which had a large rural connection. As the crook had absorbed most of Gabriel's money, he attempted, and carried out, an exchange of his overcoat for a shepherd's regulation smock-frock.

This transaction having been completed, he again hurried off to the centre of the town, and stood on the kerb of the pavement, as a shepherd, crook in hand.

Now that Oak had turned himself into a shepherd, it seemed that bailiffs were most in demand. However, two or three farmers noticed him and drew near. Dialogues followed, more or less in the subjoined form:—

"Where do you come from?"

"Norcombe."

"That's a long way.

"Fifteen miles."

"Who's farm were you upon last?"

"My own."

This reply invariably operated like a rumour of cholera. The inquiring farmer would edge away and shake his head dubiously. Gabriel, like his dog, was too good to be trustworthy, and he never made advance beyond this point.

It is safer to accept any chance that offers itself, and extemporize a procedure to fit it, than to get a good plan matured, and wait for a chance of using it. Gabriel wished he had not nailed up his colours as a shepherd, but had laid himself out for anything in the whole cycle of labour that was required in the fair. It grew dusk. Some merry men were whistling and singing by the corn-exchange. Gabriel's hand, which had lain for some time idle in his smock-frock pocket, touched his flute which he carried there. Here was an opportunity for putting his dearly bought wisdom into practice.

He drew out his flute and began to play "Jockey to the Fair" in the style of a man who had never known moment's sorrow. Oak could pipe with Arcadian sweetness, and the sound of the well-known notes cheered his own heart as well as those of the loungers. He played on with spirit, and in half an hour had earned in pence what was a small fortune to a destitute man.

By making inquiries he learnt that there was another fair at Shottsford the next day.

"How far is Shottsford?"

"Ten miles t'other side of Weatherbury."

Weatherbury! It was where Bathsheba had gone two months before. This information was like coming from night into noon.

"How far is it to Weatherbury?"

"Five or six miles."

Bathsheba had probably left Weatherbury long before this time, but the place had enough interest attaching to it to lead Oak to choose Shottsford fair as his next field of inquiry, because it lay in the Weatherbury quarter. Moreover, the Weatherbury folk were by no means uninteresting intrinsically. If report spoke truly they were as hardy, merry, thriving, wicked a set as any in the whole county. Oak resolved to sleep at Weatherbury that night on his way to Shottsford, and struck out at once into the high road which had been recommended as the direct route to the village in question.

The road stretched through water-meadows traversed by little brooks, whose quivering surfaces were braided along their centres, and folded into creases at the sides; or, where the flow was more rapid, the stream was pied with spots of white froth, which rode on in undisturbed serenity. On the higher levels the dead and dry carcasses of leaves tapped the ground as they bowled along helter-skelter upon the shoulders of the wind, and little birds in the hedges were rustling their feathers and tucking themselves in comfortably for the night, retaining their places if Oak kept moving, but flying away if he stopped to look at them. He passed by Yalbury Wood where the game-birds were rising to their roosts, and heard the crack-voiced cock-pheasants "cu-uck, cuck," and the wheezy whistle of the hens.

By the time he had walked three or four miles every shape in the landscape had assumed a uniform hue of blackness. He descended Yalbury Hill and could just discern ahead of him a waggon, drawn up under a great over-hanging tree by the roadside.

On coming close, he found there were no horses attached to it, the spot being apparently quite deserted. The waggon, from its position, seemed to have been left there for the night, for beyond about half a truss of hay which was heaped in the bottom, it was quite empty. Gabriel sat down on the shafts of the vehicle and considered his position. He calculated that he had walked a very fair proportion of the journey; and having been on foot since daybreak, he felt tempted to lie down upon the hay in the waggon instead of pushing on to the village of Weatherbury, and having to pay for a lodging.

Eating his last slices of bread and ham, and drinking from the bottle of cider he had taken the precaution to bring with him, he got into the lonely waggon. Here he spread half of the hay as a bed, and, as well as he could in the darkness, pulled the other half over him by way of bed-clothes, covering himself entirely, and feeling, physically, as comfortable as ever he had been in his life. Inward melancholy it was impossible for a man like Oak, introspective far beyond his neighbours, to banish quite, whilst conning the present untoward page of his history. So, thinking of his misfortunes, amorous and pastoral, he fell asleep, shepherds enjoying, in common with sailors, the privilege of being able to summon the god instead of having to wait for him.

On somewhat suddenly awaking, after a sleep of whose length he had no idea, Oak found that the waggon was in motion. He was being carried along the road at a rate rather considerable for a vehicle without springs, and under circumstances of physical uneasiness, his head being dandled up and down on the bed of the waggon like a kettledrum-stick. He then distinguished voices in conversation, coming from the forpart of the waggon. His concern at this dilemma (which would have been alarm, had he been a thriving man; but misfortune is a fine opiate to personal terror) led him to peer cautiously from the hay, and the first sight he beheld was the stars above him. Charles's Wain was getting towards a right angle with the Pole star, and Gabriel concluded that it must be about nine o'clock—in other words, that he had slept two hours. This small astronomical calculation was made without any positive effort, and whilst he was stealthily turning to discover, if possible, into whose hands he had fallen.

Two figures were dimly visible in front, sitting with their legs outside the waggon, one of whom was driving. Gabriel soon found that this was the waggoner, and it appeared they had come from Casterbridge fair, like himself.

A conversation was in progress, which continued thus:—

"Be as 'twill, she's a fine handsome body as far's looks be concerned. But that's only the skin of the woman, and these dandy cattle be as proud as a lucifer in their insides."

"Ay—so 'a do seem, Billy Smallbury—so 'a do seem." This utterance was very shaky by nature, and more so by circumstance, the jolting of the waggon not being without its effect upon the speaker's larynx. It came from the man who held the reins.

"She's a very vain feymell—so 'tis said here and there."

"Ah, now. If so be 'tis like that, I can't look her in the face. Lord, no: not I—heh-heh-heh! Such a shy man as I be!"

"Yes—she's very vain. 'Tis said that every night at going to bed she looks in the glass to put on her night-cap properly."

"And not a married woman. Oh, the world!"

"And 'a can play the peanner, so 'tis said. Can play so clever that 'a can make a psalm tune sound as well as the merriest loose song a man can wish for."

"D'ye tell o't! A happy time for us, and I feel quite a new man! And how do she pay?"

"That I don't know, Master Poorgrass."

On hearing these and other similar remarks, a wild thought flashed into Gabriel's mind that they might be speaking of Bathsheba. There were, however, no grounds for retaining such a supposition, for the waggon, though going in the direction of Weatherbury, might be going beyond it, and the woman alluded to seemed to be the mistress of some estate. They were now apparently close upon Weatherbury and not to alarm the speakers unnecessarily, Gabriel slipped out of the waggon unseen.

He turned to an opening in the hedge, which he found to be a gate, and mounting thereon, he sat meditating whether to seek a cheap lodging in the village, or to ensure a cheaper one by lying under some hay or corn-stack. The crunching jangle of the waggon died upon his ear. He was about to walk on, when he noticed on his left hand an unusual light—appearing about half a mile distant. Oak watched it, and the glow increased. Something was on fire.

Gabriel again mounted the gate, and, leaping down on the other side upon what he found to be ploughed soil, made across the field in the exact direction of the fire. The blaze, enlarging in a double ratio by his approach and its own increase, showed him as he drew nearer the outlines of ricks beside it, lighted up to great distinctness. A rick-yard was the source of the fire. His weary face now began to be painted over with a rich orange glow, and the whole front of his smock-frock and gaiters was covered with a dancing shadow pattern of thorn-twigs—the light reaching him through a leafless intervening hedge—and the metallic curve of his sheep-crook shone silver-bright in the same abounding rays. He came up to the boundary fence, and stood to regain breath. It seemed as if the spot was unoccupied by a living soul.

The fire was issuing from a long straw-stack, which was so far gone as to preclude a possibility of saving it. A rick burns differently from a house. As the wind blows the fire inwards, the portion in flames completely disappears like melting sugar, and the outline is lost to the eye. However, a hay or a wheat-rick, well put together, will resist combustion for a length of time, if it begins on the outside.

This before Gabriel's eyes was a rick of straw, loosely put together, and the flames darted into it with lightning swiftness. It glowed on the windward side, rising and falling in intensity, like the coal of a cigar. Then a superincumbent bundle rolled down, with a whisking noise; flames elongated, and bent themselves about with a quiet roar, but no crackle. Banks of smoke went off horizontally at the back like passing clouds, and behind these burned hidden pyres, illuminating the semi-transparent sheet of smoke to a lustrous yellow uniformity. Individual straws in the foreground were consumed in a creeping movement of ruddy heat, as if they were knots of red worms, and above shone imaginary fiery faces, tongues hanging from lips, glaring eyes, and other impish forms, from which at intervals sparks flew in clusters like birds from a nest.

Oak suddenly ceased from being a mere spectator by discovering the case to be more serious than he had at first imagined. A scroll of smoke blew aside and revealed to him a wheat-rick in startling juxtaposition with the decaying one, and behind this a series of others, composing the main corn produce of the farm; so that instead of the straw-stack standing, as he had imagined comparatively isolated, there was a regular connection between it and the remaining stacks of the group.

Gabriel leapt over the hedge, and saw that he was not alone. The first man he came to was running about in a great hurry, as if his thoughts were several yards in advance of his body, which they could never drag on fast enough.

"O, man—fire, fire! A good master and a bad servant is fire, fire!—I mane a bad servant and a good master. Oh, Mark Clark—come! And you, Billy Smallbury—and you, Maryann Money—and you, Jan Coggan, and Matthew there!" Other figures now appeared behind this shouting man and among the smoke, and Gabriel found that, far from being alone he was in a great company—whose shadows danced merrily up and down, timed by the jigging of the flames, and not at all by their owners' movements. The assemblage—belonging to that class of society which casts its thoughts into the form of feeling, and its feelings into the form of commotion—set to work with a remarkable confusion of purpose.

"Stop the draught under the wheat-rick!" cried Gabriel to those nearest to him. The corn stood on stone staddles, and between these, tongues of yellow hue from the burning straw licked and darted playfully. If the fire once got under this stack, all would be lost.

"Get a tarpaulin—quick!" said Gabriel.

A rick-cloth was brought, and they hung it like a curtain across the channel. The flames immediately ceased to go under the bottom of the corn-stack, and stood up vertical.

"Stand here with a bucket of water and keep the cloth wet." said Gabriel again.

The flames, now driven upwards, began to attack the angles of the huge roof covering the wheat-stack.

"A ladder," cried Gabriel.

"The ladder was against the straw-rick and is burnt to a cinder," said a spectre-like form in the smoke.

Oak seized the cut ends of the sheaves, as if he were going to engage in the operation of "reed-drawing," and digging in his feet, and occasionally sticking in the stem of his sheep-crook, he clambered up the beetling face. He at once sat astride the very apex, and began with his crook to beat off the fiery fragments which had lodged thereon, shouting to the others to get him a bough and a ladder, and some water.

Billy Smallbury—one of the men who had been on the waggon—by this time had found a ladder, which Mark Clark ascended, holding on beside Oak upon the thatch. The smoke at this corner was stifling, and Clark, a nimble fellow, having been handed a bucket of water, bathed Oak's face and sprinkled him generally, whilst Gabriel, now with a long beech-bough in one hand, in addition to his crook in the other, kept sweeping the stack and dislodging all fiery particles.

On the ground the groups of villagers were still occupied in doing all they could to keep down the conflagration, which was not much. They were all tinged orange, and backed up by shadows of varying pattern. Round the corner of the largest stack, out of the direct rays of the fire, stood a pony, bearing a young woman on its back. By her side was another woman, on foot. These two seemed to keep at a distance from the fire, that the horse might not become restive.

Analysis: In sharp contrast to the way he has been portrayed in the preceding chapters – as a hapless victim – Hardy now presents Oak as a hero: his quickness of mind, his knowledge of how fire spreads, his calmness under pressure enable him to rescue the wheat ricks from certain destruction. Notice how Hardy builds suspense through his mixture of panic-stricken dialogue and vivid imagery: Oak's intervention immediately ceases the fire.

Discussion point: How does Hardy generate drama during his description of the fire?

"He's a shepherd," said the woman on foot. "Yes—he is. See how his crook shines as he beats the rick with it. And his smock-frock is burnt in two holes, I declare! A fine young shepherd he is too, ma'am."

"Whose shepherd is he?" said the equestrian in a clear voice.

"Don't know, ma'am."

"Don't any of the others know?"

"Nobody at all—I've asked 'em. Quite a stranger, they say."

The young woman on the pony rode out from the shade and looked anxiously around.

"Do you think the barn is safe?" she said.

"D'ye think the barn is safe, Jan Coggan?" said the second woman, passing on the question to the nearest man in that direction.

"Safe-now—leastwise I think so. If this rick had gone the barn would have followed. 'Tis that bold shepherd up there that have done the most good— he sitting on the top o' rick, whizzing his great long-arms about like a windmill."

"He does work hard," said the young woman on horseback, looking up at Gabriel through her thick woollen veil. "I wish he was shepherd here. Don't any of you know his name."

"Never heard the man's name in my life, or seed his form afore."

The fire began to get worsted, and Gabriel's elevated position being no longer required of him, he made as if to descend.

"Maryann," said the girl on horseback, "go to him as he comes down, and say that the farmer wishes to thank him for the great service he has done."

Maryann stalked off towards the rick and met Oak at the foot of the ladder. She delivered her message.

"Where is your master the farmer?" asked Gabriel, kindling with the idea of getting employment that seemed to strike him now.

"'Tisn't a master; 'tis a mistress, shepherd."

"A woman farmer?"

"Ay, 'a b'lieve, and a rich one too!" said a bystander. "Lately 'a came here from a distance. Took on her uncle's farm, who died suddenly. Used to measure his money in half-pint cups. They say now that she've business in every bank in Casterbridge, and thinks no more of playing pitch-and-toss sovereign than you and I do pitch-halfpenny—not a bit in the world, shepherd."

"That's she, back there upon the pony," said Maryann; "wi' her face a-covered up in that black cloth with holes in it."

Oak, his features smudged, grimy, and undiscoverable from the smoke and heat, his smock-frock burnt into holes and dripping with water, the ash stem of his sheep-crook charred six inches shorter, advanced with the humility stern adversity had thrust upon him up to the slight female form in the saddle. He lifted his hat with respect, and not without gallantry: stepping close to her hanging feet he said in a hesitating voice,—

"Do you happen to want a shepherd, ma'am?"

She lifted the wool veil tied round her face, and looked all astonishment. Gabriel and his cold-hearted darling, Bathsheba Everdene, were face to face.

Bathsheba did not speak, and he mechanically repeated in an abashed and sad voice,—

"Do you want a shepherd, ma'am?"

Analysis: The themes of fate and love intertwine here. The description of Oak is marvellous: his clothes full of holes, his face smudged, he comes towards Bathsheba. Here he is characterised almost as an action hero, stepping out of the fire like Bruce Willis in *Diehard*. However, it is interesting to note how Oak is entirely humble, asking the absurdly plaintive question: "Do you want a shepherd, ma'am?" His tone is very respectful, almost begging. Unlike an action hero, he does not have the luxury of being free from monetary concerns: he must find work in order to live. Hardy wrote for serial and deliberately ends this chapter with a cliff-hanger, making sure that his readers would want more next week.

Discussion point: What is fateful about this encounter? How does Hardy develop the theme of love here?

Questions

What is a bailiff?

Why does Oak fail to get work as a shepherd or a bailiff?

Who is Joseph Poorgrass talking about?

How does Gabriel help put out the fire in the hay ricks?

Who does Gabriel discover is the mistress of the farm?

How are the roles reversed between Bathsheba and Gabriel?

GCSE style question: how does Hardy make the fire in the hayricks such an exciting scene?

A Level style question: compare and contrast the representation of the fire with another scene in literature where there is a fire, e.g. Jane rescuing Rochester in his burning bed in *Jane Eyre*.

Creative response: write a story/poem/description called 'The Fire'.

CHAPTER VII
RECOGNITION—A TIMID GIRL

Bathsheba withdrew into the shade. She scarcely knew whether most to be amused at the singularity of the meeting, or to be concerned at its awkwardness. There was room for a little pity, also for a very little exultation: the former at his position, the latter at her own. Embarrassed she was not, and she remembered Gabriel's declaration of love to her at Norcombe only to think she had nearly forgotten it.

"Yes," she murmured, putting on an air of dignity, and turning again to him with a little warmth of cheek; "I do want a shepherd. But—"

"He's the very man, ma'am," said one of the villagers, quietly.

Conviction breeds conviction. "Ay, that 'a is," said a second, decisively.

"The man, truly!" said a third, with heartiness.

"He's all there!" said number four, fervidly.

"Then will you tell him to speak to the bailiff," said Bathsheba.

All was practical again now. A summer eve and loneliness would have been necessary to give the meeting its proper fulness of romance.

The bailiff was pointed out to Gabriel, who, checking the palpitation within his breast at discovering that this Ashtoreth of strange report was only a modification of Venus the well-known and admired, retired with him to talk over the necessary preliminaries of hiring.

The fire before them wasted away. "Men," said Bathsheba, "you shall take a little refreshment after this extra work. Will you come to the house?"

"We could knock in a bit and a drop a good deal freer, Miss, if so be ye'd send it to Warren's Malthouse," replied the spokesman.

Bathsheba then rode off into the darkness, and the men straggled on to the village in twos and threes—Oak and the bailiff being left by the rick alone.

"And now," said the bailiff, finally, "all is settled, I think, about your coming, and I am going home-along. Good-night to ye, shepherd."

"Can you get me a lodging?" inquired Gabriel.

"That I can't, indeed," he said, moving past Oak as a Christian edges past an offertory-plate when he does not mean to contribute. "If you follow on the road till you come to Warren's Malthouse, where they are all gone to have their snap of victuals, I daresay some of 'em will tell you of a place. Good-night to ye, shepherd."

The bailiff who showed this nervous dread of loving his neighbour as himself, went up the hill, and Oak walked on to the village, still astonished at the reencounter with Bathsheba, glad of his nearness to her, and perplexed at the rapidity with which the unpractised girl of Norcombe had developed into the supervising and cool woman here. But some women only require an emergency to make them fit for one.

Obliged, to some extent, to forgo dreaming in order to find the way, he reached the churchyard, and passed round it under the wall where several ancient trees grew. There was a wide margin of grass along here, and Gabriel's footsteps were deadened by its softness, even at this indurating period of the year. When abreast of a trunk which appeared to be the oldest of the old, he became aware that a figure was standing behind it. Gabriel did not pause in his walk, and in another moment he accidentally kicked a loose stone. The noise was enough to disturb the motionless stranger, who started and assumed a careless position.

It was a slim girl, rather thinly clad.

"Good-night to you," said Gabriel, heartily.

"Good-night," said the girl to Gabriel.

The voice was unexpectedly attractive; it was the low and dulcet note suggestive of romance; common in descriptions, rare in experience.

"I'll thank you to tell me if I'm in the way for Warren's Malthouse?" Gabriel resumed, primarily to gain the information, indirectly to get more of the music.

"Quite right. It's at the bottom of the hill. And do you know—" The girl hesitated and then went on again. "Do you know how late they keep open the Buck's Head Inn?" She seemed to be won by Gabriel's heartiness, as Gabriel had been won by her modulations.

"I don't know where the Buck's Head is, or anything about it. Do you think of going there to-night?"

"Yes—" The woman again paused. There was no necessity for any continuance of speech, and the fact that she did add more seemed to proceed from an unconscious desire to show unconcern by making a remark, which is noticeable in the ingenuous when they are acting by stealth. "You are not a Weatherbury man?" she said, timorously.

"I am not. I am the new shepherd—just arrived."

"Only a shepherd—and you seem almost a farmer by your ways."

"Only a shepherd," Gabriel repeated, in a dull cadence of finality. His thoughts were directed to the past, his eyes to the feet of the girl; and for the first time he saw lying there a bundle of some sort. She may have perceived the direction of his face, for she said coaxingly,—

"You won't say anything in the parish about having seen me here, will you—at least, not for a day or two?"

"I won't if you wish me not to," said Oak.

"Thank you, indeed," the other replied. "I am rather poor, and I don't want people to know anything about me." Then she was silent and shivered.

"You ought to have a cloak on such a cold night," Gabriel observed. "I would advise 'ee to get indoors."

"O no! Would you mind going on and leaving me? I thank you much for what you have told me."

"I will go on," he said; adding hesitatingly,—"Since you are not very well off, perhaps you would accept this trifle from me. It is only a shilling, but it is all I have to spare."

"Yes, I will take it," said the stranger gratefully.

She extended her hand; Gabriel his. In feeling for each other's palm in the gloom before the money could be passed, a minute incident occurred which told much. Gabriel's fingers alighted on the young woman's wrist. It was beating with a throb of tragic intensity. He had frequently felt the same quick, hard beat in the femoral artery of his lambs when overdriven. It suggested a consumption too great of a vitality which, to judge from her figure and stature, was already too little.

Analysis: Now that Hardy has established the main setting for the whole novel – Weatherbury farm and its surroundings – he proceeds to introduce the sub-plots which will come together at the end of the novel to form the dramatic climax of the book. Like Dickens before him, he is a master at introducing mystery into the novel: the appearance of Fanny Robin here is full of suspense. Oak, now in love himself and sensitive to the pulses of his lambs, notices that there is a "throb of tragic intensity". Thus he sets up the whole Fanny Robin sub-plot: presenting us with a woman who is a victim of the cruel society of the time.

Discussion point: How does Hardy create mystery here?

"What is the matter?"

"Nothing."

"But there is?"

"No, no, no! Let your having seen me be a secret!"

"Very well; I will. Good-night, again."

"Good-night."

The young girl remained motionless by the tree, and Gabriel descended into the village of Weatherbury, or Lower Longpuddle as it was sometimes called. He fancied that he had felt himself in the penumbra of a very deep sadness when touching that slight and fragile creature. But wisdom lies in moderating mere impressions, and Gabriel endeavoured to think little of this.

Questions

What job does Bathsheba give Oak?

Why is Gabriel amazed at Bathsheba?

Who does he meet by the churchyard and what does he give her?

Why does the girl shock him and what does he promise to do?

GCSE style question: how does Hardy make Fanny Robin a mysterious and poignant figure?

A Level style question: compare and contrast the representation of Bathsheba with Fanny.

Creative response: write a poem/story/description of a person who is suffering from poverty.

CHAPTER VIII
THE MALTHOUSE—THE CHAT—NEWS

Warren's Malthouse was enclosed by an old wall inwrapped with ivy, and though not much of the exterior was visible at this hour, the character and purposes of the building were clearly enough shown by its outline upon the sky. From the walls an overhanging thatched roof sloped up to a point in the centre, upon which rose a small wooden lantern, fitted with louvre-boards on all the four sides, and from these openings a mist was dimly perceived to be escaping into the night air. There was no window in front; but a square hole in the door was glazed with a single pane, through which red, comfortable rays now stretched out upon the ivied wall in front. Voices were to be heard inside.

Oak's hand skimmed the surface of the door with fingers extended to an Elymas-the-Sorcerer pattern, till he found a leathern strap, which he pulled. This lifted a wooden latch, and the door swung open.

The room inside was lighted only by the ruddy glow from the kiln mouth, which shone over the floor with the streaming horizontality of the setting sun, and threw upwards the shadows of all facial irregularities in those assembled around. The stone-flag floor was worn into a path from the doorway to the kiln, and into undulations everywhere. A curved settle of unplaned oak stretched along one side, and in a remote corner was a small bed and bedstead, the owner and frequent occupier of which was the maltster.

This aged man was now sitting opposite the fire, his frosty white hair and beard overgrowing his gnarled figure like the grey moss and lichen upon a leafless apple-tree. He wore breeches and the laced-up shoes called ankle-jacks; he kept his eyes fixed upon the fire.

Gabriel's nose was greeted by an atmosphere laden with the sweet smell of new malt. The conversation (which seemed to have been concerning the origin of the fire) immediately ceased, and every one ocularly criticised him to the degree expressed by contracting the flesh of their foreheads and looking at him with narrowed eyelids, as if he had been a light too strong for their sight. Several exclaimed meditatively, after this operation had been completed:—

"Oh, 'tis the new shepherd, 'a b'lieve."

"We thought we heard a hand pawing about the door for the bobbin, but weren't sure 'twere not a dead leaf blowed across," said another. "Come in, shepherd; sure ye be welcome, though we don't know yer name."

"Gabriel Oak, that's my name, neighbours."

The ancient maltster sitting in the midst turned at this—his turning being as the turning of a rusty crane.

"That's never Gable Oak's grandson over at Norcombe—never!" he said, as a formula expressive of surprise, which nobody was supposed for a moment to take literally.

"My father and my grandfather were old men of the name of Gabriel," said the shepherd, placidly.

"Thought I knowed the man's face as I seed him on the rick!—thought I did! And where be ye trading o't to now, shepherd?"

"I'm thinking of biding here," said Mr. Oak.

"Knowed yer grandfather for years and years!" continued the maltster, the words coming forth of their own accord as if the momentum previously imparted had been sufficient.

"Ah—and did you!"

"Knowed yer grandmother."

"And her too!"

"Likewise knowed yer father when he was a child. Why, my boy Jacob there and your father were sworn brothers—that they were sure—weren't ye, Jacob?"

"Ay, sure," said his son, a young man about sixty-five, with a semi-bald head and one tooth in the left centre of his upper jaw, which made much of itself by standing prominent, like a milestone in a bank. "But 'twas Joe had most to do with him. However, my son William must have knowed the very man afore us—didn't ye, Billy, afore ye left Norcombe?"

"No, 'twas Andrew," said Jacob's son Billy, a child of forty, or thereabouts, who manifested the peculiarity of possessing a cheerful soul in a gloomy body, and whose whiskers were assuming a chinchilla shade here and there.

"I can mind Andrew," said Oak, "as being a man in the place when I was quite a child."

"Ay—the other day I and my youngest daughter, Liddy, were over at my grandson's christening," continued Billy. "We were talking about this very family, and 'twas only last Purification Day in this very world, when the use-money is gied away to the second-best poor folk, you know, shepherd, and I can mind the day because they all had to traypse up to the vestry— yes, this very man's family."

"Come, shepherd, and drink. 'Tis gape and swaller with us—a drap of sommit, but not of much account," said the maltster, removing from the fire his eyes, which were vermilion-red and bleared by gazing into it for so many years. "Take up the God-forgive-me, Jacob. See if 'tis warm, Jacob."

Jacob stooped to the God-forgive-me, which was a two-handled tall mug standing in the ashes, cracked and charred with heat: it was rather furred with extraneous matter about the outside, especially in the crevices of the handles, the innermost curves of which may not have seen daylight for several years by reason of this encrustation thereon—formed of ashes accidentally wetted with cider and baked hard; but to the mind of any sensible drinker the cup was no worse for that, being incontestably clean on the inside and about the rim. It may be observed that such a class of mug is called a God-forgive-me in Weatherbury and its vicinity for uncertain reasons; probably because its size makes any given toper feel ashamed of himself when he sees its bottom in drinking it empty.

Jacob, on receiving the order to see if the liquor was warm enough, placidly dipped his forefinger into it by way of thermometer, and having pronounced it nearly of the proper degree, raised the cup and very civilly attempted to dust some of the ashes from the bottom with the skirt of his smock-frock, because Shepherd Oak was a stranger.

"A clane cup for the shepherd," said the maltster commandingly.

"No—not at all," said Gabriel, in a reproving tone of considerateness. "I never fuss about dirt in its pure state, and when I know what sort it is." Taking the mug he drank an inch or more from the depth of its contents, and duly passed it to the next man. "I wouldn't think of giving such trouble to neighbours in washing up when there's so much work to be done in the world already." continued Oak in a moister tone, after recovering from the stoppage of breath which is occasioned by pulls at large mugs.

"A right sensible man," said Jacob.

"True, true; it can't be gainsaid!" observed a brisk young man—Mark Clark by name, a genial and pleasant gentleman, whom to meet anywhere in your travels was to know, to know was to drink with, and to drink with was, unfortunately, to pay for.

"And here's a mouthful of bread and bacon that mis'ess have sent, shepherd. The cider will go down better with a bit of victuals. Don't ye chaw quite close, shepherd, for I let the bacon fall in the road outside as I was bringing it along, and may be 'tis rather gritty. There, 'tis clane dirt; and we all know what that is, as you say, and you bain't a particular man we see, shepherd."

"True, true—not at all," said the friendly Oak.

Analysis: Hardy is perhaps most famous for two things: being obsessed with the destructive forces of Fate, and describing in vivid and entertaining detail the lives of the Dorset yokels who he grew up with. This is perhaps the most vivid example of this: Oak has a mug of cider, which is "cracked and charred with heat." The attention to detail is both comic and illuminating: the instructions that Oak receives make the reader recoil because it all sounds rather disgusting and unhygienic. There is comedy here, but it is affectionate. There is also a deeper message as well though: the country-folk seem to rejoice and enjoy the simple pleasures of a mug of cider, a little bit of gritty bacon. This is "far from the madding crowd": we are in a different world here, the world of Dorset of the 1840s, the Dorset of Hardy's childhood. A place that had vanished by the time Hardy had written the book in 1872.

Discussion point: Why does Hardy depict the locals like this?

"Don't let your teeth quite meet, and you won't feel the sandiness at all. Ah! 'tis wonderful what can be done by contrivance!"

"My own mind exactly, neighbour."

"Ah, he's his grandfer's own grandson!—his grandfer were just such a nice unparticular man!" said the maltster.

"Drink, Henry Fray—drink," magnanimously said Jan Coggan, a person who held Saint-Simonian notions of share and share alike where liquor was concerned, as the vessel showed signs of approaching him in its gradual revolution among them.

Having at this moment reached the end of a wistful gaze into mid-air, Henry did not refuse. He was a man of more than middle age, with eyebrows high up in his forehead, who laid it down that the law of the world was bad, with a long-suffering look through his listeners at the world alluded to, as it presented itself to his imagination. He always signed his name "Henery"—strenuously insisting upon that spelling, and if any passing schoolmaster ventured to remark that the second "e" was superfluous and old-fashioned, he received the reply that "H-e-n-e-r-y" was the name he was christened and the name he would stick to—in the tone of one to whom orthographical differences were matters which had a great deal to do with personal character.

Mr. Jan Coggan, who had passed the cup to Henery, was a crimson man with a spacious countenance and private glimmer in his eye, whose name had appeared on the marriage register of Weatherbury and neighbouring parishes as best man and chief witness in countless unions of the previous twenty years; he also very frequently filled the post of head godfather in baptisms of the subtly-jovial kind.

"Come, Mark Clark—come. Ther's plenty more in the barrel," said Jan.

"Ay—that I will, 'tis my only doctor," replied Mr. Clark, who, twenty years younger than Jan Coggan, revolved in the same orbit. He secreted mirth on all occasions for special discharge at popular parties.

"Why, Joseph Poorgrass, ye han't had a drop!" said Mr. Coggan to a self-conscious man in the background, thrusting the cup towards him.

"Such a modest man as he is!" said Jacob Smallbury. "Why, ye've hardly had strength of eye enough to look in our young mis'ess's face, so I hear, Joseph?"

All looked at Joseph Poorgrass with pitying reproach.

"No—I've hardly looked at her at all," simpered Joseph, reducing his body smaller whilst talking, apparently from a meek sense of undue prominence. "And when I seed her, 'twas nothing but blushes with me!"

"Poor feller," said Mr. Clark.

"'Tis a curious nature for a man," said Jan Coggan.

"Yes," continued Joseph Poorgrass—his shyness, which was so painful as a defect, filling him with a mild complacency now that it was regarded as an interesting study. "'Twere blush, blush, blush with me every minute of the time, when she was speaking to me."

"I believe ye, Joseph Poorgrass, for we all know ye to be a very bashful man."

"'Tis a' awkward gift for a man, poor soul," said the maltster. "And how long have ye have suffered from it, Joseph?"

"Oh, ever since I was a boy. Yes—mother was concerned to her heart about it—yes. But 'twas all nought."

"Did ye ever go into the world to try and stop it, Joseph Poorgrass?"

"Oh ay, tried all sorts o' company. They took me to Greenhill Fair, and into a great gay jerry-go-nimble show, where there were women-folk riding round—standing upon horses, with hardly anything on but their smocks; but it didn't cure me a morsel. And then I was put errand-man at the Women's Skittle Alley at the back of the Tailor's Arms in Casterbridge. 'Twas a horrible sinful situation, and a very curious place for a good man. I had to stand and look ba'dy people in the face from morning till night; but 'twas no use—I was just as bad as ever after all. Blushes hev been in the family for generations. There, 'tis a happy providence that I be no worse."

"True," said Jacob Smallbury, deepening his thoughts to a profounder view of the subject. "'Tis a thought to look at, that ye might have been worse; but even as you be, 'tis a very bad affliction for 'ee, Joseph. For ye see, shepherd, though 'tis very well for a woman, dang it all, 'tis awkward for a man like him, poor feller?"

"'Tis—'tis," said Gabriel, recovering from a meditation. "Yes, very awkward for the man."

"Ay, and he's very timid, too," observed Jan Coggan. "Once he had been working late at Yalbury Bottom, and had had a drap of drink, and lost his way as he was coming home-along through Yalbury Wood, didn't ye, Master Poorgrass?"

"No, no, no; not that story!" expostulated the modest man, forcing a laugh to bury his concern.

"—And so 'a lost himself quite," continued Mr. Coggan, with an impassive face, implying that a true narrative, like time and tide, must run its course and would respect no man. "And as he was coming along in the middle of the night, much afeared, and not able to find his way out of the trees nohow, 'a cried out, 'Man-a-lost! man-a-lost!' A owl in a tree happened to be crying 'Whoo-whoo-whoo!' as owls do, you know, shepherd" (Gabriel nodded), "and Joseph, all in a tremble, said, 'Joseph Poorgrass, of Weatherbury, sir!'"

"No, no, now—that's too much!" said the timid man, becoming a man of brazen courage all of a sudden. "I didn't say sir. I'll take my oath I didn't say 'Joseph Poorgrass o' Weatherbury, sir.' No, no; what's right is right, and I never said sir to the bird, knowing very well that no man of a gentleman's rank would be hollering there at that time o' night. 'Joseph Poorgrass of Weatherbury,'—that's every word I said, and I shouldn't ha' said that if 't hadn't been for Keeper Day's metheglin... There, 'twas a merciful thing it ended where it did."

The question of which was right being tacitly waived by the company, Jan went on meditatively:—

"And he's the fearfullest man, bain't ye, Joseph? Ay, another time ye were lost by Lambing-Down Gate, weren't ye, Joseph?"

"I was," replied Poorgrass, as if there were some conditions too serious even for modesty to remember itself under, this being one.

"Yes; that were the middle of the night, too. The gate would not open, try how he would, and knowing there was the Devil's hand in it, he kneeled down."

"Ay," said Joseph, acquiring confidence from the warmth of the fire, the cider, and a perception of the narrative capabilities of the experience alluded to. "My heart died within me, that time; but I kneeled down and said the Lord's Prayer, and then the Belief right through, and then the Ten Commandments, in earnest prayer. But no, the gate wouldn't open; and then I went on with Dearly Beloved Brethren, and, thinks I, this makes four, and 'tis all I know out of book, and if this don't do it nothing will, and I'm a lost man. Well, when I got to Saying After Me, I rose from my knees and found the gate would open—yes, neighbours, the gate opened the same as ever."

A meditation on the obvious inference was indulged in by all, and during its continuance each directed his vision into the ashpit, which glowed like a desert in the tropics under a vertical sun, shaping their eyes long and liny, partly because of the light, partly from the depth of the subject discussed.

Gabriel broke the silence. "What sort of a place is this to live at, and what sort of a mis'ess is she to work under?" Gabriel's bosom thrilled gently as he thus slipped under the notice of the assembly the inner-most subject of his heart.

"We d' know little of her—nothing. She only showed herself a few days ago. Her uncle was took bad, and the doctor was called with his world-wide skill; but he couldn't save the man. As I take it, she's going to keep on the farm.

"That's about the shape o't, 'a b'lieve," said Jan Coggan. "Ay, 'tis a very good family. I'd as soon be under 'em as under one here and there. Her uncle was a very fair sort of man. Did ye know en, shepherd—a bachelor-man?"

"Not at all."

"I used to go to his house a-courting my first wife, Charlotte, who was his dairymaid. Well, a very good-hearted man were Farmer Everdene, and I being a respectable young fellow was allowed to call and see her and drink as much ale as I liked, but not to carry away any—outside my skin I mane of course."

"Ay, ay, Jan Coggan; we know yer maning."

"And so you see 'twas beautiful ale, and I wished to value his kindness as much as I could, and not to be so ill-mannered as to drink only a thimbleful, which would have been insulting the man's generosity—"

"True, Master Coggan, 'twould so," corroborated Mark Clark.

"—And so I used to eat a lot of salt fish afore going, and then by the time I got there I were as dry as a lime-basket—so thorough dry that that ale would slip down—ah, 'twould slip down sweet! Happy times! Heavenly times! Such lovely drunks as I used to have at that house! You can mind, Jacob? You used to go wi' me sometimes."

"I can—I can," said Jacob. "That one, too, that we had at Buck's Head on a White Monday was a pretty tipple."

"'Twas. But for a wet of the better class, that brought you no nearer to the horned man than you were afore you begun, there was none like those in Farmer Everdene's kitchen. Not a single damn allowed; no, not a bare poor one, even at the most cheerful moment when all were blindest, though the good old word of sin thrown in here and there at such times is a great relief to a merry soul."

"True," said the maltster. "Nater requires her swearing at the regular times, or she's not herself; and unholy exclamations is a necessity of life."

"But Charlotte," continued Coggan—"not a word of the sort would Charlotte allow, nor the smallest item of taking in vain... Ay, poor Charlotte, I wonder if she had the good fortune to get into Heaven when 'a died! But 'a was never much in luck's way, and perhaps 'a went downwards after all, poor soul."

"And did any of you know Miss Everdene's father and mother?" inquired the shepherd, who found some difficulty in keeping the conversation in the desired channel.

"I knew them a little," said Jacob Smallbury; "but they were townsfolk, and didn't live here. They've been dead for years. Father, what sort of people were mis'ess' father and mother?"

"Well," said the maltster, "he wasn't much to look at; but she was a lovely woman. He was fond enough of her as his sweetheart."

"Used to kiss her scores and long-hundreds o' times, so 'twas said," observed Coggan.

"He was very proud of her, too, when they were married, as I've been told," said the maltster. "Ay," said Coggan. "He admired her so much that he used to light the candle three times a night to look at her."

"Boundless love; I shouldn't have supposed it in the universe!" murmured Joseph Poorgrass, who habitually spoke on a large scale in his moral reflections.

"Well, to be sure," said Gabriel.

"Oh, 'tis true enough. I knowed the man and woman both well. Levi Everdene—that was the man's name, sure. 'Man,' saith I in my hurry, but he were of a higher circle of life than that—'a was a gentleman-tailor really, worth scores of pounds. And he became a very celebrated bankrupt two or three times."

"Oh, I thought he was quite a common man!" said Joseph.

"Oh no, no! That man failed for heaps of money; hundreds in gold and silver."

The maltster being rather short of breath, Mr. Coggan, after absently scrutinising a coal which had fallen among the ashes, took up the narrative, with a private twirl of his eye:—

"Well, now, you'd hardly believe it, but that man—our Miss Everdene's father—was one of the ficklest husbands alive, after a while. Understand? 'a didn't want to be fickle, but he couldn't help it. The pore feller were faithful and true enough to her in his wish, but his heart would rove, do what he would. He spoke to me in real tribulation about it once. 'Coggan,' he said, 'I could never wish for a handsomer woman than I've got, but feeling she's ticketed as my lawful wife, I can't help my wicked heart wandering, do what I will.' But at last I believe he cured it by making her take off her wedding-ring and calling her by her maiden name as they sat together after the shop was shut, and so 'a would get to fancy she was only his sweetheart, and not married to him at all. And as soon as he could thoroughly fancy he was doing wrong and committing the seventh, 'a got to like her as well as ever, and they lived on a perfect picture of mutel love."

"Well, 'twas a most ungodly remedy," murmured Joseph Poorgrass; "but we ought to feel deep cheerfulness that a happy Providence kept it from being any worse. You see, he might have gone the bad road and given his eyes to unlawfulness entirely—yes, gross unlawfulness, so to say it."

"You see," said Billy Smallbury, "The man's will was to do right, sure enough, but his heart didn't chime in."

"He got so much better, that he was quite godly in his later years, wasn't he, Jan?" said Joseph Poorgrass. "He got himself confirmed over again in a more serious way, and took to saying 'Amen' almost as loud as the clerk, and he liked to copy comforting verses from the tombstones. He used, too, to hold the money-plate at Let Your Light so Shine, and stand godfather to poor little come-by-chance children; and he kept a missionary box upon his table to nab folks unawares when they called; yes, and he would box the charity-boys' ears, if they laughed in church, till they could hardly stand upright, and do other deeds of piety natural to the saintly inclined."

"Ay, at that time he thought of nothing but high things," added Billy Smallbury. "One day Parson Thirdly met him and said, 'Good-Morning, Mister Everdene; 'tis a fine day!' 'Amen' said Everdene, quite absent-like, thinking only of religion when he seed a parson. Yes, he was a very Christian man."

"Their daughter was not at all a pretty chiel at that time," said Henery Fray. "Never should have thought she'd have growed up such a handsome body as she is."

"'Tis to be hoped her temper is as good as her face."

"Well, yes; but the baily will have most to do with the business and ourselves. Ah!" Henery gazed into the ashpit, and smiled volumes of ironical knowledge.

"A queer Christian, like the Devil's head in a cowl, as the saying is," volunteered Mark Clark.

"He is," said Henery, implying that irony must cease at a certain point. "Between we two, man and man, I believe that man would as soon tell a lie Sundays as working-days—that I do so."

"Good faith, you do talk!" said Gabriel.

"True enough," said the man of bitter moods, looking round upon the company with the antithetic laughter that comes from a keener appreciation of the miseries of life than ordinary men are capable of. "Ah, there's people of one sort, and people of another, but that man—bless your souls!"

Gabriel thought fit to change the subject. "You must be a very aged man, malter, to have sons growed mild and ancient," he remarked.

"Father's so old that 'a can't mind his age, can ye, father?" interposed Jacob. "And he's growed terrible crooked too, lately," Jacob continued, surveying his father's figure, which was rather more bowed than his own. "Really one may say that father there is three-double."

"Crooked folk will last a long while," said the maltster, grimly, and not in the best humour.

"Shepherd would like to hear the pedigree of yer life, father—wouldn't ye, shepherd?"

"Ay that I should," said Gabriel with the heartiness of a man who had longed to hear it for several months. "What may your age be, malter?"

The maltster cleared his throat in an exaggerated form for emphasis, and elongating his gaze to the remotest point of the ashpit, said, in the slow speech justifiable when the importance of a subject is so generally felt that any mannerism must be tolerated in getting at it, "Well, I don't mind the year I were born in, but perhaps I can reckon up the places I've lived at, and so get it that way. I bode at Upper Longpuddle across there" (nodding to the north) "till I were eleven. I bode seven at Kingsbere" (nodding to the east) "where I took to malting. I went therefrom to Norcombe, and malted there two-and-twenty years, and-two-and-twenty years I was there turnip-hoeing and harvesting. Ah, I knowed that old place, Norcombe, years afore you were thought of, Master Oak" (Oak smiled sincere belief in the fact). "Then I malted at Durnover four year, and four year turnip-hoeing; and I was fourteen times eleven months at Millpond St. Jude's" (nodding north-west-by-north). "Old Twills wouldn't hire me for more than eleven months at a time, to keep me from being chargeable to the parish if so be I was disabled. Then I was three year at Mellstock, and I've been here one-and-thirty year come Candlemas. How much is that?"

"Hundred and seventeen," chuckled another old gentleman, given to mental arithmetic and little conversation, who had hitherto sat unobserved in a corner.

"Well, then, that's my age," said the maltster, emphatically.

"O no, father!" said Jacob. "Your turnip-hoeing were in the summer and your malting in the winter of the same years, and ye don't ought to count both halves, father."

"Chok' it all! I lived through the summers, didn't I? That's my question. I suppose ye'll say next I be no age at all to speak of?"

"Sure we shan't," said Gabriel, soothingly.

"Ye be a very old aged person, malter," attested Jan Coggan, also soothingly. "We all know that, and ye must have a wonderful talented constitution to be able to live so long, mustn't he, neighbours?"

"True, true; ye must, malter, wonderful," said the meeting unanimously.

The maltster, being now pacified, was even generous enough to voluntarily disparage in a slight degree the virtue of having lived a great many years, by mentioning that the cup they were drinking out of was three years older than he.

While the cup was being examined, the end of Gabriel Oak's flute became visible over his smock-frock pocket, and Henery Fray exclaimed, "Surely, shepherd, I seed you blowing into a great flute by now at Casterbridge?"

"You did," said Gabriel, blushing faintly. "I've been in great trouble, neighbours, and was driven to it. I used not to be so poor as I be now."

"Never mind, heart!" said Mark Clark. You should take it careless-like, shepherd, and your time will come. But we could thank ye for a tune, if ye bain't too tired?"

"Neither drum nor trumpet have I heard since Christmas," said Jan Coggan. "Come, raise a tune, Master Oak!"

"Ay, that I will," said Gabriel, pulling out his flute and putting it together. "A poor tool, neighbours; but such as I can do ye shall have and welcome."

Oak then struck up "Jockey to the Fair," and played that sparkling melody three times through, accenting the notes in the third round in a most artistic and lively manner by bending his body in small jerks and tapping with his foot to beat time.

"He can blow the flute very well—that 'a can," said a young married man, who having no individuality worth mentioning was known as "Susan Tall's husband." He continued, "I'd as lief as not be able to blow into a flute as well as that."

"He's a clever man, and 'tis a true comfort for us to have such a shepherd," murmured Joseph Poorgrass, in a soft cadence. "We ought to feel full o' thanksgiving that he's not a player of ba'dy songs instead of these merry tunes; for 'twould have been just as easy for God to have made the shepherd a loose low man—a man of iniquity, so to speak it—as what he is. Yes, for our wives' and daughters' sakes we should feel real thanksgiving."

"True, true,—real thanksgiving!" dashed in Mark Clark conclusively, not feeling it to be of any consequence to his opinion that he had only heard about a word and three-quarters of what Joseph had said.

"Yes," added Joseph, beginning to feel like a man in the Bible; "for evil do thrive so in these times that ye may be as much deceived in the cleanest shaved and whitest shirted man as in the raggedest tramp upon the turnpike, if I may term it so."

"Ay, I can mind yer face now, shepherd," said Henery Fray, criticising Gabriel with misty eyes as he entered upon his second tune. "Yes—now I see 'ee blowing into the flute I know 'ee to be the same man I see play at Casterbridge, for yer mouth were scrimped up and yer eyes a-staring out like a strangled man's—just as they be now."

"'Tis a pity that playing the flute should make a man look such a scarecrow," observed Mr. Mark Clark, with additional criticism of Gabriel's countenance, the latter person jerking out, with the ghastly grimace required by the instrument, the chorus of "Dame Durden:"—

'Twas Moll' and Bet', and Doll' and Kate', And Dor'-othy Drag'-gle Tail'.

"I hope you don't mind that young man's bad manners in naming your features?" whispered Joseph to Gabriel.

"Not at all," said Mr. Oak.

"For by nature ye be a very handsome man, shepherd," continued Joseph Poorgrass, with winning sauvity.

"Ay, that ye be, shepard," said the company.

"Thank you very much," said Oak, in the modest tone good manners demanded, thinking, however, that he would never let Bathsheba see him playing the flute; in this resolve showing a discretion equal to that related to its sagacious inventress, the divine Minerva herself.

"Ah, when I and my wife were married at Norcombe Church," said the old maltster, not pleased at finding himself left out of the subject, "we were called the handsomest couple in the neighbourhood—everybody said so."

"Danged if ye bain't altered now, malter," said a voice with the vigour natural to the enunciation of a remarkably evident truism. It came from the old man in the background, whose offensiveness and spiteful ways were barely atoned for by the occasional chuckle he contributed to general laughs.

"O no, no," said Gabriel.

"Don't ye play no more shepherd" said Susan Tall's husband, the young married man who had spoken once before. "I must be moving and when there's tunes going on I seem as if hung in wires. If I thought after I'd left that music was still playing, and I not there, I should be quite melancholy-like."

"What's yer hurry then, Laban?" inquired Coggan. "You used to bide as late as the latest."

"Well, ye see, neighbours, I was lately married to a woman, and she's my vocation now, and so ye see—" The young man halted lamely.

"New Lords new laws, as the saying is, I suppose," remarked Coggan.

"Ay, 'a b'lieve—ha, ha!" said Susan Tall's husband, in a tone intended to imply his habitual reception of jokes without minding them at all. The young man then wished them good-night and withdrew.

Henery Fray was the first to follow. Then Gabriel arose and went off with Jan Coggan, who had offered him a lodging. A few minutes later, when the remaining ones were on their legs and about to depart, Fray came back again in a hurry. Flourishing his finger ominously he threw a gaze teeming with tidings just where his eye alighted by accident, which happened to be in Joseph Poorgrass's face.

"O—what's the matter, what's the matter, Henery?" said Joseph, starting back.

"What's a-brewing, Henrey?" asked Jacob and Mark Clark.

"Baily Pennyways—Baily Pennyways—I said so; yes, I said so!"

"What, found out stealing anything?"

"Stealing it is. The news is, that after Miss Everdene got home she went out again to see all was safe, as she usually do, and coming in found Baily Pennyways creeping down the granary steps with half a a bushel of barley. She fleed at him like a cat—never such a tomboy as she is—of course I speak with closed doors?"

"You do—you do, Henery."

"She fleed at him, and, to cut a long story short, he owned to having carried off five sack altogether, upon her promising not to persecute him. Well, he's turned out neck and crop, and my question is, who's going to be baily now?"

The question was such a profound one that Henery was obliged to drink there and then from the large cup till the bottom was distinctly visible inside. Before he had replaced it on the table, in came the young man, Susan Tall's husband, in a still greater hurry.

"Have ye heard the news that's all over parish?"

"About Baily Pennyways?"

"But besides that?"

"No—not a morsel of it!" they replied, looking into the very midst of Laban Tall as if to meet his words half-way down his throat.

"What a night of horrors!" murmured Joseph Poorgrass, waving his hands spasmodically. "I've had the news-bell ringing in my left ear quite bad enough for a murder, and I've seen a magpie all alone!"

"Fanny Robin—Miss Everdene's youngest servant—can't be found. They've been wanting to lock up the door these two hours, but she isn't come in. And they don't know what to do about going to bed for fear of locking her out. They wouldn't be so concerned if she hadn't been noticed in such low spirits these last few days, and Maryann d' think the beginning of a crowner's inquest has happened to the poor girl."

"Oh—'tis burned—'tis burned!" came from Joseph Poorgrass's dry lips.

"No—'tis drowned!" said Tall.

"Or 'tis her father's razor!" suggested Billy Smallbury, with a vivid sense of detail.

"Well—Miss Everdene wants to speak to one or two of us before we go to bed. What with this trouble about the baily, and now about the girl, mis'ess is almost wild."

Analysis: Now that Bathsheba is running the farm, she is in the thick of things: her bailiff has stolen from her and one of her workers has disappeared. Thus Hardy seeks to present us with a vibrant, close-knit, caring community which is by and large honest: it is clear that Pennyways' dishonesty is an aberration, not the norm. The way the community look for Fanny shows that everyone pulls together and looks after each other. There would have been many communities where the odd farm worker going missing would not have been noticed.

Discussion point: What is Hardy revealing about the community here?

They all hastened up the lane to the farmhouse, excepting the old maltster, whom neither news, fire, rain, nor thunder could draw from his hole. There, as the others' footsteps died away he sat down again and continued gazing as usual into the furnace with his red, bleared eyes.

From the bedroom window above their heads Bathsheba's head and shoulders, robed in mystic white, were dimly seen extended into the air.

"Are any of my men among you?" she said anxiously.

"Yes, ma'am, several," said Susan Tall's husband.

"To-morrow morning I wish two or three of you to make inquiries in the villages round if they have seen such a person as Fanny Robin. Do it quietly; there is no reason for alarm as yet. She must have left whilst we were all at the fire."

"I beg yer pardon, but had she any young man courting her in the parish, ma'am?" asked Jacob Smallbury.

"I don't know," said Bathsheba.

"I've never heard of any such thing, ma'am," said two or three.

"It is hardly likely, either," continued Bathsheba. "For any lover of hers might have come to the house if he had been a respectable lad. The most mysterious matter connected with her absence—indeed, the only thing which gives me serious alarm—is that she was seen to go out of the house by Maryann with only her indoor working gown on—not even a bonnet."

"And you mean, ma'am, excusing my words, that a young woman would hardly go to see her young man without dressing up," said Jacob, turning his mental vision upon past experiences. "That's true—she would not, ma'am."

"She had, I think, a bundle, though I couldn't see very well," said a female voice from another window, which seemed that of Maryann. "But she had no young man about here. Hers lives in Casterbridge, and I believe he's a soldier."

"Do you know his name?" Bathsheba said.

"No, mistress; she was very close about it."

"Perhaps I might be able to find out if I went to Casterbridge barracks," said William Smallbury.

"Very well; if she doesn't return to-morrow, mind you go there and try to discover which man it is, and see him. I feel more responsible than I should if she had had any friends or relations alive. I do hope she has come to no harm through a man of that kind... And then there's this disgraceful affair of the bailiff—but I can't speak of him now."

Bathsheba had so many reasons for uneasiness that it seemed she did not think it worth while to dwell upon any particular one. "Do as I told you, then," she said in conclusion, closing the casement.

"Ay, ay, mistress; we will," they replied, and moved away.

That night at Coggan's, Gabriel Oak, beneath the screen of closed eyelids, was busy with fancies, and full of movement, like a river flowing rapidly under its ice. Night had always been the time at which he saw Bathsheba most vividly, and through the slow hours of shadow he tenderly regarded her image now. It is rarely that the pleasures of the imagination will compensate for the pain of sleeplessness, but they possibly did with Oak to-night, for the delight of merely seeing her effaced for the time his perception of the great difference between seeing and possessing.

He also thought of plans for fetching his few utensils and books from Norcombe. The Young Man's Best Companion, The Farrier's Sure Guide, The Veterinary Surgeon, Paradise Lost, The Pilgrim's Progress, Robinson Crusoe, Ash's Dictionary, and Walkingame's Arithmetic, constituted his library; and though a limited series, it was one from which he had acquired more sound information by diligent perusal than many a man of opportunities has done from a furlong of laden shelves.

Questions

How do the villagers feel about Gabriel and how do we know this?

What is a malster and a Malthouse?

Who did the malster know of Gabriel's family?

Where does Gabriel stay?

What news is there in Warren's Malthouse?

What does Bathsheba do about Fanny Robin?

GCSE style question: how does Hardy represent the local people in this chapter?

A Level style question: compare and contrast the representation of drinking alcohol in *FFMC* with another text of your choice.

Creative response: write a description/poem of a bar/café or place where people gather to socialize.

CHAPTER IX
THE HOMESTEAD—A VISITOR—
HALF-CONFIDENCES

By daylight, the bower of Oak's new-found mistress, Bathsheba Everdene, presented itself as a hoary building, of the early stage of Classic Renaissance as regards its architecture, and of a proportion which told at a glance that, as is so frequently the case, it had once been the memorial hall upon a small estate around it, now altogether effaced as a distinct property, and merged in the vast tract of a non-resident landlord, which comprised several such modest demesnes.

Fluted pilasters, worked from the solid stone, decorated its front, and above the roof the chimneys were panelled or columnar, some coped gables with finials and like features still retaining traces of their Gothic extraction. Soft brown mosses, like faded velveteen, formed cushions upon the stone tiling, and tufts of the houseleek or sengreen sprouted from the eaves of the low surrounding buildings. A gravel walk leading from the door to the road in front was encrusted at the sides with more moss—here it was a silver-green variety, the nut-brown of the gravel being visible to the width of only a foot or two in the centre. This circumstance, and the generally sleepy air of the whole prospect here, together with the animated and contrasting state of the reverse façade, suggested to the imagination that on the adaptation of the building for farming purposes the vital principle of the house had turned round inside its body to face the other way. Reversals of this kind, strange deformities, tremendous paralyses, are often seen to be inflicted by trade upon edifices—either individual or in the aggregate as streets and towns—which were originally planned for pleasure alone.

Lively voices were heard this morning in the upper rooms, the main staircase to which was of hard oak, the balusters, heavy as bed-posts, being turned and moulded in the quaint fashion of their century, the handrail as stout as a parapet-top, and the stairs themselves continually twisting round like a person trying to look over his shoulder. Going up, the floors above were found to have a very irregular surface, rising to ridges, sinking into valleys; and being just then uncarpeted, the face of the boards was seen to be eaten into innumerable vermiculations. Every window replied by a clang to the opening and shutting of every door, a tremble followed every bustling movement, and a creak accompanied a walker about the house, like a spirit, wherever he went.

In the room from which the conversation proceeded Bathsheba and her servant-companion, Liddy Smallbury, were to be discovered sitting upon the floor, and sorting a complication of papers, books, bottles, and rubbish spread out thereon—remnants from the household stores of the late occupier. Liddy, the maltster's great-granddaughter, was about Bathsheba's equal in age, and her face was a prominent advertisement of the light-hearted English country girl. The beauty her features might have lacked in form was amply made up for by perfection of hue, which at this winter-time was the softened ruddiness on a surface of high rotundity that we meet with in a Terburg or a Gerard Douw; and, like the presentations of those great colourists, it was a face which kept well back from the boundary between comeliness and the ideal. Though elastic in nature she was less daring than Bathsheba, and occasionally showed some earnestness, which consisted half of genuine feeling, and half of mannerliness superadded by way of duty.

Through a partly-opened door the noise of a scrubbing-brush led up to the charwoman, Maryann Money, a person who for a face had a circular disc, furrowed less by age than by long gazes of perplexity at distant objects. To think of her was to get good-humoured; to speak of her was to raise the image of a dried Normandy pippin.

"Stop your scrubbing a moment," said Bathsheba through the door to her. "I hear something."

Maryann suspended the brush.

The tramp of a horse was apparent, approaching the front of the building. The paces slackened, turned in at the wicket, and, what was most unusual, came up the mossy path close to the door. The door was tapped with the end of a crop or stick.

"What impertinence!" said Liddy, in a low voice. "To ride up the footpath like that! Why didn't he stop at the gate? Lord! 'Tis a gentleman! I see the top of his hat."

"Be quiet!" said Bathsheba.

The further expression of Liddy's concern was continued by aspect instead of narrative.

"Why doesn't Mrs. Coggan go to the door?" Bathsheba continued.

Rat-tat-tat-tat resounded more decisively from Bathsheba's oak.

"Maryann, you go!" said she, fluttering under the onset of a crowd of romantic possibilities.

"Oh ma'am—see, here's a mess!"

The argument was unanswerable after a glance at Maryann.

"Liddy—you must," said Bathsheba.

Liddy held up her hands and arms, coated with dust from the rubbish they were sorting, and looked imploringly at her mistress.

"There—Mrs. Coggan is going!" said Bathsheba, exhaling her relief in the form of a long breath which had lain in her bosom a minute or more.

The door opened, and a deep voice said—

"Is Miss Everdene at home?"

"I'll see, sir," said Mrs. Coggan, and in a minute appeared in the room.

"Dear, what a thirtover place this world is!" continued Mrs. Coggan (a wholesome-looking lady who had a voice for each class of remark according to the emotion involved; who could toss a pancake or twirl a mop with the accuracy of pure mathematics, and who at this moment showed hands shaggy with fragments of dough and arms encrusted with flour). "I am never up to my elbows, Miss, in making a pudding but one of two things do happen—either my nose must needs begin tickling, and I can't live without scratching it, or somebody knocks at the door. Here's Mr. Boldwood wanting to see you, Miss Everdene."

A woman's dress being a part of her countenance, and any disorder in the one being of the same nature with a malformation or wound in the other, Bathsheba said at once—

"I can't see him in this state. Whatever shall I do?"

Not-at-homes were hardly naturalized in Weatherbury farmhouses, so Liddy suggested—"Say you're a fright with dust, and can't come down."

"Yes—that sounds very well," said Mrs. Coggan, critically.

"Say I can't see him—that will do."

Mrs. Coggan went downstairs, and returned the answer as requested, adding, however, on her own responsibility, "Miss is dusting bottles, sir, and is quite a object—that's why 'tis."

"Oh, very well," said the deep voice indifferently. "All I wanted to ask was, if anything had been heard of Fanny Robin?"

"Nothing, sir—but we may know to-night. William Smallbury is gone to Casterbridge, where her young man lives, as is supposed, and the other men be inquiring about everywhere."

The horse's tramp then recommenced and retreated, and the door closed.

"Who is Mr. Boldwood?" said Bathsheba.

"A gentleman-farmer at Little Weatherbury."

"Married?"

"No, miss."

"How old is he?"

"Forty, I should say—very handsome—rather stern-looking—and rich."

"What a bother this dusting is! I am always in some unfortunate plight or other," Bathsheba said, complainingly. "Why should he inquire about Fanny?"

"Oh, because, as she had no friends in her childhood, he took her and put her to school, and got her her place here under your uncle. He's a very kind man that way, but Lord—there!"

"What?"

"Never was such a hopeless man for a woman! He's been courted by sixes and sevens—all the girls, gentle and simple, for miles round, have tried him. Jane Perkins worked at him for two months like a slave, and the two Miss Taylors spent a year upon him, and he cost Farmer Ives's daughter nights of tears and twenty pounds' worth of new clothes; but Lord—the money might as well have been thrown out of the window."

A little boy came up at this moment and looked in upon them. This child was one of the Coggans, who, with the Smallburys, were as common among the families of this district as the Avons and Derwents among our rivers. He always had a loosened tooth or a cut finger to show to particular friends, which he did with an air of being thereby elevated above the common herd of afflictionless humanity—to which exhibition people were expected to say "Poor child!" with a dash of congratulation as well as pity.

"I've got a pen-nee!" said Master Coggan in a scanning measure.

"Well—who gave it you, Teddy?" said Liddy.

"Mis-terr Bold-wood! He gave it to me for opening the gate."

"What did he say?"

"He said, 'Where are you going, my little man?' and I said, 'To Miss Everdene's please,' and he said, 'She is a staid woman, isn't she, my little man?' and I said, 'Yes.'"

"You naughty child! What did you say that for?"

"'Cause he gave me the penny!"

"What a pucker everything is in!" said Bathsheba, discontentedly when the child had gone. "Get away, Maryann, or go on with your scrubbing, or do something! You ought to be married by this time, and not here troubling me!"

"Ay, mistress—so I did. But what between the poor men I won't have, and the rich men who won't have me, I stand as a pelican in the wilderness!"

"Did anybody ever want to marry you miss?" Liddy ventured to ask when they were again alone. "Lots of 'em, I daresay?"

Bathsheba paused, as if about to refuse a reply, but the temptation to say yes, since it was really in her power was irresistible by aspiring virginity, in spite of her spleen at having been published as old.

"A man wanted to once," she said, in a highly experienced tone, and the image of Gabriel Oak, as the farmer, rose before her.

"How nice it must seem!" said Liddy, with the fixed features of mental realization. "And you wouldn't have him?"

"He wasn't quite good enough for me."

"How sweet to be able to disdain, when most of us are glad to say, 'Thank you!' I seem I hear it. 'No, sir—I'm your better.' or 'Kiss my foot, sir; my face is for mouths of consequence.' And did you love him, miss?"

"Oh, no. But I rather liked him."

"Do you now?"

"Of course not—what footsteps are those I hear?"

Liddy looked from a back window into the courtyard behind, which was now getting low-toned and dim with the earliest films of night. A crooked file of men was approaching the back door. The whole string of trailing individuals advanced in the completest balance of intention, like the remarkable creatures known as Chain Salpæ, which, distinctly organized in other respects, have one will common to a whole family. Some were, as usual, in snow-white smock-frocks of Russia duck, and some in whitey-brown ones of drabbet—marked on the wrists, breasts, backs, and sleeves with honeycomb-work. Two or three women in pattens brought up the rear.

"The Philistines be upon us," said Liddy, making her nose white against the glass.

"Oh, very well. Maryann, go down and keep them in the kitchen till I am dressed, and then show them in to me in the hall."

Questions

Why does Bathsheba refuse to see Boldwood?

Why has Boldwood called?

What does she learn about Boldwood from Liddy?

What did Boldwood do for Fanny?

Why is Bathsheba cross with Coggan's son?

What does she tell Liddy about her love life?

GCSE style question: how does Hardy represent the relationship between Liddy and Bathsheba here?

A Level style question: compare and contrast the representation of female friendship in the novel with another important female friendship in another text.

Creative response: write a poem/description of a friendship.

CHAPTER X
MISTRESS AND MEN

Half-an-hour later Bathsheba, in finished dress, and followed by Liddy, entered the upper end of the old hall to find that her men had all deposited themselves on a long form and a settle at the lower extremity. She sat down at a table and opened the time-book, pen in her hand, with a canvas money-bag beside her. From this she poured a small heap of coin. Liddy chose a position at her elbow and began to sew, sometimes pausing and looking round, or, with the air of a privileged person, taking up one of the half-sovereigns lying before her and surveying it merely as a work of art, while strictly preventing her countenance from expressing any wish to possess it as money.

"Now before I begin, men," said Bathsheba, "I have two matters to speak of. The first is that the bailiff is dismissed for thieving, and that I have formed a resolution to have no bailiff at all, but to manage everything with my own head and hands."

The men breathed an audible breath of amazement.

"The next matter is, have you heard anything of Fanny?"

"Nothing, ma'am."

"Have you done anything?"

"I met Farmer Boldwood," said Jacob Smallbury, "and I went with him and two of his men, and dragged Newmill Pond, but we found nothing."

"And the new shepherd have been to Buck's Head, by Yalbury, thinking she had gone there, but nobody had seed her," said Laban Tall.

"Hasn't William Smallbury been to Casterbridge?"

"Yes, ma'am, but he's not yet come home. He promised to be back by six."

"It wants a quarter to six at present," said Bathsheba, looking at her watch. "I daresay he'll be in directly. Well, now then"—she looked into the book—"Joseph Poorgrass, are you there?"

"Yes, sir—ma'am I mane," said the person addressed. "I be the personal name of Poorgrass."

"And what are you?"

"Nothing in my own eye. In the eye of other people—well, I don't say it; though public thought will out."

"What do you do on the farm?"

"I do do carting things all the year, and in seed time I shoots the rooks and sparrows, and helps at pig-killing, sir."

"How much to you?"

"Please nine and ninepence and a good halfpenny where 'twas a bad one, sir—ma'am I mane."

"Quite correct. Now here are ten shillings in addition as a small present, as I am a new comer."

Bathsheba blushed slightly at the sense of being generous in public, and Henery Fray, who had drawn up towards her chair, lifted his eyebrows and fingers to express amazement on a small scale.

"How much do I owe you—that man in the corner—what's your name?" continued Bathsheba.

"Matthew Moon, ma'am," said a singular framework of clothes with nothing of any consequence inside them, which advanced with the toes in no definite direction forwards, but turned in or out as they chanced to swing.

"Matthew Mark, did you say?—speak out—I shall not hurt you," inquired the young farmer, kindly.

"Matthew Moon, mem," said Henery Fray, correctingly, from behind her chair, to which point he had edged himself.

"Matthew Moon," murmured Bathsheba, turning her bright eyes to the book. "Ten and twopence halfpenny is the sum put down to you, I see?"

"Yes, mis'ess," said Matthew, as the rustle of wind among dead leaves.

"Here it is, and ten shillings. Now the next—Andrew Randle, you are a new man, I hear. How come you to leave your last farm?"

"P-p-p-p-p-pl-pl-pl-pl-l-l-l-l-ease, ma'am, p-p-p-p-pl-pl- pl-pl-please, ma'am-please'm-please'm—"

"'A's a stammering man, mem," said Henery Fray in an undertone, "and they turned him away because the only time he ever did speak plain he said his soul was his own, and other iniquities, to the squire. 'A can cuss, mem, as well as you or I, but 'a can't speak a common speech to save his life."

"Andrew Randle, here's yours—finish thanking me in a day or two. Temperance Miller—oh, here's another, Soberness—both women I suppose?"

"Yes'm. Here we be, 'a b'lieve," was echoed in shrill unison.

"What have you been doing?"

"Tending thrashing-machine and wimbling haybonds, and saying 'Hoosh!' to the cocks and hens when they go upon your seeds, and planting Early Flourballs and Thompson's Wonderfuls with a dibble."

"Yes—I see. Are they satisfactory women?" she inquired softly of Henery Fray.

"Oh mem—don't ask me! Yielding women—as scarlet a pair as ever was!"

groaned Henery under his breath.

"Sit down."

"Who, mem?"

"Sit down."

Joseph Poorgrass, in the background twitched, and his lips became dry with fear of some terrible consequences, as he saw Bathsheba summarily speaking, and Henery slinking off to a corner.

"Now the next. Laban Tall, you'll stay on working for me?"

"For you or anybody that pays me well, ma'am," replied the young married man.

"True—the man must live!" said a woman in the back quarter, who had just entered with clicking pattens.

"What woman is that?" Bathsheba asked.

"I be his lawful wife!" continued the voice with greater prominence of manner and tone. This lady called herself five-and-twenty, looked thirty, passed as thirty-five, and was forty. She was a woman who never, like some newly married, showed conjugal tenderness in public, perhaps because she had none to show.

"Oh, you are," said Bathsheba. "Well, Laban, will you stay on?"

"Yes, he'll stay, ma'am!" said again the shrill tongue of Laban's lawful wife.

"Well, he can speak for himself, I suppose."

"Oh Lord, not he, ma'am! A simple tool. Well enough, but a poor gawkhammer mortal," the wife replied.

"Heh-heh-heh!" laughed the married man with a hideous effort of appreciation, for he was as irrepressibly good-humoured under ghastly snubs as a parliamentary candidate on the hustings.

The names remaining were called in the same manner.

"Now I think I have done with you," said Bathsheba, closing the book and shaking back a stray twine of hair. "Has William Smallbury returned?"

"No, ma'am."

"The new shepherd will want a man under him," suggested Henery Fray, trying to make himself official again by a sideway approach towards her chair.

"Oh—he will. Who can he have?"

"Young Cain Ball is a very good lad," Henery said, "and Shepherd Oak don't mind his youth?" he added, turning with an apologetic smile to the shepherd, who had just appeared on the scene, and was now leaning against the doorpost with his arms folded.

"No, I don't mind that," said Gabriel.

"How did Cain come by such a name?" asked Bathsheba.

"Oh you see, mem, his pore mother, not being a Scripture-read woman, made a mistake at his christening, thinking 'twas Abel killed Cain, and called en Cain, meaning Abel all the time. The parson put it right, but 'twas too late, for the name could never be got rid of in the parish. 'Tis very unfortunate for the boy."

"It is rather unfortunate."

"Yes. However, we soften it down as much as we can, and call him Cainy. Ah, pore widow-woman! she cried her heart out about it almost. She was brought up by a very heathen father and mother, who never sent her to church or school, and it shows how the sins of the parents are visited upon the children, mem."

Mr. Fray here drew up his features to the mild degree of melancholy required when the persons involved in the given misfortune do not belong to your own family.

"Very well then, Cainey Ball to be under-shepherd. And you quite understand your duties?—you I mean, Gabriel Oak?"

"Quite well, I thank you, Miss Everdene," said Shepherd Oak from the doorpost. "If I don't, I'll inquire." Gabriel was rather staggered by the remarkable coolness of her manner. Certainly nobody without previous information would have dreamt that Oak and the handsome woman before whom he stood had ever been other than strangers. But perhaps her air was the inevitable result of the social rise which had advanced her from a cottage to a large house and fields. The case is not unexampled in high places. When, in the writings of the later poets, Jove and his family are found to have moved from their cramped quarters on the peak of Olympus into the wide sky above it, their words show a proportionate increase of arrogance and reserve.

Footsteps were heard in the passage, combining in their character the qualities both of weight and measure, rather at the expense of velocity.

(All.) "Here's Billy Smallbury come from Casterbridge."

"And what's the news?" said Bathsheba, as William, after marching to the middle of the hall, took a handkerchief from his hat and wiped his forehead from its centre to its remoter boundaries.

"I should have been sooner, miss," he said, "if it hadn't been for the weather." He then stamped with each foot severely, and on looking down his boots were perceived to be clogged with snow.

"Come at last, is it?" said Henery.

"Well, what about Fanny?" said Bathsheba.

"Well, ma'am, in round numbers, she's run away with the soldiers," said William.

"No; not a steady girl like Fanny!"

"I'll tell ye all particulars. When I got to Casterbridge Barracks, they said, 'The Eleventh Dragoon-Guards be gone away, and new troops have come.' The Eleventh left last week for Melchester and onwards. The Route came from Government like a thief in the night, as is his nature to, and afore the Eleventh knew it almost, they were on the march. They passed near here."

Gabriel had listened with interest. "I saw them go," he said.

"Yes," continued William, "they pranced down the street playing 'The Girl I Left Behind Me,' so 'tis said, in glorious notes of triumph. Every looker-on's inside shook with the blows of the great drum to his deepest vitals, and there was not a dry eye throughout the town among the public-house people and the nameless women!"

"But they're not gone to any war?"

"No, ma'am; but they be gone to take the places of them who may, which is very close connected. And so I said to myself, Fanny's young man was one of the regiment, and she's gone after him. There, ma'am, that's it in black and white."

"Did you find out his name?"

"No; nobody knew it. I believe he was higher in rank than a private."

Gabriel remained musing and said nothing, for he was in doubt.

"Well, we are not likely to know more to-night, at any rate," said Bathsheba. "But one of you had better run across to Farmer Boldwood's and tell him that much."

She then rose; but before retiring, addressed a few words to them with a pretty dignity, to which her mourning dress added a soberness that was hardly to be found in the words themselves.

"Now mind, you have a mistress instead of a master. I don't yet know my powers or my talents in farming; but I shall do my best, and if you serve me well, so shall I serve you. Don't any unfair ones among you (if there are any such, but I hope not) suppose that because I'm a woman I don't understand the difference between bad goings-on and good."

Analysis: Perhaps the best part of the 1960s film of *Far From The Madding Crowd* is when Julie Christie delivers this speech, which she does admirably. In such a way, the film becomes more than a historical drama but a clarion call for women's liberation: evidence that women can be just as good at running things as men. Bathsheba has decided to sack Pennyways and become bailiff herself: she will supervise the day-to-day running of the farm. She is showing us what we were told earlier that she wishes to be "independent". She wishes to be a worth-while, active member of the farm that she owns. This is, thus, a decisive moment not only in the book but also the whole of English Literature: the first time that a heroine actually supplants the man in the running of a business.

Discussion point: What is the effect of this speech upon the listeners and the readers? How might have a Victorian readership responded?

(All.) "No'm!"

(Liddy.) "Excellent well said."

"I shall be up before you are awake; I shall be afield before you are up; and I shall have breakfasted before you are afield. In short, I shall astonish you all."

(All.) "Yes'm!"

"And so good-night."

(All.) "Good-night, ma'am."

Then this small thesmothete stepped from the table, and surged out of the hall, her black silk dress licking up a few straws and dragging them along with a scratching noise upon the floor. Liddy, elevating her feelings to the occasion from a sense of grandeur, floated off behind Bathsheba with a milder dignity not entirely free from travesty, and the door was closed.

Questions

How does Bathsheba pay her workmen?

What is she going to do about the position of bailiff?

Why does she shock the locals? Who becomes Gabriel's assistant?

What is the news of Fanny?

GCSE style question: how does Hardy represent Bathsheba as a powerful character in this chapter?

A Level style question: compare and contrast the representation of Bathsheba with another working woman in another text of your choice.

Creative response: write a poem/description/story about some issue connected with gender politics, e.g. a woman working in a traditionally male profession/sport etc, or vice versa.

CHAPTER XI
OUTSIDE THE BARRACKS—
SNOW—A MEETING

For dreariness nothing could surpass a prospect in the outskirts of a certain town and military station, many miles north of Weatherbury, at a later hour on this same snowy evening—if that may be called a prospect of which the chief constituent was darkness.

It was a night when sorrow may come to the brightest without causing any great sense of incongruity: when, with impressible persons, love becomes solicitousness, hope sinks to misgiving, and faith to hope: when the exercise of memory does not stir feelings of regret at opportunities for ambition that have been passed by, and anticipation does not prompt to enterprise.

The scene was a public path, bordered on the left hand by a river, behind which rose a high wall. On the right was a tract of land, partly meadow and partly moor, reaching, at its remote verge, to a wide undulating upland.

The changes of the seasons are less obtrusive on spots of this kind than amid woodland scenery. Still, to a close observer, they are just as perceptible; the difference is that their media of manifestation are less trite and familiar than such well-known ones as the bursting of the buds or the fall of the leaf. Many are not so stealthy and gradual as we may be apt to imagine in considering the general torpidity of a moor or waste. Winter, in coming to the country hereabout, advanced in well-marked stages, wherein might have been successively observed the retreat of the snakes, the transformation of the ferns, the filling of the pools, a rising of fogs, the embrowning by frost, the collapse of the fungi, and an obliteration by snow.

This climax of the series had been reached to-night on the aforesaid moor, and for the first time in the season its irregularities were forms without features; suggestive of anything, proclaiming nothing, and without more character than that of being the limit of something else—the lowest layer of a firmament of snow. From this chaotic skyful of crowding flakes the mead and moor momentarily received additional clothing, only to appear momentarily more naked thereby. The vast arch of cloud above was strangely low, and formed as it were the roof of a large dark cavern, gradually sinking in upon its floor; for the instinctive thought was that the snow lining the heavens and that encrusting the earth would soon unite into one mass without any intervening stratum of air at all.

We turn our attention to the left-hand characteristics; which were flatness in respect of the river, verticality in respect of the wall behind it, and darkness as to both. These features made up the mass. If anything could be darker than the sky, it was the wall, and if any thing could be gloomier than the wall it was the river beneath. The indistinct summit of the facade was notched and pronged by chimneys here and there, and upon its face were faintly signified the oblong shapes of windows, though only in the upper part. Below, down to the water's edge, the flat was unbroken by hole or projection.

An indescribable succession of dull blows, perplexing in their regularity, sent their sound with difficulty through the fluffy atmosphere. It was a neighbouring clock striking ten. The bell was in the open air, and being overlaid with several inches of muffling snow, had lost its voice for the time.

About this hour the snow abated: ten flakes fell where twenty had fallen, then one had the room of ten. Not long after a form moved by the brink of the river.

By its outline upon the colourless background, a close observer might have seen that it was small. This was all that was positively discoverable, though it seemed human.

The shape went slowly along, but without much exertion, for the snow, though sudden, was not as yet more than two inches deep. At this time some words were spoken aloud:—

"One. Two. Three. Four. Five."

Between each utterance the little shape advanced about half a dozen yards. It was evident now that the windows high in the wall were being counted. The word "Five" represented the fifth window from the end of the wall.

Here the spot stopped, and dwindled smaller. The figure was stooping. Then a morsel of snow flew across the river towards the fifth window. It smacked against the wall at a point several yards from its mark. The throw was the idea of a man conjoined with the execution of a woman. No man who had ever seen bird, rabbit, or squirrel in his childhood, could possibly have thrown with such utter imbecility as was shown here.

Another attempt, and another; till by degrees the wall must have become pimpled with the adhering lumps of snow. At last one fragment struck the fifth window.

The river would have been seen by day to be of that deep smooth sort which races middle and sides with the same gliding precision, any irregularities of speed being immediately corrected by a small whirlpool. Nothing was heard in reply to the signal but the gurgle and cluck of one of these invisible wheels—together with a few small sounds which a sad man would have called moans, and a happy man laughter—caused by the flapping of the waters against trifling objects in other parts of the stream.

The window was struck again in the same manner.

Then a noise was heard, apparently produced by the opening of the window. This was followed by a voice from the same quarter.

"Who's there?"

The tones were masculine, and not those of surprise. The high wall being that of a barrack, and marriage being looked upon with disfavour in the army, assignations and communications had probably been made across the river before to-night.

"Is it Sergeant Troy?" said the blurred spot in the snow, tremulously.

This person was so much like a mere shade upon the earth, and the other speaker so much a part of the building, that one would have said the wall was holding a conversation with the snow.

"Yes," came suspiciously from the shadow. "What girl are you?"

"Oh, Frank—don't you know me?" said the spot. "Your wife, Fanny Robin."

"Fanny!" said the wall, in utter astonishment.

"Yes," said the girl, with a half-suppressed gasp of emotion.

There was something in the woman's tone which is not that of the wife, and there was a manner in the man which is rarely a husband's. The dialogue went on:

"How did you come here?"

"I asked which was your window. Forgive me!"

"I did not expect you to-night. Indeed, I did not think you would come at all. It was a wonder you found me here. I am orderly to-morrow."

"You said I was to come."

"Well—I said that you might."

"Yes, I mean that I might. You are glad to see me, Frank?"

"Oh yes—of course."

"Can you—come to me!"

My dear Fan, no! The bugle has sounded, the barrack gates are closed, and I have no leave. We are all of us as good as in the county gaol till to-morrow morning."

"Then I shan't see you till then!" The words were in a faltering tone of disappointment.

"How did you get here from Weatherbury?"

"I walked—some part of the way—the rest by the carriers."

"I am surprised."

"Yes—so am I. And Frank, when will it be?"

"What?"

"That you promised."

"I don't quite recollect."

"O you do! Don't speak like that. It weighs me to the earth. It makes me say what ought to be said first by you."

"Never mind—say it."

"O, must I?—it is, when shall we be married, Frank?"

"Oh, I see. Well—you have to get proper clothes."

"I have money. Will it be by banns or license?"

"Banns, I should think."

"And we live in two parishes."

"Do we? What then?"

"My lodgings are in St. Mary's, and this is not. So they will have to be published in both."

"Is that the law?"

"Yes. O Frank—you think me forward, I am afraid! Don't, dear Frank— will you—for I love you so. And you said lots of times you would marry me, and—and—I—I—I—"

"Don't cry, now! It is foolish. If I said so, of course I will."

"And shall I put up the banns in my parish, and will you in yours?"

"Yes"

"To-morrow?"

"Not to-morrow. We'll settle in a few days."

"You have the permission of the officers?"

"No, not yet."

"O—how is it? You said you almost had before you left Casterbridge."

"The fact is, I forgot to ask. Your coming like this is so sudden and unexpected."

"Yes—yes—it is. It was wrong of me to worry you. I'll go away now. Will you come and see me to-morrow, at Mrs. Twills's, in North Street? I don't like to come to the Barracks. There are bad women about, and they think me one."

"Quite, so. I'll come to you, my dear. Good-night."

"Good-night, Frank—good-night!"

And the noise was again heard of a window closing. The little spot moved away. When she passed the corner a subdued exclamation was heard inside the wall.

"Ho—ho—Sergeant—ho—ho!" An expostulation followed, but it was indistinct; and it became lost amid a low peal of laughter, which was hardly distinguishable from the gurgle of the tiny whirlpools outside.

Analysis: Hardy starts developing the subplot of Fanny Robin. He is clearly at pains to present Fanny as a victim throughout the narrative, to elicit as much sympathy as possible for her from his Victorian audience. Here she is just a "little spot" in the snow, while Troy is high above her in the barracks, his colleagues laughing about his attracting a young woman to his window. The shift in setting to Casterbridge is important too: this is the town where the environment is harsher, more unforgiving than at the farm. Fanny's plea to get married is doubly pathetic because it was not the done thing in those days for a woman to propose to a man, but we realise that Fanny is desperate so she has too. Again Hardy generates mystery here because we don't know exactly why Fanny is so keen to get married very soon, but we can guess that she might be pregnant.

Discussion point: What do you think of the characterisations of Fanny and Troy here?

Questions

What is the weather and time of day when Fanny arrives at the barracks?
What does Fanny plead with Troy for him to do?
What is stopping them getting married, according to Troy?
Where does he agree to meet Fanny the next day?
GCSE style question: how does Hardy present Troy and Fanny's relationship in this chapter?
A Level style question: compare and contrast this snowy scene with another snowy scene in a literary text of your choosing.
Creative response: write a poem/story/description called 'Meeting in the Snow'.

CHAPTER XII
FARMERS—A RULE—AN EXCEPTION

The first public evidence of Bathsheba's decision to be a farmer in her own person and by proxy no more was her appearance the following market-day in the cornmarket at Casterbridge.

The low though extensive hall, supported by beams and pillars, and latterly dignified by the name of Corn Exchange, was thronged with hot men who talked among each other in twos and threes, the speaker of the minute looking sideways into his auditor's face and concentrating his argument by a contraction of one eyelid during delivery. The greater number carried in their hands ground-ash saplings, using them partly as walking-sticks and partly for poking up pigs, sheep, neighbours with their backs turned, and restful things in general, which seemed to require such treatment in the course of their peregrinations. During conversations each subjected his sapling to great varieties of usage—bending it round his back, forming an arch of it between his two hands, overweighting it on the ground till it reached nearly a semicircle; or perhaps it was hastily tucked under the arm whilst the sample-bag was pulled forth and a handful of corn poured into the palm, which, after criticism, was flung upon the floor, an issue of events perfectly well known to half-a-dozen acute town-bred fowls which had as usual crept into the building unobserved, and waited the fulfilment of their anticipations with a high-stretched neck and oblique eye.

Among these heavy yeomen a feminine figure glided, the single one of her sex that the room contained. She was prettily and even daintily dressed. She moved between them as a chaise between carts, was heard after them as a romance after sermons, was felt among them like a breeze among furnaces. It had required a little determination—far more than she had at first imagined—to take up a position here, for at her first entry the lumbering dialogues had ceased, nearly every face had been turned towards her, and those that were already turned rigidly fixed there.

Two or three only of the farmers were personally known to Bathsheba, and to these she had made her way. But if she was to be the practical woman she had intended to show herself, business must be carried on, introductions or none, and she ultimately acquired confidence enough to speak and reply boldly to men merely known to her by hearsay. Bathsheba too had her sample-bags, and by degrees adopted the professional pour into the hand—holding up the grains in her narrow palm for inspection, in perfect Casterbridge manner.

Something in the exact arch of her upper unbroken row of teeth, and in the keenly pointed corners of her red mouth when, with parted lips, she somewhat defiantly turned up her face to argue a point with a tall man, suggested that there was potentiality enough in that lithe slip of humanity for alarming exploits of sex, and daring enough to carry them out. But her eyes had a softness—invariably a softness—which, had they not been dark, would have seemed mistiness; as they were, it lowered an expression that might have been piercing to simple clearness.

Strange to say of a woman in full bloom and vigor, she always allowed her interlocutors to finish their statements before rejoining with hers. In arguing on prices, she held to her own firmly, as was natural in a dealer, and reduced theirs persistently, as was inevitable in a woman. But there was an elasticity in her firmness which removed it from obstinacy, as there was a naïveté in her cheapening which saved it from meanness.

Those of the farmers with whom she had no dealings (by far the greater part) were continually asking each other, "Who is she?" The reply would be—

"Farmer Everdene's niece; took on Weatherbury Upper Farm; turned away the baily, and swears she'll do everything herself."

The other man would then shake his head.

"Yes, 'tis a pity she's so headstrong," the first would say. "But we ought to be proud of her here—she lightens up the old place. 'Tis such a shapely maid, however, that she'll soon get picked up."

It would be ungallant to suggest that the novelty of her engagement in such an occupation had almost as much to do with the magnetism as had the beauty of her face and movements. However, the interest was general, and this Saturday's début in the forum, whatever it may have been to Bathsheba as the buying and selling farmer, was unquestionably a triumph to her as the maiden. Indeed, the sensation was so pronounced that her instinct on two or three occasions was merely to walk as a queen among these gods of the fallow, like a little sister of a little Jove, and to neglect closing prices altogether.

The numerous evidences of her power to attract were only thrown into greater relief by a marked exception. Women seem to have eyes in their ribbons for such matters as these. Bathsheba, without looking within a right angle of him, was conscious of a black sheep among the flock.

It perplexed her first. If there had been a respectable minority on either side, the case would have been most natural. If nobody had regarded her, she would have taken the matter indifferently—such cases had occurred. If everybody, this man included, she would have taken it as a matter of course—people had done so before. But the smallness of the exception made the mystery.

She soon knew thus much of the recusant's appearance. He was a gentlemanly man, with full and distinctly outlined Roman features, the prominences of which glowed in the sun with a bronze-like richness of tone. He was erect in attitude, and quiet in demeanour. One characteristic pre-eminently marked him—dignity.

Apparently he had some time ago reached that entrance to middle age at which a man's aspect naturally ceases to alter for the term of a dozen years or so; and, artificially, a woman's does likewise. Thirty-five and fifty were his limits of variation—he might have been either, or anywhere between the two.

It may be said that married men of forty are usually ready and generous enough to fling passing glances at any specimen of moderate beauty they may discern by the way. Probably, as with persons playing whist for love, the consciousness of a certain immunity under any circumstances from that worst possible ultimate, the having to pay, makes them unduly speculative. Bathsheba was convinced that this unmoved person was not a married man.

When marketing was over, she rushed off to Liddy, who was waiting for her beside the yellow gig in which they had driven to town. The horse was put in, and on they trotted—Bathsheba's sugar, tea, and drapery parcels being packed behind, and expressing in some indescribable manner, by their colour, shape, and general lineaments, that they were that young lady-farmer's property, and the grocer's and draper's no more.

"I've been through it, Liddy, and it is over. I shan't mind it again, for they will all have grown accustomed to seeing me there; but this morning it was as bad as being married—eyes everywhere!"

"I knowed it would be," Liddy said. "Men be such a terrible class of society to look at a body."

"But there was one man who had more sense than to waste his time upon me." The information was put in this form that Liddy might not for a moment suppose her mistress was at all piqued. "A very good-looking man," she continued, "upright; about forty, I should think. Do you know at all who he could be?"

Liddy couldn't think.

"Can't you guess at all?" said Bathsheba with some disappointment.

"I haven't a notion; besides, 'tis no difference, since he took less notice of you than any of the rest. Now, if he'd taken more, it would have mattered a great deal."

Bathsheba was suffering from the reverse feeling just then, and they bowled along in silence. A low carriage, bowling along still more rapidly behind a horse of unimpeachable breed, overtook and passed them.

"Why, there he is!" she said.

Liddy looked. "That! That's Farmer Boldwood—of course 'tis—the man you couldn't see the other day when he called."

Analysis: The presentation of Fanny is thrown into marked relief by Bathsheba's appearance at the Farmer's Market. Being the only woman there, she makes a big impression: she is not duped by the farmers' attempts to get the better of her during bargaining for the buying and selling of produce, and she is moreover hugely attractive to them, leaving the red-faced farmers gawping at the way she glides around the market. There is only person who she does not attract: Farmer Boldwood. Notice how Bathsheba describes Boldwood as "very good looking". Boldwood is described as having "Roman features", and being "erect in attitude". Boldwood is, above all else, a proper, straight-forward man, not given over to dreaming and wild fancies. Unlike Hardy's characterisation of Fanny, his portrayal of Boldwood who too becomes a victim of his desires, is complex: Boldwood is not a victim at the beginning of the novel. He is triumphant, handsome, and wants for nothing. By the end of the novel, he will be an utterly broken man.

Discussion point: Why does Hardy present Boldwood as such an important person at the beginning of the novel?

"Oh, Farmer Boldwood," murmured Bathsheba, and looked at him as he outstripped them. The farmer had never turned his head once, but with eyes fixed on the most advanced point along the road, passed as unconsciously and abstractedly as if Bathsheba and her charms were thin air.

"He's an interesting man—don't you think so?" she remarked.

"O yes, very. Everybody owns it," replied Liddy.

"I wonder why he is so wrapt up and indifferent, and seemingly so far away from all he sees around him."

"It is said—but not known for certain—that he met with some bitter disappointment when he was a young man and merry. A woman jilted him, they say."

"People always say that—and we know very well women scarcely ever jilt men; 'tis the men who jilt us. I expect it is simply his nature to be so reserved."

"Simply his nature—I expect so, miss—nothing else in the world."

"Still, 'tis more romantic to think he has been served cruelly, poor thing'! Perhaps, after all, he has!"

"Depend upon it he has. Oh yes, miss, he has! I feel he must have."

"However, we are very apt to think extremes of people. I shouldn't wonder after all if it wasn't a little of both—just between the two—rather cruelly used and rather reserved."

"Oh dear no, miss—I can't think it between the two!"

"That's most likely."

"Well, yes, so it is. I am convinced it is most likely. You may take my word, miss, that that's what's the matter with him."

Questions

What makes Bathsheba stand out in the cornmarket?

What is her response to the contempt and sexism of the farmers?

Who is the only person who is indifferent to Bathsheba?

Why is she curious about Boldwood?

GCSE style question: how does Hardy make the scene in the cornmarket such a telling and revealing scene about Bathsheba and the world of the farmers?

A Level style question: compare and contrast the presentation of the male world of the farmers with another presentation of masculinity in another text of your choice.

Creative response: write a poem/story/description of a world/scene which is dominated by one gender, either male or female.

CHAPTER XIII
SORTES SANCTORUM—THE VALENTINE

It was Sunday afternoon in the farmhouse, on the thirteenth of February. Dinner being over, Bathsheba, for want of a better companion, had asked Liddy to come and sit with her. The mouldy pile was dreary in winter-time before the candles were lighted and the shutters closed; the atmosphere of the place seemed as old as the walls; every nook behind the furniture had a temperature of its own, for the fire was not kindled in this part of the house early in the day; and Bathsheba's new piano, which was an old one in other annals, looked particularly sloping and out of level on the warped floor before night threw a shade over its less prominent angles and hid the unpleasantness. Liddy, like a little brook, though shallow, was always rippling; her presence had not so much weight as to task thought, and yet enough to exercise it.

On the table lay an old quarto Bible, bound in leather. Liddy looking at it said,—

"Did you ever find out, miss, who you are going to marry by means of the Bible and key?"

"Don't be so foolish, Liddy. As if such things could be."

"Well, there's a good deal in it, all the same."

"Nonsense, child."

"And it makes your heart beat fearful. Some believe in it; some don't; I do."

"Very well, let's try it," said Bathsheba, bounding from her seat with that total disregard of consistency which can be indulged in towards a dependent, and entering into the spirit of divination at once. "Go and get the front door key."

Liddy fetched it. "I wish it wasn't Sunday," she said, on returning. "Perhaps 'tis wrong."

"What's right week days is right Sundays," replied her mistress in a tone which was a proof in itself.

The book was opened—the leaves, drab with age, being quite worn away at much-read verses by the forefingers of unpractised readers in former days, where they were moved along under the line as an aid to the vision. The special verse in the Book of Ruth was sought out by Bathsheba, and the sublime words met her eye. They slightly thrilled and abashed her. It was Wisdom in the abstract facing Folly in the concrete. Folly in the concrete blushed, persisted in her intention, and placed the key on the book. A rusty patch immediately upon the verse, caused by previous pressure of an iron substance thereon, told that this was not the first time the old volume had been used for the purpose.

"Now keep steady, and be silent," said Bathsheba.

The verse was repeated; the book turned round; Bathsheba blushed guiltily.

"Who did you try?" said Liddy curiously.

"I shall not tell you."

"Did you notice Mr. Boldwood's doings in church this morning, miss?" Liddy continued, adumbrating by the remark the track her thoughts had taken.

"No, indeed," said Bathsheba, with serene indifference.

"His pew is exactly opposite yours, miss."

"I know it."

"And you did not see his goings on!"

"Certainly I did not, I tell you."

Liddy assumed a smaller physiognomy, and shut her lips decisively.

This move was unexpected, and proportionately disconcerting. "What did he do?" Bathsheba said perforce.

"Didn't turn his head to look at you once all the service."

"Why should he?" again demanded her mistress, wearing a nettled look. "I didn't ask him to."

"Oh no. But everybody else was noticing you; and it was odd he didn't. There, 'tis like him. Rich and gentlemanly, what does he care?"

Bathsheba dropped into a silence intended to express that she had opinions on the matter too abstruse for Liddy's comprehension, rather than that she had nothing to say.

"Dear me—I had nearly forgotten the valentine I bought yesterday," she exclaimed at length.

"Valentine! who for, miss?" said Liddy. "Farmer Boldwood?"

It was the single name among all possible wrong ones that just at this moment seemed to Bathsheba more pertinent than the right.

"Well, no. It is only for little Teddy Coggan. I have promised him something, and this will be a pretty surprise for him. Liddy, you may as well bring me my desk and I'll direct it at once."

Bathsheba took from her desk a gorgeously illuminated and embossed design in post-octavo, which had been bought on the previous market-day at the chief stationer's in Casterbridge. In the centre was a small oval enclosure; this was left blank, that the sender might insert tender words more appropriate to the special occasion than any generalities by a printer could possibly be.

"Here's a place for writing," said Bathsheba. "What shall I put?"

"Something of this sort, I should think," returned Liddy promptly:—

> "The rose is red,
> The violet blue,
> Carnation's sweet,
> And so are you."

"Yes, that shall be it. It just suits itself to a chubby-faced child like him," said Bathsheba. She inserted the words in a small though legible handwriting; enclosed the sheet in an envelope, and dipped her pen for the direction.

"What fun it would be to send it to the stupid old Boldwood, and how he would wonder!" said the irrepressible Liddy, lifting her eyebrows, and indulging in an awful mirth on the verge of fear as she thought of the moral and social magnitude of the man contemplated.

Bathsheba paused to regard the idea at full length. Boldwood's had begun to be a troublesome image—a species of Daniel in her kingdom who persisted in kneeling eastward when reason and common sense said that he might just as well follow suit with the rest, and afford her the official glance of admiration which cost nothing at all. She was far from being seriously concerned about his nonconformity. Still, it was faintly depressing that the most dignified and valuable man in the parish should withhold his eyes, and that a girl like Liddy should talk about it. So Liddy's idea was at first rather harassing than piquant.

"No, I won't do that. He wouldn't see any humour in it."

"He'd worry to death," said the persistent Liddy.

"Really, I don't care particularly to send it to Teddy," remarked her mistress. "He's rather a naughty child sometimes."

"Yes—that he is."

"Let's toss as men do," said Bathsheba, idly. "Now then, head, Boldwood; tail, Teddy. No, we won't toss money on a Sunday, that would be tempting the devil indeed."

"Toss this hymn-book; there can't be no sinfulness in that, miss."

"Very well. Open, Boldwood—shut, Teddy. No; it's more likely to fall open. Open, Teddy—shut, Boldwood."

The book went fluttering in the air and came down shut.

Bathsheba, a small yawn upon her mouth, took the pen, and with off-hand serenity directed the missive to Boldwood.

"Now light a candle, Liddy. Which seal shall we use? Here's a unicorn's head—there's nothing in that. What's this?—two doves—no. It ought to be something extraordinary, ought it not, Liddy? Here's one with a motto—I remember it is some funny one, but I can't read it. We'll try this, and if it doesn't do we'll have another."

A large red seal was duly affixed. Bathsheba looked closely at the hot wax to discover the words.

"Capital!" she exclaimed, throwing down the letter frolicsomely. "'Twould upset the solemnity of a parson and clerke too."

Liddy looked at the words of the seal, and read—

"Marry Me."

The same evening the letter was sent, and was duly sorted in Casterbridge post-office that night, to be returned to Weatherbury again in the morning.

So very idly and unreflectingly was this deed done. Of love as a spectacle Bathsheba had a fair knowledge; but of love subjectively she knew nothing.

Questions

What does Liddy persuade Bathsheba to do?

What does Bathsheba decide to do with her Valentine card, which she had bought to send to a child?

What does the seal on the card say?

Why does she send the card to Boldwood?

GCSE style question: how does Hardy make the sending of the Valentine such an interesting scene?

A Level style question: compare and contrast the presentation of Bathsheba's interest in Boldwood with another similar relationship in another text of your choice.

Creative response: write a poem/story/description called 'The Valentine Card', or write Liddy or Bathsheba's diary for this chapter.

CHAPTER XIV
EFFECT OF THE LETTER—
SUNRISE

At dusk, on the evening of St. Valentine's Day, Boldwood sat down to supper as usual, by a beaming fire of aged logs. Upon the mantel-shelf before him was a time-piece, surmounted by a spread eagle, and upon the eagle's wings was the letter Bathsheba had sent. Here the bachelor's gaze was continually fastening itself, till the large red seal became as a blot of blood on the retina of his eye; and as he ate and drank he still read in fancy the words thereon, although they were too remote for his sight—

"Marry Me."

The pert injunction was like those crystal substances which, colourless themselves, assume the tone of objects about them. Here, in the quiet of Boldwood's parlour, where everything that was not grave was extraneous, and where the atmosphere was that of a Puritan Sunday lasting all the week, the letter and its dictum changed their tenor from the thoughtlessness of their origin to a deep solemnity, imbibed from their accessories now.

Since the receipt of the missive in the morning, Boldwood had felt the symmetry of his existence to be slowly getting distorted in the direction of an ideal passion. The disturbance was as the first floating weed to Columbus—the contemptibly little suggesting possibilities of the infinitely great.

The letter must have had an origin and a motive. That the latter was of the smallest magnitude compatible with its existence at all, Boldwood, of course, did not know. And such an explanation did not strike him as a possibility even. It is foreign to a mystified condition of mind to realize of the mystifier that the processes of approving a course suggested by circumstance, and of striking out a course from inner impulse, would look the same in the result. The vast difference between starting a train of events, and directing into a particular groove a series already started, is rarely apparent to the person confounded by the issue.

When Boldwood went to bed he placed the valentine in the corner of the looking-glass. He was conscious of its presence, even when his back was turned upon it. It was the first time in Boldwood's life that such an event had occurred.

Analysis: The tossing of the hymn book is the event which causes so much chaos in the life of Bathsheba. Here we see Hardy being at pains to present two main things: the insidious role of fate and Bathsheba's lack of knowledge about the world of men. Bathsheba appears to want to send the Valentine to Teddy Coggan: the Bible is more likely to fall open than shut. However, fate decrees that it is shut and it is sent to Boldwood. Throughout Bathsheba, unlike Liddy, her servant, is not aware of the magnitude of what she is doing, she stifles a "yawn". There is an "off-hand serenity" about the way she carries out the whole thing. It is clear that she believes she is like anyone else, that the Valentine will be interpreted as a joke. Her naivety is breath-taking but believable: she has not yet mastered the rules of attraction or understood properly the power of her beauty or wealth.

Discussion point: Why does this become such an important event in the novel?

The same fascination that caused him to think it an act which had a deliberate motive prevented him from regarding it as an impertinence. He looked again at the direction. The mysterious influences of night invested the writing with the presence of the unknown writer. Somebody's—some woman's—hand had travelled softly over the paper bearing his name; her unrevealed eyes had watched every curve as she formed it; her brain had seen him in imagination the while. Why should she have imagined him? Her mouth—were the lips red or pale, plump or creased?—had curved itself to a certain expression as the pen went on—the corners had moved with all their natural tremulousness: what had been the expression?

The vision of the woman writing, as a supplement to the words written, had no individuality. She was a misty shape, and well she might be, considering that her original was at that moment sound asleep and oblivious of all love and letter-writing under the sky. Whenever Boldwood dozed she took a form, and comparatively ceased to be a vision: when he awoke there was the letter justifying the dream.

The moon shone to-night, and its light was not of a customary kind. His window admitted only a reflection of its rays, and the pale sheen had that reversed direction which snow gives, coming upward and lighting up his ceiling in an unnatural way, casting shadows in strange places, and putting lights where shadows had used to be.

The substance of the epistle had occupied him but little in comparison with the fact of its arrival. He suddenly wondered if anything more might be found in the envelope than what he had withdrawn. He jumped out of bed in the weird light, took the letter, pulled out the flimsy sheet, shook the envelope—searched it. Nothing more was there. Boldwood looked, as he had a hundred times the preceding day, at the insistent red seal: "Marry me," he said aloud.

The solemn and reserved yeoman again closed the letter, and stuck it in the frame of the glass. In doing so he caught sight of his reflected features, wan in expression, and insubstantial in form. He saw how closely compressed was his mouth, and that his eyes were wide-spread and vacant. Feeling uneasy and dissatisfied with himself for this nervous excitability, he returned to bed.

Then the dawn drew on. The full power of the clear heaven was not equal to that of a cloudy sky at noon, when Boldwood arose and dressed himself. He descended the stairs and went out towards the gate of a field to the east, leaning over which he paused and looked around.

It was one of the usual slow sunrises of this time of the year, and the sky, pure violet in the zenith, was leaden to the northward, and murky to the east, where, over the snowy down or ewe-lease on Weatherbury Upper Farm, and apparently resting upon the ridge, the only half of the sun yet visible burnt rayless, like a red and flameless fire shining over a white hearthstone. The whole effect resembled a sunset as childhood resembles age.

In other directions, the fields and sky were so much of one colour by the snow, that it was difficult in a hasty glance to tell whereabouts the horizon occurred; and in general there was here, too, that before-mentioned preternatural inversion of light and shade which attends the prospect when the garish brightness commonly in the sky is found on the earth, and the shades of earth are in the sky. Over the west hung the wasting moon, now dull and greenish-yellow, like tarnished brass.

Boldwood was listlessly noting how the frost had hardened and glazed the surface of the snow, till it shone in the red eastern light with the polish of marble; how, in some portions of the slope, withered grass-bents, encased in icicles, bristled through the smooth wan coverlet in the twisted and curved shapes of old Venetian glass; and how the footprints of a few birds, which had hopped over the snow whilst it lay in the state of a soft fleece, were now frozen to a short permanency. A half-muffled noise of light wheels interrupted him. Boldwood turned back into the road. It was the mail-cart—a crazy, two-wheeled vehicle, hardly heavy enough to resist a puff of wind. The driver held out a letter. Boldwood seized it and opened it, expecting another anonymous one—so greatly are people's ideas of probability a mere sense that precedent will repeat itself.

"I don't think it is for you, sir," said the man, when he saw Boldwood's action. "Though there is no name, I think it is for your shepherd."

Boldwood looked then at the address—

> To the New Shepherd,
> Weatherbury Farm,
> Near Casterbridge

"Oh—what a mistake!—it is not mine. Nor is it for my shepherd. It is for Miss Everdene's. You had better take it on to him—Gabriel Oak—and say I opened it in mistake."

At this moment, on the ridge, up against the blazing sky, a figure was visible, like the black snuff in the midst of a candle-flame. Then it moved and began to bustle about vigorously from place to place, carrying square skeleton masses, which were riddled by the same rays. A small figure on all fours followed behind. The tall form was that of Gabriel Oak; the small one that of George; the articles in course of transit were hurdles.

"Wait," said Boldwood. "That's the man on the hill. I'll take the letter to him myself."

To Boldwood it was now no longer merely a letter to another man. It was an opportunity. Exhibiting a face pregnant with intention, he entered the snowy field.

Gabriel, at that minute, descended the hill towards the right. The glow stretched down in this direction now, and touched the distant roof of Warren's Malthouse—whither the shepherd was apparently bent: Boldwood followed at a distance.

Questions

What does Boldwood initially do with the Valentine Card?
How does the card haunt him?

Who does he stare at when wakes early?

GCSE style question: how does Hardy develop Boldwood's character in this scene?

A Level style question: compare and contrast the representation of Boldwood with another similar character in another text of your choice.

Creative response: write a story/poem/description called 'The Obsession' or write Boldwood's diary for this scene.

CHAPTER XV
A MORNING MEETING—THE LETTER AGAIN

The scarlet and orange light outside the malthouse did not penetrate to its interior, which was, as usual, lighted by a rival glow of similar hue, radiating from the hearth.

The maltster, after having lain down in his clothes for a few hours, was now sitting beside a three-legged table, breakfasting off bread and bacon. This was eaten on the plateless system, which is performed by placing a slice of bread upon the table, the meat flat upon the bread, a mustard plaster upon the meat, and a pinch of salt upon the whole, then cutting them vertically downwards with a large pocket-knife till wood is reached, when the severed lump is impaled on the knife, elevated, and sent the proper way of food.

The maltster's lack of teeth appeared not to sensibly diminish his powers as a mill. He had been without them for so many years that toothlessness was felt less to be a defect than hard gums an acquisition. Indeed, he seemed to approach the grave as a hyperbolic curve approaches a straight line—less directly as he got nearer, till it was doubtful if he would ever reach it at all.

In the ashpit was a heap of potatoes roasting, and a boiling pipkin of charred bread, called "coffee", for the benefit of whomsoever should call, for Warren's was a sort of clubhouse, used as an alternative to the inn.

"I say, says I, we get a fine day, and then down comes a snapper at night," was a remark now suddenly heard spreading into the malthouse from the door, which had been opened the previous moment. The form of Henery Fray advanced to the fire, stamping the snow from his boots when about half-way there. The speech and entry had not seemed to be at all an abrupt beginning to the maltster, introductory matter being often omitted in this neighbourhood, both from word and deed, and the maltster having the same latitude allowed him, did not hurry to reply. He picked up a fragment of cheese, by pecking upon it with his knife, as a butcher picks up skewers.

Henery appeared in a drab kerseymere great-coat, buttoned over his smock-frock, the white skirts of the latter being visible to the distance of about a foot below the coat-tails, which, when you got used to the style of dress, looked natural enough, and even ornamental—it certainly was comfortable.

Matthew Moon, Joseph Poorgrass, and other carters and waggoners followed at his heels, with great lanterns dangling from their hands, which showed that they had just come from the cart-horse stables, where they had been busily engaged since four o'clock that morning.

"And how is she getting on without a baily?" the maltster inquired. Henery shook his head, and smiled one of the bitter smiles, dragging all the flesh of his forehead into a corrugated heap in the centre.

"She'll rue it—surely, surely!" he said. "Benjy Pennyways were not a true man or an honest baily—as big a betrayer as Judas Iscariot himself. But to think she can carr' on alone!" He allowed his head to swing laterally three or four times in silence. "Never in all my creeping up—never!"

This was recognized by all as the conclusion of some gloomy speech which had been expressed in thought alone during the shake of the head; Henery meanwhile retained several marks of despair upon his face, to imply that they would be required for use again directly he should go on speaking.

"All will be ruined, and ourselves too, or there's no meat in gentlemen's houses!" said Mark Clark.

"A headstrong maid, that's what she is—and won't listen to no advice at all. Pride and vanity have ruined many a cobbler's dog. Dear, dear, when I think o' it, I sorrows like a man in travel!"

"True, Henery, you do, I've heard ye," said Joseph Poorgrass in a voice of thorough attestation, and with a wire-drawn smile of misery.

"'Twould do a martel man no harm to have what's under her bonnet," said Billy Smallbury, who had just entered, bearing his one tooth before him. "She can spaik real language, and must have some sense somewhere. Do ye foller me?"

"I do, I do; but no baily—I deserved that place," wailed Henery, signifying wasted genius by gazing blankly at visions of a high destiny apparently visible to him on Billy Smallbury's smock-frock. "There, 'twas to be, I suppose. Your lot is your lot, and Scripture is nothing; for if you do good you don't get rewarded according to your works, but be cheated in some mean way out of your recompense."

"No, no; I don't agree with'ee there," said Mark Clark. "God's a perfect gentleman in that respect."

"Good works good pay, so to speak it," attested Joseph Poorgrass.

A short pause ensued, and as a sort of entr'acte Henery turned and blew out the lanterns, which the increase of daylight rendered no longer necessary even in the malthouse, with its one pane of glass.

"I wonder what a farmer-woman can want with a harpsichord, dulcimer, pianner, or whatever 'tis they d'call it?" said the maltster. "Liddy saith she've a new one."

"Got a pianner?"

"Ay. Seems her old uncle's things were not good enough for her. She've bought all but everything new. There's heavy chairs for the stout, weak and wiry ones for the slender; great watches, getting on to the size of clocks, to stand upon the chimbley-piece."

"Pictures, for the most part wonderful frames."

"And long horse-hair settles for the drunk, with horse-hair pillows at each end," said Mr. Clark. "Likewise looking-glasses for the pretty, and lying books for the wicked."

A firm loud tread was now heard stamping outside; the door was opened about six inches, and somebody on the other side exclaimed—

"Neighbours, have ye got room for a few new-born lambs?"

"Ay, sure, shepherd," said the conclave.

The door was flung back till it kicked the wall and trembled from top to bottom with the blow. Mr. Oak appeared in the entry with a steaming face, hay-bands wound about his ankles to keep out the snow, a leather strap round his waist outside the smock-frock, and looking altogether an epitome of the world's health and vigour. Four lambs hung in various embarrassing attitudes over his shoulders, and the dog George, whom Gabriel had contrived to fetch from Norcombe, stalked solemnly behind.

"Well, Shepherd Oak, and how's lambing this year, if I mid say it?" inquired Joseph Poorgrass.

"Terrible trying," said Oak. "I've been wet through twice a-day, either in snow or rain, this last fortnight. Cainy and I haven't tined our eyes to-night."

"A good few twins, too, I hear?"

"Too many by half. Yes; 'tis a very queer lambing this year. We shan't have done by Lady Day."

"And last year 'twer all over by Sexajessamine Sunday," Joseph remarked.

"Bring on the rest Cain," said Gabriel, "and then run back to the ewes. I'll follow you soon."

Cainy Ball—a cheery-faced young lad, with a small circular orifice by way of mouth, advanced and deposited two others, and retired as he was bidden. Oak lowered the lambs from their unnatural elevation, wrapped them in hay, and placed them round the fire.

"We've no lambing-hut here, as I used to have at Norcombe," said Gabriel, "and 'tis such a plague to bring the weakly ones to a house. If 'twasn't for your place here, malter, I don't know what I should do i' this keen weather. And how is it with you to-day, malter?"

"Oh, neither sick nor sorry, shepherd; but no younger."

"Ay—I understand."

"Sit down, Shepherd Oak," continued the ancient man of malt. "And how was the old place at Norcombe, when ye went for your dog? I should like to see the old familiar spot; but faith, I shouldn't know a soul there now."

"I suppose you wouldn't. 'Tis altered very much."

"Is it true that Dicky Hill's wooden cider-house is pulled down?"

"Oh yes—years ago, and Dicky's cottage just above it."

"Well, to be sure!"

"Yes; and Tompkins's old apple-tree is rooted that used to bear two hogsheads of cider; and no help from other trees."

"Rooted?—you don't say it! Ah! stirring times we live in—stirring times."

"And you can mind the old well that used to be in the middle of the place? That's turned into a solid iron pump with a large stone trough, and all complete."

"Dear, dear—how the face of nations alter, and what we live to see nowadays! Yes—and 'tis the same here. They've been talking but now of the mis'ess's strange doings."

"What have you been saying about her?" inquired Oak, sharply turning to the rest, and getting very warm.

"These middle-aged men have been pulling her over the coals for pride and vanity," said Mark Clark; "but I say, let her have rope enough. Bless her pretty face—shouldn't I like to do so—upon her cherry lips!" The gallant Mark Clark here made a peculiar and well known sound with his own.

"Mark," said Gabriel, sternly, "now you mind this! none of that dalliance-talk—that smack-and-coddle style of yours—about Miss Everdene. I don't allow it. Do you hear?"

"With all my heart, as I've got no chance," replied Mr. Clark, cordially.

"I suppose you've been speaking against her?" said Oak, turning to Joseph Poorgrass with a very grim look.

"No, no—not a word I—'tis a real joyful thing that she's no worse, that's what I say," said Joseph, trembling and blushing with terror. "Matthew just said—"

"Matthew Moon, what have you been saying?" asked Oak.

"I? Why ye know I wouldn't harm a worm—no, not one underground worm?" said Matthew Moon, looking very uneasy.

"Well, somebody has—and look here, neighbours," Gabriel, though one of the quietest and most gentle men on earth, rose to the occasion, with martial promptness and vigour. "That's my fist." Here he placed his fist, rather smaller in size than a common loaf, in the mathematical centre of the maltster's little table, and with it gave a bump or two thereon, as if to ensure that their eyes all thoroughly took in the idea of fistiness before he went further. "Now—the first man in the parish that I hear prophesying bad of our mistress, why" (here the fist was raised and let fall as Thor might have done with his hammer in assaying it)—"he'll smell and taste that—or I'm a Dutchman."

All earnestly expressed by their features that their minds did not wander to Holland for a moment on account of this statement, but were deploring the difference which gave rise to the figure; and Mark Clark cried "Hear, hear; just what I should ha' said." The dog George looked up at the same time after the shepherd's menace, and though he understood English but imperfectly, began to growl.

"Now, don't ye take on so, shepherd, and sit down!" said Henery, with a deprecating peacefulness equal to anything of the kind in Christianity.

"We hear that ye be a extraordinary good and clever man, shepherd," said Joseph Poorgrass with considerable anxiety from behind the maltster's bedstead, whither he had retired for safety. "'Tis a great thing to be clever, I'm sure," he added, making movements associated with states of mind rather than body; "we wish we were, don't we, neighbours?"

"Ay, that we do, sure," said Matthew Moon, with a small anxious laugh towards Oak, to show how very friendly disposed he was likewise.

"Who's been telling you I'm clever?" said Oak.

"'Tis blowed about from pillar to post quite common," said Matthew. "We hear that ye can tell the time as well by the stars as we can by the sun and moon, shepherd."

"Yes, I can do a little that way," said Gabriel, as a man of medium sentiments on the subject.

"And that ye can make sun-dials, and prent folks' names upon their waggons almost like copper-plate, with beautiful flourishes, and great long tails. A excellent fine thing for ye to be such a clever man, shepherd. Joseph Poorgrass used to prent to Farmer James Everdene's waggons before you came, and 'a could never mind which way to turn the J's and E's—could ye, Joseph?" Joseph shook his head to express how absolute was the fact that he couldn't. "And so you used to do 'em the wrong way, like this, didn't ye, Joseph?" Matthew marked on the dusty floor with his whip-handle

"And how Farmer James would cuss, and call thee a fool, wouldn't he, Joseph, when 'a seed his name looking so inside-out-like?" continued Matthew Moon with feeling.

"Ay—'a would," said Joseph, meekly. "But, you see, I wasn't so much to blame, for them J's and E's be such trying sons o' witches for the memory to mind whether they face backward or forward; and I always had such a forgetful memory, too."

"'Tis a very bad affliction for ye, being such a man of calamities in other ways."

"Well, 'tis; but a happy Providence ordered that it should be no worse, and I feel my thanks. As to shepherd, there, I'm sure mis'ess ought to have made ye her baily—such a fitting man for't as you be."

"I don't mind owning that I expected it," said Oak, frankly. "Indeed, I hoped for the place. At the same time, Miss Everdene has a right to be her own baily if she choose—and to keep me down to be a common shepherd only." Oak drew a slow breath, looked sadly into the bright ashpit, and seemed lost in thoughts not of the most hopeful hue.

The genial warmth of the fire now began to stimulate the nearly lifeless lambs to bleat and move their limbs briskly upon the hay, and to recognize for the first time the fact that they were born. Their noise increased to a chorus of baas, upon which Oak pulled the milk-can from before the fire, and taking a small tea-pot from the pocket of his smock-frock, filled it with milk, and taught those of the helpless creatures which were not to be restored to their dams how to drink from the spout—a trick they acquired with astonishing aptitude.

"And she don't even let ye have the skins of the dead lambs, I hear?" resumed Joseph Poorgrass, his eyes lingering on the operations of Oak with the necessary melancholy.

"I don't have them," said Gabriel.

"Ye be very badly used, shepherd," hazarded Joseph again, in the hope of getting Oak as an ally in lamentation after all. "I think she's took against ye—that I do."

"Oh no—not at all," replied Gabriel, hastily, and a sigh escaped him, which the deprivation of lamb skins could hardly have caused.

Before any further remark had been added a shade darkened the door, and Boldwood entered the malthouse, bestowing upon each a nod of a quality between friendliness and condescension.

"Ah! Oak, I thought you were here," he said. "I met the mail-cart ten minutes ago, and a letter was put into my hand, which I opened without reading the address. I believe it is yours. You must excuse the accident please."

"Oh yes—not a bit of difference, Mr. Boldwood—not a bit," said Gabriel, readily. He had not a correspondent on earth, nor was there a possible letter coming to him whose contents the whole parish would not have been welcome to peruse.

Oak stepped aside, and read the following in an unknown hand:—

Dear Friend,—I do not know your name, but I think these few lines will reach you, which I wrote to thank you for your kindness to me the night I left Weatherbury in a reckless way. I also return the money I owe you, which you will excuse my not keeping as a gift. All has ended well, and I am happy to say I am going to be married to the young man who has courted me for some time—Sergeant Troy, of the 11th Dragoon Guards, now quartered in this town. He would, I know, object to my having received anything except as a loan, being a man of great respectability and high honour—indeed, a nobleman by blood.

I should be much obliged to you if you would keep the contents of this letter a secret for the present, dear friend. We mean to surprise Weatherbury by coming there soon as husband and wife, though I blush to state it to one nearly a stranger. The sergeant grew up in Weatherbury. Thanking you again for your kindness,

I am, your sincere well-wisher,
Fanny Robin.

"Have you read it, Mr. Boldwood?" said Gabriel; "if not, you had better do so. I know you are interested in Fanny Robin."

Boldwood read the letter and looked grieved.

"Fanny—poor Fanny! the end she is so confident of has not yet come, she should remember—and may never come. I see she gives no address."

"What sort of a man is this Sergeant Troy?" said Gabriel.

"H'm—I'm afraid not one to build much hope upon in such a case as this," the farmer murmured, "though he's a clever fellow, and up to everything. A slight romance attaches to him, too. His mother was a French governess, and it seems that a secret attachment existed between her and the late Lord Severn. She was married to a poor medical man, and soon after an infant was born; and while money was forthcoming all went on well. Unfortunately for her boy, his best friends died; and he got then a situation as second clerk at a lawyer's in Casterbridge. He stayed there for some time, and might have worked himself into a dignified position of some sort had he not indulged in the wild freak of enlisting. I have much doubt if ever little Fanny will surprise us in the way she mentions—very much doubt. A silly girl!—silly girl!"

The door was hurriedly burst open again, and in came running Cainy Ball out of breath, his mouth red and open, like the bell of a penny trumpet, from which he coughed with noisy vigour and great distension of face.

"Now, Cain Ball," said Oak, sternly, "why will you run so fast and lose your breath so? I'm always telling you of it."

"Oh—I—a puff of mee breath—went—the—wrong way, please, Mister Oak, and made me cough—hok—hok!"

"Well—what have you come for?"

"I've run to tell ye," said the junior shepherd, supporting his exhausted youthful frame against the doorpost, "that you must come directly. Two more ewes have twinned—that's what's the matter, Shepherd Oak."

"Oh, that's it," said Oak, jumping up, and dimissing for the present his thoughts on poor Fanny. "You are a good boy to run and tell me, Cain, and you shall smell a large plum pudding some day as a treat. But, before we go, Cainy, bring the tarpot, and we'll mark this lot and have done with 'em."

Oak took from his illimitable pockets a marking iron, dipped it into the pot, and imprinted on the buttocks of the infant sheep the initials of her he delighted to muse on—"B. E.," which signified to all the region round that henceforth the lambs belonged to Farmer Bathsheba Everdene, and to no one else.

"Now, Cainy, shoulder your two, and off. Good morning, Mr. Boldwood." The shepherd lifted the sixteen large legs and four small bodies he had himself brought, and vanished with them in the direction of the lambing field hard by—their frames being now in a sleek and hopeful state, pleasantly contrasting with their death's-door plight of half an hour before.

Boldwood followed him a little way up the field, hesitated, and turned back. He followed him again with a last resolve, annihilating return. On approaching the nook in which the fold was constructed, the farmer drew out his pocket-book, unfastened it, and allowed it to lie open on his hand. A letter was revealed—Bathsheba's.

"I was going to ask you, Oak," he said, with unreal carelessness, "if you know whose writing this is?"

Oak glanced into the book, and replied instantly, with a flushed face, "Miss Everdene's."

Oak had coloured simply at the consciousness of sounding her name. He now felt a strangely distressing qualm from a new thought. The letter could of course be no other than anonymous, or the inquiry would not have been necessary.

Analysis: Fanny's letter to Oak is crucial for a few reasons. The letter means that both Oak and Boldwood know that Troy is cheating upon Fanny by taking up with Bathsheba, which he does later on in the novel. And yet, neither man tells Bathsheba the truth, wanting to protect her from the full horror of Troy's betrayal. Oak warns her most strongly about Troy, while Boldwood actually tries to bribe and attack Troy for he does. Boldwood is fully aware of what Troy is like: that he is clever but "up to everything" – meaning he is happy to seduce anyone he likes. The sympathy that Boldwood has is important because it makes the reader feel concerned for Fanny.

Discussion point: Why does Hardy manipulate the narrative so that both Oak and Boldwood know what a scoundrel Troy is very early on before he has been introduced to Bathsheba?

Boldwood mistook his confusion: sensitive persons are always ready with their "Is it I?" in preference to objective reasoning.

"The question was perfectly fair," he returned—and there was something incongruous in the serious earnestness with which he applied himself to an argument on a valentine. "You know it is always expected that privy inquiries will be made: that's where the—fun lies." If the word "fun" had been "torture," it could not have been uttered with a more constrained and restless countenance than was Boldwood's then.

Soon parting from Gabriel, the lonely and reserved man returned to his house to breakfast—feeling twinges of shame and regret at having so far exposed his mood by those fevered questions to a stranger. He again placed the letter on the mantelpiece, and sat down to think of the circumstances attending it by the light of Gabriel's information.

Questions

What does Oak bring to the Malthouse?

What does Fanny's letter say?

Whose handwriting does Oak recognise on the Valentine?

GCSE style question: how does Hardy develop suspense in this chapter?

A Level style question: explore how Hardy and another author of your choice investigate the theme of naivety.

Creative response: write a story/poem about a naïve person.

CHAPTER XVI
ALL SAINTS' AND ALL SOULS'

On a week-day morning a small congregation, consisting mainly of women and girls, rose from its knees in the mouldy nave of a church called All Saints', in the distant barrack-town before-mentioned, at the end of a service without a sermon. They were about to disperse, when a smart footstep, entering the porch and coming up the central passage, arrested their attention. The step echoed with a ring unusual in a church; it was the clink of spurs. Everybody looked. A young cavalry soldier in a red uniform, with the three chevrons of a sergeant upon his sleeve, strode up the aisle, with an embarrassment which was only the more marked by the intense vigour of his step, and by the determination upon his face to show none. A slight flush had mounted his cheek by the time he had run the gauntlet between these women; but, passing on through the chancel arch, he never paused till he came close to the altar railing. Here for a moment he stood alone.

The officiating curate, who had not yet doffed his surplice, perceived the new-comer, and followed him to the communion-space. He whispered to the soldier, and then beckoned to the clerk, who in his turn whispered to an elderly woman, apparently his wife, and they also went up the chancel steps.

"'Tis a wedding!" murmured some of the women, brightening. "Let's wait!"

The majority again sat down.

There was a creaking of machinery behind, and some of the young ones turned their heads. From the interior face of the west wall of the tower projected a little canopy with a quarter-jack and small bell beneath it, the automaton being driven by the same clock machinery that struck the large bell in the tower. Between the tower and the church was a close screen, the door of which was kept shut during services, hiding this grotesque clockwork from sight. At present, however, the door was open, and the egress of the jack, the blows on the bell, and the mannikin's retreat into the nook again, were visible to many, and audible throughout the church.

The jack had struck half-past eleven.

"Where's the woman?" whispered some of the spectators.

The young sergeant stood still with the abnormal rigidity of the old pillars around. He faced the south-east, and was as silent as he was still.

The silence grew to be a noticeable thing as the minutes went on, and nobody else appeared, and not a soul moved. The rattle of the quarter-jack again from its niche, its blows for three-quarters, its fussy retreat, were almost painfully abrupt, and caused many of the congregation to start palpably.

"I wonder where the woman is!" a voice whispered again.

There began now that slight shifting of feet, that artificial coughing among several, which betrays a nervous suspense. At length there was a titter. But the soldier never moved. There he stood, his face to the south-east, upright as a column, his cap in his hand.

The clock ticked on. The women threw off their nervousness, and titters and giggling became more frequent. Then came a dead silence. Every one was waiting for the end. Some persons may have noticed how extraordinarily the striking of quarters seems to quicken the flight of time. It was hardly credible that the jack had not got wrong with the minutes when the rattle began again, the puppet emerged, and the four quarters were struck fitfully as before. One could almost be positive that there was a malicious leer upon the hideous creature's face, and a mischievous delight in its twitchings. Then followed the dull and remote resonance of the twelve heavy strokes in the tower above. The women were impressed, and there was no giggle this time.

The clergyman glided into the vestry, and the clerk vanished. The sergeant had not yet turned; every woman in the church was waiting to see his face, and he appeared to know it. At last he did turn, and stalked resolutely down the nave, braving them all, with a compressed lip. Two bowed and toothless old almsmen then looked at each other and chuckled, innocently enough; but the sound had a strange weird effect in that place.

Opposite to the church was a paved square, around which several overhanging wood buildings of old time cast a picturesque shade. The young man on leaving the door went to cross the square, when, in the middle, he met a little woman. The expression of her face, which had been one of intense anxiety, sank at the sight of his nearly to terror.

"Well?" he said, in a suppressed passion, fixedly looking at her.

"Oh, Frank—I made a mistake!—I thought that church with the spire was All Saints', and I was at the door at half-past eleven to a minute as you said. I waited till a quarter to twelve, and found then that I was in All Souls'. But I wasn't much frightened, for I thought it could be to-morrow as well."

"You fool, for so fooling me! But say no more."

"Shall it be to-morrow, Frank?" she asked blankly.

"To-morrow!" and he gave vent to a hoarse laugh. "I don't go through that experience again for some time, I warrant you!"

"But after all," she expostulated in a trembling voice, "the mistake was not such a terrible thing! Now, dear Frank, when shall it be?"

"Ah, when? God knows!" he said, with a light irony, and turning from her walked rapidly away.

Analysis: Again, the role of fate is vital here. It is clear that Troy would have married Fanny if she had gone to the right church, but that the public humiliation of waiting at the wrong church has changed his mind. Thus we see how Troy is very much a man concerned with how he appears: the ridicule which he perceived he endured shapes his response to the whole relationship. He rejects her. Whether he is using her mistake as an excuse or the reason for rejecting her, we never quite know. Unlike Boldwood, Bathsheba and Oak's characterisations, Troy's characterisation never quite rises above the stereotype of the dashing cad.

Discussion point: Why does Hardy show us Troy behaving like this at this point in the novel before he has met Bathsheba?

Questions

Where does Troy wait for Fanny and for how long?
What happens when he leaves?

Where had Fanny been?

What does she plead with Troy to do and what is his response?

GCSE style question: how does Hardy represent Troy and Fanny in this chapter?

A Level style question: compare and contrast Fanny with another person in a literary text who is presented as a victim.

Creative response: write a story/poem/description called 'Late' or write Troy and/or Fanny's diaries for this chapter.

CHAPTER XVII
IN THE MARKET-PLACE

On Saturday Boldwood was in Casterbridge market house as usual, when the disturber of his dreams entered and became visible to him. Adam had awakened from his deep sleep, and behold! there was Eve. The farmer took courage, and for the first time really looked at her.

Material causes and emotional effects are not to be arranged in regular equation. The result from capital employed in the production of any movement of a mental nature is sometimes as tremendous as the cause itself is absurdly minute. When women are in a freakish mood, their usual intuition, either from carelessness or inherent defect, seemingly fails to teach them this, and hence it was that Bathsheba was fated to be astonished to-day.

Boldwood looked at her—not slily, critically, or understandingly, but blankly at gaze, in the way a reaper looks up at a passing train—as something foreign to his element, and but dimly understood. To Boldwood women had been remote phenomena rather than necessary complements— comets of such uncertain aspect, movement, and permanence, that whether their orbits were as geometrical, unchangeable, and as subject to laws as his own, or as absolutely erratic as they superficially appeared, he had not deemed it his duty to consider.

He saw her black hair, her correct facial curves and profile, and the roundness of her chin and throat. He saw then the side of her eyelids, eyes, and lashes, and the shape of her ear. Next he noticed her figure, her skirt, and the very soles of her shoes.

Boldwood thought her beautiful, but wondered whether he was right in his thought, for it seemed impossible that this romance in the flesh, if so sweet as he imagined, could have been going on long without creating a commotion of delight among men, and provoking more inquiry than Bathsheba had done, even though that was not a little. To the best of his judgement neither nature nor art could improve this perfect one of an imperfect many. His heart began to move within him. Boldwood, it must be remembered, though forty years of age, had never before inspected a woman with the very centre and force of his glance; they had struck upon all his senses at wide angles.

Was she really beautiful? He could not assure himself that his opinion was true even now. He furtively said to a neighbour, "Is Miss Everdene considered handsome?"

"Oh yes; she was a good deal noticed the first time she came, if you remember. A very handsome girl indeed."

A man is never more credulous than in receiving favourable opinions on the beauty of a woman he is half, or quite, in love with; a mere child's word on the point has the weight of an R.A.'s. Boldwood was satisfied now.

And this charming woman had in effect said to him, "Marry me." Why should she have done that strange thing? Boldwood's blindness to the difference between approving of what circumstances suggest, and originating what they do not suggest, was well matched by Bathsheba's insensibility to the possibly great issues of little beginnings.

She was at this moment coolly dealing with a dashing young farmer, adding up accounts with him as indifferently as if his face had been the pages of a ledger. It was evident that such a nature as his had no attraction for a woman of Bathsheba's taste. But Boldwood grew hot down to his hands with an incipient jealousy; he trod for the first time the threshold of "the injured lover's hell." His first impulse was to go and thrust himself between them. This could be done, but only in one way—by asking to see a sample of her corn. Boldwood renounced the idea. He could not make the request; it was debasing loveliness to ask it to buy and sell, and jarred with his conceptions of her.

All this time Bathsheba was conscious of having broken into that dignified stronghold at last. His eyes, she knew, were following her everywhere. This was a triumph; and had it come naturally, such a triumph would have been the sweeter to her for this piquing delay. But it had been brought about by misdirected ingenuity, and she valued it only as she valued an artificial flower or a wax fruit.

Being a woman with some good sense in reasoning on subjects wherein her heart was not involved, Bathsheba genuinely repented that a freak which had owed its existence as much to Liddy as to herself, should ever have been undertaken, to disturb the placidity of a man she respected too highly to deliberately tease.

She that day nearly formed the intention of begging his pardon on the very next occasion of their meeting. The worst features of this arrangement were that, if he thought she ridiculed him, an apology would increase the offence by being disbelieved; and if he thought she wanted him to woo her, it would read like additional evidence of her forwardness.

Questions

What does Boldwood do and feel at Casterbridge market?

What does Bathsheba think and feel about Boldwood?

Why is Bathsheba worried about apologizing to Boldwood about the Valentine?

GCSE style question: how does Hardy represent Boldwood and

Bathsheba's relationship in this scene?

A Level style question: compare and contrast the presentation of the theme of jealousy in this text with another text of your choice.

Creative response: write a poem/story/description called 'Jealousy'; or write Bathsheba and/or Boldwood's diary for this chapter.

CHAPTER XVIII
BOLDWOOD IN MEDITATION -- REGRET

Boldwood was tenant of what was called Little Weatherbury Farm, and his person was the nearest approach to aristocracy that this remoter quarter of the parish could boast of. Genteel strangers, whose god was their town, who might happen to be compelled to linger about this nook for a day, heard the sound of light wheels, and prayed to see good society, to the degree of a solitary lord, or squire at the very least, but it was only Mr. Boldwood going out for the day. They heard the sound of wheels yet once more, and were re-animated to expectancy: it was only Mr. Boldwood coming home again.

His house stood recessed from the road, and the stables, which are to a farm what a fireplace is to a room, were behind, their lower portions being lost amid bushes of laurel. Inside the blue door, open half-way down, were to be seen at this time the backs and tails of half-a-dozen warm and contented horses standing in their stalls; and as thus viewed, they presented alternations of roan and bay, in shapes like a Moorish arch, the tail being a streak down the midst of each. Over these, and lost to the eye gazing in from the outer light, the mouths of the same animals could be heard busily sustaining the above-named warmth and plumpness by quantities of oats and hay. The restless and shadowy figure of a colt wandered about a loose-box at the end, whilst the steady grind of all the eaters was occasionally diversified by the rattle of a rope or the stamp of a foot.

Pacing up and down at the heels of the animals was Farmer Boldwood himself. This place was his almonry and cloister in one: here, after looking to the feeding of his four-footed dependants, the celibate would walk and meditate of an evening till the moon's rays streamed in through the cobwebbed windows, or total darkness enveloped the scene.

His square-framed perpendicularity showed more fully now than in the crowd and bustle of the market-house. In this meditative walk his foot met the floor with heel and toe simultaneously, and his fine reddish-fleshed face was bent downwards just enough to render obscure the still mouth and the well-rounded though rather prominent and broad chin. A few clear and thread-like horizontal lines were the only interruption to the otherwise smooth surface of his large forehead.

The phases of Boldwood's life were ordinary enough, but his was not an ordinary nature. That stillness, which struck casual observers more than anything else in his character and habit, and seemed so precisely like the rest of inanition, may have been the perfect balance of enormous antagonistic forces—positives and negatives in fine adjustment. His equilibrium disturbed, he was in extremity at once. If an emotion possessed him at all, it ruled him; a feeling not mastering him was entirely latent. Stagnant or rapid, it was never slow. He was always hit mortally, or he was missed.

He had no light and careless touches in his constitution, either for good or for evil. Stern in the outlines of action, mild in the details, he was serious throughout all. He saw no absurd sides to the follies of life, and thus, though not quite companionable in the eyes of merry men and scoffers, and those to whom all things show life as a jest, he was not intolerable to the earnest and those acquainted with grief. Being a man who read all the dramas of life seriously, if he failed to please when they were comedies, there was no frivolous treatment to reproach him for when they chanced to end tragically.

Bathsheba was far from dreaming that the dark and silent shape upon which she had so carelessly thrown a seed was a hotbed of tropic intensity. Had she known Boldwood's moods, her blame would have been fearful, and the stain upon her heart ineradicable. Moreover, had she known her present power for good or evil over this man, she would have trembled at her responsibility. Luckily for her present, unluckily for her future tranquillity, her understanding had not yet told her what Boldwood was. Nobody knew entirely; for though it was possible to form guesses concerning his wild capabilities from old floodmarks faintly visible, he had never been seen at the high tides which caused them.

Farmer Boldwood came to the stable-door and looked forth across the level fields. Beyond the first enclosure was a hedge, and on the other side of this a meadow belonging to Bathsheba's farm.

It was now early spring—the time of going to grass with the sheep, when they have the first feed of the meadows, before these are laid up for mowing. The wind, which had been blowing east for several weeks, had veered to the southward, and the middle of spring had come abruptly—almost without a beginning. It was that period in the vernal quarter when we may suppose the Dryads to be waking for the season. The vegetable world begins to move and swell and the saps to rise, till in the completest silence of lone gardens and trackless plantations, where everything seems helpless and still after the bond and slavery of frost, there are bustlings, strainings, united thrusts, and pulls-all-together, in comparison with which the powerful tugs of cranes and pulleys in a noisy city are but pigmy efforts.

Boldwood, looking into the distant meadows, saw there three figures. They were those of Miss Everdene, Shepherd Oak, and Cainy Ball.

When Bathsheba's figure shone upon the farmer's eyes it lighted him up as the moon lights up a great tower. A man's body is as the shell, or the tablet, of his soul, as he is reserved or ingenuous, overflowing or self-contained. There was a change in Boldwood's exterior from its former impassibleness; and his face showed that he was now living outside his defences for the first time, and with a fearful sense of exposure. It is the usual experience of strong natures when they love.

At last he arrived at a conclusion. It was to go across and inquire boldly of her.

The insulation of his heart by reserve during these many years, without a channel of any kind for disposable emotion, had worked its effect. It has been observed more than once that the causes of love are chiefly subjective, and Boldwood was a living testimony to the truth of the proposition. No mother existed to absorb his devotion, no sister for his tenderness, no idle ties for sense. He became surcharged with the compound, which was genuine lover's love.

He approached the gate of the meadow. Beyond it the ground was melodious with ripples, and the sky with larks; the low bleating of the flock mingling with both. Mistress and man were engaged in the operation of making a lamb "take," which is performed whenever an ewe has lost her own offspring, one of the twins of another ewe being given her as a substitute. Gabriel had skinned the dead lamb, and was tying the skin over the body of the live lamb, in the customary manner, whilst Bathsheba was holding open a little pen of four hurdles, into which the Mother and foisted lamb were driven, where they would remain till the old sheep conceived an affection for the young one.

Bathsheba looked up at the completion of the manœuvre and saw the farmer by the gate, where he was overhung by a willow tree in full bloom. Gabriel, to whom her face was as the uncertain glory of an April day, was ever regardful of its faintest changes, and instantly discerned thereon the mark of some influence from without, in the form of a keenly self-conscious reddening. He also turned and beheld Boldwood.

At once connecting these signs with the letter Boldwood had shown him, Gabriel suspected her of some coquettish procedure begun by that means, and carried on since, he knew not how.

Farmer Boldwood had read the pantomime denoting that they were aware of his presence, and the perception was as too much light turned upon his new sensibility. He was still in the road, and by moving on he hoped that neither would recognize that he had originally intended to enter the field. He passed by with an utter and overwhelming sensation of ignorance, shyness, and doubt. Perhaps in her manner there were signs that she wished to see him—perhaps not—he could not read a woman. The cabala of this erotic philosophy seemed to consist of the subtlest meanings expressed in misleading ways. Every turn, look, word, and accent contained a mystery quite distinct from its obvious import, and not one had ever been pondered by him until now.

As for Bathsheba, she was not deceived into the belief that Farmer Boldwood had walked by on business or in idleness. She collected the probabilities of the case, and concluded that she was herself responsible for Boldwood's appearance there. It troubled her much to see what a great flame a little wildfire was likely to kindle. Bathsheba was no schemer for marriage, nor was she deliberately a trifler with the affections of men, and a censor's experience on seeing an actual flirt after observing her would have been a feeling of surprise that Bathsheba could be so different from such a one, and yet so like what a flirt is supposed to be.

She resolved never again, by look or by sign, to interrupt the steady flow of this man's life. But a resolution to avoid an evil is seldom framed till the evil is so far advanced as to make avoidance impossible.

Analysis: One of the most modern aspects of Hardy's narrative is his detailed portrayal of Boldwood's growing obsession for Bathsheba. Once again, the theme of voyeurism is important: after receiving the Valentine, Boldwood watches Bathsheba intently from afar, developing and nurturing his obsession for her. For the modern reader, we are perhaps keen to leap to the judgement that he is psychologically disturbed, perhaps immediately labelling him as a 'pervert'. The Victorian readers would have seen him very differently. He is, above all, the most eminent member of the community, the local landowner. Victorian readers would have been more sympathetic towards his obsession because they lived in a society which prohibited the discussion of feelings in public. Sexual appetites were not aired or discussed. Yet, it is clear here that Boldwood is sexually obsessed with Bathsheba, that he is undergoing some sort of sexual awakening with her, enduring feelings that he does not understand or comprehend. Hardy portrays him as "living outside his defences for the first time" – he is weakened by his desire for her – and clearly ashamed by his feelings for her. His lack of knowledge of women is painfully but sympathetically portrayed here. He does not know how to approach Bathsheba: "he could not read a woman". His emotions contrast with Bathsheba's determination to avoid him.

Discussion point: How does Hardy show us that Boldwood is becoming obsessed by Bathsheba?

Questions

What does Boldwood do in his stable-yard?

What has happened to his feelings?

What does Boldwood do which causes Bathsheba embarrassment?

GCSE style question: how does Hardy represent nature in this chapter?

A Level style question: how does Hardy explore the theme of embarrassment in this chapter?

Creative response: write a poem/story called 'The admirer' or write Boldwood's diary for this chapter.

CHAPTER XIX
THE SHEEP-WASHING—THE OFFER

Boldwood did eventually call upon her. She was not at home. "Of course not," he murmured. In contemplating Bathsheba as a woman, he had forgotten the accidents of her position as an agriculturist—that being as much of a farmer, and as extensive a farmer, as himself, her probable whereabouts was out-of-doors at this time of the year. This, and the other oversights Boldwood was guilty of, were natural to the mood, and still more natural to the circumstances. The great aids to idealization in love were present here: occasional observation of her from a distance, and the absence of social intercourse with her—visual familiarity, oral strangeness. The smaller human elements were kept out of sight; the pettinesses that enter so largely into all earthly living and doing were disguised by the accident of lover and loved-one not being on visiting terms; and there was hardly awakened a thought in Boldwood that sorry household realities appertained to her, or that she, like all others, had moments of commonplace, when to be least plainly seen was to be most prettily remembered. Thus a mild sort of apotheosis took place in his fancy, whilst she still lived and breathed within his own horizon, a troubled creature like himself.

It was the end of May when the farmer determined to be no longer repulsed by trivialities or distracted by suspense. He had by this time grown used to being in love; the passion now startled him less even when it tortured him more, and he felt himself adequate to the situation. On inquiring for her at her house they had told him she was at the sheep-washing, and he went off to seek her there.

The sheep-washing pool was a perfectly circular basin of brickwork in the meadows, full of the clearest water. To birds on the wing its glassy surface, reflecting the light sky, must have been visible for miles around as a glistening Cyclops' eye in a green face. The grass about the margin at this season was a sight to remember long—in a minor sort of way. Its activity in sucking the moisture from the rich damp sod was almost a process observable by the eye. The outskirts of this level water-meadow were diversified by rounded and hollow pastures, where just now every flower that was not a buttercup was a daisy. The river slid along noiselessly as a shade, the swelling reeds and sedge forming a flexible palisade upon its moist brink. To the north of the mead were trees, the leaves of which were new, soft, and moist, not yet having stiffened and darkened under summer sun and drought, their colour being yellow beside a green—green beside a yellow. From the recesses of this knot of foliage the loud notes of three cuckoos were resounding through the still air.

Boldwood went meditating down the slopes with his eyes on his boots, which the yellow pollen from the buttercups had bronzed in artistic gradations. A tributary of the main stream flowed through the basin of the pool by an inlet and outlet at opposite points of its diameter. Shepherd Oak, Jan Coggan, Moon, Poorgrass, Cain Ball, and several others were assembled here, all dripping wet to the very roots of their hair, and Bathsheba was standing by in a new riding-habit—the most elegant she had ever worn—the reins of her horse being looped over her arm. Flagons of cider were rolling about upon the green. The meek sheep were pushed into the pool by Coggan and Matthew Moon, who stood by the lower hatch, immersed to their waists; then Gabriel, who stood on the brink, thrust them under as they swam along, with an instrument like a crutch, formed for the purpose, and also for assisting the exhausted animals when the wool became saturated and they began to sink. They were let out against the stream, and through the upper opening, all impurities flowing away below. Cainy Ball and Joseph, who performed this latter operation, were if possible wetter than the rest; they resembled dolphins under a fountain, every protuberance and angle of their clothes dribbling forth a small rill.

Boldwood came close and bade her good morning, with such constraint that she could not but think he had stepped across to the washing for its own sake, hoping not to find her there; more, she fancied his brow severe and his eye slighting. Bathsheba immediately contrived to withdraw, and glided along by the river till she was a stone's throw off. She heard footsteps brushing the grass, and had a consciousness that love was encircling her like a perfume. Instead of turning or waiting, Bathsheba went further among the high sedges, but Boldwood seemed determined, and pressed on till they were completely past the bend of the river. Here, without being seen, they could hear the splashing and shouts of the washers above.

"Miss Everdene!" said the farmer.

She trembled, turned, and said "Good morning." His tone was so utterly removed from all she had expected as a beginning. It was lowness and quiet accentuated: an emphasis of deep meanings, their form, at the same time, being scarcely expressed. Silence has sometimes a remarkable power of showing itself as the disembodied soul of feeling wandering without its carcase, and it is then more impressive than speech. In the same way, to say a little is often to tell more than to say a great deal. Boldwood told everything in that word.

As the consciousness expands on learning that what was fancied to be the rumble of wheels is the reverberation of thunder, so did Bathsheba's at her intuitive conviction.

"I feel—almost too much—to think," he said, with a solemn simplicity. "I have come to speak to you without preface. My life is not my own since I have beheld you clearly, Miss Everdene—I come to make you an offer of marriage."

Bathsheba tried to preserve an absolutely neutral countenance, and all the motion she made was that of closing lips which had previously been a little parted.

"I am now forty-one years old," he went on. "I may have been called a confirmed bachelor, and I was a confirmed bachelor. I had never any views of myself as a husband in my earlier days, nor have I made any calculation on the subject since I have been older. But we all change, and my change, in this matter, came with seeing you. I have felt lately, more and more, that my present way of living is bad in every respect. Beyond all things, I want you as my wife."

"I feel, Mr. Boldwood, that though I respect you much, I do not feel— what would justify me to—in accepting your offer," she stammered.

This giving back of dignity for dignity seemed to open the sluices of feeling that Boldwood had as yet kept closed.

"My life is a burden without you," he exclaimed, in a low voice. "I want you—I want you to let me say I love you again and again!"

Bathsheba answered nothing, and the horse upon her arm seemed so impressed that instead of cropping the herbage she looked up.

"I think and hope you care enough for me to listen to what I have to tell!"

Bathsheba's momentary impulse at hearing this was to ask why he thought that, till she remembered that, far from being a conceited assumption on Boldwood's part, it was but the natural conclusion of serious reflection based on deceptive premises of her own offering.

"I wish I could say courteous flatteries to you," the farmer continued in an easier tone, "and put my rugged feeling into a graceful shape: but I have neither power nor patience to learn such things. I want you for my wife—so wildly that no other feeling can abide in me; but I should not have spoken out had I not been led to hope."

"The valentine again! O that valentine!" she said to herself, but not a word to him.

"If you can love me say so, Miss Everdene. If not—don't say no!"

"Mr. Boldwood, it is painful to have to say I am surprised, so that I don't know how to answer you with propriety and respect—but am only just able to speak out my feeling—I mean my meaning; that I am afraid I can't marry you, much as I respect you. You are too dignified for me to suit you, sir."

"But, Miss Everdene!"

"I—I didn't—I know I ought never to have dreamt of sending that valentine—forgive me, sir—it was a wanton thing which no woman with any self-respect should have done. If you will only pardon my thoughtlessness, I promise never to—"

"No, no, no. Don't say thoughtlessness! Make me think it was something more—that it was a sort of prophetic instinct—the beginning of a feeling that you would like me. You torture me to say it was done in thoughtlessness—I never thought of it in that light, and I can't endure it. Ah! I wish I knew how to win you! but that I can't do—I can only ask if I have already got you. If I have not, and it is not true that you have come unwittingly to me as I have to you, I can say no more."

"I have not fallen in love with you, Mr. Boldwood—certainly I must say that." She allowed a very small smile to creep for the first time over her serious face in saying this, and the white row of upper teeth, and keenly-cut lips already noticed, suggested an idea of heartlessness, which was immediately contradicted by the pleasant eyes.

"But you will just think—in kindness and condescension think—if you cannot bear with me as a husband! I fear I am too old for you, but believe me I will take more care of you than would many a man of your own age. I will protect and cherish you with all my strength—I will indeed! You shall have no cares—be worried by no household affairs, and live quite at ease, Miss Everdene. The dairy superintendence shall be done by a man—I can afford it well—you shall never have so much as to look out of doors at haymaking time, or to think of weather in the harvest. I rather cling to the chaise, because it is the same my poor father and mother drove, but if you don't like it I will sell it, and you shall have a pony-carriage of your own. I cannot say how far above every other idea and object on earth you seem to me—nobody knows—God only knows— how much you are to me!"

Bathsheba's heart was young, and it swelled with sympathy for the deep-natured man who spoke so simply.

"Don't say it! don't! I cannot bear you to feel so much, and me to feel nothing. And I am afraid they will notice us, Mr. Boldwood. Will you let the matter rest now? I cannot think collectedly. I did not know you were going to say this to me. Oh, I am wicked to have made you suffer so!" She was frightened as well as agitated at his vehemence.

"Say then, that you don't absolutely refuse. Do not quite refuse?"

"I can do nothing. I cannot answer."

"I may speak to you again on the subject?"

"Yes."

"I may think of you?"

"Yes, I suppose you may think of me."

Analysis: This is the second proposal scene in the novel and is in marked contrast to Oak's proposal. However, before we look at the differences, let's examine the similarities. The tone is overwhelmingly pastoral: Hardy takes some time to describe the sheep-washing, the lushness and moistness of spring, the glittering sun. We are indeed far from the madding crowd. But there is a difference: Boldwood's unease, his growing obsession for Bathsheba. Hardy's characterisation of him here is masterful: we really see a man struggling to grapple with his own desire and achieve his own ends, but failing, despite all of his social standing, to do so. His passionate plea is broken up with parenthesis (-) always a sign in the book that a character is emotionally disturbed. Unlike Oak, he does not seek to charm Bathsheba initially with a vision of their life together, but to attempt to describe his feelings. Unfortunately for him, he can't articulate them in words and seems to have lost the power of his rational thought; he can offer her no "courteous flatteries". In other words, he is not able to make Bathsheba feel good about herself by offering her an enticing vision of herself; he doesn't stimulate her imagination or desire. Instead of trying to speak positively of her, to listen to her, to work with her, he emotionally blackmails her, by saying that he has been led to hope – implying that having stirred his hopes she would be immoral to refuse him now. Unlike Oak – and indeed Troy at the beginning of the courtship – he is not keen to spend time with her at her work, to get to know, but prefers to watch her from afar, to keep her as his "tower". The vision he offers her of married life is of preserving her like a doll in his grand house; he promises her that she will never have to work again.

Discussion point: If you were Bathsheba, would you marry Troy? What do you think most Victorian women would have done in her position?

"And hope to obtain you?"

"No—do not hope! Let us go on."

"I will call upon you again to-morrow."

"No—please not. Give me time."

"Yes—I will give you any time," he said earnestly and gratefully. "I am happier now."

"No—I beg you! Don't be happier if happiness only comes from my agreeing. Be neutral, Mr. Boldwood! I must think."

"I will wait," he said.

And then she turned away. Boldwood dropped his gaze to the ground, and stood long like a man who did not know where he was. Realities then returned upon him like the pain of a wound received in an excitement which eclipses it, and he, too, then went on.

Questions

What is Bathsheba doing when Boldwood calls?

What does Boldwood do as soon as they are alone?

What does Boldwood feel gave him hope?

What is Bathsheba's response?

What alarms Bathsheba about Boldwood and how does she manage to get rid of him?

GCSE style question: how does Hardy make Boldwood's proposal such a tense moment in the novel?

A Level style question: to what extent is Bathsheba the victim of a patriarchal system in this chapter?

Creative response: write Bathsheba's diary for this chapter.

CHAPTER XX
PERPLEXITY—GRINDING THE
SHEARS—A QUARREL

"He is so disinterested and kind to offer me all that I can desire," Bathsheba mused.

Yet Farmer Boldwood, whether by nature kind or the reverse to kind, did not exercise kindness, here. The rarest offerings of the purest loves are but a self-indulgence, and no generosity at all.

Bathsheba, not being the least in love with him, was eventually able to look calmly at his offer. It was one which many women of her own station in the neighbourhood, and not a few of higher rank, would have been wild to accept and proud to publish. In every point of view, ranging from politic to passionate, it was desirable that she, a lonely girl, should marry, and marry this earnest, well-to-do, and respected man. He was close to her doors: his standing was sufficient: his qualities were even supererogatory. Had she felt, which she did not, any wish whatever for the married state in the abstract, she could not reasonably have rejected him, being a woman who frequently appealed to her understanding for deliverance from her whims. Boldwood as a means to marriage was unexceptionable: she esteemed and liked him, yet she did not want him. It appears that ordinary men take wives because possession is not possible without marriage, and that ordinary women accept husbands because marriage is not possible without possession; with totally differing aims the method is the same on both sides. But the understood incentive on the woman's part was wanting here. Besides, Bathsheba's position as absolute mistress of a farm and house was a novel one, and the novelty had not yet begun to wear off.

But a disquiet filled her which was somewhat to her credit, for it would have affected few. Beyond the mentioned reasons with which she combated her objections, she had a strong feeling that, having been the one who began the game, she ought in honesty to accept the consequences. Still the reluctance remained. She said in the same breath that it would be ungenerous not to marry Boldwood, and that she couldn't do it to save her life.

Bathsheba's was an impulsive nature under a deliberative aspect. An Elizabeth in brain and a Mary Stuart in spirit, she often performed actions of the greatest temerity with a manner of extreme discretion. Many of her thoughts were perfect syllogisms; unluckily they always remained thoughts. Only a few were irrational assumptions; but, unfortunately, they were the ones which most frequently grew into deeds.

The next day to that of the declaration she found Gabriel Oak at the bottom of her garden, grinding his shears for the sheep-shearing. All the surrounding cottages were more or less scenes of the same operation; the scurr of whetting spread into the sky from all parts of the village as from an armoury previous to a campaign. Peace and war kiss each other at their hours of preparation—sickles, scythes, shears, and pruning-hooks, ranking with swords, bayonets, and lances, in their common necessity for point and edge.

Cainy Ball turned the handle of Gabriel's grindstone, his head performing a melancholy see-saw up and down with each turn of the wheel. Oak stood somewhat as Eros is represented when in the act of sharpening his arrows: his figure slightly bent, the weight of his body thrown over on the shears, and his head balanced side-ways, with a critical compression of the lips and contraction of the eyelids to crown the attitude.

His mistress came up and looked upon them in silence for a minute or two; then she said—

"Cain, go to the lower mead and catch the bay mare. I'll turn the winch of the grindstone. I want to speak to you, Gabriel."

Cain departed, and Bathsheba took the handle. Gabriel had glanced up in intense surprise, quelled its expression, and looked down again. Bathsheba turned the winch, and Gabriel applied the shears.

The peculiar motion involved in turning a wheel has a wonderful tendency to benumb the mind. It is a sort of attenuated variety of Ixion's punishment, and contributes a dismal chapter to the history of gaols. The brain gets muddled, the head grows heavy, and the body's centre of gravity seems to settle by degrees in a leaden lump somewhere between the eyebrows and the crown. Bathsheba felt the unpleasant symptoms after two or three dozen turns.

"Will you turn, Gabriel, and let me hold the shears?" she said. "My head is in a whirl, and I can't talk."

Gabriel turned. Bathsheba then began, with some awkwardness, allowing her thoughts to stray occasionally from her story to attend to the shears, which required a little nicety in sharpening.

"I wanted to ask you if the men made any observations on my going behind the sedge with Mr. Boldwood yesterday?"

"Yes, they did," said Gabriel. "You don't hold the shears right, miss—I knew you wouldn't know the way—hold like this."

He relinquished the winch, and inclosing her two hands completely in his own (taking each as we sometimes slap a child's hand in teaching him to write), grasped the shears with her. "Incline the edge so," he said.

Hands and shears were inclined to suit the words, and held thus for a peculiarly long time by the instructor as he spoke.

"That will do," exclaimed Bathsheba. "Loose my hands. I won't have them held! Turn the winch."

Gabriel freed her hands quietly, retired to his handle, and the grinding went on.

"Did the men think it odd?" she said again.

"Odd was not the idea, miss."

"What did they say?"

"That Farmer Boldwood's name and your own were likely to be flung over pulpit together before the year was out."

"I thought so by the look of them! Why, there's nothing in it. A more foolish remark was never made, and I want you to contradict it! that's what I came for."

Gabriel looked incredulous and sad, but between his moments of incredulity, relieved.

"They must have heard our conversation," she continued.

"Well, then, Bathsheba!" said Oak, stopping the handle, and gazing into her face with astonishment.

"Miss Everdene, you mean," she said, with dignity.

"I mean this, that if Mr. Boldwood really spoke of marriage, I bain't going to tell a story and say he didn't to please you. I have already tried to please you too much for my own good!"

Bathsheba regarded him with round-eyed perplexity. She did not know whether to pity him for disappointed love of her, or to be angry with him for having got over it—his tone being ambiguous.

"I said I wanted you just to mention that it was not true I was going to be married to him," she murmured, with a slight decline in her assurance.

"I can say that to them if you wish, Miss Everdene. And I could likewise give an opinion to 'ee on what you have done."

"I daresay. But I don't want your opinion."

"I suppose not," said Gabriel bitterly, and going on with his turning, his words rising and falling in a regular swell and cadence as he stooped or rose with the winch, which directed them, according to his position, perpendicularly into the earth, or horizontally along the garden, his eyes being fixed on a leaf upon the ground.

With Bathsheba a hastened act was a rash act; but, as does not always happen, time gained was prudence insured. It must be added, however, that time was very seldom gained. At this period the single opinion in the parish on herself and her doings that she valued as sounder than her own was Gabriel Oak's. And the outspoken honesty of his character was such that on any subject, even that of her love for, or marriage with, another man, the same disinterestedness of opinion might be calculated on, and be had for the asking. Thoroughly convinced of the impossibility of his own suit, a high resolve constrained him not to injure that of another. This is a lover's most stoical virtue, as the lack of it is a lover's most venial sin. Knowing he would reply truly she asked the question, painful as she must have known the subject would be. Such is the selfishness of some charming women. Perhaps it was some excuse for her thus torturing honesty to her own advantage, that she had absolutely no other sound judgment within easy reach.

"Well, what is your opinion of my conduct," she said, quietly.

"That it is unworthy of any thoughtful, and meek, and comely woman."

In an instant Bathsheba's face coloured with the angry crimson of a Danby sunset. But she forbore to utter this feeling, and the reticence of her tongue only made the loquacity of her face the more noticeable.

The next thing Gabriel did was to make a mistake.

"Perhaps you don't like the rudeness of my reprimanding you, for I know it is rudeness; but I thought it would do good."

She instantly replied sarcastically—

"On the contrary, my opinion of you is so low, that I see in your abuse the praise of discerning people!"

"I am glad you don't mind it, for I said it honestly and with every serious meaning."

"I see. But, unfortunately, when you try not to speak in jest you are amusing—just as when you wish to avoid seriousness you sometimes say a sensible word."

It was a hard hit, but Bathsheba had unmistakably lost her temper, and on that account Gabriel had never in his life kept his own better. He said nothing. She then broke out—

"I may ask, I suppose, where in particular my unworthiness lies? In my not marrying you, perhaps!"

"Not by any means," said Gabriel quietly. "I have long given up thinking of that matter."

"Or wishing it, I suppose," she said; and it was apparent that she expected an unhesitating denial of this supposition.

Whatever Gabriel felt, he coolly echoed her words—

"Or wishing it either."

A woman may be treated with a bitterness which is sweet to her, and with a rudeness which is not offensive. Bathsheba would have submitted to an indignant chastisement for her levity had Gabriel protested that he was loving her at the same time; the impetuosity of passion unrequited is bearable, even if it stings and anathematizes—there is a triumph in the humiliation, and a tenderness in the strife. This was what she had been expecting, and what she had not got. To be lectured because the lecturer saw her in the cold morning light of open-shuttered disillusion was exasperating. He had not finished, either. He continued in a more agitated voice:—

"My opinion is (since you ask it) that you are greatly to blame for playing pranks upon a man like Mr. Boldwood, merely as a pastime. Leading on a man you don't care for is not a praiseworthy action. And even, Miss Everdene, if you seriously inclined towards him, you might have let him find it out in some way of true loving-kindness, and not by sending him a valentine's letter."

Bathsheba laid down the shears.

"I cannot allow any man to—to criticise my private conduct!" she exclaimed. "Nor will I for a minute. So you'll please leave the farm at the end of the week!"

It may have been a peculiarity—at any rate it was a fact—that when Bathsheba was swayed by an emotion of an earthly sort her lower lip trembled: when by a refined emotion, her upper or heavenward one. Her nether lip quivered now.

"Very well, so I will," said Gabriel calmly. He had been held to her by a beautiful thread which it pained him to spoil by breaking, rather than by a chain he could not break. "I should be even better pleased to go at once," he added.

"Go at once then, in Heaven's name!" said she, her eyes flashing at his, though never meeting them. "Don't let me see your face any more."

"Very well, Miss Everdene—so it shall be."

And he took his shears and went away from her in placid dignity, as Moses left the presence of Pharaoh.

> **Analysis:** Gabriel now becomes moralistic, speaking for the Victorian readership when he says that her conduct is "unworthy of any thoughtful, and meek, and comely woman." His adjectives here are worth analysing because they embody the qualities that Victorian men looked for in women: they should be 'comely' – attractive but not too attractive --, 'meek' – humble and subservient – and 'thoughtful' – in other words always consider men's desires above themselves. All of which Bathsheba has resolutely refused to do. Bathsheba promptly sacks him in a fit of fury. She is bitterly upset because Gabriel is not only her friend, but increasingly becoming a vital cog in the working of the farm: Gabriel and she have a working relationship, a true friendship, and a former 'dalliance' of sorts. The evolution of their friendship here is perhaps one of the most convincing aspects of the novel: they are constantly shifting in power, with one person being more important, and the other less so. Here we see Bathsheba achieving a Pyrrhic victory over him by sacking him.

> **Discussion point:** What would you do in Bathsheba's position? What would you have done in Oak's position?

Questions

What is Bathsheba's decision regarding Boldwood's proposal and why does she make this decision?

What does she ask Gabriel to do while he is grinding sheep-shears in the barn?

What is Gabriel's response?

What does Gabriel say about her conduct when she asks for his opinion of her?

What does Bathsheba do when faced with Gabriel's criticism of her?

What does Gabriel do?

GCSE style question: how does Hardy make the conversation between Bathsheba and Oak so compelling?

A Level style question: how does Hardy explore the "battle of the sexes" in this chapter?

Creative response: write a story/poem called 'Criticism' in which one person criticizes another person.

CHAPTER XXI
TROUBLES IN THE FOLD—A MESSAGE

Gabriel Oak had ceased to feed the Weatherbury flock for about four-and-twenty hours, when on Sunday afternoon the elderly gentlemen Joseph Poorgrass, Matthew Moon, Fray, and half-a-dozen others, came running up to the house of the mistress of the Upper Farm.

"Whatever is the matter, men?" she said, meeting them at the door just as she was coming out on her way to church, and ceasing in a moment from the close compression of her two red lips, with which she had accompanied the exertion of pulling on a tight glove.

"Sixty!" said Joseph Poorgrass.

"Seventy!" said Moon.

"Fifty-nine!" said Susan Tall's husband.

"—Sheep have broke fence," said Fray.

"—And got into a field of young clover," said Tall.

"—Young clover!" said Moon.

"—Clover!" said Joseph Poorgrass.

"And they be getting blasted," said Henery Fray.

"That they be," said Joseph.

"And will all die as dead as nits, if they bain't got out and cured!" said Tall.

Joseph's countenance was drawn into lines and puckers by his concern. Fray's forehead was wrinkled both perpendicularly and crosswise, after the pattern of a portcullis, expressive of a double despair. Laban Tall's lips were thin, and his face was rigid. Matthew's jaws sank, and his eyes turned whichever way the strongest muscle happened to pull them.

"Yes," said Joseph, "and I was sitting at home, looking for Ephesians, and says I to myself, ''Tis nothing but Corinthians and Thessalonians in this danged Testament,' when who should come in but Henery there: 'Joseph,' he said, 'the sheep have blasted theirselves—'"

With Bathsheba it was a moment when thought was speech and speech exclamation. Moreover, she had hardly recovered her equanimity since the disturbance which she had suffered from Oak's remarks.

"That's enough—that's enough!—oh, you fools!" she cried, throwing the parasol and Prayer-book into the passage, and running out of doors in the direction signified. "To come to me, and not go and get them out directly! Oh, the stupid numskulls!"

Her eyes were at their darkest and brightest now. Bathsheba's beauty belonging rather to the demonian than to the angelic school, she never looked so well as when she was angry—and particularly when the effect was heightened by a rather dashing velvet dress, carefully put on before a glass.

All the ancient men ran in a jumbled throng after her to the clover-field, Joseph sinking down in the midst when about half-way, like an individual withering in a world which was more and more insupportable. Having once received the stimulus that her presence always gave them they went round among the sheep with a will. The majority of the afflicted animals were lying down, and could not be stirred. These were bodily lifted out, and the others driven into the adjoining field. Here, after the lapse of a few minutes, several more fell down, and lay helpless and livid as the rest.

Bathsheba, with a sad, bursting heart, looked at these primest specimens of her prime flock as they rolled there—

Swoln with wind and the rank mist they drew.

Many of them foamed at the mouth, their breathing being quick and short, whilst the bodies of all were fearfully distended.

"Oh, what can I do, what can I do!" said Bathsheba, helplessly. "Sheep are such unfortunate animals!—there's always something happening to them! I never knew a flock pass a year without getting into some scrape or other."

"There's only one way of saving them," said Tall.

"What way? Tell me quick!"

"They must be pierced in the side with a thing made on purpose."

"Can you do it? Can I?"

"No, ma'am. We can't, nor you neither. It must be done in a particular spot. If ye go to the right or left but an inch you stab the ewe and kill her. Not even a shepherd can do it, as a rule."

"Then they must die," she said, in a resigned tone.

"Only one man in the neighbourhood knows the way," said Joseph, now just come up. "He could cure 'em all if he were here."

"Who is he? Let's get him!"

"Shepherd Oak," said Matthew. "Ah, he's a clever man in talents!"

"Ah, that he is so!" said Joseph Poorgrass.

"True—he's the man," said Laban Tall.

"How dare you name that man in my presence!" she said excitedly. "I told you never to allude to him, nor shall you if you stay with me. Ah!" she added, brightening, "Farmer Boldwood knows!"

"O no, ma'am" said Matthew. "Two of his store ewes got into some vetches t'other day, and were just like these. He sent a man on horseback here post-haste for Gable, and Gable went and saved 'em. Farmer Boldwood hev got the thing they do it with. 'Tis a holler pipe, with a sharp pricker inside. Isn't it, Joseph?"

"Ay—a holler pipe," echoed Joseph. "That's what 'tis."

"Ay, sure—that's the machine," chimed in Henery Fray, reflectively, with an Oriental indifference to the flight of time.

"Well," burst out Bathsheba, "don't stand there with your 'ayes' and your 'sures' talking at me! Get somebody to cure the sheep instantly!"

All then stalked off in consternation, to get somebody as directed, without any idea of who it was to be. In a minute they had vanished through the gate, and she stood alone with the dying flock.

"Never will I send for him—never!" she said firmly.

One of the ewes here contracted its muscles horribly, extended itself, and jumped high into the air. The leap was an astonishing one. The ewe fell heavily, and lay still.

Bathsheba went up to it. The sheep was dead.

"Oh, what shall I do—what shall I do!" she again exclaimed, wringing her hands. "I won't send for him. No, I won't!"

The most vigorous expression of a resolution does not always coincide with the greatest vigour of the resolution itself. It is often flung out as a sort of prop to support a decaying conviction which, whilst strong, required no enunciation to prove it so. The "No, I won't" of Bathsheba meant virtually, "I think I must."

She followed her assistants through the gate, and lifted her hand to one of them. Laban answered to her signal.

"Where is Oak staying?"

"Across the valley at Nest Cottage!"

"Jump on the bay mare, and ride across, and say he must return instantly—that I say so."

Tall scrambled off to the field, and in two minutes was on Poll, the bay, bare-backed, and with only a halter by way of rein. He diminished down the hill.

Bathsheba watched. So did all the rest. Tall cantered along the bridle-path through Sixteen Acres, Sheeplands, Middle Field, The Flats, Cappel's Piece, shrank almost to a point, crossed the bridge, and ascended from the valley through Springmead and Whitepits on the other side. The cottage to which Gabriel had retired before taking his final departure from the locality was visible as a white spot on the opposite hill, backed by blue firs. Bathsheba walked up and down. The men entered the field and endeavoured to ease the anguish of the dumb creatures by rubbing them. Nothing availed.

Bathsheba continued walking. The horse was seen descending the hill, and the wearisome series had to be repeated in reverse order: Whitepits, Springmead, Cappel's Piece, The Flats, Middle Field, Sheeplands, Sixteen Acres. She hoped Tall had had presence of mind enough to give the mare up to Gabriel, and return himself on foot. The rider neared them. It was Tall.

"Oh, what folly!" said Bathsheba.

Gabriel was not visible anywhere.

"Perhaps he is already gone!" she said.

Tall came into the inclosure, and leapt off, his face tragic as Morton's after the battle of Shrewsbury.

"Well?" said Bathsheba, unwilling to believe that her verbal lettre-de-cachet could possibly have miscarried.

"He says beggars mustn't be choosers," replied Laban.

"What!" said the young farmer, opening her eyes and drawing in her breath for an outburst. Joseph Poorgrass retired a few steps behind a hurdle.

"He says he shall not come onless you request en to come civilly and in a proper manner, as becomes any 'ooman begging a favour."

"Oh, oh, that's his answer! Where does he get his airs? Who am I, then, to be treated like that? Shall I beg to a man who has begged to me?"

Another of the flock sprang into the air, and fell dead.

The men looked grave, as if they suppressed opinion.

Bathsheba turned aside, her eyes full of tears. The strait she was in through pride and shrewishness could not be disguised longer: she burst out crying bitterly; they all saw it; and she attempted no further concealment.

"I wouldn't cry about it, miss," said William Smallbury, compassionately. "Why not ask him softer like? I'm sure he'd come then. Gable is a true man in that way."

Bathsheba checked her grief and wiped her eyes. "Oh, it is a wicked cruelty to me—it is—it is!" she murmured. "And he drives me to do what I wouldn't; yes, he does!—Tall, come indoors."

After this collapse, not very dignified for the head of an establishment, she went into the house, Tall at her heels. Here she sat down and hastily scribbled a note between the small convulsive sobs of convalescence which follow a fit of crying as a ground-swell follows a storm. The note was none the less polite for being written in a hurry. She held it at a distance, was about to fold it, then added these words at the bottom:—

"Do not desert me, Gabriel!"

She looked a little redder in refolding it, and closed her lips, as if thereby to suspend till too late the action of conscience in examining whether such strategy were justifiable. The note was despatched as the message had been, and Bathsheba waited indoors for the result.

It was an anxious quarter of an hour that intervened between the messenger's departure and the sound of the horse's tramp again outside. She could not watch this time, but, leaning over the old bureau at which she had written the letter, closed her eyes, as if to keep out both hope and fear.

The case, however, was a promising one. Gabriel was not angry: he was simply neutral, although her first command had been so haughty. Such imperiousness would have damned a little less beauty; and on the other hand, such beauty would have redeemed a little less imperiousness.

She went out when the horse was heard, and looked up. A mounted figure passed between her and the sky, and drew on towards the field of sheep, the rider turning his face in receding. Gabriel looked at her. It was a moment when a woman's eyes and tongue tell distinctly opposite tales. Bathsheba looked full of gratitude, and she said:—

"Oh, Gabriel, how could you serve me so unkindly!"

Such a tenderly-shaped reproach for his previous delay was the one speech in the language that he could pardon for not being commendation of his readiness now.

Gabriel murmured a confused reply, and hastened on. She knew from the look which sentence in her note had brought him. Bathsheba followed to the field.

Gabriel was already among the turgid, prostrate forms. He had flung off his coat, rolled up his shirt-sleeves, and taken from his pocket the instrument of salvation. It was a small tube or trochar, with a lance passing down the inside; and Gabriel began to use it with a dexterity that would have graced a hospital surgeon. Passing his hand over the sheep's left flank, and selecting the proper point, he punctured the skin and rumen with the lance as it stood in the tube; then he suddenly withdrew the lance, retaining the tube in its place. A current of air rushed up the tube, forcible enough to have extinguished a candle held at the orifice.

It has been said that mere ease after torment is delight for a time; and the countenances of these poor creatures expressed it now. Forty-nine operations were successfully performed. Owing to the great hurry necessitated by the far-gone state of some of the flock, Gabriel missed his aim in one case, and in one only—striking wide of the mark, and inflicting a mortal blow at once upon the suffering ewe. Four had died; three recovered without an operation. The total number of sheep which had thus strayed and injured themselves so dangerously was fifty-seven.

When the love-led man had ceased from his labours, Bathsheba came and looked him in the face.

"Gabriel, will you stay on with me?" she said, smiling winningly, and not troubling to bring her lips quite together again at the end, because there was going to be another smile soon.

"I will," said Gabriel.

And she smiled on him again.

Analysis:
It is the working of the farm which forces Bathsheba to renew her friendship with Oak: her sheep are dying and Oak is the only person who can save them. It is one of the most unusual, poignant and telling scenes in the book. Here we see Oak revealing his true skill as a shepherd and farmer, and Hardy revelling in his technical knowledge of country matters. It was the details of the sheep's illness and Oak's remedy which Hardy's readership absolutely loved: ever after, his readers wanted him to write about sheep farming, but he never did.

The relationship between Bathsheba is marvellously drawn because it is complex: the two of them need each other in very practical senses, but also for psychological support. Oak's rescuing of the sheep, his deflation of their stomachs works on a symbolic level; in getting Bathsheba to beg him to return, he deflates and humbles her. He never leaves her again after this moment – even she sacks him again and he tries to leave at the very end of the novel.

Discussion point:
Why is the rescuing of the sheep such an important moment in the novel?

Questions

What happens to Bathsheba's sheep the next day?

What does Bathsheba do after one of the sheep die?

What is Oak's response to Bathsheba's curt message?

What does Bathsheba do after another sheep dies?

What happens when Oak returns?

What does Bathsheba ask of Oak after this?

GCSE style question: how does Hardy make the bloating of the sheep both a comic and suspenseful scene?

A Level style question: compare and contrast Hardy's representation of the farming world with another text which depicts some aspect of farming.

Creative response: write Bathsheba's diary for this chapter, including her thoughts and feelings about the sheep, the farm workers and Oak.

CHAPTER XXII
THE GREAT BARN AND THE SHEEP-SHEARERS

Men thin away to insignificance and oblivion quite as often by not making the most of good spirits when they have them as by lacking good spirits when they are indispensable. Gabriel lately, for the first time since his prostration by misfortune, had been independent in thought and vigorous in action to a marked extent—conditions which, powerless without an opportunity as an opportunity without them is barren, would have given him a sure lift upwards when the favourable conjunction should have occurred. But this incurable loitering beside Bathsheba Everdene stole his time ruinously. The spring tides were going by without floating him off, and the neap might soon come which could not.

It was the first day of June, and the sheep-shearing season culminated, the landscape, even to the leanest pasture, being all health and colour. Every green was young, every pore was open, and every stalk was swollen with racing currents of juice. God was palpably present in the country, and the devil had gone with the world to town. Flossy catkins of the later kinds, fern-sprouts like bishops' croziers, the square-headed moschatel, the odd cuckoo-pint,—like an apoplectic saint in a niche of malachite,—snow-white ladies'-smocks, the toothwort, approximating to human flesh, the enchanter's night-shade, and the black-petaled doleful-bells, were among the quainter objects of the vegetable world in and about Weatherbury at this teeming time; and of the animal, the metamorphosed figures of Mr. Jan Coggan, the master-shearer; the second and third shearers, who travelled in the exercise of their calling, and do not require definition by name; Henery Fray the fourth shearer, Susan Tall's husband the fifth, Joseph Poorgrass the sixth, young Cain Ball as assistant-shearer, and Gabriel Oak as general supervisor. None of these were clothed to any extent worth mentioning, each appearing to have hit in the matter of raiment the decent mean between a high and low caste Hindoo. An angularity of lineament, and a fixity of facial machinery in general, proclaimed that serious work was the order of the day.

They sheared in the great barn, called for the nonce the Shearing-barn, which on ground-plan resembled a church with transepts. It not only emulated the form of the neighbouring church of the parish, but vied with it in antiquity. Whether the barn had ever formed one of a group of conventual buildings nobody seemed to be aware; no trace of such surroundings remained. The vast porches at the sides, lofty enough to admit a waggon laden to its highest with corn in the sheaf, were spanned by heavy-pointed arches of stone, broadly and boldly cut, whose very simplicity was the origin of a grandeur not apparent in erections where more ornament has been attempted. The dusky, filmed, chestnut roof, braced and tied in by huge collars, curves, and diagonals, was far nobler in design, because more wealthy in material, than nine-tenths of those in our modern churches. Along each side wall was a range of striding buttresses, throwing deep shadows on the spaces between them, which were perforated by lancet openings, combining in their proportions the precise requirements both of beauty and ventilation.

One could say about this barn, what could hardly be said of either the church or the castle, akin to it in age and style, that the purpose which had dictated its original erection was the same with that to which it was still applied. Unlike and superior to either of those two typical remnants of mediævalism, the old barn embodied practices which had suffered no mutilation at the hands of time. Here at least the spirit of the ancient builders was at one with the spirit of the modern beholder. Standing before this abraded pile, the eye regarded its present usage, the mind dwelt upon its past history, with a satisfied sense of functional continuity throughout— a feeling almost of gratitude, and quite of pride, at the permanence of the idea which had heaped it up. The fact that four centuries had neither proved it to be founded on a mistake, inspired any hatred of its purpose, nor given rise to any reaction that had battered it down, invested this simple grey effort of old minds with a repose, if not a grandeur, which a too curious reflection was apt to disturb in its ecclesiastical and military compeers. For once mediævalism and modernism had a common stand-point. The lanceolate windows, the time-eaten archstones and chamfers, the orientation of the axis, the misty chestnut work of the rafters, referred to no exploded fortifying art or worn-out religious creed. The defence and salvation of the body by daily bread is still a study, a religion, and a desire.

To-day the large side doors were thrown open towards the sun to admit a bountiful light to the immediate spot of the shearers' operations, which was the wood threshing-floor in the centre, formed of thick oak, black with age and polished by the beating of flails for many generations, till it had grown as slippery and as rich in hue as the state-room floors of an Elizabethan mansion. Here the shearers knelt, the sun slanting in upon their bleached shirts, tanned arms, and the polished shears they flourished, causing these to bristle with a thousand rays strong enough to blind a weak-eyed man. Beneath them a captive sheep lay panting, quickening its pants as misgiving merged in terror, till it quivered like the hot landscape outside.

This picture of to-day in its frame of four hundred years ago did not produce that marked contrast between ancient and modern which is implied by the contrast of date. In comparison with cities, Weatherbury was immutable. The citizen's Then is the rustic's Now. In London, twenty or thirty-years ago are old times; in Paris ten years, or five; in Weatherbury three or four score years were included in the mere present, and nothing less than a century set a mark on its face or tone. Five decades hardly modified the cut of a gaiter, the embroidery of a smock-frock, by the breadth of a hair. Ten generations failed to alter the turn of a single phrase. In these Wessex nooks the busy outsider's ancient times are only old; his old times are still new; his present is futurity.

So the barn was natural to the shearers, and the shearers were in harmony with the barn.

The spacious ends of the building, answering ecclesiastically to nave and chancel extremities, were fenced off with hurdles, the sheep being all collected in a crowd within these two enclosures; and in one angle a catching-pen was formed, in which three or four sheep were continuously kept ready for the shearers to seize without loss of time. In the background, mellowed by tawny shade, were the three women, Maryann Money, and Temperance and Soberness Miller, gathering up the fleeces and twisting ropes of wool with a wimble for tying them round. They were indifferently well assisted by the old maltster, who, when the malting season from October to April had passed, made himself useful upon any of the bordering farmsteads.

Behind all was Bathsheba, carefully watching the men to see that there was no cutting or wounding through carelessness, and that the animals were shorn close. Gabriel, who flitted and hovered under her bright eyes like a moth, did not shear continuously, half his time being spent in attending to the others and selecting the sheep for them. At the present moment he was engaged in handing round a mug of mild liquor, supplied from a barrel in the corner, and cut pieces of bread and cheese.

Bathsheba, after throwing a glance here, a caution there, and lecturing one of the younger operators who had allowed his last finished sheep to go off among the flock without re-stamping it with her initials, came again to Gabriel, as he put down the luncheon to drag a frightened ewe to his shear-station, flinging it over upon its back with a dexterous twist of the arm. He lopped off the tresses about its head, and opened up the neck and collar, his mistress quietly looking on.

"She blushes at the insult," murmured Bathsheba, watching the pink flush which arose and overspread the neck and shoulders of the ewe where they were left bare by the clicking shears—a flush which was enviable, for its delicacy, by many queens of coteries, and would have been creditable, for its promptness, to any woman in the world.

Poor Gabriel's soul was fed with a luxury of content by having her over him, her eyes critically regarding his skilful shears, which apparently were going to gather up a piece of the flesh at every close, and yet never did so. Like Guildenstern, Oak was happy in that he was not over happy. He had no wish to converse with her: that his bright lady and himself formed one group, exclusively their own, and containing no others in the world, was enough.

So the chatter was all on her side. There is a loquacity that tells nothing, which was Bathsheba's; and there is a silence which says much: that was Gabriel's. Full of this dim and temperate bliss, he went on to fling the ewe over upon her other side, covering her head with his knee, gradually running the shears line after line round her dewlap; thence about her flank and back, and finishing over the tail.

"Well done, and done quickly!" said Bathsheba, looking at her watch as the last snip resounded.

"How long, miss?" said Gabriel, wiping his brow.

"Three-and-twenty minutes and a half since you took the first lock from its forehead. It is the first time that I have ever seen one done in less than half an hour."

The clean, sleek creature arose from its fleece—how perfectly like Aphrodite rising from the foam should have been seen to be realized—looking startled and shy at the loss of its garment, which lay on the floor in one soft cloud, united throughout, the portion visible being the inner surface only, which, never before exposed, was white as snow, and without flaw or blemish of the minutest kind.

"Cain Ball!"

"Yes, Mister Oak; here I be!"

Cainy now runs forward with the tar-pot. "B. E." is newly stamped upon the shorn skin, and away the simple dam leaps, panting, over the board into the shirtless flock outside. Then up comes Maryann; throws the loose locks into the middle of the fleece, rolls it up, and carries it into the background as three-and-a-half pounds of unadulterated warmth for the winter enjoyment of persons unknown and far away, who will, however, never experience the superlative comfort derivable from the wool as it here exists, new and pure—before the unctuousness of its nature whilst in a living state has dried, stiffened, and been washed out—rendering it just now as superior to anything woollen as cream is superior to milk-and-water.

But heartless circumstance could not leave entire Gabriel's happiness of this morning. The rams, old ewes, and two-shear ewes had duly undergone their stripping, and the men were proceeding with the shear-lings and hogs, when Oak's belief that she was going to stand pleasantly by and time him through another performance was painfully interrupted by Farmer Boldwood's appearance in the extremest corner of the barn. Nobody seemed to have perceived his entry, but there he certainly was. Boldwood always carried with him a social atmosphere of his own, which everybody felt who came near him; and the talk, which Bathsheba's presence had somewhat suppressed, was now totally suspended.

He crossed over towards Bathsheba, who turned to greet him with a carriage of perfect ease. He spoke to her in low tones, and she instinctively modulated her own to the same pitch, and her voice ultimately even caught the inflection of his. She was far from having a wish to appear mysteriously connected with him; but woman at the impressionable age gravitates to the larger body not only in her choice of words, which is apparent every day, but even in her shades of tone and humour, when the influence is great.

What they conversed about was not audible to Gabriel, who was too independent to get near, though too concerned to disregard. The issue of their dialogue was the taking of her hand by the courteous farmer to help her over the spreading-board into the bright June sunlight outside. Standing beside the sheep already shorn, they went on talking again. Concerning the flock? Apparently not. Gabriel theorized, not without truth, that in quiet discussion of any matter within reach of the speakers' eyes, these are usually fixed upon it. Bathsheba demurely regarded a contemptible straw lying upon the ground, in a way which suggested less ovine criticism than womanly embarrassment. She became more or less red in the cheek, the blood wavering in uncertain flux and reflux over the sensitive space between ebb and flood. Gabriel sheared on, constrained and sad.

She left Boldwood's side, and he walked up and down alone for nearly a quarter of an hour. Then she reappeared in her new riding-habit of myrtle green, which fitted her to the waist as a rind fits its fruit; and young Bob Coggan led on her mare, Boldwood fetching his own horse from the tree under which it had been tied.

Oak's eyes could not forsake them; and in endeavouring to continue his shearing at the same time that he watched Boldwood's manner, he snipped the sheep in the groin. The animal plunged; Bathsheba instantly gazed towards it, and saw the blood.

"Oh, Gabriel!" she exclaimed, with severe remonstrance, "you who are so strict with the other men—see what you are doing yourself!"

To an outsider there was not much to complain of in this remark; but to Oak, who knew Bathsheba to be well aware that she herself was the cause of the poor ewe's wound, because she had wounded the ewe's shearer in a still more vital part, it had a sting which the abiding sense of his inferiority to both herself and Boldwood was not calculated to heal. But a manly resolve to recognize boldly that he had no longer a lover's interest in her, helped him occasionally to conceal a feeling.

"Bottle!" he shouted, in an unmoved voice of routine. Cainy Ball ran up, the wound was anointed, and the shearing continued.

Boldwood gently tossed Bathsheba into the saddle, and before they turned away she again spoke out to Oak with the same dominative and tantalizing graciousness.

"I am going now to see Mr. Boldwood's Leicesters. Take my place in the barn, Gabriel, and keep the men carefully to their work."

The horses' heads were put about, and they trotted away.

Boldwood's deep attachment was a matter of great interest among all around him; but, after having been pointed out for so many years as the perfect exemplar of thriving bachelorship, his lapse was an anticlimax somewhat resembling that of St. John Long's death by consumption in the midst of his proofs that it was not a fatal disease.

"That means matrimony," said Temperance Miller, following them out of sight with her eyes.

"I reckon that's the size o't," said Coggan, working along without looking up.

"Well, better wed over the mixen than over the moor," said Laban Tall, turning his sheep.

Henery Fray spoke, exhibiting miserable eyes at the same time: "I don't see why a maid should take a husband when she's bold enough to fight her own battles, and don't want a home; for 'tis keeping another woman out. But let it be, for 'tis a pity he and she should trouble two houses."

As usual with decided characters, Bathsheba invariably provoked the criticism of individuals like Henery Fray. Her emblazoned fault was to be too pronounced in her objections, and not sufficiently overt in her likings. We learn that it is not the rays which bodies absorb, but those which they reject, that give them the colours they are known by; and in the same way people are specialized by their dislikes and antagonisms, whilst their goodwill is looked upon as no attribute at all.

Henery continued in a more complaisant mood: "I once hinted my mind to her on a few things, as nearly as a battered frame dared to do so to such a froward piece. You all know, neighbours, what a man I be, and how I come down with my powerful words when my pride is boiling wi' scarn?"

"We do, we do, Henery."

"So I said, 'Mistress Everdene, there's places empty, and there's gifted men willing; but the spite'—no, not the spite—I didn't say spite—'but the villainy of the contrarikind,' I said (meaning womankind), 'keeps 'em out.' That wasn't too strong for her, say?"

"Passably well put."

"Yes; and I would have said it, had death and salvation overtook me for it. Such is my spirit when I have a mind."

"A true man, and proud as a lucifer."

"You see the artfulness? Why, 'twas about being baily really; but I didn't put it so plain that she could understand my meaning, so I could lay it on all the stronger. That was my depth! ... However, let her marry an she will. Perhaps 'tis high time. I believe Farmer Boldwood kissed her behind the spear-bed at the sheep-washing t'other day—that I do."

"What a lie!" said Gabriel.

"Ah, neighbour Oak—how'st know?" said, Henery, mildly.

"Because she told me all that passed," said Oak, with a pharisaical sense that he was not as other shearers in this matter.

"Ye have a right to believe it," said Henery, with dudgeon; "a very true right. But I mid see a little distance into things! To be long-headed enough for a baily's place is a poor mere trifle—yet a trifle more than nothing. However, I look round upon life quite cool. Do you heed me, neighbours?

My words, though made as simple as I can, mid be rather deep for some heads."

"O yes, Henery, we quite heed ye."

"A strange old piece, goodmen—whirled about from here to yonder, as if I were nothing! A little warped, too. But I have my depths; ha, and even my great depths! I might gird at a certain shepherd, brain to brain. But no—O no!"

"A strange old piece, ye say!" interposed the maltster, in a querulous voice. "At the same time ye be no old man worth naming—no old man at all. Yer teeth bain't half gone yet; and what's a old man's standing if so be his teeth bain't gone? Weren't I stale in wedlock afore ye were out of arms? 'Tis a poor thing to be sixty, when there's people far past four-score—a boast weak as water."

It was the unvarying custom in Weatherbury to sink minor differences when the maltster had to be pacified.

"Weak as water! yes," said Jan Coggan. "Malter, we feel ye to be a wonderful veteran man, and nobody can gainsay it."

"Nobody," said Joseph Poorgrass. "Ye be a very rare old spectacle, malter, and we all admire ye for that gift."

"Ay, and as a young man, when my senses were in prosperity, I was likewise liked by a good-few who knowed me," said the maltster.

"'Ithout doubt you was—'ithout doubt."

The bent and hoary man was satisfied, and so apparently was Henery Fray. That matters should continue pleasant Maryann spoke, who, what with her brown complexion, and the working wrapper of rusty linsey, had at present the mellow hue of an old sketch in oils—notably some of Nicholas Poussin's:—

"Do anybody know of a crooked man, or a lame, or any second-hand fellow at all that would do for poor me?" said Maryann. "A perfect one I don't expect to get at my time of life. If I could hear of such a thing twould do me more good than toast and ale."

Coggan furnished a suitable reply. Oak went on with his shearing, and said not another word. Pestilent moods had come, and teased away his quiet. Bathsheba had shown indications of anointing him above his fellows by installing him as the bailiff that the farm imperatively required. He did not covet the post relatively to the farm: in relation to herself, as beloved by him and unmarried to another, he had coveted it. His readings of her seemed now to be vapoury and indistinct. His lecture to her was, he thought, one of the absurdest mistakes. Far from coquetting with Boldwood, she had trifled with himself in thus feigning that she had trifled with another. He was inwardly convinced that, in accordance with the anticipations of his easy-going and worse-educated comrades, that day would see Boldwood the accepted husband of Miss Everdene. Gabriel at this time of his life had out-grown the instinctive dislike which every Christian boy has for reading the Bible, perusing it now quite frequently, and he inwardly said, "'I find more bitter than death the woman whose heart is snares and nets!'" This was mere exclamation—the froth of the storm. He adored Bathsheba just the same.

"We workfolk shall have some lordly junketing to-night," said Cainy Ball, casting forth his thoughts in a new direction. "This morning I see 'em making the great puddens in the milking-pails—lumps of fat as big as yer thumb, Mister Oak! I've never seed such splendid large knobs of fat before in the days of my life—they never used to be bigger then a horse-bean. And there was a great black crock upon the brandish with his legs a-sticking out, but I don't know what was in within."

"And there's two bushels of biffins for apple-pies," said Maryann.

"Well, I hope to do my duty by it all," said Joseph Poorgrass, in a pleasant, masticating manner of anticipation. "Yes; victuals and drink is a cheerful thing, and gives nerves to the nerveless, if the form of words may be used. 'Tis the gospel of the body, without which we perish, so to speak it."

Questions

What does Bathsheba admire about Oak?

What does Oak do when Boldwood enters and why?

Why is it ironic that Oak stops the workmen gossiping about the possible marriage between Boldwood and Bathsheba?

GCSE style question: how does Hardy create a sense of mystery in this chapter? We don't know what Bathsheba's intentions are.

Creative response: write a story/poem called 'The Gossips'.

CHAPTER XXIII
EVENTIDE—A SECOND
DECLARATION

For the shearing-supper a long table was placed on the grass-plot beside the house, the end of the table being thrust over the sill of the wide parlour window and a foot or two into the room. Miss Everdene sat inside the window, facing down the table. She was thus at the head without mingling with the men.

This evening Bathsheba was unusually excited, her red cheeks and lips contrasting lustrously with the mazy skeins of her shadowy hair. She seemed to expect assistance, and the seat at the bottom of the table was at her request left vacant until after they had begun the meal. She then asked Gabriel to take the place and the duties appertaining to that end, which he did with great readiness.

At this moment Mr. Boldwood came in at the gate, and crossed the green to Bathsheba at the window. He apologized for his lateness: his arrival was evidently by arrangement.

"Gabriel," said she, "will you move again, please, and let Mr. Boldwood come there?"

Oak moved in silence back to his original seat.

The gentleman-farmer was dressed in cheerful style, in a new coat and white waistcoat, quite contrasting with his usual sober suits of grey. Inwardy, too, he was blithe, and consequently chatty to an exceptional degree. So also was Bathsheba now that he had come, though the uninvited presence of Pennyways, the bailiff who had been dismissed for theft, disturbed her equanimity for a while.

Supper being ended, Coggan began on his own private account, without reference   to   listeners:—

> I've lost my love, and I care not,
> I've lost my love, and I care not;
> I shall soon have another
> That's better than t'other;
> I've lost my love, and I care not.

This lyric, when concluded, was received with a silently appreciative gaze at the table, implying that the performance, like a work by those established authors who are independent of notices in the papers, was a well-known delight which required no applause.

"Now, Master Poorgrass, your song!" said Coggan.

"I be all but in liquor, and the gift is wanting in me," said Joseph, diminishing himself.

"Nonsense; wou'st never be so ungrateful, Joseph—never!" said Coggan, expressing hurt feelings by an inflection of voice. "And mistress is looking hard at ye, as much as to say, 'Sing at once, Joseph Poorgrass.'"

"Faith, so she is; well, I must suffer it! ... Just eye my features, and see if the tell-tale blood overheats me much, neighbours?"

"No, yer blushes be quite reasonable," said Coggan.

"I always tries to keep my colours from rising when a beauty's eyes get fixed on me," said Joseph, differently; "but if so be 'tis willed they do, they must."

"Now, Joseph, your song, please," said Bathsheba, from the window.

"Well, really, ma'am," he replied, in a yielding tone, "I don't know what to say. It would be a poor plain ballet of my own composure."

"Hear, hear!" said the supper-party.

Poorgrass, thus assured, trilled forth a flickering yet commendable piece of sentiment, the tune of which consisted of the key-note and another, the latter being the sound chiefly dwelt upon. This was so successful that he rashly plunged into a second in the same breath, after a few false starts:—

> I sow'-ed th'-e ...
> I sow'-ed ...
> I sow'-ed th'-e seeds' of' love',
> I-it was' all' i'-in the'-e spring',
> I-in A'-pril', Ma'-ay, a'-nd sun'-ny' June',
> When sma'-all bi'-irds they' do' sing.

"Well put out of hand," said Coggan, at the end of the verse. "'They do sing' was a very taking paragraph."

"Ay; and there was a pretty place at 'seeds of love.' and 'twas well heaved out. Though 'love' is a nasty high corner when a man's voice is getting crazed. Next verse, Master Poorgrass."

But during this rendering young Bob Coggan exhibited one of those anomalies which will afflict little people when other persons are particularly serious: in trying to check his laughter, he pushed down his throat as much of the tablecloth as he could get hold of, when, after continuing hermetically sealed for a short time, his mirth burst out through his nose. Joseph perceived it, and with hectic cheeks of indignation instantly ceased singing. Coggan boxed Bob's ears immediately.

"Go on, Joseph—go on, and never mind the young scamp," said Coggan. "'Tis a very catching ballet. Now then again—the next bar; I'll help ye to flourish up the shrill notes where yer wind is rather wheezy:—

"Oh the wi'-il-lo'-ow tree' will' twist',
And the wil'-low' tre'-ee wi'-ill twine'."

But the singer could not be set going again. Bob Coggan was sent home for his ill manners, and tranquility was restored by Jacob Smallbury, who volunteered a ballad as inclusive and interminable as that with which the worthy toper old Silenus amused on a similar occasion the swains Chromis and Mnasylus, and other jolly dogs of his day.

It was still the beaming time of evening, though night was stealthily making itself visible low down upon the ground, the western lines of light raking the earth without alighting upon it to any extent, or illuminating the dead levels at all. The sun had crept round the tree as a last effort before death, and then began to sink, the shearers' lower parts becoming steeped in embrowning twilight, whilst their heads and shoulders were still enjoying day, touched with a yellow of self-sustained brilliancy that seemed inherent rather than acquired.

The sun went down in an ochreous mist; but they sat, and talked on, and grew as merry as the gods in Homer's heaven. Bathsheba still remained enthroned inside the window, and occupied herself in knitting, from which she sometimes looked up to view the fading scene outside. The slow twilight expanded and enveloped them completely before the signs of moving were shown.

Gabriel suddenly missed Farmer Boldwood from his place at the bottom of the table. How long he had been gone Oak did not know; but he had apparently withdrawn into the encircling dusk. Whilst he was thinking of this, Liddy brought candles into the back part of the room overlooking the shearers, and their lively new flames shone down the table and over the men, and dispersed among the green shadows behind. Bathsheba's form, still in its original position, was now again distinct between their eyes and the light, which revealed that Boldwood had gone inside the room, and was sitting near her.

Next came the question of the evening. Would Miss Everdene sing to them the song she always sang so charmingly—"The Banks of Allan Water"—before they went home?

After a moment's consideration Bathsheba assented, beckoning to Gabriel, who hastened up into the coveted atmosphere.

"Have you brought your flute?" she whispered.

"Yes, miss."

"Play to my singing, then."

She stood up in the window-opening, facing the men, the candles behind her, Gabriel on her right hand, immediately outside the sash-frame. Boldwood had drawn up on her left, within the room. Her singing was soft and rather tremulous at first, but it soon swelled to a steady clearness. Subsequent events caused one of the verses to be remembered for many months, and even years, by more than one of those who were gathered there:—

> For his bride a soldier sought her,
> And a winning tongue had he:
> On the banks of Allan Water
> None was gay as she!

In addition to the dulcet piping of Gabriel's flute, Boldwood supplied a bass in his customary profound voice, uttering his notes so softly, however, as to abstain entirely from making anything like an ordinary duet of the song; they rather formed a rich unexplored shadow, which threw her tones into relief. The shearers reclined against each other as at suppers in the early ages of the world, and so silent and absorbed were they that her breathing could almost be heard between the bars; and at the end of the ballad, when the last tone loitered on to an inexpressible close, there arose that buzz of pleasure which is the attar of applause.

It is scarcely necessary to state that Gabriel could not avoid noting the farmer's bearing to-night towards their entertainer. Yet there was nothing exceptional in his actions beyond what appertained to his time of performing them. It was when the rest were all looking away that Boldwood observed her; when they regarded her he turned aside; when they thanked or praised he was silent; when they were inattentive he murmured his thanks. The meaning lay in the difference between actions, none of which had any meaning of itself; and the necessity of being jealous, which lovers are troubled with, did not lead Oak to underestimate these signs.

Bathsheba then wished them good-night, withdrew from the window, and retired to the back part of the room, Boldwood thereupon closing the sash and the shutters, and remaining inside with her. Oak wandered away under the quiet and scented trees. Recovering from the softer impressions produced by Bathsheba's voice, the shearers rose to leave, Coggan turning to Pennyways as he pushed back the bench to pass out:—

"I like to give praise where praise is due, and the man deserves it—that 'a do so," he remarked, looking at the worthy thief, as if he were the masterpiece of some world-renowned artist.

"I'm sure I should never have believed it if we hadn't proved it, so to allude," hiccupped Joseph Poorgrass, "that every cup, every one of the best knives and forks, and every empty bottle be in their place as perfect now as at the beginning, and not one stole at all."

"I'm sure I don't deserve half the praise you give me," said the virtuous thief, grimly.

"Well, I'll say this for Pennyways," added Coggan, "that whenever he do really make up his mind to do a noble thing in the shape of a good action, as I could see by his face he did to-night afore sitting down, he's generally able to carry it out. Yes, I'm proud to say, neighbours, that he's stole nothing at all."

"Well, 'tis an honest deed, and we thank ye for it, Pennyways," said Joseph; to which opinion the remainder of the company subscribed unanimously.

At this time of departure, when nothing more was visible of the inside of the parlour than a thin and still chink of light between the shutters, a passionate scene was in course of enactment there.

Miss Everdene and Boldwood were alone. Her cheeks had lost a great deal of their healthful fire from the very seriousness of her position; but her eye was bright with the excitement of a triumph—though it was a triumph which had rather been contemplated than desired.

She was standing behind a low arm-chair, from which she had just risen, and he was kneeling in it—inclining himself over its back towards her, and holding her hand in both his own. His body moved restlessly, and it was with what Keats daintily calls a too happy happiness. This unwonted abstraction by love of all dignity from a man of whom it had ever seemed the chief component, was, in its distressing incongruity, a pain to her which quenched much of the pleasure she derived from the proof that she was idolized.

"I will try to love you," she was saying, in a trembling voice quite unlike her usual self-confidence. "And if I can believe in any way that I shall make you a good wife I shall indeed be willing to marry you. But, Mr. Boldwood, hesitation on so high a matter is honourable in any woman, and I don't want to give a solemn promise to-night. I would rather ask you to wait a few weeks till I can see my situation better.

"But you have every reason to believe that then—"

"I have every reason to hope that at the end of the five or six weeks, between this time and harvest, that you say you are going to be away from home, I shall be able to promise to be your wife," she said, firmly. "But remember this distinctly, I don't promise yet."

"It is enough; I don't ask more. I can wait on those dear words. And now, Miss Everdene, good-night!"

"Good-night," she said, graciously—almost tenderly; and Boldwood withdrew with a serene smile.

Bathsheba knew more of him now; he had entirely bared his heart before her, even until he had almost worn in her eyes the sorry look of a grand bird without the feathers that make it grand. She had been awe-struck at her past temerity, and was struggling to make amends without thinking whether the sin quite deserved the penalty she was schooling herself to pay. To have brought all this about her ears was terrible; but after a while the situation was not without a fearful joy. The facility with which even the most timid women sometimes acquire a relish for the dreadful when that is amalgamated with a little triumph, is marvellous.

Questions

What happens at the shearing supper?

What does Bathsheba sing about?

What happens after the supper?

What is Bathsheba's response?

GCSE style question: how does Hardy present the rural ways of life in this chapter?

A Level style question: how does Bathsheba's song foreshadow what is to come?

Creative response: write a poem/story/description about a sociable supper. Or write Bathsheba's diary for this chapter.

CHAPTER XXIV
THE SAME NIGHT—THE FIR PLANTATION

Among the multifarious duties which Bathsheba had voluntarily imposed upon herself by dispensing with the services of a bailiff, was the particular one of looking round the homestead before going to bed, to see that all was right and safe for the night. Gabriel had almost constantly preceded her in this tour every evening, watching her affairs as carefully as any specially appointed officer of surveillance could have done; but this tender devotion was to a great extent unknown to his mistress, and as much as was known was somewhat thanklessly received. Women are never tired of bewailing man's fickleness in love, but they only seem to snub his constancy.

As watching is best done invisibly, she usually carried a dark lantern in her hand, and every now and then turned on the light to examine nooks and corners with the coolness of a metropolitan policeman. This coolness may have owed its existence not so much to her fearlessness of expected danger as to her freedom from the suspicion of any; her worst anticipated discovery being that a horse might not be well bedded, the fowls not all in, or a door not closed.

This night the buildings were inspected as usual, and she went round to the farm paddock. Here the only sounds disturbing the stillness were steady munchings of many mouths, and stentorian breathings from all but invisible noses, ending in snores and puffs like the blowing of bellows slowly. Then the munching would recommence, when the lively imagination might assist the eye to discern a group of pink-white nostrils, shaped as caverns, and very clammy and humid on their surfaces, not exactly pleasant to the touch until one got used to them; the mouths beneath having a great partiality for closing upon any loose end of Bathsheba's apparel which came within reach of their tongues. Above each of these a still keener vision suggested a brown forehead and two staring though not unfriendly eyes, and above all a pair of whitish crescent-shaped horns like two particularly new moons, an occasional stolid "moo!" proclaiming beyond the shade of a doubt that these phenomena were the features and persons of Daisy, Whitefoot, Bonny-lass, Jolly-O, Spot, Twinkle-eye, etc., etc.—the respectable dairy of Devon cows belonging to Bathsheba aforesaid.

Her way back to the house was by a path through a young plantation of tapering firs, which had been planted some years earlier to shelter the premises from the north wind. By reason of the density of the interwoven foliage overhead, it was gloomy there at cloudless noontide, twilight in the evening, dark as midnight at dusk, and black as the ninth plague of Egypt at midnight. To describe the spot is to call it a vast, low, naturally formed hall, the plumy ceiling of which was supported by slender pillars of living wood, the floor being covered with a soft dun carpet of dead spikelets and mildewed cones, with a tuft of grass-blades here and there.

This bit of the path was always the crux of the night's ramble, though, before starting, her apprehensions of danger were not vivid enough to lead her to take a companion. Slipping along here covertly as Time, Bathsheba fancied she could hear footsteps entering the track at the opposite end. It was certainly a rustle of footsteps. Her own instantly fell as gently as snowflakes. She reassured herself by a remembrance that the path was public, and that the traveller was probably some villager returning home; regretting, at the same time, that the meeting should be about to occur in the darkest point of her route, even though only just outside her own door.

The noise approached, came close, and a figure was apparently on the point of gliding past her when something tugged at her skirt and pinned it forcibly to the ground. The instantaneous check nearly threw Bathsheba off her balance. In recovering she struck against warm clothes and buttons.

"A rum start, upon my soul!" said a masculine voice, a foot or so above her head. "Have I hurt you, mate?"

"No," said Bathsheba, attempting to shrink away.

"We have got hitched together somehow, I think."

"Yes."

"Are you a woman?"

"Yes."

"A lady, I should have said."

"It doesn't matter."

"I am a man."

"Oh!"

Bathsheba softly tugged again, but to no purpose.

"Is that a dark lantern you have? I fancy so," said the man.

"Yes."

"If you'll allow me I'll open it, and set you free."

A hand seized the lantern, the door was opened, the rays burst out from their prison, and Bathsheba beheld her position with astonishment.

The man to whom she was hooked was brilliant in brass and scarlet. He was a soldier. His sudden appearance was to darkness what the sound of a trumpet is to silence. Gloom, the genius loci at all times hitherto, was now totally overthrown, less by the lantern-light than by what the lantern lighted. The contrast of this revelation with her anticipations of some sinister figure in sombre garb was so great that it had upon her the effect of a fairy transformation.

It was immediately apparent that the military man's spur had become entangled in the gimp which decorated the skirt of her dress. He caught a view of her face.

"I'll unfasten you in one moment, miss," he said, with new-born gallantry.

"Oh no—I can do it, thank you," she hastily replied, and stooped for the performance.

The unfastening was not such a trifling affair. The rowel of the spur had so wound itself among the gimp cords in those few moments, that separation was likely to be a matter of time.

He too stooped, and the lantern standing on the ground betwixt them threw the gleam from its open side among the fir-tree needles and the blades of long damp grass with the effect of a large glowworm. It radiated upwards into their faces, and sent over half the plantation gigantic shadows of both man and woman, each dusky shape becoming distorted and mangled upon the tree-trunks till it wasted to nothing.

He looked hard into her eyes when she raised them for a moment; Bathsheba looked down again, for his gaze was too strong to be received point-blank with her own. But she had obliquely noticed that he was young and slim, and that he wore three chevrons upon his sleeve.

Bathsheba pulled again.

"You are a prisoner, miss; it is no use blinking the matter," said the soldier, drily. "I must cut your dress if you are in such a hurry."

"Yes—please do!" she exclaimed, helplessly.

"It wouldn't be necessary if you could wait a moment," and he unwound a cord from the little wheel. She withdrew her own hand, but, whether by accident or design, he touched it. Bathsheba was vexed; she hardly knew why.

His unravelling went on, but it nevertheless seemed coming to no end. She looked at him again.

"Thank you for the sight of such a beautiful face!" said the young sergeant, without ceremony.

She coloured with embarrassment. "'Twas unwillingly shown," she replied, stiffly, and with as much dignity—which was very little—as she could infuse into a position of captivity.

"I like you the better for that incivility, miss," he said.

"I should have liked—I wish—you had never shown yourself to me by intruding here!" She pulled again, and the gathers of her dress began to give way like liliputian musketry.

"I deserve the chastisement your words give me. But why should such a fair and dutiful girl have such an aversion to her father's sex?"

"Go on your way, please."

"What, Beauty, and drag you after me? Do but look; I never saw such a tangle!"

"Oh, 'tis shameful of you; you have been making it worse on purpose to keep me here—you have!"

"Indeed, I don't think so," said the sergeant, with a merry twinkle.

"I tell you you have!" she exclaimed, in high temper. "I insist upon undoing it. Now, allow me!"

"Certainly, miss; I am not of steel." He added a sigh which had as much archness in it as a sigh could possess without losing its nature altogether. "I am thankful for beauty, even when 'tis thrown to me like a bone to a dog. These moments will be over too soon!"

She closed her lips in a determined silence.

Bathsheba was revolving in her mind whether by a bold and desperate rush she could free herself at the risk of leaving her skirt bodily behind her. The thought was too dreadful. The dress—which she had put on to appear stately at the supper—was the head and front of her wardrobe; not another in her stock became her so well. What woman in Bathsheba's position, not naturally timid, and within call of her retainers, would have bought escape from a dashing soldier at so dear a price?

"All in good time; it will soon be done, I perceive," said her cool friend.

"This trifling provokes, and—and—"

"Not too cruel!"

"—Insults me!"

"It is done in order that I may have the pleasure of apologizing to so charming a woman, which I straightway do most humbly, madam," he said, bowing low.

Bathsheba really knew not what to say.

"I've seen a good many women in my time," continued the young man in a murmur, and more thoughtfully than hitherto, critically regarding her bent head at the same time; "but I've never seen a woman so beautiful as you. Take it or leave it—be offended or like it—I don't care."

"Who are you, then, who can so well afford to despise opinion?"

"No stranger. Sergeant Troy. I am staying in this place.—There! it is undone at last, you see. Your light fingers were more eager than mine. I wish it had been the knot of knots, which there's no untying!"

This was worse and worse. She started up, and so did he. How to decently get away from him—that was her difficulty now. She sidled off inch by inch,

the lantern in her hand, till she could see the redness of his coat no longer.
"Ah, Beauty; good-bye!" he said.

Analysis: The tangling up of Troy with Bathsheba in the fir plantation is wonderfully evocation and dramatic: the descriptions of the hideous shadows and Troy's appearance under the lamp. Her flustered response to his cheesy flirtation is very instructive and humanises her in a way she hasn't been humanised before: now we find her, shortly after being vulnerable in a practical fashion because of the sheep's illnesses, being vulnerable emotionally. Her country naivety now is exposed. Whereas many more seasoned readers may find Troy's rather obvious chat-up lines about her being beautiful rather clichéd, she doesn't know how to respond. She flounders.

Notice too how fate plays a vital role in their meeting. Clearly, we realise that Troy is looking for Fanny on his night-time walk around the farm, but bumps into Bathsheba and forgets about her.

Discussion point: What does this scene reveal about Bathsheba?

She made no reply, and, reaching a distance of twenty or thirty yards, turned about, and ran indoors.

Liddy had just retired to rest. In ascending to her own chamber, Bathsheba opened the girl's door an inch or two, and, panting, said—

"Liddy, is any soldier staying in the village—sergeant somebody—rather gentlemanly for a sergeant, and good looking—a red coat with blue facings?"

"No, miss ... No, I say; but really it might be Sergeant Troy home on furlough, though I have not seen him. He was here once in that way when the regiment was at Casterbridge."

"Yes; that's the name. Had he a moustache—no whiskers or beard?"

"He had."

"What kind of a person is he?"

"Oh! miss—I blush to name it—a gay man! But I know him to be very quick and trim, who might have made his thousands, like a squire. Such a clever young dandy as he is! He's a doctor's son by name, which is a great deal; and he's an earl's son by nature!"

Analysis: Liddy's comments about Troy hold back on the full truth about him but hints what we know as a reader: "a walking ruin to honest girls". His aristocratic background is also hinted at: "an earl's son by nature". In other words, he has an aristocratic exoticism about him which isn't entirely explained by his station in life. In truth, Troy is a chronic under-achiever, never amounting to much despite early promise. He is not even an officer in the army, but simply a lowly sergeant, one rank above private.

Discussion point: What do we learn about Troy here?

"Which is a great deal more. Fancy! Is it true?"

"Yes. And, he was brought up so well, and sent to Casterbridge Grammar School for years and years. Learnt all languages while he was there; and it was said he got on so far that he could take down Chinese in shorthand; but that I don't answer for, as it was only reported. However, he wasted his gifted lot, and listed a soldier; but even then he rose to be a sergeant without trying at all. Ah! such a blessing it is to be high-born; nobility of blood will shine out even in the ranks and files. And is he really come home, miss?"

"I believe so. Good-night, Liddy."

After all, how could a cheerful wearer of skirts be permanently offended with the man? There are occasions when girls like Bathsheba will put up with a great deal of unconventional behaviour. When they want to be praised, which is often, when they want to be mastered, which is sometimes; and when they want no nonsense, which is seldom. Just now the first feeling was in the ascendant with Bathsheba, with a dash of the second. Moreover, by chance or by devilry, the ministrant was antecedently made interesting by being a handsome stranger who had evidently seen better days.

So she could not clearly decide whether it was her opinion that he had insulted her or not.

"Was ever anything so odd!" she at last exclaimed to herself, in her own room. "And was ever anything so meanly done as what I did—to skulk away like that from a man who was only civil and kind!" Clearly she did not think his barefaced praise of her person an insult now.

It was a fatal omission of Boldwood's that he had never once told her she was beautiful.

Analysis: Here Hardy gets to the heart of the matter: Troy speaks to Bathsheba in a way that stimulates her imagination, makes her feel good about herself, he feeds her vanity. This is something that Boldwood is incapable of doing because he is, above all, a practical farmer, not an imaginative or empathetic man.

Discussion point: Do you think that being told pleasant things during a courtship is vital for its success? What kind of talk stimulates you?!

Questions

Why does Bathsheba go out at night?

What happens to her skirt?

What does the soldier say to her as he is trying to untangle himself?

What is Bathsheba shocked by?

Why does she ask Liddy for more information on Troy?

GCSE style question: how does Hardy make the meeting with Troy and Bathsheba such a charged and gripping scene?

A Level style question: compare Troy's flirtation with Bathsheba with another scene where two characters flirt from another text.

Creative response: write Bathsheba's diary for this chapter.

CHAPTER XXV
THE NEW ACQUAINTANCE
DESCRIBED

Idiosyncrasy and vicissitude had combined to stamp Sergeant Troy as an exceptional being.

He was a man to whom memories were an incumbrance, and anticipations a superfluity. Simply feeling, considering, and caring for what was before his eyes, he was vulnerable only in the present. His outlook upon time was as a transient flash of the eye now and then: that projection of consciousness into days gone by and to come, which makes the past a synonym for the pathetic and the future a word for circumspection, was foreign to Troy. With him the past was yesterday; the future, to-morrow; never, the day after.

On this account he might, in certain lights, have been regarded as one of the most fortunate of his order. For it may be argued with great plausibility that reminiscence is less an endowment than a disease, and that expectation in its only comfortable form—that of absolute faith—is practically an impossibility; whilst in the form of hope and the secondary compounds, patience, impatience, resolve, curiosity, it is a constant fluctuation between pleasure and pain.

Sergeant Troy, being entirely innocent of the practice of expectation, was never disappointed. To set against this negative gain there may have been some positive losses from a certain narrowing of the higher tastes and sensations which it entailed. But limitation of the capacity is never recognized as a loss by the loser therefrom: in this attribute moral or æsthetic poverty contrasts plausibly with material, since those who suffer do not mind it, whilst those who mind it soon cease to suffer. It is not a denial of anything to have been always without it, and what Troy had never enjoyed he did not miss; but, being fully conscious that what sober people missed he enjoyed, his capacity, though really less, seemed greater than theirs.

He was moderately truthful towards men, but to women lied like a Cretan—a system of ethics above all others calculated to win popularity at the first flush of admission into lively society; and the possibility of the favour gained being transitory had reference only to the future.

He never passed the line which divides the spruce vices from the ugly; and hence, though his morals had hardly been applauded, disapproval of them had frequently been tempered with a smile. This treatment had led to his becoming a sort of regrater of other men's gallantries, to his own aggrandizement as a Corinthian, rather than to the moral profit of his hearers.

His reason and his propensities had seldom any reciprocating influence, having separated by mutual consent long ago: thence it sometimes happened that, while his intentions were as honourable as could be wished, any particular deed formed a dark background which threw them into fine relief. The sergeant's vicious phases being the offspring of impulse, and his virtuous phases of cool meditation, the latter had a modest tendency to be oftener heard of than seen.

Troy was full of activity, but his activities were less of a locomotive than a vegetative nature; and, never being based upon any original choice of foundation or direction, they were exercised on whatever object chance might place in their way. Hence, whilst he sometimes reached the brilliant in speech because that was spontaneous, he fell below the commonplace in action, from inability to guide incipient effort. He had a quick comprehension and considerable force of character; but, being without the power to combine them, the comprehension became engaged with trivialities whilst waiting for the will to direct it, and the force wasted itself in useless grooves through unheeding the comprehension.

He was a fairly well-educated man for one of middle class—exceptionally well educated for a common soldier. He spoke fluently and unceasingly. He could in this way be one thing and seem another: for instance, he could speak of love and think of dinner; call on the husband to look at the wife; be eager to pay and intend to owe.

The wondrous power of flattery in passados at woman is a perception so universal as to be remarked upon by many people almost as automatically as they repeat a proverb, or say that they are Christians and the like, without thinking much of the enormous corollaries which spring from the proposition. Still less is it acted upon for the good of the complemental being alluded to. With the majority such an opinion is shelved with all those trite aphorisms which require some catastrophe to bring their tremendous meanings thoroughly home. When expressed with some amount of reflectiveness it seems co-ordinate with a belief that this flattery must be reasonable to be effective. It is to the credit of men that few attempt to settle the question by experiment, and it is for their happiness, perhaps, that accident has never settled it for them. Nevertheless, that a male dissembler who by deluging her with untenable fictions charms the female wisely, may acquire powers reaching to the extremity of perdition, is a truth taught to many by unsought and wringing occurrences. And some profess to have attained to the same knowledge by experiment as aforesaid, and jauntily continue their indulgence in such experiments with terrible effect. Sergeant Troy was one.

He had been known to observe casually that in dealing with womankind the only alternative to flattery was cursing and swearing. There was no third method. "Treat them fairly, and you are a lost man." he would say.

This person's public appearance in Weatherbury promptly followed his arrival there. A week or two after the shearing, Bathsheba, feeling a nameless relief of spirits on account of Boldwood's absence, approached her hayfields and looked over the hedge towards the haymakers. They consisted in about equal proportions of gnarled and flexuous forms, the former being the men, the latter the women, who wore tilt bonnets covered with nankeen, which hung in a curtain upon their shoulders. Coggan and Mark Clark were mowing in a less forward meadow, Clark humming a tune to the strokes of his scythe, to which Jan made no attempt to keep time with his. In the first mead they were already loading hay, the women raking it into cocks and windrows, and the men tossing it upon the waggon.

From behind the waggon a bright scarlet spot emerged, and went on loading unconcernedly with the rest. It was the gallant sergeant, who had come haymaking for pleasure; and nobody could deny that he was doing the mistress of the farm real knight-service by this voluntary contribution of his labour at a busy time.

As soon as she had entered the field Troy saw her, and sticking his pitchfork into the ground and picking up his crop or cane, he came forward. Bathsheba blushed with half-angry embarrassment, and adjusted her eyes as well as her feet to the direct line of her path.

Analysis: Troy also manages to see that one way to Bathsheba's heart is to join her in her work. He mucks in and gets involved. He realises that his presence there can stimulate her desire further, make her think she could live a life with him. He is hunting for her now.

Discussion point: Why does Hardy set the next love scene between Bathsheba and Troy at hay-making time? How does the juxtaposition of the night scene in the fir plantation and bright day of the hay-making work to excite the readers' imagination?

Questions

What do we learn about Troy in this chapter?
Why is Bathsheba more relaxed than normal?
How does Troy embarrass Bathsheba?
GCSE style question: how does Hardy present Troy in this chapter?
Creative response: write a description of a flirtatious person, exploring why he or she is like that.

CHAPTER XXVI
SCENE ON THE VERGE OF THE HAY-MEAD

"Ah, Miss Everdene!" said the sergeant, touching his diminutive cap. "Little did I think it was you I was speaking to the other night. And yet, if I had reflected, the 'Queen of the Corn-market' (truth is truth at any hour of the day or night, and I heard you so named in Casterbridge yesterday), the 'Queen of the Corn-market.' I say, could be no other woman. I step across now to beg your forgiveness a thousand times for having been led by my feelings to express myself too strongly for a stranger. To be sure I am no stranger to the place—I am Sergeant Troy, as I told you, and I have assisted your uncle in these fields no end of times when I was a lad. I have been doing the same for you to-day."

"I suppose I must thank you for that, Sergeant Troy," said the Queen of the Corn-market, in an indifferently grateful tone.

The sergeant looked hurt and sad. "Indeed you must not, Miss Everdene," he said. "Why could you think such a thing necessary?"

"I am glad it is not."

"Why? if I may ask without offence."

"Because I don't much want to thank you for anything."

"I am afraid I have made a hole with my tongue that my heart will never mend. O these intolerable times: that ill-luck should follow a man for honestly telling a woman she is beautiful! 'Twas the most I said—you must own that; and the least I could say—that I own myself."

"There is some talk I could do without more easily than money."

"Indeed. That remark is a sort of digression."

"No. It means that I would rather have your room than your company."

"And I would rather have curses from you than kisses from any other woman; so I'll stay here."

Bathsheba was absolutely speechless. And yet she could not help feeling that the assistance he was rendering forbade a harsh repulse.

"Well," continued Troy, "I suppose there is a praise which is rudeness, and that may be mine. At the same time there is a treatment which is injustice, and that may be yours. Because a plain blunt man, who has never been taught concealment, speaks out his mind without exactly intending it, he's to be snapped off like the son of a sinner."

"Indeed there's no such case between us," she said, turning away. "I don't allow strangers to be bold and impudent—even in praise of me."

"Ah—it is not the fact but the method which offends you," he said, carelessly. "But I have the sad satisfaction of knowing that my words, whether pleasing or offensive, are unmistakably true. Would you have had me look at you, and tell my acquaintance that you are quite a common-place woman, to save you the embarrassment of being stared at if they come near you? Not I. I couldn't tell any such ridiculous lie about a beauty to encourage a single woman in England in too excessive a modesty."

"It is all pretence—what you are saying!" exclaimed Bathsheba, laughing in spite of herself at the sly method. "You have a rare invention, Sergeant Troy. Why couldn't you have passed by me that night, and said nothing?—that was all I meant to reproach you for."

"Because I wasn't going to. Half the pleasure of a feeling lies in being able to express it on the spur of the moment, and I let out mine. It would have been just the same if you had been the reverse person—ugly and old—I should have exclaimed about it in the same way."

"How long is it since you have been so afflicted with strong feeling, then?"

"Oh, ever since I was big enough to know loveliness from deformity."

"'Tis to be hoped your sense of the difference you speak of doesn't stop at faces, but extends to morals as well."

"I won't speak of morals or religion—my own or anybody else's. Though perhaps I should have been a very good Christian if you pretty women hadn't made me an idolater."

Bathsheba moved on to hide the irrepressible dimplings of merriment. Troy followed, whirling his crop.

"But—Miss Everdene—you do forgive me?"

"Hardly."

"Why?"

"You say such things."

"I said you were beautiful, and I'll say so still; for, by G—— so you are! The most beautiful ever I saw, or may I fall dead this instant! Why, upon my ——"

"Don't—don't! I won't listen to you—you are so profane!" she said, in a restless state between distress at hearing him and a penchant to hear more.

"I again say you are a most fascinating woman. There's nothing remarkable in my saying so, is there? I'm sure the fact is evident enough. Miss Everdene, my opinion may be too forcibly let out to please you, and, for the matter of that, too insignificant to convince you, but surely it is honest, and why can't it be excused?"

"Because it—it isn't a correct one," she femininely murmured.

"Oh, fie—fie! Am I any worse for breaking the third of that Terrible Ten than you for breaking the ninth?"

"Well, it doesn't seem quite true to me that I am fascinating," she replied evasively.

"Not so to you: then I say with all respect that, if so, it is owing to your modesty, Miss Everdene. But surely you must have been told by everybody of what everybody notices? And you should take their words for it."

"They don't say so exactly."

"Oh yes, they must!"

"Well, I mean to my face, as you do," she went on, allowing herself to be further lured into a conversation that intention had rigorously forbidden.

"But you know they think so?"

"No—that is—I certainly have heard Liddy say they do, but—" She paused.

Capitulation—that was the purport of the simple reply, guarded as it was—capitulation, unknown to herself. Never did a fragile tailless sentence convey a more perfect meaning. The careless sergeant smiled within himself, and probably too the devil smiled from a loop-hole in Tophet, for the moment was the turning-point of a career. Her tone and mien signified beyond mistake that the seed which was to lift the foundation had taken root in the chink: the remainder was a mere question of time and natural changes.

"There the truth comes out!" said the soldier, in reply. "Never tell me that a young lady can live in a buzz of admiration without knowing something about it. Ah, well, Miss Everdene, you are—pardon my blunt way—you are rather an injury to our race than otherwise."

"How—indeed?" she said, opening her eyes.

"Oh, it is true enough. I may as well be hung for a sheep as a lamb (an old country saying, not of much account, but it will do for a rough soldier), and so I will speak my mind, regardless of your pleasure, and without hoping or intending to get your pardon. Why, Miss Everdene, it is in this manner that your good looks may do more harm than good in the world." The sergeant looked down the mead in critical abstraction. "Probably some one man on an average falls in love with each ordinary woman. She can marry him: he is content, and leads a useful life. Such women as you a hundred men always covet—your eyes will bewitch scores on scores into an unavailing fancy for you—you can only marry one of that many. Out of these say twenty will endeavour to drown the bitterness of despised love in drink; twenty more will mope away their lives without a wish or attempt to make a mark in he world, because they have no ambition apart from their attachment to you; twenty more—the susceptible person myself possibly among them—will be always draggling after you, getting where they may just see you, doing desperate things. Men are such constant fools! The rest may try to get over their passion with more or less success. But all these men will be saddened. And not only those ninety-nine men, but the ninety-nine women they might have married are saddened with them. There's my tale. That's why I say that a woman so charming as yourself, Miss Everdene, is hardly a blessing to her race."

The handsome sergeant's features were during this speech as rigid and stern as John Knox's in addressing his gay young queen.

Seeing she made no reply, he said, "Do you read French?"

"No; I began, but when I got to the verbs, father died," she said simply.

"I do—when I have an opportunity, which latterly has not been often (my mother was a Parisienne)—and there's a proverb they have, Qui aime bien, châtie bien—'He chastens who loves well.' Do you understand me?"

"Ah!" she replied, and there was even a little tremulousness in the usually cool girl's voice; "if you can only fight half as winningly as you can talk, you are able to make a pleasure of a bayonet wound!" And then poor Bathsheba instantly perceived her slip in making this admission: in hastily trying to retrieve it, she went from bad to worse. "Don't, however, suppose that I derive any pleasure from what you tell me."

"I know you do not—I know it perfectly," said Troy, with much hearty conviction on the exterior of his face: and altering the expression to moodiness; "when a dozen men are ready to speak tenderly to you, and give the admiration you deserve without adding the warning you need, it stands to reason that my poor rough-and-ready mixture of praise and blame cannot convey much pleasure. Fool as I may be, I am not so conceited as to suppose that!"

"I think you—are conceited, nevertheless," said Bathsheba, looking askance at a reed she was fitfully pulling with one hand, having lately grown feverish under the soldier's system of procedure—not because the nature of his cajolery was entirely unperceived, but because its vigour was overwhelming.

"I would not own it to anybody else—nor do I exactly to you. Still, there might have been some self-conceit in my foolish supposition the other night. I knew that what I said in admiration might be an opinion too often forced upon you to give any pleasure, but I certainly did think that the kindness of your nature might prevent you judging an uncontrolled tongue harshly—which you have done—and thinking badly of me and wounding me this morning, when I am working hard to save your hay."

"Well, you need not think more of that: perhaps you did not mean to be rude to me by speaking out your mind: indeed, I believe you did not," said the shrewd woman, in painfully innocent earnest. "And I thank you for giving help here. But—but mind you don't speak to me again in that way, or in any other, unless I speak to you."

"Oh, Miss Bathsheba! That is too hard!"

"No, it isn't. Why is it?"

"You will never speak to me; for I shall not be here long. I am soon going back again to the miserable monotony of drill—and perhaps our regiment will be ordered out soon. And yet you take away the one little ewe-lamb of pleasure that I have in this dull life of mine. Well, perhaps generosity is not a woman's most marked characteristic."

"When are you going from here?" she asked, with some interest.

"In a month."

"But how can it give you pleasure to speak to me?"

"Can you ask Miss Everdene—knowing as you do—what my offence is based on?"

"If you do care so much for a silly trifle of that kind, then, I don't mind doing it," she uncertainly and doubtingly answered. "But you can't really care for a word from me? you only say so—I think you only say so."

"That's unjust—but I won't repeat the remark. I am too gratified to get such a mark of your friendship at any price to cavil at the tone. I do, Miss Everdene, care for it. You may think a man foolish to want a mere word— just a good morning. Perhaps he is—I don't know. But you have never been a man looking upon a woman, and that woman yourself."

"Well."

"Then you know nothing of what such an experience is like—and Heaven forbid that you ever should!"

"Nonsense, flatterer! What is it like? I am interested in knowing."

"Put shortly, it is not being able to think, hear, or look in any direction except one without wretchedness, nor there without torture."

"Ah, sergeant, it won't do—you are pretending!" she said, shaking her head. "Your words are too dashing to be true."

"I am not, upon the honour of a soldier."

"But why is it so?—Of course I ask for mere pastime."

"Because you are so distracting—and I am so distracted."

"You look like it."

"I am indeed."

"Why, you only saw me the other night!"

"That makes no difference. The lightning works instantaneously. I loved you then, at once—as I do now."

Bathsheba surveyed him curiously, from the feet upward, as high as she liked to venture her glance, which was not quite so high as his eyes.

"You cannot and you don't," she said demurely. "There is no such sudden feeling in people. I won't listen to you any longer. Hear me, I wish I knew what o'clock it is—I am going—I have wasted too much time here already!"

The sergeant looked at his watch and told her. "What, haven't you a watch, miss?" he inquired.

"I have not just at present—I am about to get a new one."

"No. You shall be given one. Yes—you shall. A gift, Miss Everdene—a gift."

And before she knew what the young man was intending, a heavy gold watch was in her hand.

"It is an unusually good one for a man like me to possess," he quietly said. "That watch has a history. Press the spring and open the back."

She did so.

"What do you see?"

"A crest and a motto."

"A coronet with five points, and beneath, Cedit amor rebus—'Love yields to circumstance.' It's the motto of the Earls of Severn. That watch belonged to the last lord, and was given to my mother's husband, a medical man, for his use till I came of age, when it was to be given to me. It was all the fortune that ever I inherited. That watch has regulated imperial interests in its time—the stately ceremonial, the courtly assignation, pompous travels, and lordly sleeps. Now it is yours."

"But, Sergeant Troy, I cannot take this—I cannot!" she exclaimed, with round-eyed wonder. "A gold watch! What are you doing? Don't be such a dissembler!"

The sergeant retreated to avoid receiving back his gift, which she held out persistently towards him. Bathsheba followed as he retired.

"Keep it—do, Miss Everdene—keep it!" said the erratic child of impulse. "The fact of your possessing it makes it worth ten times as much to me. A more plebeian one will answer my purpose just as well, and the pleasure of knowing whose heart my old one beats against—well, I won't speak of that.

It is in far worthier hands than ever it has been in before."

Analysis: Troy's impulse to give Bathsheba the watch is a very important moment. It is from then that he begins to gain real control over her. We can see too that he is besotted with her to give her such a valuable item. His expensive, aristocratic watch contrasts with Oak's ridiculous watch.

Discussion point: Why is the giving of the watch so important?

"But indeed I can't have it!" she said, in a perfect simmer of distress. "Oh, how can you do such a thing; that is if you really mean it! Give me your dead father's watch, and such a valuable one! You should not be so reckless, indeed, Sergeant Troy!"

"I loved my father: good; but better, I love you more. That's how I can do it," said the sergeant, with an intonation of such exquisite fidelity to nature that it was evidently not all acted now. Her beauty, which, whilst it had been quiescent, he had praised in jest, had in its animated phases moved him to earnest; and though his seriousness was less than she imagined, it was probably more than he imagined himself.

Bathsheba was brimming with agitated bewilderment, and she said, in half-suspicious accents of feeling, "Can it be! Oh, how can it be, that you care for me, and so suddenly! You have seen so little of me: I may not be really so—so nice-looking as I seem to you. Please, do take it; Oh, do! I cannot and will not have it. Believe me, your generosity is too great. I have never done you a single kindness, and why should you be so kind to me?"

A factitious reply had been again upon his lips, but it was again suspended, and he looked at her with an arrested eye. The truth was, that as she now stood—excited, wild, and honest as the day—her alluring beauty bore out so fully the epithets he had bestowed upon it that he was quite startled at his temerity in advancing them as false. He said mechanically, "Ah, why?" and continued to look at her.

"And my workfolk see me following you about the field, and are wondering. Oh, this is dreadful!" she went on, unconscious of the transmutation she was effecting.

"I did not quite mean you to accept it at first, for it was my one poor patent of nobility," he broke out, bluntly; "but, upon my soul, I wish you would now. Without any shamming, come! Don't deny me the happiness of wearing it for my sake? But you are too lovely even to care to be kind as others are."

"No, no; don't say so! I have reasons for reserve which I cannot explain."

"Let it be, then, let it be," he said, receiving back the watch at last; "I must be leaving you now. And will you speak to me for these few weeks of my stay?"

"Indeed I will. Yet, I don't know if I will! Oh, why did you come and disturb me so!"

Analysis: Troy's flippant, flirtatious romanticism is important here because it contrasts so much with Boldwood's intense, leaden protestations of love. Troy is like a hawk playing with his pray, having snared her, whereas Boldwood is more like a wolf howling at a bird in the tree. Bathsheba is both entranced but disturbed by Troy's flirtatious behaviour: "I won't listen to you any longer". But, of course, she carries on listening. She is clearly increasingly vulnerable towards his charms after her acceptance of the watch.

Discussion point: What do we feel for Bathsheba here?

"Perhaps in setting a gin, I have caught myself. Such things have happened. Well, will you let me work in your fields?" he coaxed.

"Yes, I suppose so; if it is any pleasure to you."

"Miss Everdene, I thank you."

"No, no."

"Good-bye!"

The sergeant brought his hand to the cap on the slope of his head, saluted, and returned to the distant group of haymakers.

Bathsheba could not face the haymakers now. Her heart erratically flitting hither and thither from perplexed excitement, hot, and almost tearful, she retreated homeward, murmuring, "Oh, what have I done! What does it mean! I wish I knew how much of it was true!"

Analysis: Now we are beginning to see the dawning of Bathsheba's sexual awakening. We have seen Boldwood's, which has been terrible and all-pervasive. Now we see Bathsheba overwhelmed with desire for Troy, but conscious that there is something desperately wrong. Of course, we, the reader, having seen Troy's behaviour towards Fanny, know what is wrong.

Discussion point: Why is Bathsheba not very aware of what is happening to her?

Questions

What does Troy apologise for?

What is the effect of Troy's flattery?

What is happening with Troy's regiment?

What does he say about his feelings towards Bathsheba?

What is Bathsheba's response to this?

What does Troy try and give her?

What does he manage to get Bathsheba's permission for?

GCSE style question: how do we see Bathsheba's dignity being compromised in this chapter?

A Level style question: compare the presentation of Troy's behavior with Boldwood's.

Creative response: continue writing Bathsheba's diary for this scene, exploring her complex feelings for Boldwood, Oak and Troy.

CHAPTER XXVII
HIVING THE BEES

The Weatherbury bees were late in their swarming this year. It was in the latter part of June, and the day after the interview with Troy in the hayfield, that Bathsheba was standing in her garden, watching a swarm in the air and guessing their probable settling place. Not only were they late this year, but unruly. Sometimes throughout a whole season all the swarms would alight on the lowest attainable bough—such as part of a currant-bush or espalier apple-tree; next year they would, with just the same unanimity, make straight off to the uppermost member of some tall, gaunt costard, or quarrenden, and there defy all invaders who did not come armed with ladders and staves to take them.

This was the case at present. Bathsheba's eyes, shaded by one hand, were following the ascending multitude against the unexplorable stretch of blue till they ultimately halted by one of the unwieldy trees spoken of. A process somewhat analogous to that of alleged formations of the universe, time and times ago, was observable. The bustling swarm had swept the sky in a scattered and uniform haze, which now thickened to a nebulous centre: this glided on to a bough and grew still denser, till it formed a solid black spot upon the light.

The men and women being all busily engaged in saving the hay—even Liddy had left the house for the purpose of lending a hand—Bathsheba resolved to hive the bees herself, if possible. She had dressed the hive with herbs and honey, fetched a ladder, brush, and crook, made herself impregnable with armour of leather gloves, straw hat, and large gauze veil—once green but now faded to snuff colour—and ascended a dozen rungs of the ladder. At once she heard, not ten yards off, a voice that was beginning to have a strange power in agitating her.

"Miss Everdene, let me assist you; you should not attempt such a thing alone."

Troy was just opening the garden gate.

Bathsheba flung down the brush, crook, and empty hive, pulled the skirt of her dress tightly round her ankles in a tremendous flurry, and as well as she could slid down the ladder. By the time she reached the bottom Troy was there also, and he stooped to pick up the hive.

"How fortunate I am to have dropped in at this moment!" exclaimed the sergeant.

She found her voice in a minute. "What! and will you shake them in for me?" she asked, in what, for a defiant girl, was a faltering way; though, for a timid girl, it would have seemed a brave way enough.

"Will I!" said Troy. "Why, of course I will. How blooming you are to-day!"

Troy flung down his cane and put his foot on the ladder to ascend.

"But you must have on the veil and gloves, or you'll be stung fearfully!"

"Ah, yes. I must put on the veil and gloves. Will you kindly show me how to fix them properly?"

"And you must have the broad-brimmed hat, too, for your cap has no brim to keep the veil off, and they'd reach your face."

"The broad-brimmed hat, too, by all means."

So a whimsical fate ordered that her hat should be taken off—veil and all attached—and placed upon his head, Troy tossing his own into a gooseberry bush. Then the veil had to be tied at its lower edge round his collar and the gloves put on him.

He looked such an extraordinary object in this guise that, flurried as she was, she could not avoid laughing outright. It was the removal of yet another stake from the palisade of cold manners which had kept him off.

Bathsheba looked on from the ground whilst he was busy sweeping and shaking the bees from the tree, holding up the hive with the other hand for them to fall into. She made use of an unobserved minute whilst his attention was absorbed in the operation to arrange her plumes a little. He came down holding the hive at arm's length, behind which trailed a cloud of bees.

"Upon my life," said Troy, through the veil, "holding up this hive makes one's arm ache worse than a week of sword-exercise." When the manœuvre was complete he approached her. "Would you be good enough to untie me and let me out? I am nearly stifled inside this silk cage."

To hide her embarrassment during the unwonted process of untying the string about his neck, she said:—

"I have never seen that you spoke of."

"What?"

"The sword-exercise."

"Ah! would you like to?" said Troy.

Bathsheba hesitated. She had heard wondrous reports from time to time by dwellers in Weatherbury, who had by chance sojourned awhile in Casterbridge, near the barracks, of this strange and glorious performance, the sword-exercise. Men and boys who had peeped through chinks or over walls into the barrack-yard returned with accounts of its being the most flashing affair conceivable; accoutrements and weapons glistening like stars—here, there, around—yet all by rule and compass. So she said mildly what she felt strongly.

"Yes; I should like to see it very much."

Analysis: One of the pleasures of the book is the way in which Hardy weaves in descriptions of farm work with descriptions of evolving human relationships. Troy's hiving of the bees is a magnetic moment: Bathsheba and he are very close, delving into honey, amidst the buzzing of the bees. There is a sense of danger, of love, of ordinary farm work. The summer shimmers in the background. Now that Troy has snared Bathsheba we sense him drawing her further and further out of her comfort zone into the realm of forbidden desire. Her acceptance to see him do his sword exercise is a sign that she is now stepping outside the bounds of respectable Victorian feminine behaviour.

Discussion point: How is Hardy generating tension in the scenes between Bathsheba and Troy at his point?

"And so you shall; you shall see me go through it."

"No! How?"

"Let me consider."

"Not with a walking-stick—I don't care to see that. It must be a real sword."

"Yes, I know; and I have no sword here; but I think I could get one by the evening. Now, will you do this?"

Troy bent over her and murmured some suggestion in a low voice.

"Oh no, indeed!" said Bathsheba, blushing. "Thank you very much, but I couldn't on any account."

"Surely you might? Nobody would know."

She shook her head, but with a weakened negation. "If I were to," she said, "I must bring Liddy too. Might I not?"

Troy looked far away. "I don't see why you want to bring her," he said coldly.

An unconscious look of assent in Bathsheba's eyes betrayed that something more than his coldness had made her also feel that Liddy would be superfluous in the suggested scene. She had felt it, even whilst making the proposal.

"Well, I won't bring Liddy—and I'll come. But only for a very short time," she added; "a very short time."

"It will not take five minutes," said Troy.

Questions

What does Troy apologise for?

What is the effect of Troy's flattering?

What is happening with Troy's regiment?

What does he say about his feelings towards Bathsheba?

What is Bathsheba's response to this?

What does Troy try and give her?

What does he manage to get Bathsheba's permission for?

GCSE style question: how do we see Bathsheba's dignity being compromised in this chapter?

A Level style question: compare the presentation of Troy's behavior with Boldwood's.

Creative response: continue writing Bathsheba's diary for this scene, exploring her complex feelings for Boldwood, Oak and Troy.

CHAPTER XXVIII
THE HOLLOW AMID THE FERNS

The hill opposite Bathsheba's dwelling extended, a mile off, into an uncultivated tract of land, dotted at this season with tall thickets of brake fern, plump and diaphanous from recent rapid growth, and radiant in hues of clear and untainted green.

At eight o'clock this midsummer evening, whilst the bristling ball of gold in the west still swept the tips of the ferns with its long, luxuriant rays, a soft brushing-by of garments might have been heard among them, and Bathsheba appeared in their midst, their soft, feathery arms caressing her up to her shoulders. She paused, turned, went back over the hill and half-way to her own door, whence she cast a farewell glance upon the spot she had just left, having resolved not to remain near the place after all.

She saw a dim spot of artificial red moving round the shoulder of the rise. It disappeared on the other side.

She waited one minute—two minutes—thought of Troy's disappointment at her non-fulfilment of a promised engagement, till she again ran along the field, clambered over the bank, and followed the original direction. She was now literally trembling and panting at this her temerity in such an errant undertaking; her breath came and went quickly, and her eyes shone with an infrequent light. Yet go she must. She reached the verge of a pit in the middle of the ferns. Troy stood in the bottom, looking up towards her.

"I heard you rustling through the fern before I saw you," he said, coming up and giving her his hand to help her down the slope.

The pit was a saucer-shaped concave, naturally formed, with a top diameter of about thirty feet, and shallow enough to allow the sunshine to reach their heads. Standing in the centre, the sky overhead was met by a circular horizon of fern: this grew nearly to the bottom of the slope and then abruptly ceased. The middle within the belt of verdure was floored with a thick flossy carpet of moss and grass intermingled, so yielding that the foot was half-buried within it.

"Now," said Troy, producing the sword, which, as he raised it into the sunlight, gleamed a sort of greeting, like a living thing, "first, we have four right and four left cuts; four right and four left thrusts. Infantry cuts and guards are more interesting than ours, to my mind; but they are not so swashing. They have seven cuts and three thrusts. So much as a preliminary. Well, next, our cut one is as if you were sowing your corn—so." Bathsheba saw a sort of rainbow, upside down in the air, and Troy's arm was still again. "Cut two, as if you were hedging—so. Three, as if you were reaping—so. Four, as if you were threshing—in that way. Then the same on the left. The thrusts are these: one, two, three, four, right; one, two, three, four, left." He repeated them. "Have 'em again?" he said. "One, two—"

She hurriedly interrupted: "I'd rather not; though I don't mind your twos and fours; but your ones and threes are terrible!"

"Very well. I'll let you off the ones and threes. Next, cuts, points and guards altogether." Troy duly exhibited them. "Then there's pursuing practice, in this way." He gave the movements as before. "There, those are the stereotyped forms. The infantry have two most diabolical upward cuts, which we are too humane to use. Like this—three, four."

"How murderous and bloodthirsty!"

"They are rather deathly. Now I'll be more interesting, and let you see some loose play—giving all the cuts and points, infantry and cavalry, quicker than lightning, and as promiscuously—with just enough rule to regulate instinct and yet not to fetter it. You are my antagonist, with this difference from real warfare, that I shall miss you every time by one hair's breadth, or perhaps two. Mind you don't flinch, whatever you do."

"I'll be sure not to!" she said invincibly.

He pointed to about a yard in front of him.

Bathsheba's adventurous spirit was beginning to find some grains of relish in these highly novel proceedings. She took up her position as directed, facing Troy.

"Now just to learn whether you have pluck enough to let me do what I wish, I'll give you a preliminary test."

He flourished the sword by way of introduction number two, and the next thing of which she was conscious was that the point and blade of the sword were darting with a gleam towards her left side, just above her hip; then of their reappearance on her right side, emerging as it were from between her ribs, having apparently passed through her body. The third item of consciousness was that of seeing the same sword, perfectly clean and free from blood held vertically in Troy's hand (in the position technically called "recover swords"). All was as quick as electricity.

"Oh!" she cried out in affright, pressing her hand to her side. "Have you run me through?—no, you have not! Whatever have you done!"

"I have not touched you," said Troy, quietly. "It was mere sleight of hand. The sword passed behind you. Now you are not afraid, are you? Because if you are I can't perform. I give my word that I will not only not hurt you, but not once touch you."

"I don't think I am afraid. You are quite sure you will not hurt me?"

"Quite sure."

"Is the sword very sharp?"

"O no—only stand as still as a statue. Now!"

In an instant the atmosphere was transformed to Bathsheba's eyes. Beams of light caught from the low sun's rays, above, around, in front of her, well-nigh shut out earth and heaven—all emitted in the marvellous evolutions of Troy's reflecting blade, which seemed everywhere at once, and yet nowhere specially. These circling gleams were accompanied by a keen rush that was almost a whistling—also springing from all sides of her at once. In short, she was enclosed in a firmament of light, and of sharp hisses, resembling a sky-full of meteors close at hand.

Never since the broadsword became the national weapon had there been more dexterity shown in its management than by the hands of Sergeant Troy, and never had he been in such splendid temper for the performance as now in the evening sunshine among the ferns with Bathsheba. It may safely be asserted with respect to the closeness of his cuts, that had it been possible for the edge of the sword to leave in the air a permanent substance wherever it flew past, the space left untouched would have been almost a mould of Bathsheba's figure.

Behind the luminous streams of this aurora militaris, she could see the hue of Troy's sword arm, spread in a scarlet haze over the space covered by its motions, like a twanged harpstring, and behind all Troy himself, mostly facing her; sometimes, to show the rear cuts, half turned away, his eye nevertheless always keenly measuring her breadth and outline, and his lips tightly closed in sustained effort. Next, his movements lapsed slower, and she could see them individually. The hissing of the sword had ceased, and he stopped entirely.

"That outer loose lock of hair wants tidying," he said, before she had moved or spoken. "Wait: I'll do it for you."

An arc of silver shone on her right side: the sword had descended. The lock dropped to the ground.

"Bravely borne!" said Troy. "You didn't flinch a shade's thickness. Wonderful in a woman!"

"It was because I didn't expect it. Oh, you have spoilt my hair!"

"Only once more."

"No—no! I am afraid of you—indeed I am!" she cried.

"I won't touch you at all—not even your hair. I am only going to kill that caterpillar settling on you. Now: still!"

It appeared that a caterpillar had come from the fern and chosen the front of her bodice as his resting place. She saw the point glisten towards her bosom, and seemingly enter it. Bathsheba closed her eyes in the full persuasion that she was killed at last. However, feeling just as usual, she opened them again.

"There it is, look," said the sergeant, holding his sword before her eyes.

The caterpillar was spitted upon its point.

"Why, it is magic!" said Bathsheba, amazed.

"Oh no—dexterity. I merely gave point to your bosom where the caterpillar was, and instead of running you through checked the extension a thousandth of an inch short of your surface."

"But how could you chop off a curl of my hair with a sword that has no edge?"

"No edge! This sword will shave like a razor. Look here."

He touched the palm of his hand with the blade, and then, lifting it, showed her a thin shaving of scarf-skin dangling therefrom.

"But you said before beginning that it was blunt and couldn't cut me!"

"That was to get you to stand still, and so make sure of your safety. The risk of injuring you through your moving was too great not to force me to tell you a fib to escape it."

She shuddered. "I have been within an inch of my life, and didn't know it!"

"More precisely speaking, you have been within half an inch of being pared alive two hundred and ninety-five times."

"Cruel, cruel, 'tis of you!"

"You have been perfectly safe, nevertheless. My sword never errs." And Troy returned the weapon to the scabbard.

Bathsheba, overcome by a hundred tumultuous feelings resulting from the scene, abstractedly sat down on a tuft of heather.

"I must leave you now," said Troy, softly. "And I'll venture to take and keep this in remembrance of you."

She saw him stoop to the grass, pick up the winding lock which he had severed from her manifold tresses, twist it round his fingers, unfasten a button in the breast of his coat, and carefully put it inside. She felt powerless to withstand or deny him. He was altogether too much for her, and Bathsheba seemed as one who, facing a reviving wind, finds it blow so strongly that it stops the breath. He drew near and said, "I must be leaving you."

He drew nearer still. A minute later and she saw his scarlet form disappear amid the ferny thicket, almost in a flash, like a brand swiftly waved.

That minute's interval had brought the blood beating into her face, set her stinging as if aflame to the very hollows of her feet, and enlarged emotion to a compass which quite swamped thought. It had brought upon her a stroke resulting, as did that of Moses in Horeb, in a liquid stream—here a stream of tears. She felt like one who has sinned a great sin.

The circumstance had been the gentle dip of Troy's mouth downwards upon her own. He had kissed her.

Analysis: The 'Sword Exercise' scene is perhaps the most famous scene in the whole of Hardy's writing. He took some time to research the nature of sword exercises and shows how Troy's attraction is primarily non-verbal: it is his dexterity with the sword which speaks more than words. There is a real tension here because there is love, wild, undisciplined love, in the air, but also Troy is savagely disciplined in the way he manages not to hurt Bathsheba. He is utterly in control. This is in sharp contrast to Bathsheba who thrilled and excited by the danger and his dexterity has the "blood beating into face" and her "aflame to the very hollows of her feet". She is extremely "turned on" – all thought is swamped. She feels guilty about what has happened: "she felt like one who has sinned a great sin."

Discussion point: Why does Hardy focus upon Bathsheba's desire here? Why does he present her as powerless?

Questions

Where does Bathsheba wait for Troy?

What does Troy show her?

How does Troy lie to Bathsheba?

What does Troy do to Bathsheba with his sword?

What does Troy do at the end of the chapter?

GCSE style question: how does Hardy make the encounter in the hollow so sexually charged?

A Level style question: compare and contrast Troy's seduction of Bathsheba with another seduction scene in a text of your choice.

Creative response: write a story/poem/description called 'The Seduction' or write Bathsheba's diary for this scene.

CHAPTER XXIX
PARTICULARS OF A TWILIGHT WALK

We now see the element of folly distinctly mingling with the many varying particulars which made up the character of Bathsheba Everdene. It was almost foreign to her intrinsic nature. Introduced as lymph on the dart of Eros, it eventually permeated and coloured her whole constitution. Bathsheba, though she had too much understanding to be entirely governed by her womanliness, had too much womanliness to use her understanding to the best advantage. Perhaps in no minor point does woman astonish her helpmate more than in the strange power she possesses of believing cajoleries that she knows to be false—except, indeed, in that of being utterly sceptical on strictures that she knows to be true.

Bathsheba loved Troy in the way that only self-reliant women love when they abandon their self-reliance. When a strong woman recklessly throws away her strength she is worse than a weak woman who has never had any strength to throw away. One source of her inadequacy is the novelty of the occasion. She has never had practice in making the best of such a condition. Weakness is doubly weak by being new.

Bathsheba was not conscious of guile in this matter. Though in one sense a woman of the world, it was, after all, that world of daylight coteries and green carpets wherein cattle form the passing crowd and winds the busy hum; where a quiet family of rabbits or hares lives on the other side of your party-wall, where your neighbour is everybody in the tything, and where calculation is confined to market-days. Of the fabricated tastes of good fashionable society she knew but little, and of the formulated self-indulgence of bad, nothing at all. Had her utmost thoughts in this direction been distinctly worded (and by herself they never were), they would only have amounted to such a matter as that she felt her impulses to be pleasanter guides than her discretion. Her love was entire as a child's, and though warm as summer it was fresh as spring. Her culpability lay in her making no attempt to control feeling by subtle and careful inquiry into consequences. She could show others the steep and thorny way, but "reck'd not her own rede."

And Troy's deformities lay deep down from a woman's vision, whilst his embellishments were upon the very surface; thus contrasting with homely Oak, whose defects were patent to the blindest, and whose virtues were as metals in a mine.

The difference between love and respect was markedly shown in her conduct. Bathsheba had spoken of her interest in Boldwood with the greatest freedom to Liddy, but she had only communed with her own heart concerning Troy.

All this infatuation Gabriel saw, and was troubled thereby from the time of his daily journey a-field to the time of his return, and on to the small hours of many a night. That he was not beloved had hitherto been his great sorrow; that Bathsheba was getting into the toils was now a sorrow greater than the first, and one which nearly obscured it. It was a result which paralleled the oft-quoted observation of Hippocrates concerning physical pains.

That is a noble though perhaps an unpromising love which not even the fear of breeding aversion in the bosom of the one beloved can deter from combating his or her errors. Oak determined to speak to his mistress. He would base his appeal on what he considered her unfair treatment of Farmer Boldwood, now absent from home.

An opportunity occurred one evening when she had gone for a short walk by a path through the neighbouring cornfields. It was dusk when Oak, who had not been far a-field that day, took the same path and met her returning, quite pensively, as he thought.

The wheat was now tall, and the path was narrow; thus the way was quite a sunken groove between the embowing thicket on either side. Two persons could not walk abreast without damaging the crop, and Oak stood aside to let her pass.

"Oh, is it Gabriel?" she said. "You are taking a walk too. Good-night."

"I thought I would come to meet you, as it is rather late," said Oak, turning and following at her heels when she had brushed somewhat quickly by him.

"Thank you, indeed, but I am not very fearful."

"Oh no; but there are bad characters about."

"I never meet them."

Now Oak, with marvellous ingenuity, had been going to introduce the gallant sergeant through the channel of "bad characters." But all at once the scheme broke down, it suddenly occurring to him that this was rather a clumsy way, and too barefaced to begin with. He tried another preamble.

"And as the man who would naturally come to meet you is away from home, too—I mean Farmer Boldwood—why, thinks I, I'll go," he said.

"Ah, yes." She walked on without turning her head, and for many steps nothing further was heard from her quarter than the rustle of her dress against the heavy corn-ears. Then she resumed rather tartly—

"I don't quite understand what you meant by saying that Mr. Boldwood would naturally come to meet me."

I meant on account of the wedding which they say is likely to take place between you and him, miss. Forgive my speaking plainly."

"They say what is not true." she returned quickly. "No marriage is likely to take place between us."

Gabriel now put forth his unobscured opinion, for the moment had come. "Well, Miss Everdene," he said, "putting aside what people say, I never in my life saw any courting if his is not a courting of you."

Bathsheba would probably have terminated the conversation there and then by flatly forbidding the subject, had not her conscious weakness of position allured her to palter and argue in endeavours to better it.

"Since this subject has been mentioned," she said very emphatically, "I am glad of the opportunity of clearing up a mistake which is very common and very provoking. I didn't definitely promise Mr. Boldwood anything. I have never cared for him. I respect him, and he has urged me to marry him. But I have given him no distinct answer. As soon as he returns I shall do so; and the answer will be that I cannot think of marrying him."

"People are full of mistakes, seemingly."

"They are."

The other day they said you were trifling with him, and you almost proved that you were not; lately they have said that you be not, and you straightway begin to show—"

"That I am, I suppose you mean."

"Well, I hope they speak the truth."

"They do, but wrongly applied. I don't trifle with him; but then, I have nothing to do with him."

Oak was unfortunately led on to speak of Boldwood's rival in a wrong tone to her after all. "I wish you had never met that young Sergeant Troy, miss," he sighed.

Bathsheba's steps became faintly spasmodic. "Why?" she asked.

"He is not good enough for 'ee."

"Did any one tell you to speak to me like this?"

"Nobody at all."

"Then it appears to me that Sergeant Troy does not concern us here," she said, intractably. "Yet I must say that Sergeant Troy is an educated man, and quite worthy of any woman. He is well born."

"His being higher in learning and birth than the ruck o' soldiers is anything but a proof of his worth. It show's his course to be down'ard."

"I cannot see what this has to do with our conversation. Mr. Troy's course is not by any means downward; and his superiority is a proof of his worth!"

"I believe him to have no conscience at all. And I cannot help begging you, miss, to have nothing to do with him. Listen to me this once—only this once! I don't say he's such a bad man as I have fancied—I pray to God he is not. But since we don't exactly know what he is, why not behave as if he might be bad, simply for your own safety? Don't trust him, mistress; I ask you not to trust him so."

"Why, pray?"

"I like soldiers, but this one I do not like," he said, sturdily. "His cleverness in his calling may have tempted him astray, and what is mirth to the neighbours is ruin to the woman. When he tries to talk to 'ee again, why not turn away with a short 'Good day'; and when you see him coming one way, turn the other. When he says anything laughable, fail to see the point and don't smile, and speak of him before those who will report your talk as 'that fantastical man,' or 'that Sergeant What's-his-name.' 'That man of a family that has come to the dogs.' Don't be unmannerly towards en, but harmless-uncivil, and so get rid of the man."

No Christmas robin detained by a window-pane ever pulsed as did Bathsheba now.

"I say—I say again—that it doesn't become you to talk about him. Why he should be mentioned passes me quite!" she exclaimed desperately. "I know this, th-th-that he is a thoroughly conscientious man—blunt sometimes even to rudeness—but always speaking his mind about you plain to your face!"

"Oh."

"He is as good as anybody in this parish! He is very particular, too, about going to church—yes, he is!"

"I am afeard nobody saw him there. I never did, certainly."

"The reason of that is," she said eagerly, "that he goes in privately by the old tower door, just when the service commences, and sits at the back of the gallery. He told me so."

This supreme instance of Troy's goodness fell upon Gabriel ears like the thirteenth stroke of crazy clock. It was not only received with utter incredulity as regarded itself, but threw a doubt on all the assurances that had preceded it.

Oak was grieved to find how entirely she trusted him. He brimmed with deep feeling as he replied in a steady voice, the steadiness of which was spoilt by the palpableness of his great effort to keep it so:—

"You know, mistress, that I love you, and shall love you always. I only mention this to bring to your mind that at any rate I would wish to do you no harm: beyond that I put it aside. I have lost in the race for money and good things, and I am not such a fool as to pretend to 'ee now I am poor, and you have got altogether above me. But Bathsheba, dear mistress, this I beg you to consider—that, both to keep yourself well honoured among the workfolk, and in common generosity to an honourable man who loves you as well as I, you should be more discreet in your bearing towards this soldier."

"Don't, don't, don't!" she exclaimed, in a choking voice.

"Are ye not more to me than my own affairs, and even life!" he went on. "Come, listen to me! I am six years older than you, and Mr. Boldwood is ten years older than I, and consider—I do beg of 'ee to consider before it is too late—how safe you would be in his hands!"

Oak's allusion to his own love for her lessened, to some extent, her anger at his interference; but she could not really forgive him for letting his wish to marry her be eclipsed by his wish to do her good, any more than for his slighting treatment of Troy.

"I wish you to go elsewhere," she commanded, a paleness of face invisible to the eye being suggested by the trembling words. "Do not remain on this farm any longer. I don't want you—I beg you to go!"

"That's nonsense," said Oak, calmly. "This is the second time you have pretended to dismiss me; and what's the use o' it?"

"Pretended! You shall go, sir—your lecturing I will not hear! I am mistress here."

"Go, indeed—what folly will you say next? Treating me like Dick, Tom and Harry when you know that a short time ago my position was as good as yours! Upon my life, Bathsheba, it is too barefaced. You know, too, that I can't go without putting things in such a strait as you wouldn't get out of I can't tell when. Unless, indeed, you'll promise to have an understanding man as bailiff, or manager, or something. I'll go at once if you'll promise that."

"I shall have no bailiff; I shall continue to be my own manager," she said decisively.

"Very well, then; you should be thankful to me for biding. How would the farm go on with nobody to mind it but a woman? But mind this, I don't wish 'ee to feel you owe me anything. Not I. What I do, I do. Sometimes I say I should be as glad as a bird to leave the place—for don't suppose I'm content to be a nobody. I was made for better things. However, I don't like to see your concerns going to ruin, as they must if you keep in this mind... I hate taking my own measure so plain, but, upon my life, your provoking ways make a man say what he wouldn't dream of at other times! I own to being rather interfering. But you know well enough how it is, and who she is that I like too well, and feel too much like a fool about to be civil to her!"

It is more than probable that she privately and unconsciously respected him a little for this grim fidelity, which had been shown in his tone even more than in his words. At any rate she murmured something to the effect that he might stay if he wished. She said more distinctly, "Will you leave me alone now? I don't order it as a mistress—I ask it as a woman, and I expect you not to be so uncourteous as to refuse."

"Certainly I will, Miss Everdene," said Gabriel, gently. He wondered that the request should have come at this moment, for the strife was over, and they were on a most desolate hill, far from every human habitation, and the hour was getting late. He stood still and allowed her to get far ahead of him till he could only see her form upon the sky.

A distressing explanation of this anxiety to be rid of him at that point now ensued. A figure apparently rose from the earth beside her. The shape beyond all doubt was Troy's. Oak would not be even a possible listener, and at once turned back till a good two hundred yards were between the lovers and himself.

Gabriel went home by way of the churchyard. In passing the tower he thought of what she had said about the sergeant's virtuous habit of entering the church unperceived at the beginning of service. Believing that the little gallery door alluded to was quite disused, he ascended the external flight of steps at the top of which it stood, and examined it. The pale lustre yet hanging in the north-western heaven was sufficient to show that a sprig of ivy had grown from the wall across the door to a length of more than a foot, delicately tying the panel to the stone jamb. It was a decisive proof that the door had not been opened at least since Troy came back to Weatherbury.

Questions

What does Gabriel realise about Bathsheba?

What does Gabriel say to Bathsheba to try and change her mind about Troy?

What is Bathsheba's response?

What does Bathsheba try to do again?

What is Gabriel's response?

How does Gabriel realise Troy has lied to Bathsheba?

GCSE style question: how does Hardy present Bathsheba in this chapter?

Creative response: write Gabriel's diary for this chapter, outlining his concerns for Bathsheba.

CHAPTER XXX
HOT CHEEKS AND TEARFUL EYES

Half an hour later Bathsheba entered her own house. There burnt upon her face when she met the light of the candles the flush and excitement which were little less than chronic with her now. The farewell words of Troy, who had accompanied her to the very door, still lingered in her ears. He had bidden her adieu for two days, which were, so he stated, to be spent at Bath in visiting some friends. He had also kissed her a second time.

It is only fair to Bathsheba to explain here a little fact which did not come to light till a long time afterwards: that Troy's presentation of himself so aptly at the roadside this evening was not by any distinctly preconcerted arrangement. He had hinted—she had forbidden; and it was only on the chance of his still coming that she had dismissed Oak, fearing a meeting between them just then.

She now sank down into a chair, wild and perturbed by all these new and fevering sequences. Then she jumped up with a manner of decision, and fetched her desk from a side table.

In three minutes, without pause or modification, she had written a letter to Boldwood, at his address beyond Casterbridge, saying mildly but firmly that she had well considered the whole subject he had brought before her and kindly given her time to decide upon; that her final decision was that she could not marry him. She had expressed to Oak an intention to wait till Boldwood came home before communicating to him her conclusive reply. But Bathsheba found that she could not wait.

It was impossible to send this letter till the next day; yet to quell her uneasiness by getting it out of her hands, and so, as it were, setting the act in motion at once, she arose to take it to any one of the women who might be in the kitchen.

She paused in the passage. A dialogue was going on in the kitchen, and Bathsheba and Troy were the subject of it.

"If he marry her, she'll gie up farming."

"'Twill be a gallant life, but may bring some trouble between the mirth—so say I."

"Well, I wish I had half such a husband."

Bathsheba had too much sense to mind seriously what her servitors said about her; but too much womanly redundance of speech to leave alone what was said till it died the natural death of unminded things. She burst in upon them.

"Who are you speaking of?" she asked.

There was a pause before anybody replied. At last Liddy said frankly, "What was passing was a bit of a word about yourself, miss."

"I thought so! Maryann and Liddy and Temperance—now I forbid you to suppose such things. You know I don't care the least for Mr. Troy—not I. Everybody knows how much I hate him.—Yes," repeated the froward young person, "hate him!"

"We know you do, miss," said Liddy; "and so do we all."

"I hate him too," said Maryann.

"Maryann—Oh you perjured woman! How can you speak that wicked story!" said Bathsheba, excitedly. "You admired him from your heart only this morning in the very world, you did. Yes, Maryann, you know it!"

"Yes, miss, but so did you. He is a wild scamp now, and you are right to hate him."

"He's not a wild scamp! How dare you to my face! I have no right to hate him, nor you, nor anybody. But I am a silly woman! What is it to me what he is? You know it is nothing. I don't care for him; I don't mean to defend his good name, not I. Mind this, if any of you say a word against him you'll be dismissed instantly!"

She flung down the letter and surged back into the parlour, with a big heart and tearful eyes, Liddy following her.

"Oh miss!" said mild Liddy, looking pitifully into Bathsheba's face. "I am sorry we mistook you so! I did think you cared for him; but I see you don't now."

"Shut the door, Liddy."

Liddy closed the door, and went on: "People always say such foolery, miss. I'll make answer hencefor'ard, 'Of course a lady like Miss Everdene can't love him'; I'll say it out in plain black and white."

Bathsheba burst out: "O Liddy, are you such a simpleton? Can't you read riddles? Can't you see? Are you a woman yourself?"

Liddy's clear eyes rounded with wonderment.

"Yes; you must be a blind thing, Liddy!" she said, in reckless abandonment and grief. "Oh, I love him to very distraction and misery and agony! Don't be frightened at me, though perhaps I am enough to frighten any innocent woman. Come closer—closer." She put her arms round Liddy's neck. "I must let it out to somebody; it is wearing me away! Don't you yet know enough of me to see through that miserable denial of mine? O

God, what a lie it was! Heaven and my Love forgive me. And don't you know that a woman who loves at all thinks nothing of perjury when it is balanced against her love? There, go out of the room; I want to be quite alone."

Liddy went towards the door.

"Liddy, come here. Solemnly swear to me that he's not a fast man; that it is all lies they say about him!"

"But, miss, how can I say he is not if—"

"You graceless girl! How can you have the cruel heart to repeat what they say? Unfeeling thing that you are... But I'll see if you or anybody else in the village, or town either, dare do such a thing!" She started off, pacing from fireplace to door, and back again.

"No, miss. I don't—I know it is not true!" said Liddy, frightened at Bathsheba's unwonted vehemence.

"I suppose you only agree with me like that to please me. But, Liddy, he cannot be bad, as is said. Do you hear?"

"Yes, miss, yes."

"And you don't believe he is?"

"I don't know what to say, miss," said Liddy, beginning to cry. "If I say No, you don't believe me; and if I say Yes, you rage at me!"

"Say you don't believe it—say you don't!"

"I don't believe him to be so bad as they make out."

"He is not bad at all... My poor life and heart, how weak I am!" she moaned, in a relaxed, desultory way, heedless of Liddy's presence. "Oh, how I wish I had never seen him! Loving is misery for women always. I shall never forgive God for making me a woman, and dearly am I beginning to pay for the honour of owning a pretty face." She freshened and turned to Liddy suddenly. "Mind this, Lydia Smallbury, if you repeat anywhere a single word of what I have said to you inside this closed door, I'll never trust you, or love you, or have you with me a moment longer—not a moment!"

"I don't want to repeat anything," said Liddy, with womanly dignity of a diminutive order; "but I don't wish to stay with you. And, if you please, I'll go at the end of the harvest, or this week, or to-day... I don't see that I deserve to be put upon and stormed at for nothing!" concluded the small woman, bigly.

"No, no, Liddy; you must stay!" said Bathsheba, dropping from haughtiness to entreaty with capricious inconsequence. "You must not notice my being in a taking just now. You are not as a servant—you are a companion to me. Dear, dear—I don't know what I am doing since this miserable ache of my heart has weighted and worn upon me so! What shall I come to! I suppose I shall get further and further into troubles. I wonder sometimes if I am doomed to die in the Union. I am friendless enough, God knows!"

"I won't notice anything, nor will I leave you!" sobbed Liddy, impulsively putting up her lips to Bathsheba's, and kissing her.

Then Bathsheba kissed Liddy, and all was smooth again.

"I don't often cry, do I, Lidd? but you have made tears come into my eyes," she said, a smile shining through the moisture. "Try to think him a good man, won't you, dear Liddy?"

"I will, miss, indeed."

"He is a sort of steady man in a wild way, you know. That's better than to be as some are, wild in a steady way. I am afraid that's how I am. And promise me to keep my secret—do, Liddy! And do not let them know that I have been crying about him, because it will be dreadful for me, and no good to him, poor thing!"

"Death's head himself shan't wring it from me, mistress, if I've a mind to keep anything; and I'll always be your friend," replied Liddy, emphatically, at the same time bringing a few more tears into her own eyes, not from any particular necessity, but from an artistic sense of making herself in keeping with the remainder of the picture, which seems to influence women at such times. "I think God likes us to be good friends, don't you?"

"Indeed I do."

"And, dear miss, you won't harry me and storm at me, will you? because you seem to swell so tall as a lion then, and it frightens me! Do you know, I fancy you would be a match for any man when you are in one o' your takings."

"Never! do you?" said Bathsheba, slightly laughing, though somewhat seriously alarmed by this Amazonian picture of herself. "I hope I am not a bold sort of maid—mannish?" she continued with some anxiety.

"Oh no, not mannish; but so almighty womanish that 'tis getting on that way sometimes. Ah! miss," she said, after having drawn her breath very sadly in and sent it very sadly out, "I wish I had half your failing that way. 'Tis a great protection to a poor maid in these illegit'mate days!"

Questions

What does Bathsheba write in her letter to Boldwood?

Why is she upset by the servants talking?

What does Bathsheba confess to Liddy?

Why does she become upset by Liddy?

Who apologizes and why?

GCSE style question: how does Hardy present Bathsheba's contradictory state of mind in this chapter?

Creative response: write a story/poem called 'Rumours' or write Bathsheba's diary for this chapter.

CHAPTER XXXI
BLAME—FURY

The next evening Bathsheba, with the idea of getting out of the way of Mr. Boldwood in the event of his returning to answer her note in person, proceeded to fulfil an engagement made with Liddy some few hours earlier. Bathsheba's companion, as a gauge of their reconciliation, had been granted a week's holiday to visit her sister, who was married to a thriving hurdler and cattle-crib-maker living in a delightful labyrinth of hazel copse not far beyond Yalbury. The arrangement was that Miss Everdene should honour them by coming there for a day or two to inspect some ingenious contrivances which this man of the woods had introduced into his wares.

Leaving her instructions with Gabriel and Maryann, that they were to see everything carefully locked up for the night, she went out of the house just at the close of a timely thunder-shower, which had refined the air, and daintily bathed the coat of the land, though all beneath was dry as ever. Freshness was exhaled in an essence from the varied contours of bank and hollow, as if the earth breathed maiden breath; and the pleased birds were hymning to the scene. Before her, among the clouds, there was a contrast in the shape of lairs of fierce light which showed themselves in the neighbourhood of a hidden sun, lingering on to the farthest north-west corner of the heavens that this midsummer season allowed.

She had walked nearly two miles of her journey, watching how the day was retreating, and thinking how the time of deeds was quietly melting into the time of thought, to give place in its turn to the time of prayer and sleep, when she beheld advancing over Yalbury hill the very man she sought so anxiously to elude. Boldwood was stepping on, not with that quiet tread of reserved strength which was his customary gait, in which he always seemed to be balancing two thoughts. His manner was stunned and sluggish now.

Boldwood had for the first time been awakened to woman's privileges in tergiversation even when it involves another person's possible blight. That Bathsheba was a firm and positive girl, far less inconsequent than her fellows, had been the very lung of his hope; for he had held that these qualities would lead her to adhere to a straight course for consistency's sake, and accept him, though her fancy might not flood him with the iridescent hues of uncritical love. But the argument now came back as sorry gleams from a broken mirror. The discovery was no less a scourge than a surprise.

He came on looking upon the ground, and did not see Bathsheba till they were less than a stone's throw apart. He looked up at the sound of her pit-pat, and his changed appearance sufficiently denoted to her the depth and strength of the feelings paralyzed by her letter.

"Oh; is it you, Mr. Boldwood?" she faltered, a guilty warmth pulsing in her face.

Those who have the power of reproaching in silence may find it a means more effective than words. There are accents in the eye which are not on the tongue, and more tales come from pale lips than can enter an ear. It is both the grandeur and the pain of the remoter moods that they avoid the pathway of sound. Boldwood's look was unanswerable.

Seeing she turned a little aside, he said, "What, are you afraid of me?"

"Why should you say that?" said Bathsheba.

"I fancied you looked so," said he. "And it is most strange, because of its contrast with my feeling for you."

She regained self-possession, fixed her eyes calmly, and waited.

"You know what that feeling is," continued Boldwood, deliberately. "A thing strong as death. No dismissal by a hasty letter affects that."

"I wish you did not feel so strongly about me," she murmured. "It is generous of you, and more than I deserve, but I must not hear it now."

"Hear it? What do you think I have to say, then? I am not to marry you, and that's enough. Your letter was excellently plain. I want you to hear nothing—not I."

Bathsheba was unable to direct her will into any definite groove for freeing herself from this fearfully awkward position. She confusedly said, "Good evening," and was moving on. Boldwood walked up to her heavily and dully.

"Bathsheba—darling—is it final indeed?"

"Indeed it is."

"Oh, Bathsheba—have pity upon me!" Boldwood burst out. "God's sake, yes—I am come to that low, lowest stage—to ask a woman for pity! Still, she is you—she is you."

Bathsheba commanded herself well. But she could hardly get a clear voice for what came instinctively to her lips: "There is little honour to the woman in that speech." It was only whispered, for something unutterably mournful no less than distressing in this spectacle of a man showing himself to be so entirely the vane of a passion enervated the feminine instinct for punctilios.

"I am beyond myself about this, and am mad," he said. "I am no stoic at all to be supplicating here; but I do supplicate to you. I wish you knew what is in me of devotion to you; but it is impossible, that. In bare human mercy to a lonely man, don't throw me off now!"

"I don't throw you off—indeed, how can I? I never had you." In her noon-clear sense that she had never loved him she forgot for a moment her thoughtless angle on that day in February.

"But there was a time when you turned to me, before I thought of you! I don't reproach you, for even now I feel that the ignorant and cold darkness that I should have lived in if you had not attracted me by that letter— valentine you call it—would have been worse than my knowledge of you, though it has brought this misery. But, I say, there was a time when I knew nothing of you, and cared nothing for you, and yet you drew me on. And if you say you gave me no encouragement, I cannot but contradict you."

"What you call encouragement was the childish game of an idle minute. I have bitterly repented of it—ay, bitterly, and in tears. Can you still go on reminding me?"

"I don't accuse you of it—I deplore it. I took for earnest what you insist was jest, and now this that I pray to be jest you say is awful, wretched earnest. Our moods meet at wrong places. I wish your feeling was more like mine, or my feeling more like yours! Oh, could I but have foreseen the torture that trifling trick was going to lead me into, how I should have cursed you; but only having been able to see it since, I cannot do that, for I love you too well! But it is weak, idle drivelling to go on like this... Bathsheba, you are the first woman of any shade or nature that I have ever looked at to love, and it is the having been so near claiming you for my own that makes this denial so hard to bear. How nearly you promised me! But I don't speak now to move your heart, and make you grieve because of my pain; it is no use, that. I must bear it; my pain would get no less by paining you."

"But I do pity you—deeply—O, so deeply!" she earnestly said.

"Do no such thing—do no such thing. Your dear love, Bathsheba, is such a vast thing beside your pity, that the loss of your pity as well as your love is no great addition to my sorrow, nor does the gain of your pity make it sensibly less. O sweet—how dearly you spoke to me behind the spear-bed at the washing-pool, and in the barn at the shearing, and that dearest last time in the evening at your home! Where are your pleasant words all gone—your earnest hope to be able to love me? Where is your firm conviction that you would get to care for me very much? Really forgotten?—really?"

She checked emotion, looked him quietly and clearly in the face, and said in her low, firm voice, "Mr. Boldwood, I promised you nothing. Would you have had me a woman of clay when you paid me that furthest, highest compliment a man can pay a woman—telling her he loves her? I was bound to show some feeling, if I would not be a graceless shrew. Yet each of those pleasures was just for the day—the day just for the pleasure. How was I to know that what is a pastime to all other men was death to you? Have reason, do, and think more kindly of me!"

"Well, never mind arguing—never mind. One thing is sure: you were all but mine, and now you are not nearly mine. Everything is changed, and that by you alone, remember. You were nothing to me once, and I was contented; you are now nothing to me again, and how different the second nothing is from the first! Would to God you had never taken me up, since it was only to throw me down!"

Bathsheba, in spite of her mettle, began to feel unmistakable signs that she was inherently the weaker vessel. She strove miserably against this femininity which would insist upon supplying unbidden emotions in stronger and stronger current. She had tried to elude agitation by fixing her mind on the trees, sky, any trivial object before her eyes, whilst his reproaches fell, but ingenuity could not save her now.

"I did not take you up—surely I did not!" she answered as heroically as she could. "But don't be in this mood with me. I can endure being told I am in the wrong, if you will only tell it me gently! O sir, will you not kindly forgive me, and look at it cheerfully?"

"Cheerfully! Can a man fooled to utter heart-burning find a reason for being merry? If I have lost, how can I be as if I had won? Heavens you must be heartless quite! Had I known what a fearfully bitter sweet this was to be, how I would have avoided you, and never seen you, and been deaf of you. I tell you all this, but what do you care! You don't care."

She returned silent and weak denials to his charges, and swayed her head desperately, as if to thrust away the words as they came showering about her ears from the lips of the trembling man in the climax of life, with his bronzed Roman face and fine frame.

"Dearest, dearest, I am wavering even now between the two opposites of recklessly renouncing you, and labouring humbly for you again. Forget that you have said No, and let it be as it was! Say, Bathsheba, that you only wrote that refusal to me in fun—come, say it to me!"

"It would be untrue, and painful to both of us. You overrate my capacity for love. I don't possess half the warmth of nature you believe me to have. An unprotected childhood in a cold world has beaten gentleness out of me."

He immediately said with more resentment: "That may be true, somewhat; but ah, Miss Everdene, it won't do as a reason! You are not the cold woman you would have me believe. No, no! It isn't because you have no feeling in you that you don't love me. You naturally would have me think so—you would hide from me that you have a burning heart like mine. You have love enough, but it is turned into a new channel. I know where."

The swift music of her heart became hubbub now, and she throbbed to extremity. He was coming to Troy. He did then know what had occurred! And the name fell from his lips the next moment.

"Why did Troy not leave my treasure alone?" he asked, fiercely. "When I had no thought of injuring him, why did he force himself upon your notice! Before he worried you your inclination was to have me; when next I should have come to you your answer would have been Yes. Can you deny it—I ask, can you deny it?"

She delayed the reply, but was too honest to withhold it. "I cannot," she whispered.

"I know you cannot. But he stole in in my absence and robbed me. Why didn't he win you away before, when nobody would have been grieved?—when nobody would have been set tale-bearing. Now the people sneer at me—the very hills and sky seem to laugh at me till I blush shamefully for my folly. I have lost my respect, my good name, my standing—lost it, never to get it again. Go and marry your man—go on!"

"Oh sir—Mr. Boldwood!"

"You may as well. I have no further claim upon you. As for me, I had better go somewhere alone, and hide—and pray. I loved a woman once. I am now ashamed. When I am dead they'll say, miserable love-sick man that he was. Heaven—heaven—if I had got jilted secretly, and the dishonour not known, and my position kept! But no matter, it is gone, and the woman not gained. Shame upon him—shame!"

His unreasonable anger terrified her, and she glided from him, without obviously moving, as she said, "I am only a girl—do not speak to me so!"

"All the time you knew—how very well you knew—that your new freak was my misery. Dazzled by brass and scarlet—Oh, Bathsheba—this is woman's folly indeed!"

She fired up at once. "You are taking too much upon yourself!" she said, vehemently. "Everybody is upon me—everybody. It is unmanly to attack a woman so! I have nobody in the world to fight my battles for me; but no mercy is shown. Yet if a thousand of you sneer and say things against me, I will not be put down!"

"You'll chatter with him doubtless about me. Say to him, 'Boldwood would have died for me.' Yes, and you have given way to him, knowing him to be not the man for you. He has kissed you—claimed you as his. Do you hear—he has kissed you. Deny it!"

The most tragic woman is cowed by a tragic man, and although Boldwood was, in vehemence and glow, nearly her own self rendered into another sex, Bathsheba's cheek quivered. She gasped, "Leave me, sir—leave me! I am nothing to you. Let me go on!"

"Deny that he has kissed you."

"I shall not."

"Ha—then he has!" came hoarsely from the farmer.

"He has," she said, slowly, and, in spite of her fear, defiantly. "I am not ashamed to speak the truth."

"Then curse him; and curse him!" said Boldwood, breaking into a whispered fury. "Whilst I would have given worlds to touch your hand, you have let a rake come in without right or ceremony and—kiss you! Heaven's mercy—kiss you! ... Ah, a time of his life shall come when he will have to repent, and think wretchedly of the pain he has caused another man; and then may he ache, and wish, and curse, and yearn—as I do now!"

"Don't, don't, oh, don't pray down evil upon him!" she implored in a miserable cry. "Anything but that—anything. Oh, be kind to him, sir, for I love him true!"

Boldwood's ideas had reached that point of fusion at which outline and consistency entirely disappear. The impending night appeared to concentrate in his eye. He did not hear her at all now.

"I'll punish him—by my soul, that will I! I'll meet him, soldier or no, and I'll horsewhip the untimely stripling for this reckless theft of my one delight. If he were a hundred men I'd horsewhip him—" He dropped his voice suddenly and unnaturally. "Bathsheba, sweet, lost coquette, pardon me! I've been blaming you, threatening you, behaving like a churl to you, when he's the greatest sinner. He stole your dear heart away with his unfathomable lies! ... It is a fortunate thing for him that he's gone back to his regiment—that he's away up the country, and not here! I hope he may not return here just yet. I pray God he may not come into my sight, for I may be tempted beyond myself. Oh, Bathsheba, keep him away—yes, keep him away from me!"

For a moment Boldwood stood so inertly after this that his soul seemed to have been entirely exhaled with the breath of his passionate words. He turned his face away, and withdrew, and his form was soon covered over by the twilight as his footsteps mixed in with the low hiss of the leafy trees.

Analysis: Boldwood's fury about Troy's seduction of Bathsheba turns him into a border-line psychotic. Here, some critics argue that the novel becomes rather too melodramatic: the animosity that Boldwood feels is too exaggerated. There is real menace about Boldwood here: he threatens to horsewhip him. The novel begins to follow the pattern of a traditional country ballad, with a young maiden being seduced by a worthless soldier and rejecting the worthy landowner as a consequence. Except Hardy is more complex than this: he is interested in presenting us with a man in the grip of a sexual obsession which can't find any release for.

Discussion point: Why does Hardy present Boldwood in this way?

Bathsheba, who had been standing motionless as a model all this latter time, flung her hands to her face, and wildly attempted to ponder on the exhibition which had just passed away. Such astounding wells of fevered feeling in a still man like Mr. Boldwood were incomprehensible, dreadful. Instead of being a man trained to repression he was—what she had seen him.

The force of the farmer's threats lay in their relation to a circumstance known at present only to herself: her lover was coming back to Weatherbury in the course of the very next day or two. Troy had not returned to his distant barracks as Boldwood and others supposed, but had merely gone to visit some acquaintance in Bath, and had yet a week or more remaining on his furlough.

She felt wretchedly certain that if he revisited her just at this nick of time, and came into contact with Boldwood, a fierce quarrel would be the consequence. She panted with solicitude when she thought of possible injury to Troy. The least spark would kindle the farmer's swift feelings of rage and jealousy; he would lose his self-mastery as he had this evening; Troy's blitheness might become aggressive; it might take the direction of derision, and Boldwood's anger might then take the direction of revenge.

With almost a morbid dread of being thought a gushing girl, this guileless woman too well concealed from the world under a manner of carelessness the warm depths of her strong emotions. But now there was no reserve. In her distraction, instead of advancing further she walked up and down, beating the air with her fingers, pressing on her brow, and sobbing brokenly to herself. Then she sat down on a heap of stones by the wayside to think. There she remained long. Above the dark margin of the earth appeared foreshores and promontories of coppery cloud, bounding a green and pellucid expanse in the western sky. Amaranthine glosses came over them then, and the unresting world wheeled her round to a contrasting prospect eastward, in the shape of indecisive and palpitating stars. She gazed upon their silent throes amid the shades of space, but realised none at all. Her troubled spirit was far away with Troy.

Questions

Who does Bathsheba meet on Yalbury Hill and what does this person ask her to do?

What does Boldwood guess?

What does Boldwood threaten?

What is Bathsheba worried about?

GCSE style question: how does Hardy represent Boldwood in this chapter?

A Level style: compare and contrast Hardy's representation of jealousy with another text which explores the theme of jealousy.

Creative response: write a story/poem called 'Jealousy' or write Boldwood's diary.

CHAPTER XXXII
NIGHT—HORSES TRAMPING

The village of Weatherbury was quiet as the graveyard in its midst, and the living were lying well-nigh as still as the dead. The church clock struck eleven. The air was so empty of other sounds that the whirr of the clock-work immediately before the strokes was distinct, and so was also the click of the same at their close. The notes flew forth with the usual blind obtuseness of inanimate things—flapping and rebounding among walls, undulating against the scattered clouds, spreading through their interstices into unexplored miles of space.

Bathsheba's crannied and mouldy halls were to-night occupied only by Maryann, Liddy being, as was stated, with her sister, whom Bathsheba had set out to visit. A few minutes after eleven had struck, Maryann turned in her bed with a sense of being disturbed. She was totally unconscious of the nature of the interruption to her sleep. It led to a dream, and the dream to an awakening, with an uneasy sensation that something had happened. She left her bed and looked out of the window. The paddock abutted on this end of the building, and in the paddock she could just discern by the uncertain gray a moving figure approaching the horse that was feeding there. The figure seized the horse by the forelock, and led it to the corner of the field. Here she could see some object which circumstances proved to be a vehicle, for after a few minutes spent apparently in harnessing, she heard the trot of the horse down the road, mingled with the sound of light wheels.

Two varieties only of humanity could have entered the paddock with the ghostlike glide of that mysterious figure. They were a woman and a gipsy man. A woman was out of the question in such an occupation at this hour, and the comer could be no less than a thief, who might probably have known the weakness of the household on this particular night, and have chosen it on that account for his daring attempt. Moreover, to raise suspicion to conviction itself, there were gipsies in Weatherbury Bottom.

Maryann, who had been afraid to shout in the robber's presence, having seen him depart had no fear. She hastily slipped on her clothes, stumped down the disjointed staircase with its hundred creaks, ran to Coggan's, the nearest house, and raised an alarm. Coggan called Gabriel, who now again lodged in his house as at first, and together they went to the paddock. Beyond all doubt the horse was gone.

"Hark!" said Gabriel.

They listened. Distinct upon the stagnant air came the sounds of a trotting horse passing up Longpuddle Lane—just beyond the gipsies' encampment in Weatherbury Bottom.

"That's our Dainty—I'll swear to her step," said Jan.

"Mighty me! Won't mis'ess storm and call us stupids when she comes back!" moaned Maryann. "How I wish it had happened when she was at home, and none of us had been answerable!"

"We must ride after," said Gabriel, decisively. "I'll be responsible to Miss Everdene for what we do. Yes, we'll follow."

"Faith, I don't see how," said Coggan. "All our horses are too heavy for that trick except little Poppet, and what's she between two of us?—If we only had that pair over the hedge we might do something."

"Which pair?"

"Mr. Boldwood's Tidy and Moll."

"Then wait here till I come hither again," said Gabriel. He ran down the hill towards Farmer Boldwood's.

"Farmer Boldwood is not at home," said Maryann.

"All the better," said Coggan. "I know what he's gone for."

Less than five minutes brought up Oak again, running at the same pace, with two halters dangling from his hand.

"Where did you find 'em?" said Coggan, turning round and leaping upon the hedge without waiting for an answer.

"Under the eaves. I knew where they were kept," said Gabriel, following him. "Coggan, you can ride bare-backed? there's no time to look for saddles."

"Like a hero!" said Jan.

"Maryann, you go to bed," Gabriel shouted to her from the top of the hedge.

Springing down into Boldwood's pastures, each pocketed his halter to hide it from the horses, who, seeing the men empty-handed, docilely allowed themselves to be seized by the mane, when the halters were dexterously slipped on. Having neither bit nor bridle, Oak and Coggan extemporized the former by passing the rope in each case through the animal's mouth and looping it on the other side. Oak vaulted astride, and Coggan clambered up by aid of the bank, when they ascended to the gate and galloped off in the direction taken by Bathsheba's horse and the robber. Whose vehicle the horse had been harnessed to was a matter of some uncertainty.

Weatherbury Bottom was reached in three or four minutes. They scanned the shady green patch by the roadside. The gipsies were gone.

"The villains!" said Gabriel. "Which way have they gone, I wonder?"

"Straight on, as sure as God made little apples," said Jan.

"Very well; we are better mounted, and must overtake em", said Oak. "Now on at full speed!"

No sound of the rider in their van could now be discovered. The road-metal grew softer and more clayey as Weatherbury was left behind, and the late rain had wetted its surface to a somewhat plastic, but not muddy state. They came to cross-roads. Coggan suddenly pulled up Moll and slipped off.

"What's the matter?" said Gabriel.

"We must try to track 'em, since we can't hear 'em," said Jan, fumbling in his pockets. He struck a light, and held the match to the ground. The rain had been heavier here, and all foot and horse tracks made previous to the storm had been abraded and blurred by the drops, and they were now so many little scoops of water, which reflected the flame of the match like eyes. One set of tracks was fresh and had no water in them; one pair of ruts was also empty, and not small canals, like the others. The footprints forming this recent impression were full of information as to pace; they were in equidistant pairs, three or four feet apart, the right and left foot of each pair being exactly opposite one another.

"Straight on!" Jan exclaimed. "Tracks like that mean a stiff gallop. No wonder we don't hear him. And the horse is harnessed—look at the ruts. Ay, that's our mare sure enough!"

"How do you know?"

"Old Jimmy Harris only shoed her last week, and I'd swear to his make among ten thousand."

"The rest of the gipsies must ha' gone on earlier, or some other way," said Oak. "You saw there were no other tracks?"

"True." They rode along silently for a long weary time. Coggan carried an old pinchbeck repeater which he had inherited from some genius in his family; and it now struck one. He lighted another match, and examined the ground again.

"'Tis a canter now," he said, throwing away the light. "A twisty, rickety pace for a gig. The fact is, they over-drove her at starting; we shall catch 'em yet."

Again they hastened on, and entered Blackmore Vale. Coggan's watch struck one. When they looked again the hoof-marks were so spaced as to form a sort of zigzag if united, like the lamps along a street.

"That's a trot, I know," said Gabriel.

"Only a trot now," said Coggan, cheerfully. "We shall overtake him in time."

They pushed rapidly on for yet two or three miles. "Ah! a moment," said Jan. "Let's see how she was driven up this hill. 'Twill help us." A light was promptly struck upon his gaiters as before, and the examination made.

"Hurrah!" said Coggan. "She walked up here—and well she might. We shall get them in two miles, for a crown."

They rode three, and listened. No sound was to be heard save a millpond trickling hoarsely through a hatch, and suggesting gloomy possibilities of drowning by jumping in. Gabriel dismounted when they came to a turning.

The tracks were absolutely the only guide as to the direction that they now had, and great caution was necessary to avoid confusing them with some others which had made their appearance lately.

"What does this mean?—though I guess," said Gabriel, looking up at Coggan as he moved the match over the ground about the turning. Coggan, who, no less than the panting horses, had latterly shown signs of weariness, again scrutinized the mystic characters. This time only three were of the regular horseshoe shape. Every fourth was a dot.

He screwed up his face and emitted a long "Whew-w-w!"

"Lame," said Oak.

"Yes. Dainty is lamed; the near-foot-afore," said Coggan slowly, staring still at the footprints.

"We'll push on," said Gabriel, remounting his humid steed.

Although the road along its greater part had been as good as any turnpike-road in the country, it was nominally only a byway. The last turning had brought them into the high road leading to Bath. Coggan recollected himself.

"We shall have him now!" he exclaimed.

"Where?"

"Sherton Turnpike. The keeper of that gate is the sleepiest man between here and London—Dan Randall, that's his name—knowed en for years, when he was at Casterbridge gate. Between the lameness and the gate 'tis a done job."

They now advanced with extreme caution. Nothing was said until, against a shady background of foliage, five white bars were visible, crossing their route a little way ahead.

"Hush—we are almost close!" said Gabriel.

"Amble on upon the grass," said Coggan.

The white bars were blotted out in the midst by a dark shape in front of them. The silence of this lonely time was pierced by an exclamation from that quarter.

"Hoy-a-hoy! Gate!"

It appeared that there had been a previous call which they had not noticed, for on their close approach the door of the turnpike-house opened, and the keeper came out half-dressed, with a candle in his hand. The rays illumined the whole group.

"Keep the gate close!" shouted Gabriel. "He has stolen the horse!"

"Who?" said the turnpike-man.

Gabriel looked at the driver of the gig, and saw a woman—Bathsheba, his mistress.

On hearing his voice she had turned her face away from the light. Coggan had, however, caught sight of her in the meanwhile.

"Why, 'tis mistress—I'll take my oath!" he said, amazed.

Bathsheba it certainly was, and she had by this time done the trick she could do so well in crises not of love, namely, mask a surprise by coolness of manner.

"Well, Gabriel," she inquired quietly, "where are you going?"

"We thought—" began Gabriel.

"I am driving to Bath," she said, taking for her own use the assurance that Gabriel lacked. "An important matter made it necessary for me to give up my visit to Liddy, and go off at once. What, then, were you following me?"

"We thought the horse was stole."

"Well—what a thing! How very foolish of you not to know that I had taken the trap and horse. I could neither wake Maryann nor get into the house, though I hammered for ten minutes against her window-sill. Fortunately, I could get the key of the coach-house, so I troubled no one further. Didn't you think it might be me?"

Analysis: Mystery is generated in the way Bathsheba behaves here. A horse disappears in the night. Gabriel, ever the careful caretaker – or spy – finds out that it's Bathsheba. However, no one, not even the reader, knows what she is up to.

Discussion point: Why does Hardy not reveal what Bathsheba is up to here?

"Why should we, miss?"

"Perhaps not. Why, those are never Farmer Boldwood's horses! Goodness mercy! what have you been doing—bringing trouble upon me in this way? What! mustn't a lady move an inch from her door without being dogged like a thief?"

"But how was we to know, if you left no account of your doings?" expostulated Coggan, "and ladies don't drive at these hours, miss, as a jineral rule of society."

"I did leave an account—and you would have seen it in the morning. I wrote in chalk on the coach-house doors that I had come back for the horse and gig, and driven off; that I could arouse nobody, and should return soon."

"But you'll consider, ma'am, that we couldn't see that till it got daylight."

"True," she said, and though vexed at first she had too much sense to blame them long or seriously for a devotion to her that was as valuable as it was rare. She added with a very pretty grace, "Well, I really thank you heartily for taking all this trouble; but I wish you had borrowed anybody's horses but Mr. Boldwood's."

"Dainty is lame, miss," said Coggan. "Can ye go on?"

"It was only a stone in her shoe. I got down and pulled it out a hundred yards back. I can manage very well, thank you. I shall be in Bath by daylight. Will you now return, please?"

She turned her head—the gateman's candle shimmering upon her quick, clear eyes as she did so—passed through the gate, and was soon wrapped in the embowering shades of mysterious summer boughs. Coggan and Gabriel put about their horses, and, fanned by the velvety air of this July night, retraced the road by which they had come.

"A strange vagary, this of hers, isn't it, Oak?" said Coggan, curiously.

"Yes," said Gabriel, shortly.

"She won't be in Bath by no daylight!"

"Coggan, suppose we keep this night's work as quiet as we can?"

"I am of one and the same mind."

"Very well. We shall be home by three o'clock or so, and can creep into the parish like lambs."

Bathsheba's perturbed meditations by the roadside had ultimately evolved a conclusion that there were only two remedies for the present desperate state of affairs. The first was merely to keep Troy away from Weatherbury till Boldwood's indignation had cooled; the second to listen to Oak's entreaties, and Boldwood's denunciations, and give up Troy altogether.

Alas! Could she give up this new love—induce him to renounce her by saying she did not like him—could no more speak to him, and beg him, for her good, to end his furlough in Bath, and see her and Weatherbury no more?

It was a picture full of misery, but for a while she contemplated it firmly, allowing herself, nevertheless, as girls will, to dwell upon the happy life she would have enjoyed had Troy been Boldwood, and the path of love the path of duty—inflicting upon herself gratuitous tortures by imagining him the lover of another woman after forgetting her; for she had penetrated Troy's nature so far as to estimate his tendencies pretty accurately, but unfortunately loved him no less in thinking that he might soon cease to love her—indeed, considerably more.

She jumped to her feet. She would see him at once. Yes, she would implore him by word of mouth to assist her in this dilemma. A letter to keep him away could not reach him in time, even if he should be disposed to listen to it.

Was Bathsheba altogether blind to the obvious fact that the support of a lover's arms is not of a kind best calculated to assist a resolve to renounce him? Or was she sophistically sensible, with a thrill of pleasure, that by adopting this course for getting rid of him she was ensuring a meeting with him, at any rate, once more?

It was now dark, and the hour must have been nearly ten. The only way to accomplish her purpose was to give up her idea of visiting Liddy at Yalbury, return to Weatherbury Farm, put the horse into the gig, and drive at once to Bath. The scheme seemed at first impossible: the journey was a fearfully heavy one, even for a strong horse, at her own estimate; and she much underrated the distance. It was most venturesome for a woman, at night, and alone.

But could she go on to Liddy's and leave things to take their course? No, no; anything but that. Bathsheba was full of a stimulating turbulence, beside which caution vainly prayed for a hearing. She turned back towards the village.

Her walk was slow, for she wished not to enter Weatherbury till the cottagers were in bed, and, particularly, till Boldwood was secure. Her plan was now to drive to Bath during the night, see Sergeant Troy in the morning before he set out to come to her, bid him farewell, and dismiss him: then to rest the horse thoroughly (herself to weep the while, she thought), starting early the next morning on her return journey. By this arrangement she could trot Dainty gently all the day, reach Liddy at Yalbury in the evening, and come home to Weatherbury with her whenever they chose—so nobody would know she had been to Bath at all. Such was Bathsheba's scheme. But in her topographical ignorance as a late comer to the place, she misreckoned the distance of her journey as not much more than half what it really was.

This idea she proceeded to carry out, with what initial success we have already seen.

Analysis: Here we find out the truth: Bathsheba's obsession for Troy must find an outlet. We find her behaving like Boldwood and Oak. Now she starts stalking her prey. She is determined to have Troy whatever the cost.

Discussion point: Why is Bathsheba obsessed by Troy?

Questions

What does Maryann see?

What do Gabriel and Coggan do?

What do they discover at Sherton turnpike?

GCSE style question: how does Hardy create tension and excitement in this chapter?

A Level style question: compare and contrast the scene where Oak catches Bathsheba with another scene where someone is caught doing something which they don't want other people to know about.

Creative response: write a poem/story called 'The Thief'; or write Oak's diary for this scene.

CHAPTER XXXIII
IN THE SUN—A HARBINGER

A week passed, and there were no tidings of Bathsheba; nor was there any explanation of her Gilpin's rig.

Then a note came for Maryann, stating that the business which had called her mistress to Bath still detained her there; but that she hoped to return in the course of another week.

Another week passed. The oat-harvest began, and all the men were a-field under a monochromatic Lammas sky, amid the trembling air and short shadows of noon. Indoors nothing was to be heard save the droning of blue-bottle flies; out-of-doors the whetting of scythes and the hiss of tressy oat-ears rubbing together as their perpendicular stalks of amber-yellow fell heavily to each swath. Every drop of moisture not in the men's bottles and flagons in the form of cider was raining as perspiration from their foreheads and cheeks. Drought was everywhere else.

They were about to withdraw for a while into the charitable shade of a tree in the fence, when Coggan saw a figure in a blue coat and brass buttons running to them across the field.

"I wonder who that is?" he said.

"I hope nothing is wrong about mistress," said Maryann, who with some other women was tying the bundles (oats being always sheafed on this farm), "but an unlucky token came to me indoors this morning. I went to unlock the door and dropped the key, and it fell upon the stone floor and broke into two pieces. Breaking a key is a dreadful bodement. I wish mis'ess was home."

"'Tis Cain Ball," said Gabriel, pausing from whetting his reaphook.

Oak was not bound by his agreement to assist in the corn-field; but the harvest month is an anxious time for a farmer, and the corn was Bathsheba's, so he lent a hand.

"He's dressed up in his best clothes," said Matthew Moon. "He hev been away from home for a few days, since he's had that felon upon his finger; for 'a said, since I can't work I'll have a hollerday."

"A good time for one—a' excellent time," said Joseph Poorgrass, straightening his back; for he, like some of the others, had a way of resting a while from his labour on such hot days for reasons preternaturally small; of which Cain Ball's advent on a week-day in his Sunday-clothes was one of the first magnitude. "Twas a bad leg allowed me to read the Pilgrim's Progress, and Mark Clark learnt All-Fours in a whitlow."

"Ay, and my father put his arm out of joint to have time to go courting," said Jan Coggan, in an eclipsing tone, wiping his face with his shirt-sleeve and thrusting back his hat upon the nape of his neck.

By this time Cainy was nearing the group of harvesters, and was perceived to be carrying a large slice of bread and ham in one hand, from which he took mouthfuls as he ran, the other being wrapped in a bandage. When he came close, his mouth assumed the bell shape, and he began to cough violently.

"Now, Cainy!" said Gabriel, sternly. "How many more times must I tell you to keep from running so fast when you be eating? You'll choke yourself some day, that's what you'll do, Cain Ball."

"Hok-hok-hok!" replied Cain. "A crumb of my victuals went the wrong way—hok-hok! That's what 'tis, Mister Oak! And I've been visiting to Bath because I had a felon on my thumb; yes, and I've seen—ahok-hok!"

Directly Cain mentioned Bath, they all threw down their hooks and forks and drew round him. Unfortunately the erratic crumb did not improve his narrative powers, and a supplementary hindrance was that of a sneeze, jerking from his pocket his rather large watch, which dangled in front of the young man pendulum-wise.

"Yes," he continued, directing his thoughts to Bath and letting his eyes follow, "I've seed the world at last—yes—and I've seed our mis'ess—ahok-hok-hok!"

"Bother the boy!" said Gabriel. "Something is always going the wrong way down your throat, so that you can't tell what's necessary to be told."

"Ahok! there! Please, Mister Oak, a gnat have just fleed into my stomach and brought the cough on again!"

"Yes, that's just it. Your mouth is always open, you young rascal!"

"'Tis terrible bad to have a gnat fly down yer throat, pore boy!" said Matthew Moon.

"Well, at Bath you saw—" prompted Gabriel.

"I saw our mistress," continued the junior shepherd, "and a sojer, walking along. And bymeby they got closer and closer, and then they went arm-in-crook, like courting complete—hok-hok! like courting complete—hok!—courting complete—" Losing the thread of his narrative at this point simultaneously with his loss of breath, their informant looked up and down the field apparently for some clue to it. "Well, I see our mis'ess and a soldier—a-ha-a-wk!"

"Damn the boy!" said Gabriel.

"'Tis only my manner, Mister Oak, if ye'll excuse it," said Cain Ball, looking reproachfully at Oak, with eyes drenched in their own dew.

"Here's some cider for him—that'll cure his throat," said Jan Coggan, lifting a flagon of cider, pulling out the cork, and applying the hole to Cainy's mouth; Joseph Poorgrass in the meantime beginning to think apprehensively of the serious consequences that would follow Cain Ball's strangulation in his cough, and the history of his Bath adventures dying with him.

"For my poor self, I always say 'please God' afore I do anything," said Joseph, in an unboastful voice; "and so should you, Cain Ball. 'Tis a great safeguard, and might perhaps save you from being choked to death some day."

Mr. Coggan poured the liquor with unstinted liberality at the suffering Cain's circular mouth; half of it running down the side of the flagon, and half of what reached his mouth running down outside his throat, and half of what ran in going the wrong way, and being coughed and sneezed around the persons of the gathered reapers in the form of a cider fog, which for a moment hung in the sunny air like a small exhalation.

"There's a great clumsy sneeze! Why can't ye have better manners, you young dog!" said Coggan, withdrawing the flagon.

"The cider went up my nose!" cried Cainy, as soon as he could speak; "and now 'tis gone down my neck, and into my poor dumb felon, and over my shiny buttons and all my best cloze!"

"The poor lad's cough is terrible unfortunate," said Matthew Moon. "And a great history on hand, too. Bump his back, shepherd."

"'Tis my nater," mourned Cain. "Mother says I always was so excitable when my feelings were worked up to a point!"

"True, true," said Joseph Poorgrass. "The Balls were always a very excitable family. I knowed the boy's grandfather—a truly nervous and modest man, even to genteel refinery. 'Twas blush, blush with him, almost as much as 'tis with me—not but that 'tis a fault in me!"

"Not at all, Master Poorgrass," said Coggan. "'Tis a very noble quality in ye."

"Heh-heh! well, I wish to noise nothing abroad—nothing at all," murmured Poorgrass, diffidently. "But we be born to things—that's true. Yet I would rather my trifle were hid; though, perhaps, a high nater is a little high, and at my birth all things were possible to my Maker, and he may have begrudged no gifts... But under your bushel, Joseph! under your bushel with 'ee! A strange desire, neighbours, this desire to hide, and no praise due. Yet there is a Sermon on the Mount with a calendar of the blessed at the head, and certain meek men may be named therein."

"Cainy's grandfather was a very clever man," said Matthew Moon. "Invented a' apple-tree out of his own head, which is called by his name to this day—the Early Ball. You know 'em, Jan? A Quarrenden grafted on a Tom Putt, and a Rathe-ripe upon top o' that again. 'Tis trew 'a used to bide about in a public-house wi' a 'ooman in a way he had no business to by rights, but there—'a were a clever man in the sense of the term."

"Now then," said Gabriel, impatiently, "what did you see, Cain?"

"I seed our mis'ess go into a sort of a park place, where there's seats, and shrubs and flowers, arm-in-crook with a sojer," continued Cainy, firmly, and with a dim sense that his words were very effective as regarded Gabriel's emotions. "And I think the sojer was Sergeant Troy. And they sat there together for more than half-an-hour, talking moving things, and she once was crying a'most to death. And when they came out her eyes were shining and she was as white as a lily; and they looked into one another's faces, as far-gone friendly as a man and woman can be."

Gabriel's features seemed to get thinner. "Well, what did you see besides?"

"Oh, all sorts."

"White as a lily? You are sure 'twas she?"

"Yes."

"Well, what besides?"

"Great glass windows to the shops, and great clouds in the sky, full of rain, and old wooden trees in the country round."

"You stun-poll! What will ye say next?" said Coggan.

"Let en alone," interposed Joseph Poorgrass. "The boy's meaning is that the sky and the earth in the kingdom of Bath is not altogether different from ours here. 'Tis for our good to gain knowledge of strange cities, and as such the boy's words should be suffered, so to speak it."

"And the people of Bath," continued Cain, "never need to light their fires except as a luxury, for the water springs up out of the earth ready boiled for use."

"'Tis true as the light," testified Matthew Moon. "I've heard other navigators say the same thing."

"They drink nothing else there," said Cain, "and seem to enjoy it, to see how they swaller it down."

"Well, it seems a barbarian practice enough to us, but I daresay the natives think nothing o' it," said Matthew.

"And don't victuals spring up as well as drink?" asked Coggan, twirling his eye.

"No—I own to a blot there in Bath—a true blot. God didn't provide 'em with victuals as well as drink, and 'twas a drawback I couldn't get over at all."

"Well, 'tis a curious place, to say the least," observed Moon; "and it must be a curious people that live therein."

"Miss Everdene and the soldier were walking about together, you say?" said Gabriel, returning to the group.

"Ay, and she wore a beautiful gold-colour silk gown, trimmed with black lace, that would have stood alone 'ithout legs inside if required. 'Twas a very winsome sight; and her hair was brushed splendid. And when the sun shone upon the bright gown and his red coat—my! how handsome they looked. You could see 'em all the length of the street."

"And what then?" murmured Gabriel.

"And then I went into Griffin's to hae my boots hobbed, and then I went to Riggs's batty-cake shop, and asked 'em for a penneth of the cheapest and nicest stales, that were all but blue-mouldy, but not quite. And whilst I was chawing 'em down I walked on and seed a clock with a face as big as a baking trendle—"

"But that's nothing to do with mistress!"

"I'm coming to that, if you'll leave me alone, Mister Oak!" remonstrated Cainy. "If you excites me, perhaps you'll bring on my cough, and then I shan't be able to tell ye nothing."

"Yes—let him tell it his own way," said Coggan.

Gabriel settled into a despairing attitude of patience, and Cainy went on:—

"And there were great large houses, and more people all the week long than at Weatherbury club-walking on White Tuesdays. And I went to grand churches and chapels. And how the parson would pray! Yes; he would kneel down and put up his hands together, and make the holy gold rings on his fingers gleam and twinkle in yer eyes, that he'd earned by praying so excellent well!—Ah yes, I wish I lived there."

"Our poor Parson Thirdly can't get no money to buy such rings," said Matthew Moon, thoughtfully. "And as good a man as ever walked. I don't believe poor Thirdly have a single one, even of humblest tin or copper. Such a great ornament as they'd be to him on a dull afternoon, when he's up in the pulpit lighted by the wax candles! But 'tis impossible, poor man. Ah, to think how unequal things be."

"Perhaps he's made of different stuff than to wear 'em," said Gabriel, grimly. "Well, that's enough of this. Go on, Cainy—quick."

"Oh—and the new style of parsons wear moustaches and long beards," continued the illustrious traveller, "and look like Moses and Aaron complete, and make we fokes in the congregation feel all over like the children of Israel."

"A very right feeling—very," said Joseph Poorgrass.

"And there's two religions going on in the nation now—High Church and

High Chapel. And, thinks I, I'll play fair; so I went to High Church in the morning, and High Chapel in the afternoon."

"A right and proper boy," said Joseph Poorgrass.

"Well, at High Church they pray singing, and worship all the colours of the rainbow; and at High Chapel they pray preaching, and worship drab and whitewash only. And then—I didn't see no more of Miss Everdene at all."

"Why didn't you say so afore, then?" exclaimed Oak, with much disappointment.

"Ah," said Matthew Moon, "she'll wish her cake dough if so be she's over intimate with that man."

"She's not over intimate with him," said Gabriel, indignantly.

"She would know better," said Coggan. "Our mis'ess has too much sense under they knots of black hair to do such a mad thing."

"You see, he's not a coarse, ignorant man, for he was well brought up," said Matthew, dubiously. "'Twas only wildness that made him a soldier, and maids rather like your man of sin."

"Now, Cain Ball," said Gabriel restlessly, "can you swear in the most awful form that the woman you saw was Miss Everdene?"

"Cain Ball, you be no longer a babe and suckling," said Joseph in the sepulchral tone the circumstances demanded, "and you know what taking an oath is. 'Tis a horrible testament mind ye, which you say and seal with your blood-stone, and the prophet Matthew tells us that on whomsoever it shall fall it will grind him to powder. Now, before all the work-folk here assembled, can you swear to your words as the shepherd asks ye?"

"Please no, Mister Oak!" said Cainy, looking from one to the other with great uneasiness at the spiritual magnitude of the position. "I don't mind saying 'tis true, but I don't like to say 'tis damn true, if that's what you mane."

"Cain, Cain, how can you!" asked Joseph sternly. "You be asked to swear in a holy manner, and you swear like wicked Shimei, the son of Gera, who cursed as he came. Young man, fie!"

"No, I don't! 'Tis you want to squander a pore boy's soul, Joseph Poorgrass—that's what 'tis!" said Cain, beginning to cry. "All I mane is that in common truth 'twas Miss Everdene and Sergeant Troy, but in the horrible so-help-me truth that ye want to make of it perhaps 'twas somebody else!"

"There's no getting at the rights of it," said Gabriel, turning to his work.

"Cain Ball, you'll come to a bit of bread!" groaned Joseph Poorgrass.

Then the reapers' hooks were flourished again, and the old sounds went on. Gabriel, without making any pretence of being lively, did nothing to show that he was particularly dull. However, Coggan knew pretty nearly how the land lay, and when they were in a nook together he said—

"Don't take on about her, Gabriel. What difference does it make whose sweetheart she is, since she can't be yours?"

"That's the very thing I say to myself," said Gabriel.

Questions

What does the letter to Maryann from Bathsheba say?

What are the workers doing?

Who is supervising the farm effectively?

What news does Cainy Ball bring?

GCSE style question: how does Hardy create humour and suspense with Cainy Ball's news?

Creative response: write Cainy Ball's diary for this chapter.

CHAPTER XXXIV
HOME AGAIN—A TRICKSTER

That same evening at dusk Gabriel was leaning over Coggan's garden-gate, taking an up-and-down survey before retiring to rest.

A vehicle of some kind was softly creeping along the grassy margin of the lane. From it spread the tones of two women talking. The tones were natural and not at all suppressed. Oak instantly knew the voices to be those of Bathsheba and Liddy.

The carriage came opposite and passed by. It was Miss Everdene's gig, and Liddy and her mistress were the only occupants of the seat. Liddy was asking questions about the city of Bath, and her companion was answering them listlessly and unconcernedly. Both Bathsheba and the horse seemed weary.

The exquisite relief of finding that she was here again, safe and sound, overpowered all reflection, and Oak could only luxuriate in the sense of it. All grave reports were forgotten.

He lingered and lingered on, till there was no difference between the eastern and western expanses of sky, and the timid hares began to limp courageously round the dim hillocks. Gabriel might have been there an additional half-hour when a dark form walked slowly by. "Good-night, Gabriel," the passer said.

It was Boldwood. "Good-night, sir," said Gabriel.

Boldwood likewise vanished up the road, and Oak shortly afterwards turned indoors to bed.

Farmer Boldwood went on towards Miss Everdene's house. He reached the front, and approaching the entrance, saw a light in the parlour. The blind was not drawn down, and inside the room was Bathsheba, looking over some papers or letters. Her back was towards Boldwood. He went to the door, knocked, and waited with tense muscles and an aching brow.

Boldwood had not been outside his garden since his meeting with Bathsheba in the road to Yalbury. Silent and alone, he had remained in moody meditation on woman's ways, deeming as essentials of the whole sex the accidents of the single one of their number he had ever closely beheld. By degrees a more charitable temper had pervaded him, and this was the reason of his sally to-night. He had come to apologize and beg forgiveness of Bathsheba with something like a sense of shame at his violence, having but just now learnt that she had returned—only from a visit to Liddy, as he supposed, the Bath escapade being quite unknown to him.

He inquired for Miss Everdene. Liddy's manner was odd, but he did not notice it. She went in, leaving him standing there, and in her absence the blind of the room containing Bathsheba was pulled down. Boldwood augured ill from that sign. Liddy came out.

"My mistress cannot see you, sir," she said.

The farmer instantly went out by the gate. He was unforgiven—that was the issue of it all. He had seen her who was to him simultaneously a delight and a torture, sitting in the room he had shared with her as a peculiarly privileged guest only a little earlier in the summer, and she had denied him an entrance there now.

Boldwood did not hurry homeward. It was ten o'clock at least, when, walking deliberately through the lower part of Weatherbury, he heard the carrier's spring van entering the village. The van ran to and from a town in a northern direction, and it was owned and driven by a Weatherbury man, at the door of whose house it now pulled up. The lamp fixed to the head of the hood illuminated a scarlet and gilded form, who was the first to alight.

"Ah!" said Boldwood to himself, "come to see her again."

Troy entered the carrier's house, which had been the place of his lodging on his last visit to his native place. Boldwood was moved by a sudden determination. He hastened home. In ten minutes he was back again, and made as if he were going to call upon Troy at the carrier's. But as he approached, some one opened the door and came out. He heard this person say "Good-night" to the inmates, and the voice was Troy's. This was strange, coming so immediately after his arrival. Boldwood, however, hastened up to him. Troy had what appeared to be a carpet-bag in his hand—the same that he had brought with him. It seemed as if he were going to leave again this very night.

Troy turned up the hill and quickened his pace. Boldwood stepped forward.

"Sergeant Troy?"

"Yes—I'm Sergeant Troy."

"Just arrived from up the country, I think?"

"Just arrived from Bath."

"I am William Boldwood."

"Indeed."

The tone in which this word was uttered was all that had been wanted to bring Boldwood to the point.

"I wish to speak a word with you," he said.

"What about?"

"About her who lives just ahead there—and about a woman you have wronged."

"I wonder at your impertinence," said Troy, moving on.

"Now look here," said Boldwood, standing in front of him, "wonder or not, you are going to hold a conversation with me."

Troy heard the dull determination in Boldwood's voice, looked at his stalwart frame, then at the thick cudgel he carried in his hand. He remembered it was past ten o'clock. It seemed worth while to be civil to Boldwood.

"Very well, I'll listen with pleasure," said Troy, placing his bag on the ground, "only speak low, for somebody or other may overhear us in the farmhouse there."

"Well then—I know a good deal concerning your Fanny Robin's attachment to you. I may say, too, that I believe I am the only person in the village, excepting Gabriel Oak, who does know it. You ought to marry her."

"I suppose I ought. Indeed, I wish to, but I cannot."

"Why?"

Troy was about to utter something hastily; he then checked himself and said, "I am too poor." His voice was changed. Previously it had had a devil-may-care tone. It was the voice of a trickster now.

Boldwood's present mood was not critical enough to notice tones. He continued, "I may as well speak plainly; and understand, I don't wish to enter into the questions of right or wrong, woman's honour and shame, or to express any opinion on your conduct. I intend a business transaction with you."

"I see," said Troy. "Suppose we sit down here."

An old tree trunk lay under the hedge immediately opposite, and they sat down.

"I was engaged to be married to Miss Everdene," said Boldwood, "but you came and—"

"Not engaged," said Troy.

"As good as engaged."

"If I had not turned up she might have become engaged to you."

"Hang might!"

"Would, then."

"If you had not come I should certainly—yes, certainly—have been accepted by this time. If you had not seen her you might have been married to Fanny. Well, there's too much difference between Miss Everdene's station and your own for this flirtation with her ever to benefit you by ending in marriage. So all I ask is, don't molest her any more. Marry Fanny. I'll make it worth your while."

"How will you?"

"I'll pay you well now, I'll settle a sum of money upon her, and I'll see that you don't suffer from poverty in the future. I'll put it clearly. Bathsheba is only playing with you: you are too poor for her as I said; so give up wasting your time about a great match you'll never make for a moderate and rightful match you may make to-morrow; take up your carpet-bag, turn about, leave Weatherbury now, this night, and you shall take fifty pounds with you. Fanny shall have fifty to enable her to prepare for the wedding, when you have told me where she is living, and she shall have five hundred paid down on her wedding-day."

In making this statement Boldwood's voice revealed only too clearly a consciousness of the weakness of his position, his aims, and his method. His manner had lapsed quite from that of the firm and dignified Boldwood of former times; and such a scheme as he had now engaged in he would have condemned as childishly imbecile only a few months ago. We discern a grand force in the lover which he lacks whilst a free man; but there is a breadth of vision in the free man which in the lover we vainly seek. Where there is much bias there must be some narrowness, and love, though added emotion, is subtracted capacity. Boldwood exemplified this to an abnormal degree: he knew nothing of Fanny Robin's circumstances or whereabouts, he knew nothing of Troy's possibilities, yet that was what he said.

"I like Fanny best," said Troy; "and if, as you say, Miss Everdene is out of my reach, why I have all to gain by accepting your money, and marrying Fan. But she's only a servant."

"Never mind—do you agree to my arrangement?"

"I do."

"Ah!" said Boldwood, in a more elastic voice. "Oh, Troy, if you like her best, why then did you step in here and injure my happiness?"

"I love Fanny best now," said Troy. "But Bathsh—Miss Everdene inflamed me, and displaced Fanny for a time. It is over now."

Analysis: The conversation between Boldwood and Troy is a classic set-piece. Finally, the two suitors for Bathsheba confront each other. Like a master storyteller, Troy keeps Boldwood guessing, goading him to new heights of folly. However, in his playing and toying with Troy, he reveals some essential truth: he likes Fanny best but went with Bathsheba because she inflamed him. He says something similar when Bathsheba opens Fanny's coffin and sees their child.

Discussion point: Why does Troy anger Boldwood so much? How does Hardy generate extra tension in this scene?

"Why should it be over so soon? And why then did you come here again?"

"There are weighty reasons. Fifty pounds at once, you said!"

"I did," said Boldwood, "and here they are—fifty sovereigns." He handed Troy a small packet.

"You have everything ready—it seems that you calculated on my accepting them," said the sergeant, taking the packet.

"I thought you might accept them," said Boldwood.

"You've only my word that the programme shall be adhered to, whilst I at any rate have fifty pounds."

"I had thought of that, and I have considered that if I can't appeal to your honour I can trust to your—well, shrewdness we'll call it—not to lose five hundred pounds in prospect, and also make a bitter enemy of a man who is willing to be an extremely useful friend."

"Stop, listen!" said Troy in a whisper.

A light pit-pat was audible upon the road just above them.

"By George—'tis she," he continued. "I must go on and meet her."

"She—who?"

"Bathsheba."

"Bathsheba—out alone at this time o' night!" said Boldwood in amazement, and starting up. "Why must you meet her?"

"She was expecting me to-night—and I must now speak to her, and wish her good-bye, according to your wish."

"I don't see the necessity of speaking."

"It can do no harm—and she'll be wandering about looking for me if I don't. You shall hear all I say to her. It will help you in your love-making when I am gone."

"Your tone is mocking."

"Oh no. And remember this, if she does not know what has become of me, she will think more about me than if I tell her flatly I have come to give her up."

"Will you confine your words to that one point?—Shall I hear every word you say?"

"Every word. Now sit still there, and hold my carpet bag for me, and mark what you hear."

The light footstep came closer, halting occasionally, as if the walker listened for a sound. Troy whistled a double note in a soft, fluty tone.

"Come to that, is it!" murmured Boldwood, uneasily.

"You promised silence," said Troy.

"I promise again."

Troy stepped forward.

"Frank, dearest, is that you?" The tones were Bathsheba's.

"O God!" said Boldwood.

"Yes," said Troy to her.

"How late you are," she continued, tenderly. "Did you come by the carrier? I listened and heard his wheels entering the village, but it was some time ago, and I had almost given you up, Frank."

"I was sure to come," said Frank. "You knew I should, did you not?"

"Well, I thought you would," she said, playfully; "and, Frank, it is so lucky! There's not a soul in my house but me to-night. I've packed them all off so nobody on earth will know of your visit to your lady's bower. Liddy wanted to go to her grandfather's to tell him about her holiday, and I said she might stay with them till to-morrow—when you'll be gone again."

"Capital," said Troy. "But, dear me, I had better go back for my bag, because my slippers and brush and comb are in it; you run home whilst I fetch it, and I'll promise to be in your parlour in ten minutes."

"Yes." She turned and tripped up the hill again.

During the progress of this dialogue there was a nervous twitching of Boldwood's tightly closed lips, and his face became bathed in a clammy dew. He now started forward towards Troy. Troy turned to him and took up the bag.

"Shall I tell her I have come to give her up and cannot marry her?" said the soldier, mockingly.

"No, no; wait a minute. I want to say more to you—more to you!" said Boldwood, in a hoarse whisper.

"Now," said Troy, "you see my dilemma. Perhaps I am a bad man—the victim of my impulses—led away to do what I ought to leave undone. I can't, however, marry them both. And I have two reasons for choosing Fanny. First, I like her best upon the whole, and second, you make it worth my while."

At the same instant Boldwood sprang upon him, and held him by the neck. Troy felt Boldwood's grasp slowly tightening. The move was absolutely unexpected.

"A moment," he gasped. "You are injuring her you love!"

"Well, what do you mean?" said the farmer.

"Give me breath," said Troy.

Boldwood loosened his hand, saying, "By Heaven, I've a mind to kill you!"

"And ruin her."

"Save her."

"Oh, how can she be saved now, unless I marry her?"

Boldwood groaned. He reluctantly released the soldier, and flung him back against the hedge. "Devil, you torture me!" said he.

Troy rebounded like a ball, and was about to make a dash at the farmer; but he checked himself, saying lightly—

"It is not worth while to measure my strength with you. Indeed it is a barbarous way of settling a quarrel. I shall shortly leave the army because of the same conviction. Now after that revelation of how the land lies with Bathsheba, 'twould be a mistake to kill me, would it not?"

"'Twould be a mistake to kill you," repeated Boldwood, mechanically, with a bowed head.

"Better kill yourself."

"Far better."

"I'm glad you see it."

Analysis: Here we see Boldwood's suicidal nature because he has learnt that Troy has slept with Bathsheba and believes that they have had pre-marital sex. The reader is in suspense too because we think that's what has happened. Bathsheba has been corrupted by Troy!

Discussion point: Why is Boldwood suicidal?

"Troy, make her your wife, and don't act upon what I arranged just now. The alternative is dreadful, but take Bathsheba; I give her up! She must love you indeed to sell soul and body to you so utterly as she has done. Wretched woman—deluded woman—you are, Bathsheba!"

"But about Fanny?"

"Bathsheba is a woman well to do," continued Boldwood, in nervous anxiety, and, Troy, she will make a good wife; and, indeed, she is worth your hastening on your marriage with her!"

"But she has a will—not to say a temper, and I shall be a mere slave to her. I could do anything with poor Fanny Robin."

"Troy," said Boldwood, imploringly, "I'll do anything for you, only don't desert her; pray don't desert her, Troy."

"Which, poor Fanny?"

"No; Bathsheba Everdene. Love her best! Love her tenderly! How shall I get you to see how advantageous it will be to you to secure her at once?"

"I don't wish to secure her in any new way."

Boldwood's arm moved spasmodically towards Troy's person again. He repressed the instinct, and his form drooped as with pain.

Troy went on—

"I shall soon purchase my discharge, and then—"

"But I wish you to hasten on this marriage! It will be better for you both. You love each other, and you must let me help you to do it."

"How?"

"Why, by settling the five hundred on Bathsheba instead of Fanny, to enable you to marry at once. No; she wouldn't have it of me. I'll pay it down to you on the wedding-day."

Troy paused in secret amazement at Boldwood's wild infatuation. He carelessly said, "And am I to have anything now?"

"Yes, if you wish to. But I have not much additional money with me. I did not expect this; but all I have is yours."

Boldwood, more like a somnambulist than a wakeful man, pulled out the large canvas bag he carried by way of a purse, and searched it.

"I have twenty-one pounds more with me," he said. "Two notes and a sovereign. But before I leave you I must have a paper signed—"

"Pay me the money, and we'll go straight to her parlour, and make any arrangement you please to secure my compliance with your wishes. But she must know nothing of this cash business."

"Nothing, nothing," said Boldwood, hastily. "Here is the sum, and if you'll come to my house we'll write out the agreement for the remainder, and the terms also."

"First we'll call upon her."

"But why? Come with me to-night, and go with me to-morrow to the surrogate's."

"But she must be consulted; at any rate informed."

"Very well; go on."

They went up the hill to Bathsheba's house. When they stood at the entrance, Troy said, "Wait here a moment." Opening the door, he glided inside, leaving the door ajar.

Boldwood waited. In two minutes a light appeared in the passage. Boldwood then saw that the chain had been fastened across the door. Troy appeared inside, carrying a bedroom candlestick.

"What, did you think I should break in?" said Boldwood, contemptuously.

"Oh, no, it is merely my humour to secure things. Will you read this a moment? I'll hold the light."

Troy handed a folded newspaper through the slit between door and doorpost, and put the candle close. "That's the paragraph," he said, placing his finger on a line.

Boldwood looked and read—

Marriages.

On the 17th inst., at St. Ambrose's Church, Bath, by the Rev. G. Mincing, B.A., Francis Troy, only son of the late Edward Troy, Esq., M.D., of Weatherbury, and sergeant with Dragoon Guards, to Bathsheba, only surviving daughter of the late Mr. John Everdene, of Casterbridge.

"This may be called Fort meeting Feeble, hey, Boldwood?" said Troy. A low gurgle of derisive laughter followed the words.

The paper fell from Boldwood's hands. Troy continued—

"Fifty pounds to marry Fanny. Good. Twenty-one pounds not to marry Fanny, but Bathsheba. Good. Finale: already Bathsheba's husband. Now, Boldwood, yours is the ridiculous fate which always attends interference between a man and his wife. And another word. Bad as I am, I am not such a villain as to make the marriage or misery of any woman a matter of huckster and sale. Fanny has long ago left me. I don't know where she is. I have searched everywhere. Another word yet. You say you love Bathsheba; yet on the merest apparent evidence you instantly believe in her dishonour. A fig for such love! Now that I've taught you a lesson, take your money back again."

"I will not; I will not!" said Boldwood, in a hiss.

"Anyhow I won't have it," said Troy, contemptuously. He wrapped the packet of gold in the notes, and threw the whole into the road.

Analysis: We have to revise our opinion of Troy when we realise that he has been tricking Boldwood all this time with his promises to marry Fanny and then Bathsheba. There is a horrible comedy here in the way Troy has played with Boldwood.

Discussion point: What do we think of Troy and Boldwood at this point?

Boldwood shook his clenched fist at him. "You juggler of Satan! You black hound! But I'll punish you yet; mark me, I'll punish you yet!"

Another peal of laughter. Troy then closed the door, and locked himself in.

Throughout the whole of that night Boldwood's dark form might have been seen walking about the hills and downs of Weatherbury like an unhappy Shade in the Mournful Fields by Acheron.

Questions

Who does Bathsheba refuse to see?

What does Boldwood confront Troy about in Weatherbury?

What does he offer Troy if he marries Fanny?

Why does Boldwood change his mind and try to bribe Troy to marry Bathsheba when he overhears Bathsheba and Troy talking?

What does Troy do?

What does Boldwood vow to do?

GCSE style question: how does Hardy make the conversation between Boldwood and Troy so suspenseful?

A Level style question: explore the representation of the trickster figure in literature in this text (Troy) and another of your choice.

Creative response: write a story/poem called 'The Trickster' or write Troy or Boldwood's diary for this scene.

CHAPTER XXXV
AT AN UPPER WINDOW

It was very early the next morning—a time of sun and dew. The confused beginnings of many birds' songs spread into the healthy air, and the wan blue of the heaven was here and there coated with thin webs of incorporeal cloud which were of no effect in obscuring day. All the lights in the scene were yellow as to colour, and all the shadows were attenuated as to form. The creeping plants about the old manor-house were bowed with rows of heavy water drops, which had upon objects behind them the effect of minute lenses of high magnifying power.

Just before the clock struck five Gabriel Oak and Coggan passed the village cross, and went on together to the fields. They were yet barely in view of their mistress's house, when Oak fancied he saw the opening of a casement in one of the upper windows. The two men were at this moment partially screened by an elder bush, now beginning to be enriched with black bunches of fruit, and they paused before emerging from its shade.

A handsome man leaned idly from the lattice. He looked east and then west, in the manner of one who makes a first morning survey. The man was Sergeant Troy. His red jacket was loosely thrown on, but not buttoned, and he had altogether the relaxed bearing of a soldier taking his ease.

Coggan spoke first, looking quietly at the window.

"She has married him!" he said.

Gabriel had previously beheld the sight, and he now stood with his back turned, making no reply.

"I fancied we should know something to-day," continued Coggan. "I heard wheels pass my door just after dark—you were out somewhere." He glanced round upon Gabriel. "Good heavens above us, Oak, how white your face is; you look like a corpse!"

"Do I?" said Oak, with a faint smile.

"Lean on the gate: I'll wait a bit."

"All right, all right."

They stood by the gate awhile, Gabriel listlessly staring at the ground. His mind sped into the future, and saw there enacted in years of leisure the scenes of repentance that would ensue from this work of haste. That they were married he had instantly decided. Why had it been so mysteriously managed? It had become known that she had had a fearful journey to Bath, owing to her miscalculating the distance: that the horse had broken down, and that she had been more than two days getting there. It was not Bathsheba's way to do things furtively. With all her faults, she was candour itself. Could she have been entrapped? The union was not only an unutterable grief to him: it amazed him, notwithstanding that he had passed the preceding week in a suspicion that such might be the issue of Troy's meeting her away from home. Her quiet return with Liddy had to some extent dispersed the dread. Just as that imperceptible motion which appears like stillness is infinitely divided in its properties from stillness itself, so had his hope undistinguishable from despair differed from despair indeed.

In a few minutes they moved on again towards the house. The sergeant still looked from the window.

"Morning, comrades!" he shouted, in a cheery voice, when they came up.

Coggan replied to the greeting. "Bain't ye going to answer the man?" he then said to Gabriel. "I'd say good morning—you needn't spend a hapenny of meaning upon it, and yet keep the man civil."

Gabriel soon decided too that, since the deed was done, to put the best face upon the matter would be the greatest kindness to her he loved.

"Good morning, Sergeant Troy," he returned, in a ghastly voice.

"A rambling, gloomy house this," said Troy, smiling.

"Why—they may not be married!" suggested Coggan. "Perhaps she's not there."

Gabriel shook his head. The soldier turned a little towards the east, and the sun kindled his scarlet coat to an orange glow.

"But it is a nice old house," responded Gabriel.

"Yes—I suppose so; but I feel like new wine in an old bottle here. My notion is that sash-windows should be put throughout, and these old wainscoted walls brightened up a bit; or the oak cleared quite away, and the walls papered."

"It would be a pity, I think."

"Well, no. A philosopher once said in my hearing that the old builders, who worked when art was a living thing, had no respect for the work of builders who went before them, but pulled down and altered as they thought fit; and why shouldn't we? 'Creation and preservation don't do well together,' says he, 'and a million of antiquarians can't invent a style.' My mind exactly. I am for making this place more modern, that we may be cheerful whilst we can."

The military man turned and surveyed the interior of the room, to assist his ideas of improvement in this direction. Gabriel and Coggan began to move on.

"Oh, Coggan," said Troy, as if inspired by a recollection "do you know if insanity has ever appeared in Mr. Boldwood's family?"

Jan reflected for a moment.

"I once heard that an uncle of his was queer in his head, but I don't know the rights o't," he said.

"It is of no importance," said Troy, lightly. "Well, I shall be down in the fields with you some time this week; but I have a few matters to attend to first. So good-day to you. We shall, of course, keep on just as friendly terms as usual. I'm not a proud man: nobody is ever able to say that of Sergeant Troy. However, what is must be, and here's half-a-crown to drink my health, men."

Troy threw the coin dexterously across the front plot and over the fence towards Gabriel, who shunned it in its fall, his face turning to an angry red. Coggan twirled his eye, edged forward, and caught the money in its ricochet upon the road.

"Very well—you keep it, Coggan," said Gabriel with disdain and almost fiercely. "As for me, I'll do without gifts from him!"

Analysis: Now that Troy is in charge of the farm we see just how out of touch he is with country ways, chucking coins at the work men as if they are hired labourers, not an organic part of the farm, as integral to it as the land and animals. In this sense, Troy represents the new type of landowner, one that believes in the power of money not loyalty. Notice how angry Oak is with him: Oak is, after all, the custodian in many ways of the ancient values of decency, fidelity and trust.

Discussion point: In what way does Troy not conform to the country ways?

"Don't show it too much," said Coggan, musingly. "For if he's married to her, mark my words, he'll buy his discharge and be our master here. Therefore 'tis well to say 'Friend' outwardly, though you say 'Troublehouse' within."

"Well—perhaps it is best to be silent; but I can't go further than that. I can't flatter, and if my place here is only to be kept by smoothing him down, my place must be lost."

A horseman, whom they had for some time seen in the distance, now appeared close beside them.

"There's Mr. Boldwood," said Oak. "I wonder what Troy meant by his question."

Coggan and Oak nodded respectfully to the farmer, just checked their paces to discover if they were wanted, and finding they were not stood back to let him pass on.

The only signs of the terrible sorrow Boldwood had been combating through the night, and was combating now, were the want of colour in his well-defined face, the enlarged appearance of the veins in his forehead and temples, and the sharper lines about his mouth. The horse bore him away, and the very step of the animal seemed significant of dogged despair. Gabriel, for a minute, rose above his own grief in noticing Boldwood's. He saw the square figure sitting erect upon the horse, the head turned to neither side, the elbows steady by the hips, the brim of the hat level and undisturbed in its onward glide, until the keen edges of Boldwood's shape sank by degrees over the hill. To one who knew the man and his story there was something more striking in this immobility than in a collapse. The clash of discord between mood and matter here was forced painfully home to the heart; and, as in laughter there are more dreadful phases than in tears, so was there in the steadiness of this agonized man an expression deeper than a cry.

Questions

Why does Troy throw down money to Coggan and Oak from the window?
What does Oak do with the money?
Who appears on horseback and what is this person's mood?
GCSE style question: how does Hardy present Troy in this chapter?
Creative response: write a poem/story/description called 'Just Married'.

CHAPTER XXXVI
WEALTH IN JEOPARDY—THE REVEL

One night, at the end of August, when Bathsheba's experiences as a married woman were still new, and when the weather was yet dry and sultry, a man stood motionless in the stockyard of Weatherbury Upper Farm, looking at the moon and sky.

The night had a sinister aspect. A heated breeze from the south slowly fanned the summits of lofty objects, and in the sky dashes of buoyant cloud were sailing in a course at right angles to that of another stratum, neither of them in the direction of the breeze below. The moon, as seen through these films, had a lurid metallic look. The fields were sallow with the impure light, and all were tinged in monochrome, as if beheld through stained glass. The same evening the sheep had trailed homeward head to tail, the behaviour of the rooks had been confused, and the horses had moved with timidity and caution.

Thunder was imminent, and, taking some secondary appearances into consideration, it was likely to be followed by one of the lengthened rains which mark the close of dry weather for the season. Before twelve hours had passed a harvest atmosphere would be a bygone thing.

Oak gazed with misgiving at eight naked and unprotected ricks, massive and heavy with the rich produce of one-half the farm for that year. He went on to the barn.

This was the night which had been selected by Sergeant Troy—ruling now in the room of his wife—for giving the harvest supper and dance. As Oak approached the building the sound of violins and a tambourine, and the regular jigging of many feet, grew more distinct. He came close to the large doors, one of which stood slightly ajar, and looked in.

The central space, together with the recess at one end, was emptied of all incumbrances, and this area, covering about two-thirds of the whole, was appropriated for the gathering, the remaining end, which was piled to the ceiling with oats, being screened off with sail-cloth. Tufts and garlands of green foliage decorated the walls, beams, and extemporized chandeliers, and immediately opposite to Oak a rostrum had been erected, bearing a table and chairs. Here sat three fiddlers, and beside them stood a frantic man with his hair on end, perspiration streaming down his cheeks, and a tambourine quivering in his hand.

The dance ended, and on the black oak floor in the midst a new row of couples formed for another.

"Now, ma'am, and no offence I hope, I ask what dance you would like next?" said the first violin.

"Really, it makes no difference," said the clear voice of Bathsheba, who stood at the inner end of the building, observing the scene from behind a table covered with cups and viands. Troy was lolling beside her.

"Then," said the fiddler, "I'll venture to name that the right and proper thing is 'The Soldier's Joy'—there being a gallant soldier married into the farm—hey, my sonnies, and gentlemen all?"

"It shall be 'The Soldier's Joy,'" exclaimed a chorus.

"Thanks for the compliment," said the sergeant gaily, taking Bathsheba by the hand and leading her to the top of the dance. "For though I have purchased my discharge from Her Most Gracious Majesty's regiment of cavalry the 11th Dragoon Guards, to attend to the new duties awaiting me here, I shall continue a soldier in spirit and feeling as long as I live."

So the dance began. As to the merits of "The Soldier's Joy," there cannot be, and never were, two opinions. It has been observed in the musical circles of Weatherbury and its vicinity that this melody, at the end of three-quarters of an hour of thunderous footing, still possesses more stimulative properties for the heel and toe than the majority of other dances at their first opening. "The Soldier's Joy" has, too, an additional charm, in being so admirably adapted to the tambourine aforesaid—no mean instrument in the hands of a performer who understands the proper convulsions, spasms, St. Vitus's dances, and fearful frenzies necessary when exhibiting its tones in their highest perfection.

The immortal tune ended, a fine DD rolling forth from the bass-viol with the sonorousness of a cannonade, and Gabriel delayed his entry no longer. He avoided Bathsheba, and got as near as possible to the platform, where Sergeant Troy was now seated, drinking brandy-and-water, though the others drank without exception cider and ale. Gabriel could not easily thrust himself within speaking distance of the sergeant, and he sent a message, asking him to come down for a moment. The sergeant said he could not attend.

"Will you tell him, then," said Gabriel, "that I only stepped ath'art to say that a heavy rain is sure to fall soon, and that something should be done to protect the ricks?"

"Mr. Troy says it will not rain," returned the messenger, "and he cannot stop to talk to you about such fidgets."

In juxtaposition with Troy, Oak had a melancholy tendency to look like a candle beside gas, and ill at ease, he went out again, thinking he would go home; for, under the circumstances, he had no heart for the scene in the barn. At the door he paused for a moment: Troy was speaking.

"Friends, it is not only the harvest home that we are celebrating to-night; but this is also a Wedding Feast. A short time ago I had the happiness to lead to the altar this lady, your mistress, and not until now have we been able to give any public flourish to the event in Weatherbury. That it may be thoroughly well done, and that every man may go happy to bed, I have ordered to be brought here some bottles of brandy and kettles of hot water. A treble-strong goblet will be handed round to each guest."

Bathsheba put her hand upon his arm, and, with upturned pale face, said imploringly, "No—don't give it to them—pray don't, Frank! It will only do them harm: they have had enough of everything."

"True—we don't wish for no more, thank ye," said one or two.

"Pooh!" said the sergeant contemptuously, and raised his voice as if lighted up by a new idea. "Friends," he said, "we'll send the women-folk home! 'Tis time they were in bed. Then we cockbirds will have a jolly carouse to ourselves! If any of the men show the white feather, let them look elsewhere for a winter's work."

Bathsheba indignantly left the barn, followed by all the women and children.

> Analysis: Here we see how Troy is intent upon asserting his supremacy, intent upon appearing the top person on the farm. There is something yobbish about his behaviour, in the way he insists upon every man taking part in the drinking, dismissing the women. He has to threaten them with the sack to get them to join him, thus exhibiting his bullying behaviour. Above all, we see him presented as someone who is out of touch with the country ways which are about consensus, inclusion, sobriety, tending to the land. Here we see him uninterested in looking after the crops which are threatened by the oncoming storm.

> Discussion point: Why does Hardy present Troy in this way?

The musicians, not looking upon themselves as "company," slipped quietly away to their spring waggon and put in the horse. Thus Troy and the men on the farm were left sole occupants of the place. Oak, not to appear unnecessarily disagreeable, stayed a little while; then he, too, arose and quietly took his departure, followed by a friendly oath from the sergeant for not staying to a second round of grog.

Gabriel proceeded towards his home. In approaching the door, his toe kicked something which felt and sounded soft, leathery, and distended, like a boxing-glove. It was a large toad humbly travelling across the path. Oak took it up, thinking it might be better to kill the creature to save it from pain; but finding it uninjured, he placed it again among the grass. He knew what this direct message from the Great Mother meant. And soon came another.

When he struck a light indoors there appeared upon the table a thin glistening streak, as if a brush of varnish had been lightly dragged across it. Oak's eyes followed the serpentine sheen to the other side, where it led up to a huge brown garden-slug, which had come indoors to-night for reasons of its own. It was Nature's second way of hinting to him that he was to prepare for foul weather.

Oak sat down meditating for nearly an hour. During this time two black spiders, of the kind common in thatched houses, promenaded the ceiling, ultimately dropping to the floor. This reminded him that if there was one class of manifestation on this matter that he thoroughly understood, it was the instincts of sheep. He left the room, ran across two or three fields towards the flock, got upon a hedge, and looked over among them.

They were crowded close together on the other side around some furze bushes, and the first peculiarity observable was that, on the sudden appearance of Oak's head over the fence, they did not stir or run away. They had now a terror of something greater than their terror of man. But this was not the most noteworthy feature: they were all grouped in such a way that their tails, without a single exception, were towards that half of the horizon from which the storm threatened. There was an inner circle closely huddled, and outside these they radiated wider apart, the pattern formed by the flock as a whole not being unlike a vandyked lace collar, to which the clump of furze-bushes stood in the position of a wearer's neck.

This was enough to re-establish him in his original opinion. He knew now that he was right, and that Troy was wrong. Every voice in nature was unanimous in bespeaking change. But two distinct translations attached to these dumb expressions. Apparently there was to be a thunder-storm, and afterwards a cold continuous rain. The creeping things seemed to know all about the later rain, but little of the interpolated thunder-storm; whilst the sheep knew all about the thunder-storm and nothing of the later rain.

This complication of weathers being uncommon, was all the more to be feared. Oak returned to the stack-yard. All was silent here, and the conical tips of the ricks jutted darkly into the sky. There were five wheat-ricks in this yard, and three stacks of barley. The wheat when threshed would average about thirty quarters to each stack; the barley, at least forty. Their value to Bathsheba, and indeed to anybody, Oak mentally estimated by the following simple calculation:—

$$5 \times 30 = 150 \text{ quarters} = 500 \text{ L.}$$

$$3 \times 40 = 120 \text{ quarters} = 250 \text{ L.}$$

$$\text{Total} \ldots 750 \text{ L.}$$

Seven hundred and fifty pounds in the divinest form that money can wear—that of necessary food for man and beast: should the risk be run of deteriorating this bulk of corn to less than half its value, because of the instability of a woman? "Never, if I can prevent it!" said Gabriel.

Such was the argument that Oak set outwardly before him. But man, even to himself, is a palimpsest, having an ostensible writing, and another beneath the lines. It is possible that there was this golden legend under the utilitarian one: "I will help to my last effort the woman I have loved so dearly."

He went back to the barn to endeavour to obtain assistance for covering the ricks that very night. All was silent within, and he would have passed on in the belief that the party had broken up, had not a dim light, yellow as saffron by contrast with the greenish whiteness outside, streamed through a knot-hole in the folding doors.

Gabriel looked in. An unusual picture met his eye.

The candles suspended among the evergreens had burnt down to their sockets, and in some cases the leaves tied about them were scorched. Many of the lights had quite gone out, others smoked and stank, grease dropping from them upon the floor. Here, under the table, and leaning against forms and chairs in every conceivable attitude except the perpendicular, were the wretched persons of all the work-folk, the hair of their heads at such low levels being suggestive of mops and brooms. In the midst of these shone red and distinct the figure of Sergeant Troy, leaning back in a chair. Coggan was on his back, with his mouth open, huzzing forth snores, as were several others; the united breathings of the horizonal assemblage forming a subdued roar like London from a distance. Joseph Poorgrass was curled round in the fashion of a hedge-hog, apparently in attempts to present the least possible portion of his surface to the air; and behind him was dimly visible an unimportant remnant of William Smallbury. The glasses and cups still stood upon the table, a water-jug being overturned, from which a small rill, after tracing its course with marvellous precision down the centre of the long table, fell into the neck of the unconscious Mark Clark, in a steady, monotonous drip, like the dripping of a stalactite in a cave.

Gabriel glanced hopelessly at the group, which, with one or two exceptions, composed all the able-bodied men upon the farm. He saw at once that if the ricks were to be saved that night, or even the next morning, he must save them with his own hands.

A faint "ting-ting" resounded from under Coggan's waistcoat. It was Coggan's watch striking the hour of two.

Oak went to the recumbent form of Matthew Moon, who usually undertook the rough thatching of the home-stead, and shook him. The shaking was without effect.

Gabriel shouted in his ear, "where's your thatching-beetle and rick-stick and spars?"

"Under the staddles," said Moon, mechanically, with the unconscious promptness of a medium.

Gabriel let go his head, and it dropped upon the floor like a bowl. He then went to Susan Tall's husband.

"Where's the key of the granary?"

No answer. The question was repeated, with the same result. To be shouted to at night was evidently less of a novelty to Susan Tall's husband than to Matthew Moon. Oak flung down Tall's head into the corner again and turned away.

To be just, the men were not greatly to blame for this painful and demoralizing termination to the evening's entertainment. Sergeant Troy had so strenuously insisted, glass in hand, that drinking should be the bond of their union, that those who wished to refuse hardly liked to be so unmannerly under the circumstances. Having from their youth up been entirely unaccustomed to any liquor stronger than cider or mild ale, it was no wonder that they had succumbed, one and all, with extraordinary uniformity, after the lapse of about an hour.

Gabriel was greatly depressed. This debauch boded ill for that wilful and fascinating mistress whom the faithful man even now felt within him as the embodiment of all that was sweet and bright and hopeless.

He put out the expiring lights, that the barn might not be endangered, closed the door upon the men in their deep and oblivious sleep, and went again into the lone night. A hot breeze, as if breathed from the parted lips of some dragon about to swallow the globe, fanned him from the south, while directly opposite in the north rose a grim misshapen body of cloud, in the very teeth of the wind. So unnaturally did it rise that one could fancy it to be lifted by machinery from below. Meanwhile the faint cloudlets had flown back into the south-east corner of the sky, as if in terror of the large cloud, like a young brood gazed in upon by some monster.

Going on to the village, Oak flung a small stone against the window of Laban Tall's bedroom, expecting Susan to open it; but nobody stirred. He went round to the back door, which had been left unfastened for Laban's entry, and passed in to the foot of the staircase.

"Mrs. Tall, I've come for the key of the granary, to get at the rick-cloths," said Oak, in a stentorian voice.

"Is that you?" said Mrs. Susan Tall, half awake.

"Yes," said Gabriel.

"Come along to bed, do, you drawlatching rogue—keeping a body awake like this!"

"It isn't Laban—'tis Gabriel Oak. I want the key of the granary."

"Gabriel! What in the name of fortune did you pretend to be Laban for?"

"I didn't. I thought you meant—"

"Yes you did! What do you want here?"

"The key of the granary."

"Take it then. 'Tis on the nail. People coming disturbing women at this time of night ought—"

Gabriel took the key, without waiting to hear the conclusion of the tirade. Ten minutes later his lonely figure might have been seen dragging four large water-proof coverings across the yard, and soon two of these heaps of treasure in grain were covered snug—two cloths to each. Two hundred pounds were secured. Three wheat-stacks remained open, and there were no more cloths. Oak looked under the staddles and found a fork. He mounted the third pile of wealth and began operating, adopting the plan of sloping the upper sheaves one over the other; and, in addition, filling the interstices with the material of some untied sheaves.

So far all was well. By this hurried contrivance Bathsheba's property in wheat was safe for at any rate a week or two, provided always that there was not much wind.

Next came the barley. This it was only possible to protect by systematic thatching. Time went on, and the moon vanished not to reappear. It was the farewell of the ambassador previous to war. The night had a haggard look, like a sick thing; and there came finally an utter expiration of air from the whole heaven in the form of a slow breeze, which might have been likened to a death. And now nothing was heard in the yard but the dull thuds of the beetle which drove in the spars, and the rustle of thatch in the intervals.

Questions

What does Oak warn Troy about on the night of the harvest supper?

Who is in charge of the farm now and why?

What does Troy order should be brought to celebrate his marriage?

Who does Troy send away?

What does Oak decide to do when he leaves the party?

What happens when he goes to the men for extra help?

What does Oak do?

GCSE style question: how does Hardy present the position of women in this chapter?

A Level style question: compare and contrast the presentation of Troy and Oak in this chapter.

Creative response: write a poem/story/description called 'The Party' or write Oak's diary for this scene.

CHAPTER XXXVII
THE STORM—THE TWO
TOGETHER

A light flapped over the scene, as if reflected from phosphorescent wings crossing the sky, and a rumble filled the air. It was the first move of the approaching storm.

The second peal was noisy, with comparatively little visible lightning. Gabriel saw a candle shining in Bathsheba's bedroom, and soon a shadow swept to and fro upon the blind.

Then there came a third flash. Manœuvres of a most extraordinary kind were going on in the vast firmamental hollows overhead. The lightning now was the colour of silver, and gleamed in the heavens like a mailed army. Rumbles became rattles. Gabriel from his elevated position could see over the landscape at least half-a-dozen miles in front. Every hedge, bush, and tree was distinct as in a line engraving. In a paddock in the same direction was a herd of heifers, and the forms of these were visible at this moment in the act of galloping about in the wildest and maddest confusion, flinging their heels and tails high into the air, their heads to earth. A poplar in the immediate foreground was like an ink stroke on burnished tin. Then the picture vanished, leaving the darkness so intense that Gabriel worked entirely by feeling with his hands.

He had stuck his ricking-rod, or poniard, as it was indifferently called—a long iron lance, polished by handling—into the stack, used to support the sheaves instead of the support called a groom used on houses. A blue light appeared in the zenith, and in some indescribable manner flickered down near the top of the rod. It was the fourth of the larger flashes. A moment later and there was a smack—smart, clear, and short. Gabriel felt his position to be anything but a safe one, and he resolved to descend.

Not a drop of rain had fallen as yet. He wiped his weary brow, and looked again at the black forms of the unprotected stacks. Was his life so valuable to him after all? What were his prospects that he should be so chary of running risk, when important and urgent labour could not be carried on without such risk? He resolved to stick to the stack. However, he took a precaution. Under the staddles was a long tethering chain, used to prevent the escape of errant horses. This he carried up the ladder, and sticking his rod through the clog at one end, allowed the other end of the chain to trail upon the ground. The spike attached to it he drove in. Under the shadow of this extemporized lightning-conductor he felt himself comparatively safe.

Before Oak had laid his hands upon his tools again out leapt the fifth flash, with the spring of a serpent and the shout of a fiend. It was green as an emerald, and the reverberation was stunning. What was this the light revealed to him? In the open ground before him, as he looked over the ridge of the rick, was a dark and apparently female form. Could it be that of the only venturesome woman in the parish—Bathsheba? The form moved on a step: then he could see no more.

"Is that you, ma'am?" said Gabriel to the darkness.

"Who is there?" said the voice of Bathsheba.

"Gabriel. I am on the rick, thatching."

"Oh, Gabriel!—and are you? I have come about them. The weather awoke me, and I thought of the corn. I am so distressed about it—can we save it anyhow? I cannot find my husband. Is he with you?"

"He is not here."

"Do you know where he is?"

"Asleep in the barn."

"He promised that the stacks should be seen to, and now they are all neglected! Can I do anything to help? Liddy is afraid to come out. Fancy finding you here at such an hour! Surely I can do something?"

"You can bring up some reed-sheaves to me, one by one, ma'am; if you are not afraid to come up the ladder in the dark," said Gabriel. "Every moment is precious now, and that would save a good deal of time. It is not very dark when the lightning has been gone a bit."

"I'll do anything!" she said, resolutely. She instantly took a sheaf upon her shoulder, clambered up close to his heels, placed it behind the rod, and descended for another. At her third ascent the rick suddenly brightened with the brazen glare of shining majolica—every knot in every straw was visible. On the slope in front of him appeared two human shapes, black as jet. The rick lost its sheen—the shapes vanished. Gabriel turned his head. It had been the sixth flash which had come from the east behind him, and the two dark forms on the slope had been the shadows of himself and Bathsheba.

Then came the peal. It hardly was credible that such a heavenly light could be the parent of such a diabolical sound.

"How terrible!" she exclaimed, and clutched him by the sleeve. Gabriel turned, and steadied her on her aerial perch by holding her arm. At the same moment, while he was still reversed in his attitude, there was more light, and he saw, as it were, a copy of the tall poplar tree on the hill drawn in black on the wall of the barn. It was the shadow of that tree, thrown across by a secondary flash in the west.

The next flare came. Bathsheba was on the ground now, shouldering another sheaf, and she bore its dazzle without flinching—thunder and all— and again ascended with the load. There was then a silence everywhere for four or five minutes, and the crunch of the spars, as Gabriel hastily drove them in, could again be distinctly heard. He thought the crisis of the storm had passed. But there came a burst of light.

"Hold on!" said Gabriel, taking the sheaf from her shoulder, and grasping her arm again.

Heaven opened then, indeed. The flash was almost too novel for its inexpressibly dangerous nature to be at once realized, and they could only comprehend the magnificence of its beauty. It sprang from east, west, north, south, and was a perfect dance of death. The forms of skeletons appeared in the air, shaped with blue fire for bones—dancing, leaping, striding, racing around, and mingling altogether in unparalleled confusion. With these were intertwined undulating snakes of green, and behind these was a broad mass of lesser light. Simultaneously came from every part of the tumbling sky what may be called a shout; since, though no shout ever came near it, it was more of the nature of a shout than of anything else earthly. In the meantime one of the grisly forms had alighted upon the point of Gabriel's rod, to run invisibly down it, down the chain, and into the earth. Gabriel was almost blinded, and he could feel Bathsheba's warm arm tremble in his hand—a sensation novel and thrilling enough; but love, life, everything human, seemed small and trifling in such close juxtaposition with an infuriated universe.

Oak had hardly time to gather up these impressions into a thought, and to see how strangely the red feather of her hat shone in this light, when the tall tree on the hill before mentioned seemed on fire to a white heat, and a new one among these terrible voices mingled with the last crash of those preceding. It was a stupefying blast, harsh and pitiless, and it fell upon their ears in a dead, flat blow, without that reverberation which lends the tones of a drum to more distant thunder. By the lustre reflected from every part of the earth and from the wide domical scoop above it, he saw that the tree was sliced down the whole length of its tall, straight stem, a huge riband of bark being apparently flung off. The other portion remained erect, and revealed the bared surface as a strip of white down the front. The lightning had struck the tree. A sulphurous smell filled the air; then all was silent, and black as a cave in Hinnom.

"We had a narrow escape!" said Gabriel, hurriedly. "You had better go down."

Bathsheba said nothing; but he could distinctly hear her rhythmical pants, and the recurrent rustle of the sheaf beside her in response to her frightened pulsations. She descended the ladder, and, on second thoughts, he followed her. The darkness was now impenetrable by the sharpest vision. They both stood still at the bottom, side by side. Bathsheba appeared to think only of the weather—Oak thought only of her just then. At last he said—

"The storm seems to have passed now, at any rate."

"I think so too," said Bathsheba. "Though there are multitudes of gleams, look!"

The sky was now filled with an incessant light, frequent repetition melting into complete continuity, as an unbroken sound results from the successive strokes on a gong.

"Nothing serious," said he. "I cannot understand no rain falling. But Heaven be praised, it is all the better for us. I am now going up again."

"Gabriel, you are kinder than I deserve! I will stay and help you yet. Oh, why are not some of the others here!"

"They would have been here if they could," said Oak, in a hesitating way.

"O, I know it all—all," she said, adding slowly: "They are all asleep in the barn, in a drunken sleep, and my husband among them. That's it, is it not? Don't think I am a timid woman and can't endure things."

"I am not certain," said Gabriel. "I will go and see."

He crossed to the barn, leaving her there alone. He looked through the chinks of the door. All was in total darkness, as he had left it, and there still arose, as at the former time, the steady buzz of many snores.

He felt a zephyr curling about his cheek, and turned. It was Bathsheba's breath—she had followed him, and was looking into the same chink.

He endeavoured to put off the immediate and painful subject of their thoughts by remarking gently, "If you'll come back again, miss—ma'am, and hand up a few more; it would save much time."

Then Oak went back again, ascended to the top, stepped off the ladder for greater expedition, and went on thatching. She followed, but without a sheaf.

"Gabriel," she said, in a strange and impressive voice.

Oak looked up at her. She had not spoken since he left the barn. The soft and continual shimmer of the dying lightning showed a marble face high against the black sky of the opposite quarter. Bathsheba was sitting almost on the apex of the stack, her feet gathered up beneath her, and resting on the top round of the ladder.

"Yes, mistress," he said.

"I suppose you thought that when I galloped away to Bath that night it was on purpose to be married?"

"I did at last—not at first," he answered, somewhat surprised at the abruptness with which this new subject was broached.

"And others thought so, too?"

"Yes."

"And you blamed me for it?"

"Well—a little."

"I thought so. Now, I care a little for your good opinion, and I want to explain something—I have longed to do it ever since I returned, and you looked so gravely at me. For if I were to die—and I may die soon—it would be dreadful that you should always think mistakenly of me. Now, listen."

Gabriel ceased his rustling.

"I went to Bath that night in the full intention of breaking off my engagement to Mr. Troy. It was owing to circumstances which occurred after I got there that—that we were married. Now, do you see the matter in a new light?"

"I do—somewhat."

"I must, I suppose, say more, now that I have begun. And perhaps it's no harm, for you are certainly under no delusion that I ever loved you, or that I can have any object in speaking, more than that object I have mentioned. Well, I was alone in a strange city, and the horse was lame. And at last I didn't know what to do. I saw, when it was too late, that scandal might seize hold of me for meeting him alone in that way. But I was coming away, when he suddenly said he had that day seen a woman more beautiful than I, and that his constancy could not be counted on unless I at once became his... And I was grieved and troubled—" She cleared her voice, and waited a moment, as if to gather breath. "And then, between jealousy and distraction, I married him!" she whispered with desperate impetuosity.

Gabriel made no reply.

"He was not to blame, for it was perfectly true about—about his seeing somebody else," she quickly added. "And now I don't wish for a single remark from you upon the subject—indeed, I forbid it. I only wanted you to know that misunderstood bit of my history before a time comes when you could never know it.—You want some more sheaves?"

She went down the ladder, and the work proceeded. Gabriel soon perceived a languor in the movements of his mistress up and down, and he said to her, gently as a mother—

"I think you had better go indoors now, you are tired. I can finish the rest alone. If the wind does not change the rain is likely to keep off."

"If I am useless I will go," said Bathsheba, in a flagging cadence. "But O, if your life should be lost!"

"You are not useless; but I would rather not tire you longer. You have done well."

"And you better!" she said, gratefully. "Thank you for your devotion, a thousand times, Gabriel! Goodnight—I know you are doing your very best for me."

She diminished in the gloom, and vanished, and he heard the latch of the gate fall as she passed through. He worked in a reverie now, musing upon her story, and upon the contradictoriness of that feminine heart which had caused her to speak more warmly to him to-night than she ever had done whilst unmarried and free to speak as warmly as she chose.

He was disturbed in his meditation by a grating noise from the coach-house. It was the vane on the roof turning round, and this change in the wind was the signal for a disastrous rain.

Analysis: Amidst the natural horrors of the storm, Bathsheba has to face the horror that she has created in her life, marrying someone out of a jealous obsession and now bitterly regretting it. This is an effective scene – as are many between Oak and Bathsheba – because the two of them are working together but also talking. We realise that there is something deeper than superficial love developing between them. Their relationship is based upon listening to each other, working together, sharing their problems. The storm is both a literal and metaphorical storm; a manifestation of the turbulent emotions that have shaped the main characters' lives.

Discussion point: Why does Hardy present the reader with Bathsheba talking to Oak like this?

Questions

Why is Oak in danger?
How does Bathsheba help him?
What does Bathsheba confess to Oak?

GCSE style question: how does Hardy make the scene in the storm such a thrilling and vivid moment in the novel?

Creative response: write a poem/story/description called 'The Storm'.

CHAPTER XXXVIII
RAIN—ONE SOLITARY MEETS ANOTHER

It was now five o'clock, and the dawn was promising to break in hues of drab and ash.

The air changed its temperature and stirred itself more vigorously. Cool breezes coursed in transparent eddies round Oak's face. The wind shifted yet a point or two and blew stronger. In ten minutes every wind of heaven seemed to be roaming at large. Some of the thatching on the wheat-stacks was now whirled fantastically aloft, and had to be replaced and weighted with some rails that lay near at hand. This done, Oak slaved away again at the barley. A huge drop of rain smote his face, the wind snarled round every corner, the trees rocked to the bases of their trunks, and the twigs clashed in strife. Driving in spars at any point and on any system, inch by inch he covered more and more safely from ruin this distracting impersonation of seven hundred pounds. The rain came on in earnest, and Oak soon felt the water to be tracking cold and clammy routes down his back. Ultimately he was reduced well-nigh to a homogeneous sop, and the dyes of his clothes trickled down and stood in a pool at the foot of the ladder. The rain stretched obliquely through the dull atmosphere in liquid spines, unbroken in continuity between their beginnings in the clouds and their points in him.

Oak suddenly remembered that eight months before this time he had been fighting against fire in the same spot as desperately as he was fighting against water now—and for a futile love of the same woman. As for her— But Oak was generous and true, and dismissed his reflections.

It was about seven o'clock in the dark leaden morning when Gabriel came down from the last stack, and thankfully exclaimed, "It is done!" He was drenched, weary, and sad, and yet not so sad as drenched and weary, for he was cheered by a sense of success in a good cause.

Faint sounds came from the barn, and he looked that way. Figures stepped singly and in pairs through the doors—all walking awkwardly, and abashed, save the foremost, who wore a red jacket, and advanced with his hands in his pockets, whistling. The others shambled after with a conscience-stricken air: the whole procession was not unlike Flaxman's group of the suitors tottering on towards the infernal regions under the conduct of Mercury. The gnarled shapes passed into the village, Troy, their leader, entering the farmhouse. Not a single one of them had turned his face to the ricks, or apparently bestowed one thought upon their condition.

Soon Oak too went homeward, by a different route from theirs. In front of him against the wet glazed surface of the lane he saw a person walking yet more slowly than himself under an umbrella. The man turned and plainly started; he was Boldwood.

"How are you this morning, sir?" said Oak.

"Yes, it is a wet day.—Oh, I am well, very well, I thank you; quite well."

"I am glad to hear it, sir."

Boldwood seemed to awake to the present by degrees. "You look tired and ill, Oak," he said then, desultorily regarding his companion.

"I am tired. You look strangely altered, sir."

"I? Not a bit of it: I am well enough. What put that into your head?"

"I thought you didn't look quite so topping as you used to, that was all."

"Indeed, then you are mistaken," said Boldwood, shortly. "Nothing hurts me. My constitution is an iron one."

"I've been working hard to get our ricks covered, and was barely in time. Never had such a struggle in my life... Yours of course are safe, sir."

"Oh yes," Boldwood added, after an interval of silence: "What did you ask, Oak?"

"Your ricks are all covered before this time?"

"No."

"At any rate, the large ones upon the stone staddles?"

"They are not."

"Them under the hedge?"

"No. I forgot to tell the thatcher to set about it."

"Nor the little one by the stile?"

"Nor the little one by the stile. I overlooked the ricks this year."

"Then not a tenth of your corn will come to measure, sir."

"Possibly not."

"Overlooked them," repeated Gabriel slowly to himself. It is difficult to describe the intensely dramatic effect that announcement had upon Oak at such a moment. All the night he had been feeling that the neglect he was labouring to repair was abnormal and isolated—the only instance of the kind within the circuit of the county. Yet at this very time, within the same parish, a greater waste had been going on, uncomplained of and disregarded. A few months earlier Boldwood's forgetting his husbandry would have been as preposterous an idea as a sailor forgetting he was in a ship. Oak was just thinking that whatever he himself might have suffered from Bathsheba's marriage, here was a man who had suffered more, when Boldwood spoke in a changed voice—that of one who yearned to make a confidence and relieve his heart by an outpouring.

"Oak, you know as well as I that things have gone wrong with me lately. I may as well own it. I was going to get a little settled in life; but in some way my plan has come to nothing."

"I thought my mistress would have married you," said Gabriel, not knowing enough of the full depths of Boldwood's love to keep silence on the farmer's account, and determined not to evade discipline by doing so on his own. "However, it is so sometimes, and nothing happens that we expect," he added, with the repose of a man whom misfortune had inured rather than subdued.

"I daresay I am a joke about the parish," said Boldwood, as if the subject came irresistibly to his tongue, and with a miserable lightness meant to express his indifference.

"Oh no—I don't think that."

"—But the real truth of the matter is that there was not, as some fancy, any jilting on—her part. No engagement ever existed between me and Miss Everdene. People say so, but it is untrue: she never promised me!" Boldwood stood still now and turned his wild face to Oak. "Oh, Gabriel," he continued, "I am weak and foolish, and I don't know what, and I can't fend off my miserable grief! ... I had some faint belief in the mercy of God till I lost that woman. Yes, He prepared a gourd to shade me, and like the prophet I thanked Him and was glad. But the next day He prepared a worm to smite the gourd and wither it; and I feel it is better to die than to live!"

A silence followed. Boldwood aroused himself from the momentary mood of confidence into which he had drifted, and walked on again, resuming his usual reserve.

"No, Gabriel," he resumed, with a carelessness which was like the smile on the countenance of a skull: "it was made more of by other people than ever it was by us. I do feel a little regret occasionally, but no woman ever had power over me for any length of time. Well, good morning; I can trust you not to mention to others what has passed between us two here."

Questions

How long does Gabriel work?

Who does Oak meet at dawn?

What has happened to Boldwood's ricks and why?

What is Boldwood thinking of doing?

GCSE style question: how does Hardy make Boldwood a poignant and broken figure in this chapter?

Creative response: write a poem/story called 'Broken' in which you describe a person/thing which is broken.

CHAPTER XXXIX
COMING HOME—A CRY

On the turnpike road, between Casterbridge and Weatherbury, and about three miles from the former place, is Yalbury Hill, one of those steep long ascents which pervade the highways of this undulating part of South Wessex. In returning from market it is usual for the farmers and other gig-gentry to alight at the bottom and walk up.

One Saturday evening in the month of October Bathsheba's vehicle was duly creeping up this incline. She was sitting listlessly in the second seat of the gig, whilst walking beside her in a farmer's marketing suit of unusually fashionable cut was an erect, well-made young man. Though on foot, he held the reins and whip, and occasionally aimed light cuts at the horse's ear with the end of the lash, as a recreation. This man was her husband, formerly Sergeant Troy, who, having bought his discharge with Bathsheba's money, was gradually transforming himself into a farmer of a spirited and very modern school. People of unalterable ideas still insisted upon calling him "Sergeant" when they met him, which was in some degree owing to his having still retained the well-shaped moustache of his military days, and the soldierly bearing inseparable from his form and training.

"Yes, if it hadn't been for that wretched rain I should have cleared two hundred as easy as looking, my love," he was saying. "Don't you see, it altered all the chances? To speak like a book I once read, wet weather is the narrative, and fine days are the episodes, of our country's history; now, isn't that true?"

"But the time of year is come for changeable weather."

"Well, yes. The fact is, these autumn races are the ruin of everybody. Never did I see such a day as 'twas! 'Tis a wild open place, just out of Budmouth, and a drab sea rolled in towards us like liquid misery. Wind and rain—good Lord! Dark? Why, 'twas as black as my hat before the last race was run. 'Twas five o'clock, and you couldn't see the horses till they were almost in, leave alone colours. The ground was as heavy as lead, and all judgment from a fellow's experience went for nothing. Horses, riders, people, were all blown about like ships at sea. Three booths were blown over, and the wretched folk inside crawled out upon their hands and knees; and in the next field were as many as a dozen hats at one time. Ay, Pimpernel regularly stuck fast, when about sixty yards off, and when I saw Policy stepping on, it did knock my heart against the lining of my ribs, I assure you, my love!"

"And you mean, Frank," said Bathsheba, sadly—her voice was painfully lowered from the fulness and vivacity of the previous summer—"that you have lost more than a hundred pounds in a month by this dreadful horse-racing? O, Frank, it is cruel; it is foolish of you to take away my money so. We shall have to leave the farm; that will be the end of it!"

"Humbug about cruel. Now, there 'tis again—turn on the waterworks; that's just like you."

"But you'll promise me not to go to Budmouth second meeting, won't you?" she implored. Bathsheba was at the full depth for tears, but she maintained a dry eye.

"I don't see why I should; in fact, if it turns out to be a fine day, I was thinking of taking you."

"Never, never! I'll go a hundred miles the other way first. I hate the sound of the very word!"

"But the question of going to see the race or staying at home has very little to do with the matter. Bets are all booked safely enough before the race begins, you may depend. Whether it is a bad race for me or a good one, will have very little to do with our going there next Monday."

"But you don't mean to say that you have risked anything on this one too!" she exclaimed, with an agonized look.

"There now, don't you be a little fool. Wait till you are told. Why, Bathsheba, you have lost all the pluck and sauciness you formerly had, and upon my life if I had known what a chicken-hearted creature you were under all your boldness, I'd never have—I know what."

A flash of indignation might have been seen in Bathsheba's dark eyes as she looked resolutely ahead after this reply. They moved on without further speech, some early-withered leaves from the trees which hooded the road at this spot occasionally spinning downward across their path to the earth.

A woman appeared on the brow of the hill. The ridge was in a cutting, so that she was very near the husband and wife before she became visible. Troy had turned towards the gig to remount, and whilst putting his foot on the step the woman passed behind him.

Though the overshadowing trees and the approach of eventide enveloped them in gloom, Bathsheba could see plainly enough to discern the extreme poverty of the woman's garb, and the sadness of her face.

"Please, sir, do you know at what time Casterbridge Union-house closes at night?"

The woman said these words to Troy over his shoulder.

Troy started visibly at the sound of the voice; yet he seemed to recover presence of mind sufficient to prevent himself from giving way to his impulse to suddenly turn and face her. He said, slowly—

"I don't know."

The woman, on hearing him speak, quickly looked up, examined the side of his face, and recognized the soldier under the yeoman's garb. Her face was drawn into an expression which had gladness and agony both among its elements. She uttered an hysterical cry, and fell down.

"Oh, poor thing!" exclaimed Bathsheba, instantly preparing to alight.

"Stay where you are, and attend to the horse!" said Troy, peremptorily throwing her the reins and the whip. "Walk the horse to the top: I'll see to the woman."

"But I—"

"Do you hear? Clk—Poppet!"

The horse, gig, and Bathsheba moved on.

"How on earth did you come here? I thought you were miles away, or dead! Why didn't you write to me?" said Troy to the woman, in a strangely gentle, yet hurried voice, as he lifted her up.

"I feared to."

"Have you any money?"

"None."

"Good Heaven—I wish I had more to give you! Here's—wretched—the merest trifle. It is every farthing I have left. I have none but what my wife gives me, you know, and I can't ask her now."

The woman made no answer.

"I have only another moment," continued Troy; "and now listen. Where are you going to-night? Casterbridge Union?"

"Yes; I thought to go there."

"You shan't go there; yet, wait. Yes, perhaps for to-night; I can do nothing better—worse luck! Sleep there to-night, and stay there to-morrow. Monday is the first free day I have; and on Monday morning, at ten exactly, meet me on Grey's Bridge just out of the town. I'll bring all the money I can muster. You shan't want—I'll see that, Fanny; then I'll get you a lodging somewhere. Good-bye till then. I am a brute—but good-bye!"

Analysis: Now we have Hardy skilfully bringing together the threads of the story: the subplot with Fanny is now colliding with the main plot of Bathsheba's search for love. In many ways, Fanny's story is the stuff of ancient ballads: she is the ruined maid. Her life provides a darkly ironic counterpoint to Bathsheba's: she has been ruined financially and physically by Troy. Bathsheba has been destroyed psychologically.

Discussion point: Why does Hardy re-introduce Fanny at this point in the novel?

After advancing the distance which completed the ascent of the hill, Bathsheba turned her head. The woman was upon her feet, and Bathsheba saw her withdrawing from Troy, and going feebly down the hill by the third milestone from Casterbridge. Troy then came on towards his wife, stepped into the gig, took the reins from her hand, and without making any observation whipped the horse into a trot. He was rather agitated.

"Do you know who that woman was?" said Bathsheba, looking searchingly into his face.

"I do," he said, looking boldly back into hers.

"I thought you did," said she, with angry hauteur, and still regarding him. "Who is she?"

He suddenly seemed to think that frankness would benefit neither of the women.

"Nothing to either of us," he said. "I know her by sight."

"What is her name?"

"How should I know her name?"

"I think you do."

"Think if you will, and be—" The sentence was completed by a smart cut of the whip round Poppet's flank, which caused the animal to start forward at a wild pace. No more was said.

Questions

What has Troy lost at the races?

Why do Bathsheba and he quarrel?

Who meets them on the highway?

What does Troy say and give to Fanny?

What is Bathsheba's response?

GCSE style question: how does Hardy make the re-appearance of Fanny such a shocking and moving moment?

Creative response; write a poem/story/description of a homeless person.

Or write Troy's diary for this chapter.

CHAPTER XL
ON CASTERBRIDGE HIGHWAY

For a considerable time the woman walked on. Her steps became feebler, and she strained her eyes to look afar upon the naked road, now indistinct amid the penumbræ of night. At length her onward walk dwindled to the merest totter, and she opened a gate within which was a haystack. Underneath this she sat down and presently slept.

When the woman awoke it was to find herself in the depths of a moonless and starless night. A heavy unbroken crust of cloud stretched across the sky, shutting out every speck of heaven; and a distant halo which hung over the town of Casterbridge was visible against the black concave, the luminosity appearing the brighter by its great contrast with the circumscribing darkness. Towards this weak, soft glow the woman turned her eyes.

"If I could only get there!" she said. "Meet him the day after to-morrow: God help me! Perhaps I shall be in my grave before then."

A manor-house clock from the far depths of shadow struck the hour, one, in a small, attenuated tone. After midnight the voice of a clock seems to lose in breadth as much as in length, and to diminish its sonorousness to a thin falsetto.

Afterwards a light—two lights—arose from the remote shade, and grew larger. A carriage rolled along the road, and passed the gate. It probably contained some late diners-out. The beams from one lamp shone for a moment upon the crouching woman, and threw her face into vivid relief. The face was young in the groundwork, old in the finish; the general contours were flexuous and childlike, but the finer lineaments had begun to be sharp and thin.

The pedestrian stood up, apparently with revived determination, and looked around. The road appeared to be familiar to her, and she carefully scanned the fence as she slowly walked along. Presently there became visible a dim white shape; it was another milestone. She drew her fingers across its face to feel the marks.

"Two more!" she said.

She leant against the stone as a means of rest for a short interval, then bestirred herself, and again pursued her way. For a slight distance she bore up bravely, afterwards flagging as before. This was beside a lone copsewood, wherein heaps of white chips strewn upon the leafy ground showed that woodmen had been faggoting and making hurdles during the day. Now there was not a rustle, not a breeze, not the faintest clash of twigs to keep her company. The woman looked over the gate, opened it, and went in. Close to the entrance stood a row of faggots, bound and un-bound, together with stakes of all sizes.

For a few seconds the wayfarer stood with that tense stillness which signifies itself to be not the end, but merely the suspension, of a previous motion. Her attitude was that of a person who listens, either to the external world of sound, or to the imagined discourse of thought. A close criticism might have detected signs proving that she was intent on the latter alternative. Moreover, as was shown by what followed, she was oddly exercising the faculty of invention upon the speciality of the clever Jacquet Droz, the designer of automatic substitutes for human limbs.

By the aid of the Casterbridge aurora, and by feeling with her hands, the woman selected two sticks from the heaps. These sticks were nearly straight to the height of three or four feet, where each branched into a fork like the letter Y. She sat down, snapped off the small upper twigs, and carried the remainder with her into the road. She placed one of these forks under each arm as a crutch, tested them, timidly threw her whole weight upon them—so little that it was—and swung herself forward. The girl had made for herself a material aid.

The crutches answered well. The pat of her feet, and the tap of her sticks upon the highway, were all the sounds that came from the traveller now. She had passed the last milestone by a good long distance, and began to look wistfully towards the bank as if calculating upon another milestone soon. The crutches, though so very useful, had their limits of power. Mechanism only transfers labour, being powerless to supersede it, and the original amount of exertion was not cleared away; it was thrown into the body and arms. She was exhausted, and each swing forward became fainter. At last she swayed sideways, and fell.

Here she lay, a shapeless heap, for ten minutes and more. The morning wind began to boom dully over the flats, and to move afresh dead leaves which had lain still since yesterday. The woman desperately turned round upon her knees, and next rose to her feet. Steadying herself by the help of one crutch, she essayed a step, then another, then a third, using the crutches now as walking-sticks only. Thus she progressed till descending Mellstock Hill another milestone appeared, and soon the beginning of an iron-railed fence came into view. She staggered across to the first post, clung to it, and looked around.

The Casterbridge lights were now individually visible. It was getting towards morning, and vehicles might be hoped for, if not expected soon. She listened. There was not a sound of life save that acme and sublimation of all dismal sounds, the bark of a fox, its three hollow notes being rendered at intervals of a minute with the precision of a funeral bell.

"Less than a mile!" the woman murmured. "No; more," she added, after a pause. "The mile is to the county hall, and my resting-place is on the other side Casterbridge. A little over a mile, and there I am!" After an interval she again spoke. "Five or six steps to a yard—six perhaps. I have to go seventeen hundred yards. A hundred times six, six hundred. Seventeen times that. O pity me, Lord!"

Holding to the rails, she advanced, thrusting one hand forward upon the rail, then the other, then leaning over it whilst she dragged her feet on beneath.

This woman was not given to soliloquy; but extremity of feeling lessens the individuality of the weak, as it increases that of the strong. She said again in the same tone, "I'll believe that the end lies five posts forward, and no further, and so get strength to pass them."

This was a practical application of the principle that a half-feigned and fictitious faith is better than no faith at all.

She passed five posts and held on to the fifth.

"I'll pass five more by believing my longed-for spot is at the next fifth. I can do it."

She passed five more.

"It lies only five further."

She passed five more.

"But it is five further."

She passed them.

"That stone bridge is the end of my journey," she said, when the bridge over the Froom was in view.

She crawled to the bridge. During the effort each breath of the woman went into the air as if never to return again.

"Now for the truth of the matter," she said, sitting down. "The truth is, that I have less than half a mile." Self-beguilement with what she had known all the time to be false had given her strength to come over half a mile that she would have been powerless to face in the lump. The artifice showed that the woman, by some mysterious intuition, had grasped the paradoxical truth that blindness may operate more vigorously than prescience, and the short-sighted effect more than the far-seeing; that limitation, and not comprehensiveness, is needed for striking a blow.

The half-mile stood now before the sick and weary woman like a stolid Juggernaut. It was an impassive King of her world. The road here ran across Durnover Moor, open to the road on either side. She surveyed the wide space, the lights, herself, sighed, and lay down against a guard-stone of the bridge.

Never was ingenuity exercised so sorely as the traveller here exercised hers. Every conceivable aid, method, stratagem, mechanism, by which these last desperate eight hundred yards could be overpassed by a human being unperceived, was revolved in her busy brain, and dismissed as impracticable. She thought of sticks, wheels, crawling—she even thought of rolling. But the exertion demanded by either of these latter two was greater than to walk erect. The faculty of contrivance was worn out. Hopelessness had come at last.

"No further!" she whispered, and closed her eyes.

From the stripe of shadow on the opposite side of the bridge a portion of shade seemed to detach itself and move into isolation upon the pale white of the road. It glided noiselessly towards the recumbent woman.

She became conscious of something touching her hand; it was softness and it was warmth. She opened her eyes, and the substance touched her face. A dog was licking her cheek.

He was a huge, heavy, and quiet creature, standing darkly against the low horizon, and at least two feet higher than the present position of her eyes. Whether Newfoundland, mastiff, bloodhound, or what not, it was impossible to say. He seemed to be of too strange and mysterious a nature to belong to any variety among those of popular nomenclature. Being thus assignable to no breed, he was the ideal embodiment of canine greatness— a generalization from what was common to all. Night, in its sad, solemn, and benevolent aspect, apart from its stealthy and cruel side, was personified in this form. Darkness endows the small and ordinary ones among mankind with poetical power, and even the suffering woman threw her idea into figure.

In her reclining position she looked up to him just as in earlier times she had, when standing, looked up to a man. The animal, who was as homeless as she, respectfully withdrew a step or two when the woman moved, and, seeing that she did not repulse him, he licked her hand again.

A thought moved within her like lightning. "Perhaps I can make use of him—I might do it then!"

She pointed in the direction of Casterbridge, and the dog seemed to misunderstand: he trotted on. Then, finding she could not follow, he came back and whined.

The ultimate and saddest singularity of woman's effort and invention was reached when, with a quickened breathing, she rose to a stooping posture, and, resting her two little arms upon the shoulders of the dog, leant firmly thereon, and murmured stimulating words. Whilst she sorrowed in her heart she cheered with her voice, and what was stranger than that the strong should need encouragement from the weak was that cheerfulness should be so well stimulated by such utter dejection. Her friend moved forward slowly, and she with small mincing steps moved forward beside him, half her weight being thrown upon the animal. Sometimes she sank as she had sunk from walking erect, from the crutches, from the rails. The dog, who now thoroughly understood her desire and her incapacity, was frantic in his distress on these occasions; he would tug at her dress and run forward. She always called him back, and it was now to be observed that the woman listened for human sounds only to avoid them. It was evident that she had an object in keeping her presence on the road and her forlorn state unknown.

Their progress was necessarily very slow. They reached the bottom of the town, and the Casterbridge lamps lay before them like fallen Pleiads as they turned to the left into the dense shade of a deserted avenue of chestnuts, and so skirted the borough. Thus the town was passed, and the goal was reached.

On this much-desired spot outside the town rose a picturesque building. Originally it had been a mere case to hold people. The shell had been so thin, so devoid of excrescence, and so closely drawn over the accommodation granted, that the grim character of what was beneath showed through it, as the shape of a body is visible under a winding-sheet.

Then Nature, as if offended, lent a hand. Masses of ivy grew up, completely covering the walls, till the place looked like an abbey; and it was discovered that the view from the front, over the Casterbridge chimneys, was one of the most magnificent in the county. A neighbouring earl once said that he would give up a year's rental to have at his own door the view enjoyed by the inmates from theirs—and very probably the inmates would have given up the view for his year's rental.

This stone edifice consisted of a central mass and two wings, whereon stood as sentinels a few slim chimneys, now gurgling sorrowfully to the slow wind. In the wall was a gate, and by the gate a bellpull formed of a hanging wire. The woman raised herself as high as possible upon her knees, and could just reach the handle. She moved it and fell forwards in a bowed attitude, her face upon her bosom.

It was getting on towards six o'clock, and sounds of movement were to be heard inside the building which was the haven of rest to this wearied soul. A little door by the large one was opened, and a man appeared inside. He discerned the panting heap of clothes, went back for a light, and came again. He entered a second time, and returned with two women.

These lifted the prostrate figure and assisted her in through the doorway. The man then closed the door.

"How did she get here?" said one of the women.

"The Lord knows," said the other.

"There is a dog outside," murmured the overcome traveller. "Where is he gone? He helped me."

"I stoned him away," said the man.

The little procession then moved forward—the man in front bearing the light, the two bony women next, supporting between them the small and supple one. Thus they entered the house and disappeared.

Questions

How much does Fanny sleep?
What does she use to help her walk?
What helps her walk as she nears Casterbridge?
Where does she collapse?
GCSE style question: how does Hardy present Fanny as a figure of pathos here?
A Level style question: explore the presentation of the vagrant in literature, using Fanny as a starting point and the look at other texts of your choice.
Creative response: write a description/poem/story about a difficult journey.

CHAPTER XLI
SUSPICION—FANNY IS SENT FOR

Bathsheba said very little to her husband all that evening of their return from market, and he was not disposed to say much to her. He exhibited the unpleasant combination of a restless condition with a silent tongue. The next day, which was Sunday, passed nearly in the same manner as regarded their taciturnity, Bathsheba going to church both morning and afternoon. This was the day before the Budmouth races. In the evening Troy said, suddenly—

"Bathsheba, could you let me have twenty pounds?"

Her countenance instantly sank. "Twenty pounds?" she said.

"The fact is, I want it badly." The anxiety upon Troy's face was unusual and very marked. It was a culmination of the mood he had been in all the day.

"Ah! for those races to-morrow."

Troy for the moment made no reply. Her mistake had its advantages to a man who shrank from having his mind inspected as he did now. "Well, suppose I do want it for races?" he said, at last.

"Oh, Frank!" Bathsheba replied, and there was such a volume of entreaty in the words. "Only such a few weeks ago you said that I was far sweeter than all your other pleasures put together, and that you would give them all up for me; and now, won't you give up this one, which is more a worry than a pleasure? Do, Frank. Come, let me fascinate you by all I can do—by pretty words and pretty looks, and everything I can think of—to stay at home. Say yes to your wife—say yes!"

The tenderest and softest phases of Bathsheba's nature were prominent now—advanced impulsively for his acceptance, without any of the disguises and defences which the wariness of her character when she was cool too frequently threw over them. Few men could have resisted the arch yet dignified entreaty of the beautiful face, thrown a little back and sideways in the well known attitude that expresses more than the words it accompanies, and which seems to have been designed for these special occasions. Had the woman not been his wife, Troy would have succumbed instantly; as it was, he thought he would not deceive her longer.

"The money is not wanted for racing debts at all," he said.

"What is it for?" she asked. "You worry me a great deal by these mysterious responsibilities, Frank."

Troy hesitated. He did not now love her enough to allow himself to be carried too far by her ways. Yet it was necessary to be civil. "You wrong me by such a suspicious manner," he said. "Such strait-waistcoating as you treat me to is not becoming in you at so early a date."

"I think that I have a right to grumble a little if I pay," she said, with features between a smile and a pout.

"Exactly; and, the former being done, suppose we proceed to the latter. Bathsheba, fun is all very well, but don't go too far, or you may have cause to regret something."

She reddened. "I do that already," she said, quickly.

"What do you regret?"

"That my romance has come to an end."

"All romances end at marriage."

"I wish you wouldn't talk like that. You grieve me to my soul by being smart at my expense."

"You are dull enough at mine. I believe you hate me."

"Not you—only your faults. I do hate them."

"'Twould be much more becoming if you set yourself to cure them. Come, let's strike a balance with the twenty pounds, and be friends."

She gave a sigh of resignation. "I have about that sum here for household expenses. If you must have it, take it."

"Very good. Thank you. I expect I shall have gone away before you are in to breakfast to-morrow."

"And must you go? Ah! there was a time, Frank, when it would have taken a good many promises to other people to drag you away from me. You used to call me darling, then. But it doesn't matter to you how my days are passed now."

"I must go, in spite of sentiment." Troy, as he spoke, looked at his watch, and, apparently actuated by non lucendo principles, opened the case at the back, revealing, snugly stowed within it, a small coil of hair.

Bathsheba's eyes had been accidentally lifted at that moment, and she saw the action and saw the hair. She flushed in pain and surprise, and some words escaped her before she had thought whether or not it was wise to utter them. "A woman's curl of hair!" she said. "Oh, Frank, whose is that?"

Troy had instantly closed his watch. He carelessly replied, as one who cloaked some feelings that the sight had stirred. "Why, yours, of course. Whose should it be? I had quite forgotten that I had it."

"What a dreadful fib, Frank!"

"I tell you I had forgotten it!" he said, loudly.

"I don't mean that—it was yellow hair."

"Nonsense."

"That's insulting me. I know it was yellow. Now whose was it? I want to know."

"Very well—I'll tell you, so make no more ado. It is the hair of a young woman I was going to marry before I knew you."

"You ought to tell me her name, then."

"I cannot do that."

"Is she married yet?"

"No."

"Is she alive?"

"Yes."

"Is she pretty?"

"Yes."

"It is wonderful how she can be, poor thing, under such an awful affliction!"

"Affliction—what affliction?" he inquired, quickly.

"Having hair of that dreadful colour."

"Oh—ho—I like that!" said Troy, recovering himself. "Why, her hair has been admired by everybody who has seen her since she has worn it loose, which has not been long. It is beautiful hair. People used to turn their heads to look at it, poor girl!"

"Pooh! that's nothing—that's nothing!" she exclaimed, in incipient accents of pique. "If I cared for your love as much as I used to I could say people had turned to look at mine."

"Bathsheba, don't be so fitful and jealous. You knew what married life would be like, and shouldn't have entered it if you feared these contingencies."

Troy had by this time driven her to bitterness: her heart was big in her throat, and the ducts to her eyes were painfully full. Ashamed as she was to show emotion, at last she burst out:—

"This is all I get for loving you so well! Ah! when I married you your life was dearer to me than my own. I would have died for you—how truly I can say that I would have died for you! And now you sneer at my foolishness in marrying you. O! is it kind to me to throw my mistake in my face? Whatever opinion you may have of my wisdom, you should not tell me of it so mercilessly, now that I am in your power."

"I can't help how things fall out," said Troy; "upon my heart, women will be the death of me!"

"Well you shouldn't keep people's hair. You'll burn it, won't you, Frank?"

Frank went on as if he had not heard her. "There are considerations even before my consideration for you; reparations to be made—ties you know nothing of. If you repent of marrying, so do I."

Trembling now, she put her hand upon his arm, saying, in mingled tones of wretchedness and coaxing, "I only repent it if you don't love me better than any woman in the world! I don't otherwise, Frank. You don't repent because you already love somebody better than you love me, do you?"

"I don't know. Why do you say that?"

"You won't burn that curl. You like the woman who owns that pretty hair—yes; it is pretty—more beautiful than my miserable black mane! Well, it is no use; I can't help being ugly. You must like her best, if you will!"

"Until to-day, when I took it from a drawer, I have never looked upon that bit of hair for several months—that I am ready to swear."

"But just now you said 'ties'; and then—that woman we met?"

"'Twas the meeting with her that reminded me of the hair."

"Is it hers, then?"

"Yes. There, now that you have wormed it out of me, I hope you are content."

"And what are the ties?"

"Oh! that meant nothing—a mere jest."

"A mere jest!" she said, in mournful astonishment. "Can you jest when I am so wretchedly in earnest? Tell me the truth, Frank. I am not a fool, you know, although I am a woman, and have my woman's moments. Come! treat me fairly," she said, looking honestly and fearlessly into his face. "I don't want much; bare justice—that's all! Ah! once I felt I could be content with nothing less than the highest homage from the husband I should choose. Now, anything short of cruelty will content me. Yes! the independent and spirited Bathsheba is come to this!"

"For Heaven's sake don't be so desperate!" Troy said, snappishly, rising as he did so, and leaving the room.

Directly he had gone, Bathsheba burst into great sobs—dry-eyed sobs, which cut as they came, without any softening by tears. But she determined to repress all evidences of feeling. She was conquered; but she would never own it as long as she lived. Her pride was indeed brought low by despairing discoveries of her spoliation by marriage with a less pure nature than her own. She chafed to and fro in rebelliousness, like a caged leopard; her whole soul was in arms, and the blood fired her face. Until she had met Troy, Bathsheba had been proud of her position as a woman; it had been a glory to her to know that her lips had been touched by no man's on earth— that her waist had never been encircled by a lover's arm. She hated herself now. In those earlier days she had always nourished a secret contempt for girls who were the slaves of the first good-looking young fellow who should choose to salute them. She had never taken kindly to the idea of marriage in the abstract as did the majority of women she saw about her. In the turmoil of her anxiety for her lover she had agreed to marry him; but the perception that had accompanied her happiest hours on this account was rather that of self-sacrifice than of promotion and honour. Although she scarcely knew the divinity's name, Diana was the goddess whom Bathsheba instinctively adored. That she had never, by look, word, or sign, encouraged a man to approach her—that she had felt herself sufficient to herself, and had in the independence of her girlish heart fancied there was a certain degradation in renouncing the simplicity of a maiden existence to become the humbler half of an indifferent matrimonial whole—were facts now bitterly remembered. Oh, if she had never stooped to folly of this kind, respectable as it was, and could only stand again, as she had stood on the hill at Norcombe, and dare Troy or any other man to pollute a hair of her head by his interference!

The next morning she rose earlier than usual, and had the horse saddled for her ride round the farm in the customary way. When she came in at half-past eight—their usual hour for breakfasting—she was informed that her husband had risen, taken his breakfast, and driven off to Casterbridge with the gig and Poppet.

After breakfast she was cool and collected—quite herself in fact—and she rambled to the gate, intending to walk to another quarter of the farm, which she still personally superintended as well as her duties in the house would permit, continually, however, finding herself preceded in forethought by Gabriel Oak, for whom she began to entertain the genuine friendship of a sister. Of course, she sometimes thought of him in the light of an old lover, and had momentary imaginings of what life with him as a husband would have been like; also of life with Boldwood under the same conditions. But Bathsheba, though she could feel, was not much given to futile dreaming, and her musings under this head were short and entirely confined to the times when Troy's neglect was more than ordinarily evident.

She saw coming up the road a man like Mr. Boldwood. It was Mr. Boldwood. Bathsheba blushed painfully, and watched. The farmer stopped when still a long way off, and held up his hand to Gabriel Oak, who was in a footpath across the field. The two men then approached each other and seemed to engage in earnest conversation.

Thus they continued for a long time. Joseph Poorgrass now passed near them, wheeling a barrow of apples up the hill to Bathsheba's residence. Boldwood and Gabriel called to him, spoke to him for a few minutes, and then all three parted, Joseph immediately coming up the hill with his barrow.

Bathsheba, who had seen this pantomime with some surprise, experienced great relief when Boldwood turned back again. "Well, what's the message, Joseph?" she said.

He set down his barrow, and, putting upon himself the refined aspect that a conversation with a lady required, spoke to Bathsheba over the gate.

"You'll never see Fanny Robin no more—use nor principal—ma'am."

"Why?"

"Because she's dead in the Union."

"Fanny dead—never!"

"Yes, ma'am."

"What did she die from?"

"I don't know for certain; but I should be inclined to think it was from general neshness of constitution. She was such a limber maid that 'a could stand no hardship, even when I knowed her, and 'a went like a candle-snoff, so 'tis said. She was took bad in the morning, and, being quite feeble and worn out, she died in the evening. She belongs by law to our parish; and Mr. Boldwood is going to send a waggon at three this afternoon to fetch her home here and bury her."

"Indeed I shall not let Mr. Boldwood do any such thing—I shall do it! Fanny was my uncle's servant, and, although I only knew her for a couple of days, she belongs to me. How very, very sad this is!—the idea of Fanny being in a workhouse." Bathsheba had begun to know what suffering was, and she spoke with real feeling... "Send across to Mr. Boldwood's, and say that Mrs. Troy will take upon herself the duty of fetching an old servant of the family... We ought not to put her in a waggon; we'll get a hearse."

"There will hardly be time, ma'am, will there?"

"Perhaps not," she said, musingly. "When did you say we must be at the door—three o'clock?"

"Three o'clock this afternoon, ma'am, so to speak it."

"Very well—you go with it. A pretty waggon is better than an ugly hearse, after all. Joseph, have the new spring waggon with the blue body and red wheels, and wash it very clean. And, Joseph—"

Analysis: Here we see how Bathsheba feels very much part of the community with her commitment to make sure that Fanny is buried properly. There is, of course, dark irony in the fact that everyone else knows the truth about Fanny but she doesn't.

Discussion point: How does Hardy ratchet up the suspense here?

"Yes, ma'am."

"Carry with you some evergreens and flowers to put upon her coffin—indeed, gather a great many, and completely bury her in them. Get some boughs of laurustinus, and variegated box, and yew, and boy's-love; ay, and some bunches of chrysanthemum. And let old Pleasant draw her, because she knew him so well."

"I will, ma'am. I ought to have said that the Union, in the form of four labouring men, will meet me when I gets to our churchyard gate, and take her and bury her according to the rites of the Board of Guardians, as by law ordained."

"Dear me—Casterbridge Union—and is Fanny come to this?" said Bathsheba, musing. "I wish I had known of it sooner. I thought she was far away. How long has she lived there?"

"On'y been there a day or two."

"Oh!—then she has not been staying there as a regular inmate?"

"No. She first went to live in a garrison-town t'other side o' Wessex, and since then she's been picking up a living at seampstering in Melchester for several months, at the house of a very respectable widow-woman who takes in work of that sort. She only got handy the Union-house on Sunday morning 'a b'lieve, and 'tis supposed here and there that she had traipsed every step of the way from Melchester. Why she left her place, I can't say, for I don't know; and as to a lie, why, I wouldn't tell it. That's the short of the story, ma'am."

"Ah-h!"

No gem ever flashed from a rosy ray to a white one more rapidly than changed the young wife's countenance whilst this word came from her in a long-drawn breath. "Did she walk along our turnpike-road?" she said, in a suddenly restless and eager voice.

"I believe she did... Ma'am, shall I call Liddy? You bain't well, ma'am, surely? You look like a lily—so pale and fainty!"

"No; don't call her; it is nothing. When did she pass Weatherbury?"

"Last Saturday night."

"That will do, Joseph; now you may go."

"Certainly, ma'am."

"Joseph, come hither a moment. What was the colour of Fanny Robin's hair?"

"Really, mistress, now that 'tis put to me so judge-and-jury like, I can't call to mind, if ye'll believe me!"

"Never mind; go on and do what I told you. Stop—well no, go on."

She turned herself away from him, that he might no longer notice the mood which had set its sign so visibly upon her, and went indoors with a distressing sense of faintness and a beating brow. About an hour after, she heard the noise of the waggon and went out, still with a painful consciousness of her bewildered and troubled look. Joseph, dressed in his best suit of clothes, was putting in the horse to start. The shrubs and flowers were all piled in the waggon, as she had directed; Bathsheba hardly saw them now.

"Died of what? did you say, Joseph?"

"I don't know, ma'am."

"Are you quite sure?"

"Yes, ma'am, quite sure."

"Sure of what?"

"I'm sure that all I know is that she arrived in the morning and died in the evening without further parley. What Oak and Mr. Boldwood told me was only these few words. 'Little Fanny Robin is dead, Joseph,' Gabriel said, looking in my face in his steady old way. I was very sorry, and I said, 'Ah!—and how did she come to die?' 'Well, she's dead in Casterbridge Union,' he said, 'and perhaps 'tisn't much matter about how she came to die. She reached the Union early Sunday morning, and died in the afternoon—that's clear enough.' Then I asked what she'd been doing lately, and Mr. Boldwood turned round to me then, and left off spitting a thistle with the end of his stick. He told me about her having lived by seampstering in Melchester, as I mentioned to you, and that she walked therefrom at the end of last week, passing near here Saturday night in the dusk. They then said I had better just name a hint of her death to you, and away they went. Her death might have been brought on by biding in the night wind, you know, ma'am; for people used to say she'd go off in a decline: she used to cough a good deal in winter time. However, 'tisn't much odds to us about that now, for 'tis all over."

"Have you heard a different story at all?" She looked at him so intently that Joseph's eyes quailed.

"Not a word, mistress, I assure 'ee!" he said. "Hardly anybody in the parish knows the news yet."

"I wonder why Gabriel didn't bring the message to me himself. He mostly makes a point of seeing me upon the most trifling errand." These words were merely murmured, and she was looking upon the ground.

"Perhaps he was busy, ma'am," Joseph suggested. "And sometimes he seems to suffer from things upon his mind, connected with the time when he was better off than 'a is now. 'A's rather a curious item, but a very understanding shepherd, and learned in books."

"Did anything seem upon his mind whilst he was speaking to you about this?"

"I cannot but say that there did, ma'am. He was terrible down, and so was Farmer Boldwood."

"Thank you, Joseph. That will do. Go on now, or you'll be late."

Bathsheba, still unhappy, went indoors again. In the course of the afternoon she said to Liddy, who had been informed of the occurrence, "What was the colour of poor Fanny Robin's hair? Do you know? I cannot recollect—I only saw her for a day or two."

"It was light, ma'am; but she wore it rather short, and packed away under her cap, so that you would hardly notice it. But I have seen her let it down when she was going to bed, and it looked beautiful then. Real golden hair."

"Her young man was a soldier, was he not?"

"Yes. In the same regiment as Mr. Troy. He says he knew him very well."

"What, Mr. Troy says so? How came he to say that?"

"One day I just named it to him, and asked him if he knew Fanny's young man. He said, 'Oh yes, he knew the young man as well as he knew himself, and that there wasn't a man in the regiment he liked better.'"

"Ah! Said that, did he?"

"Yes; and he said there was a strong likeness between himself and the other young man, so that sometimes people mistook them—"

"Liddy, for Heaven's sake stop your talking!" said Bathsheba, with the nervous petulance that comes from worrying perceptions.

Questions

How much money does Troy get from Bathsheba?

What does Bathsheba notice when Troy opens his watch?

What does Troy tell Bathsheba about the lock of hair?

What does Bathsheba guess about the woman on the highway?

GCSE style question: how does Hardy present marriage in this chapter?

A Level style question: compare and contrast Hardy's presentation of marriage with another text which explores the theme.

Creative response: write a story/poem/description about an item which is treasured by someone because it is connected to a former love like a lock of hair etc., call it 'The Memento'.

CHAPTER XLII
JOSEPH AND HIS BURDEN—
BUCK'S HEAD

A wall bounded the site of Casterbridge Union-house, except along a portion of the end. Here a high gable stood prominent, and it was covered like the front with a mat of ivy. In this gable was no window, chimney, ornament, or protuberance of any kind. The single feature appertaining to it, beyond the expanse of dark green leaves, was a small door.

The situation of the door was peculiar. The sill was three or four feet above the ground, and for a moment one was at a loss for an explanation of this exceptional altitude, till ruts immediately beneath suggested that the door was used solely for the passage of articles and persons to and from the level of a vehicle standing on the outside. Upon the whole, the door seemed to advertise itself as a species of Traitor's Gate translated to another sphere. That entry and exit hereby was only at rare intervals became apparent on noting that tufts of grass were allowed to flourish undisturbed in the chinks of the sill.

As the clock over the South-street Alms-house pointed to five minutes to three, a blue spring waggon, picked out with red, and containing boughs and flowers, passed the end of the street, and up towards this side of the building. Whilst the chimes were yet stammering out a shattered form of "Malbrook," Joseph Poorgrass rang the bell, and received directions to back his waggon against the high door under the gable. The door then opened, and a plain elm coffin was slowly thrust forth, and laid by two men in fustian along the middle of the vehicle.

One of the men then stepped up beside it, took from his pocket a lump of chalk, and wrote upon the cover the name and a few other words in a large scrawling hand. (We believe that they do these things more tenderly now, and provide a plate.) He covered the whole with a black cloth, threadbare, but decent, the tail-board of the waggon was returned to its place, one of the men handed a certificate of registry to Poorgrass, and both entered the door, closing it behind them. Their connection with her, short as it had been, was over for ever.

Joseph then placed the flowers as enjoined, and the evergreens around the flowers, till it was difficult to divine what the waggon contained; he smacked his whip, and the rather pleasing funeral car crept down the hill, and along the road to Weatherbury.

The afternoon drew on apace, and, looking to the right towards the sea as he walked beside the horse, Poorgrass saw strange clouds and scrolls of mist rolling over the long ridges which girt the landscape in that quarter. They came in yet greater volumes, and indolently crept across the intervening valleys, and around the withered papery flags of the moor and river brinks. Then their dank spongy forms closed in upon the sky. It was a sudden overgrowth of atmospheric fungi which had their roots in the neighbouring sea, and by the time that horse, man, and corpse entered Yalbury Great Wood, these silent workings of an invisible hand had reached them, and they were completely enveloped, this being the first arrival of the autumn fogs, and the first fog of the series.

The air was as an eye suddenly struck blind. The waggon and its load rolled no longer on the horizontal division between clearness and opacity, but were imbedded in an elastic body of a monotonous pallor throughout. There was no perceptible motion in the air, not a visible drop of water fell upon a leaf of the beeches, birches, and firs composing the wood on either side. The trees stood in an attitude of intentness, as if they waited longingly for a wind to come and rock them. A startling quiet overhung all surrounding things—so completely, that the crunching of the waggon-wheels was as a great noise, and small rustles, which had never obtained a hearing except by night, were distinctly individualized.

Joseph Poorgrass looked round upon his sad burden as it loomed faintly through the flowering laurustinus, then at the unfathomable gloom amid the high trees on each hand, indistinct, shadowless, and spectre-like in their monochrome of grey. He felt anything but cheerful, and wished he had the company even of a child or dog. Stopping the horse, he listened. Not a footstep or wheel was audible anywhere around, and the dead silence was broken only by a heavy particle falling from a tree through the evergreens and alighting with a smart rap upon the coffin of poor Fanny. The fog had by this time saturated the trees, and this was the first dropping of water from the overbrimming leaves. The hollow echo of its fall reminded the waggoner painfully of the grim Leveller. Then hard by came down another drop, then two or three. Presently there was a continual tapping of these heavy drops upon the dead leaves, the road, and the travellers. The nearer boughs were beaded with the mist to the greyness of aged men, and the rusty-red leaves of the beeches were hung with similar drops, like diamonds on auburn hair.

At the roadside hamlet called Roy-Town, just beyond this wood, was the old inn Buck's Head. It was about a mile and a half from Weatherbury, and in the meridian times of stage-coach travelling had been the place where many coaches changed and kept their relays of horses. All the old stabling was now pulled down, and little remained besides the habitable inn itself, which, standing a little way back from the road, signified its existence to people far up and down the highway by a sign hanging from the horizontal bough of an elm on the opposite side of the way.

Travellers—for the variety tourist had hardly developed into a distinct species at this date—sometimes said in passing, when they cast their eyes up to the sign-bearing tree, that artists were fond of representing the signboard hanging thus, but that they themselves had never before noticed so perfect an instance in actual working order. It was near this tree that the waggon was standing into which Gabriel Oak crept on his first journey to Weatherbury; but, owing to the darkness, the sign and the inn had been unobserved.

The manners of the inn were of the old-established type. Indeed, in the minds of its frequenters they existed as unalterable formulæ: e.g.—

> Rap with the bottom of your pint for more liquor.
> For tobacco, shout.
> In calling for the girl in waiting, say, "Maid!"
> Ditto for the landlady, "Old Soul!" etc., etc.

It was a relief to Joseph's heart when the friendly signboard came in view, and, stopping his horse immediately beneath it, he proceeded to fulfil an intention made a long time before. His spirits were oozing out of him quite. He turned the horse's head to the green bank, and entered the hostel for a mug of ale.

Going down into the kitchen of the inn, the floor of which was a step below the passage, which in its turn was a step below the road outside, what should Joseph see to gladden his eyes but two copper-coloured discs, in the form of the countenances of Mr. Jan Coggan and Mr. Mark Clark.

These owners of the two most appreciative throats in the neighbourhood, within the pale of respectability, were now sitting face to face over a three-legged circular table, having an iron rim to keep cups and pots from being accidentally elbowed off; they might have been said to resemble the setting sun and the full moon shining vis-à-vis across the globe.

"Why, 'tis neighbour Poorgrass!" said Mark Clark. "I'm sure your face don't praise your mistress's table, Joseph."

"I've had a very pale companion for the last four miles," said Joseph, indulging in a shudder toned down by resignation. "And to speak the truth, 'twas beginning to tell upon me. I assure ye, I ha'n't seed the colour of victuals or drink since breakfast time this morning, and that was no more than a dew-bit afield."

"Then drink, Joseph, and don't restrain yourself!" said Coggan, handing him a hooped mug three-quarters full.

Joseph drank for a moderately long time, then for a longer time, saying, as he lowered the jug, "'Tis pretty drinking—very pretty drinking, and is more than cheerful on my melancholy errand, so to speak it."

"True, drink is a pleasant delight," said Jan, as one who repeated a truism so familiar to his brain that he hardly noticed its passage over his tongue; and, lifting the cup, Coggan tilted his head gradually backwards, with closed eyes, that his expectant soul might not be diverted for one instant from its bliss by irrelevant surroundings.

"Well, I must be on again," said Poorgrass. "Not but that I should like another nip with ye; but the parish might lose confidence in me if I was seed here."

"Where be ye trading o't to to-day, then, Joseph?"

"Back to Weatherbury. I've got poor little Fanny Robin in my waggon outside, and I must be at the churchyard gates at a quarter to five with her."

"Ay—I've heard of it. And so she's nailed up in parish boards after all, and nobody to pay the bell shilling and the grave half-crown."

"The parish pays the grave half-crown, but not the bell shilling, because the bell's a luxery: but 'a can hardly do without the grave, poor body. However, I expect our mistress will pay all."

"A pretty maid as ever I see! But what's yer hurry, Joseph? The pore woman's dead, and you can't bring her to life, and you may as well sit down comfortable, and finish another with us."

"I don't mind taking just the least thimbleful ye can dream of more with ye, sonnies. But only a few minutes, because 'tis as 'tis."

"Of course, you'll have another drop. A man's twice the man afterwards. You feel so warm and glorious, and you whop and slap at your work without any trouble, and everything goes on like sticks a-breaking. Too much liquor is bad, and leads us to that horned man in the smoky house; but after all, many people haven't the gift of enjoying a wet, and since we be highly favoured with a power that way, we should make the most o't."

"True," said Mark Clark. "'Tis a talent the Lord has mercifully bestowed upon us, and we ought not to neglect it. But, what with the parsons and clerks and school-people and serious tea-parties, the merry old ways of good life have gone to the dogs—upon my carcase, they have!"

"Well, really, I must be onward again now," said Joseph.

"Now, now, Joseph; nonsense! The poor woman is dead, isn't she, and what's your hurry?"

"Well, I hope Providence won't be in a way with me for my doings," said Joseph, again sitting down. "I've been troubled with weak moments lately, 'tis true. I've been drinky once this month already, and I did not go to church a-Sunday, and I dropped a curse or two yesterday; so I don't want to go too far for my safety. Your next world is your next world, and not to be squandered offhand."

"I believe ye to be a chapelmember, Joseph. That I do."

"Oh, no, no! I don't go so far as that."

"For my part," said Coggan, "I'm staunch Church of England."

"Ay, and faith, so be I," said Mark Clark.

"I won't say much for myself; I don't wish to," Coggan continued, with that tendency to talk on principles which is characteristic of the barley-corn. "But I've never changed a single doctrine: I've stuck like a plaster to the old faith I was born in. Yes; there's this to be said for the Church, a man can belong to the Church and bide in his cheerful old inn, and never trouble or worry his mind about doctrines at all. But to be a meetinger, you must go to chapel in all winds and weathers, and make yerself as frantic as a skit. Not but that chapel members be clever chaps enough in their way. They can lift up beautiful prayers out of their own heads, all about their families and shipwrecks in the newspaper."

"They can—they can," said Mark Clark, with corroborative feeling; "but we Churchmen, you see, must have it all printed aforehand, or, dang it all, we should no more know what to say to a great gaffer like the Lord than babes unborn."

"Chapelfolk be more hand-in-glove with them above than we," said Joseph, thoughtfully.

"Yes," said Coggan. "We know very well that if anybody do go to heaven, they will. They've worked hard for it, and they deserve to have it, such as 'tis. I bain't such a fool as to pretend that we who stick to the Church have the same chance as they, because we know we have not. But I hate a feller who'll change his old ancient doctrines for the sake of getting to heaven. I'd as soon turn king's-evidence for the few pounds you get. Why, neighbours, when every one of my taties were frosted, our Parson Thirdly were the man who gave me a sack for seed, though he hardly had one for his own use, and no money to buy 'em. If it hadn't been for him, I shouldn't hae had a tatie to put in my garden. D'ye think I'd turn after that? No, I'll stick to my side; and if we be in the wrong, so be it: I'll fall with the fallen!"

"Well said—very well said," observed Joseph.—"However, folks, I must be moving now: upon my life I must. Pa'son Thirdly will be waiting at the church gates, and there's the woman a-biding outside in the waggon."

"Joseph Poorgrass, don't be so miserable! Pa'son Thirdly won't mind. He's a generous man; he's found me in tracts for years, and I've consumed a good many in the course of a long and shady life; but he's never been the man to cry out at the expense. Sit down."

The longer Joseph Poorgrass remained, the less his spirit was troubled by the duties which devolved upon him this afternoon. The minutes glided by uncounted, until the evening shades began perceptibly to deepen, and the eyes of the three were but sparkling points on the surface of darkness. Coggan's repeater struck six from his pocket in the usual still small tones.

At that moment hasty steps were heard in the entry, and the door opened to admit the figure of Gabriel Oak, followed by the maid of the inn bearing a candle. He stared sternly at the one lengthy and two round faces of the sitters, which confronted him with the expressions of a fiddle and a couple of warming-pans. Joseph Poorgrass blinked, and shrank several inches into the background.

"Upon my soul, I'm ashamed of you; 'tis disgraceful, Joseph, disgraceful!" said Gabriel, indignantly. "Coggan, you call yourself a man, and don't know better than this."

Coggan looked up indefinitely at Oak, one or other of his eyes occasionally opening and closing of its own accord, as if it were not a member, but a dozy individual with a distinct personality.

"Don't take on so, shepherd!" said Mark Clark, looking reproachfully at the candle, which appeared to possess special features of interest for his eyes.

"Nobody can hurt a dead woman," at length said Coggan, with the precision of a machine. "All that could be done for her is done—she's beyond us: and why should a man put himself in a tearing hurry for lifeless clay that can neither feel nor see, and don't know what you do with her at all? If she'd been alive, I would have been the first to help her. If she now wanted victuals and drink, I'd pay for it, money down. But she's dead, and no speed of ours will bring her to life. The woman's past us—time spent upon her is throwed away: why should we hurry to do what's not required? Drink, shepherd, and be friends, for to-morrow we may be like her."

"We may," added Mark Clark, emphatically, at once drinking himself, to run no further risk of losing his chance by the event alluded to, Jan meanwhile merging his additional thoughts of to-morrow in a song:—

> To-mor-row, to-mor-row!
> And while peace and plen-ty I find at my board,
> With a heart free from sick-ness and sor-row,
> With my friends will I share what to-day may af-ford,
> And let them spread the ta-ble to-mor-row.
> To-mor-row', to-mor—

"Do hold thy horning, Jan!" said Oak; and turning upon Poorgrass, "as for you, Joseph, who do your wicked deeds in such confoundedly holy ways, you are as drunk as you can stand."

"No, Shepherd Oak, no! Listen to reason, shepherd. All that's the matter with me is the affliction called a multiplying eye, and that's how it is I look double to you—I mean, you look double to me."

"A multiplying eye is a very bad thing," said Mark Clark.

"It always comes on when I have been in a public-house a little time," said Joseph Poorgrass, meekly. "Yes; I see two of every sort, as if I were some holy man living in the times of King Noah and entering into the ark... Y-y-y-yes," he added, becoming much affected by the picture of himself as a person thrown away, and shedding tears; "I feel too good for England: I ought to have lived in Genesis by rights, like the other men of sacrifice, and then I shouldn't have b-b-been called a d-d-drunkard in such a way!"

"I wish you'd show yourself a man of spirit, and not sit whining there!"

"Show myself a man of spirit? ... Ah, well! let me take the name of drunkard humbly—let me be a man of contrite knees—let it be! I know that I always do say 'Please God' afore I do anything, from my getting up to my going down of the same, and I be willing to take as much disgrace as there is in that holy act. Hah, yes! ... But not a man of spirit? Have I ever allowed the toe of pride to be lifted against my hinder parts without groaning manfully that I question the right to do so? I inquire that query boldly?"

"We can't say that you have, Hero Poorgrass," admitted Jan.

"Never have I allowed such treatment to pass unquestioned! Yet the shepherd says in the face of that rich testimony that I be not a man of spirit! Well, let it pass by, and death is a kind friend!"

Gabriel, seeing that neither of the three was in a fit state to take charge of the waggon for the remainder of the journey, made no reply, but, closing the door again upon them, went across to where the vehicle stood, now getting indistinct in the fog and gloom of this mildewy time. He pulled the horse's head from the large patch of turf it had eaten bare, readjusted the boughs over the coffin, and drove along through the unwholesome night.

Analysis: Amidst the gloomy atmosphere of the novel at this point, Hardy lightens the mood with some dark comedy. Joseph Poorgrass in pursuit of the "multiplying eye" gets drunk at the Malthouse and, as a result, abandons the coffin outside, forgetting his mission to return it to Weatherbury farm. It is Hardy's seamless ability to merge incidental characters such as Poorgrass with the main narrative which give the novel its rich texture, the feeling that we are experiencing a whole community rather just a few characters.

Discussion point: Why does Hardy include this incident at the novel here?

It had gradually become rumoured in the village that the body to be brought and buried that day was all that was left of the unfortunate Fanny Robin who had followed the Eleventh from Casterbridge through Melchester and onwards. But, thanks to Boldwood's reticence and Oak's generosity, the lover she had followed had never been individualized as Troy. Gabriel hoped that the whole truth of the matter might not be published till at any rate the girl had been in her grave for a few days, when the interposing barriers of earth and time, and a sense that the events had been somewhat shut into oblivion, would deaden the sting that revelation and invidious remark would have for Bathsheba just now.

By the time that Gabriel reached the old manor-house, her residence, which lay in his way to the church, it was quite dark. A man came from the gate and said through the fog, which hung between them like blown flour—

"Is that Poorgrass with the corpse?"

Gabriel recognized the voice as that of the parson.

"The corpse is here, sir," said Gabriel.

"I have just been to inquire of Mrs. Troy if she could tell me the reason of the delay. I am afraid it is too late now for the funeral to be performed with proper decency. Have you the registrar's certificate?"

"No," said Gabriel. "I expect Poorgrass has that; and he's at the Buck's Head. I forgot to ask him for it."

"Then that settles the matter. We'll put off the funeral till to-morrow morning. The body may be brought on to the church, or it may be left here at the farm and fetched by the bearers in the morning. They waited more than an hour, and have now gone home."

Gabriel had his reasons for thinking the latter a most objectionable plan, notwithstanding that Fanny had been an inmate of the farm-house for several years in the lifetime of Bathsheba's uncle. Visions of several unhappy contingencies which might arise from this delay flitted before him. But his will was not law, and he went indoors to inquire of his mistress what were her wishes on the subject. He found her in an unusual mood: her eyes as she looked up to him were suspicious and perplexed as with some antecedent thought. Troy had not yet returned. At first Bathsheba assented with a mien of indifference to his proposition that they should go on to the church at once with their burden; but immediately afterwards, following Gabriel to the gate, she swerved to the extreme of solicitousness on Fanny's account, and desired that the girl might be brought into the house. Oak argued upon the convenience of leaving her in the waggon, just as she lay now, with her flowers and green leaves about her, merely wheeling the vehicle into the coach-house till the morning, but to no purpose. "It is unkind and unchristian," she said, "to leave the poor thing in a coach-house all night."

"Very well, then," said the parson. "And I will arrange that the funeral shall take place early to-morrow. Perhaps Mrs. Troy is right in feeling that we cannot treat a dead fellow-creature too thoughtfully. We must remember that though she may have erred grievously in leaving her home, she is still our sister: and it is to be believed that God's uncovenanted mercies are extended towards her, and that she is a member of the flock of Christ."

The parson's words spread into the heavy air with a sad yet unperturbed cadence, and Gabriel shed an honest tear. Bathsheba seemed unmoved. Mr. Thirdly then left them, and Gabriel lighted a lantern. Fetching three other men to assist him, they bore the unconscious truant indoors, placing the coffin on two benches in the middle of a little sitting-room next the hall, as Bathsheba directed.

Every one except Gabriel Oak then left the room. He still indecisively lingered beside the body. He was deeply troubled at the wretchedly ironical aspect that circumstances were putting on with regard to Troy's wife, and at his own powerlessness to counteract them. In spite of his careful manœuvering all this day, the very worst event that could in any way have happened in connection with the burial had happened now. Oak imagined a terrible discovery resulting from this afternoon's work that might cast over Bathsheba's life a shade which the interposition of many lapsing years might but indifferently lighten, and which nothing at all might altogether remove.

Suddenly, as in a last attempt to save Bathsheba from, at any rate, immediate anguish, he looked again, as he had looked before, at the chalk writing upon the coffin-lid. The scrawl was this simple one, "Fanny Robin and child." Gabriel took his handkerchief and carefully rubbed out the two latter words, leaving visible the inscription "Fanny Robin" only. He then left the room, and went out quietly by the front door.

Analysis: Oak's desire to protect Bathsheba has been evident since he came back and rescued her sheep from dying: since then he has been vigilantly watching over her like a guardian angel, living up to his namesake. Now he takes the step of attempting to protect Bathsheba from the full knowledge of what her husband has done.

Discussion point: Why does Hardy present Oak like this do you think?

Questions

Where does Joseph collect the coffin from?
Where does Joseph stop and what happens to him there?
Who takes the coffin back to Weatherbury?
Where does Bathsheba insist the coffin is brought to?
What words does Gabriel remove from the coffin lid?
GCSE style question: why do you think Hardy makes both Boldwood and Oak not reveal the identity of Fanny's lover to the villagers or Bathsheba?
A Level style question: examine Hardy's portrayal of the death of Fanny, analyzing the way he juxtaposes the comic banter of the villagers with her tragic death.
Creative response: write Gabriel's diary for this chapter.

CHAPTER XLIII
FANNY'S REVENGE

"Do you want me any longer ma'am?" inquired Liddy, at a later hour the same evening, standing by the door with a chamber candlestick in her hand and addressing Bathsheba, who sat cheerless and alone in the large parlour beside the first fire of the season.

"No more to-night, Liddy."

"I'll sit up for master if you like, ma'am. I am not at all afraid of Fanny, if I may sit in my own room and have a candle. She was such a childlike, nesh young thing that her spirit couldn't appear to anybody if it tried, I'm quite sure."

"Oh no, no! You go to bed. I'll sit up for him myself till twelve o'clock, and if he has not arrived by that time, I shall give him up and go to bed too."

"It is half-past ten now."

"Oh! is it?"

"Why don't you sit upstairs, ma'am?"

"Why don't I?" said Bathsheba, desultorily. "It isn't worth while—there's a fire here, Liddy." She suddenly exclaimed in an impulsive and excited whisper, "Have you heard anything strange said of Fanny?" The words had no sooner escaped her than an expression of unutterable regret crossed her face, and she burst into tears.

"No—not a word!" said Liddy, looking at the weeping woman with astonishment. "What is it makes you cry so, ma'am; has anything hurt you?" She came to Bathsheba's side with a face full of sympathy.

"No, Liddy—I don't want you any more. I can hardly say why I have taken to crying lately: I never used to cry. Good-night."

Liddy then left the parlour and closed the door.

Bathsheba was lonely and miserable now; not lonelier actually than she had been before her marriage; but her loneliness then was to that of the present time as the solitude of a mountain is to the solitude of a cave. And within the last day or two had come these disquieting thoughts about her husband's past. Her wayward sentiment that evening concerning Fanny's temporary resting-place had been the result of a strange complication of impulses in Bathsheba's bosom. Perhaps it would be more accurately described as a determined rebellion against her prejudices, a revulsion from a lower instinct of uncharitableness, which would have withheld all sympathy from the dead woman, because in life she had preceded Bathsheba in the attentions of a man whom Bathsheba had by no means ceased from loving, though her love was sick to death just now with the gravity of a further misgiving.

In five or ten minutes there was another tap at the door. Liddy reappeared, and coming in a little way stood hesitating, until at length she said, "Maryann has just heard something very strange, but I know it isn't true. And we shall be sure to know the rights of it in a day or two."

"What is it?"

"Oh, nothing connected with you or us, ma'am. It is about Fanny. That same thing you have heard."

"I have heard nothing."

"I mean that a wicked story is got to Weatherbury within this last hour—that—" Liddy came close to her mistress and whispered the remainder of the sentence slowly into her ear, inclining her head as she spoke in the direction of the room where Fanny lay.

Bathsheba trembled from head to foot.

"I don't believe it!" she said, excitedly. "And there's only one name written on the coffin-cover."

"Nor I, ma'am. And a good many others don't; for we should surely have been told more about it if it had been true—don't you think so, ma'am?"

"We might or we might not."

Bathsheba turned and looked into the fire, that Liddy might not see her face. Finding that her mistress was going to say no more, Liddy glided out, closed the door softly, and went to bed.

Bathsheba's face, as she continued looking into the fire that evening, might have excited solicitousness on her account even among those who loved her least. The sadness of Fanny Robin's fate did not make Bathsheba's glorious, although she was the Esther to this poor Vashti, and their fates might be supposed to stand in some respects as contrasts to each other. When Liddy came into the room a second time the beautiful eyes which met hers had worn a listless, weary look. When she went out after telling the story they had expressed wretchedness in full activity. Her simple country nature, fed on old-fashioned principles, was troubled by that which would have troubled a woman of the world very little, both Fanny and her child, if she had one, being dead.

Bathsheba had grounds for conjecturing a connection between her own history and the dimly suspected tragedy of Fanny's end which Oak and Boldwood never for a moment credited her with possessing. The meeting with the lonely woman on the previous Saturday night had been unwitnessed and unspoken of. Oak may have had the best of intentions in withholding for as many days as possible the details of what had happened to Fanny; but had he known that Bathsheba's perceptions had already been exercised in the matter, he would have done nothing to lengthen the minutes of suspense she was now undergoing, when the certainty which must terminate it would be the worst fact suspected after all.

She suddenly felt a longing desire to speak to some one stronger than herself, and so get strength to sustain her surmised position with dignity and her lurking doubts with stoicism. Where could she find such a friend? nowhere in the house. She was by far the coolest of the women under her roof. Patience and suspension of judgement for a few hours were what she wanted to learn, and there was nobody to teach her. Might she but go to Gabriel Oak!—but that could not be. What a way Oak had, she thought, of enduring things. Boldwood, who seemed so much deeper and higher and stronger in feeling than Gabriel, had not yet learnt, any more than she herself, the simple lesson which Oak showed a mastery of by every turn and look he gave—that among the multitude of interests by which he was surrounded, those which affected his personal well-being were not the most absorbing and important in his eyes. Oak meditatively looked upon the horizon of circumstances without any special regard to his own standpoint in the midst. That was how she would wish to be. But then Oak was not racked by incertitude upon the inmost matter of his bosom, as she was at this moment. Oak knew all about Fanny that he wished to know—she felt convinced of that. If she were to go to him now at once and say no more than these few words, "What is the truth of the story?" he would feel bound in honour to tell her. It would be an inexpressible relief. No further speech would need to be uttered. He knew her so well that no eccentricity of behaviour in her would alarm him.

She flung a cloak round her, went to the door and opened it. Every blade, every twig was still. The air was yet thick with moisture, though somewhat less dense than during the afternoon, and a steady smack of drops upon the fallen leaves under the boughs was almost musical in its soothing regularity. It seemed better to be out of the house than within it, and Bathsheba closed the door, and walked slowly down the lane till she came opposite to Gabriel's cottage, where he now lived alone, having left Coggan's house through being pinched for room. There was a light in one window only, and that was downstairs. The shutters were not closed, nor was any blind or curtain drawn over the window, neither robbery nor observation being a contingency which could do much injury to the occupant of the domicile. Yes, it was Gabriel himself who was sitting up: he was reading. From her standing-place in the road she could see him plainly, sitting quite still, his light curly head upon his hand, and only occasionally looking up to snuff the candle which stood beside him. At length he looked at the clock, seemed surprised at the lateness of the hour, closed his book, and arose. He was going to bed, she knew, and if she tapped it must be done at once.

Alas for her resolve! She felt she could not do it. Not for worlds now could she give a hint about her misery to him, much less ask him plainly for information on the cause of Fanny's death. She must suspect, and guess, and chafe, and bear it all alone.

Like a homeless wanderer she lingered by the bank, as if lulled and fascinated by the atmosphere of content which seemed to spread from that little dwelling, and was so sadly lacking in her own. Gabriel appeared in an upper room, placed his light in the window-bench, and then—knelt down to pray. The contrast of the picture with her rebellious and agitated existence at this same time was too much for her to bear to look upon longer. It was not for her to make a truce with trouble by any such means. She must tread her giddy distracting measure to its last note, as she had begun it. With a swollen heart she went again up the lane, and entered her own door.

More fevered now by a reaction from the first feelings which Oak's example had raised in her, she paused in the hall, looking at the door of the room wherein Fanny lay. She locked her fingers, threw back her head, and strained her hot hands rigidly across her forehead, saying, with a hysterical sob, "Would to God you would speak and tell me your secret, Fanny! ... Oh, I hope, hope it is not true that there are two of you! ... If I could only look in upon you for one little minute, I should know all!"

A few moments passed, and she added, slowly, "And I will."

Bathsheba in after times could never gauge the mood which carried her through the actions following this murmured resolution on this memorable evening of her life. She went to the lumber-closet for a screw-driver. At the end of a short though undefined time she found herself in the small room, quivering with emotion, a mist before her eyes, and an excruciating pulsation in her brain, standing beside the uncovered coffin of the girl whose conjectured end had so entirely engrossed her, and saying to herself in a husky voice as she gazed within—

"It was best to know the worst, and I know it now!"

She was conscious of having brought about this situation by a series of actions done as by one in an extravagant dream; of following that idea as to method, which had burst upon her in the hall with glaring obviousness, by gliding to the top of the stairs, assuring herself by listening to the heavy breathing of her maids that they were asleep, gliding down again, turning the handle of the door within which the young girl lay, and deliberately setting herself to do what, if she had anticipated any such undertaking at night and alone, would have horrified her, but which, when done, was not so dreadful as was the conclusive proof of her husband's conduct which came with knowing beyond doubt the last chapter of Fanny's story.

Bathsheba's head sank upon her bosom, and the breath which had been bated in suspense, curiosity, and interest, was exhaled now in the form of a whispered wail: "Oh-h-h!" she said, and the silent room added length to her moan.

Her tears fell fast beside the unconscious pair in the coffin: tears of a complicated origin, of a nature indescribable, almost indefinable except as other than those of simple sorrow. Assuredly their wonted fires must have lived in Fanny's ashes when events were so shaped as to chariot her hither in this natural, unobtrusive, yet effectual manner. The one feat alone—that of dying—by which a mean condition could be resolved into a grand one, Fanny had achieved. And to that had destiny subjoined this reencounter to-night, which had, in Bathsheba's wild imagining, turned her companion's failure to success, her humiliation to triumph, her lucklessness to ascendency; it had thrown over herself a garish light of mockery, and set upon all things about her an ironical smile.

Fanny's face was framed in by that yellow hair of hers; and there was no longer much room for doubt as to the origin of the curl owned by Troy. In Bathsheba's heated fancy the innocent white countenance expressed a dim triumphant consciousness of the pain she was retaliating for her pain with all the merciless rigour of the Mosaic law: "Burning for burning; wound for wound: strife for strife."

Bathsheba indulged in contemplations of escape from her position by immediate death, which, thought she, though it was an inconvenient and awful way, had limits to its inconvenience and awfulness that could not be overpassed; whilst the shames of life were measureless. Yet even this scheme of extinction by death was but tamely copying her rival's method without the reasons which had glorified it in her rival's case. She glided rapidly up and down the room, as was mostly her habit when excited, her hands hanging clasped in front of her, as she thought and in part expressed in broken words: "O, I hate her, yet I don't mean that I hate her, for it is grievous and wicked; and yet I hate her a little! Yes, my flesh insists upon hating her, whether my spirit is willing or no! ... If she had only lived, I could have been angry and cruel towards her with some justification; but to be vindictive towards a poor dead woman recoils upon myself. O God, have mercy! I am miserable at all this!"

Bathsheba became at this moment so terrified at her own state of mind that she looked around for some sort of refuge from herself. The vision of Oak kneeling down that night recurred to her, and with the imitative instinct which animates women she seized upon the idea, resolved to kneel, and, if possible, pray. Gabriel had prayed; so would she.

She knelt beside the coffin, covered her face with her hands, and for a time the room was silent as a tomb. Whether from a purely mechanical, or from any other cause, when Bathsheba arose it was with a quieted spirit, and a regret for the antagonistic instincts which had seized upon her just before.

In her desire to make atonement she took flowers from a vase by the window, and began laying them around the dead girl's head. Bathsheba knew no other way of showing kindness to persons departed than by giving them flowers. She knew not how long she remained engaged thus. She forgot time, life, where she was, what she was doing. A slamming together of the coach-house doors in the yard brought her to herself again. An instant after, the front door opened and closed, steps crossed the hall, and her husband appeared at the entrance to the room, looking in upon her.

He beheld it all by degrees, stared in stupefaction at the scene, as if he thought it an illusion raised by some fiendish incantation. Bathsheba, pallid as a corpse on end, gazed back at him in the same wild way.

So little are instinctive guesses the fruit of a legitimate induction that, at this moment, as he stood with the door in his hand, Troy never once thought of Fanny in connection with what he saw. His first confused idea was that somebody in the house had died.

"Well—what?" said Troy, blankly.

"I must go! I must go!" said Bathsheba, to herself more than to him. She came with a dilated eye towards the door, to push past him.

"What's the matter, in God's name? who's dead?" said Troy.

"I cannot say; let me go out. I want air!" she continued.

"But no; stay, I insist!" He seized her hand, and then volition seemed to leave her, and she went off into a state of passivity. He, still holding her, came up the room, and thus, hand in hand, Troy and Bathsheba approached the coffin's side.

The candle was standing on a bureau close by them, and the light slanted down, distinctly enkindling the cold features of both mother and babe. Troy looked in, dropped his wife's hand, knowledge of it all came over him in a lurid sheen, and he stood still.

So still he remained that he could be imagined to have left in him no motive power whatever. The clashes of feeling in all directions confounded one another, produced a neutrality, and there was motion in none.

"Do you know her?" said Bathsheba, in a small enclosed echo, as from the interior of a cell.

"I do," said Troy.

"Is it she?"

"It is."

He had originally stood perfectly erect. And now, in the well-nigh congealed immobility of his frame could be discerned an incipient movement, as in the darkest night may be discerned light after a while. He was gradually sinking forwards. The lines of his features softened, and dismay modulated to illimitable sadness. Bathsheba was regarding him from the other side, still with parted lips and distracted eyes. Capacity for intense feeling is proportionate to the general intensity of the nature, and perhaps in all Fanny's sufferings, much greater relatively to her strength, there never was a time she suffered in an absolute sense what Bathsheba suffered now.

What Troy did was to sink upon his knees with an indefinable union of remorse and reverence upon his face, and, bending over Fanny Robin, gently kissed her, as one would kiss an infant asleep to avoid awakening it.

At the sight and sound of that, to her, unendurable act, Bathsheba sprang towards him. All the strong feelings which had been scattered over her existence since she knew what feeling was, seemed gathered together into one pulsation now. The revulsion from her indignant mood a little earlier, when she had meditated upon compromised honour, forestalment, eclipse in maternity by another, was violent and entire. All that was forgotten in the simple and still strong attachment of wife to husband. She had sighed for her self-completeness then, and now she cried aloud against the severance of the union she had deplored. She flung her arms round Troy's neck, exclaiming wildly from the deepest deep of her heart—

"Don't—don't kiss them! O, Frank, I can't bear it—I can't! I love you better than she did: kiss me too, Frank—kiss me! You will, Frank, kiss me too!"

There was something so abnormal and startling in the childlike pain and simplicity of this appeal from a woman of Bathsheba's calibre and independence, that Troy, loosening her tightly clasped arms from his neck, looked at her in bewilderment. It was such an unexpected revelation of all women being alike at heart, even those so different in their accessories as Fanny and this one beside him, that Troy could hardly seem to believe her to be his proud wife Bathsheba. Fanny's own spirit seemed to be animating her frame. But this was the mood of a few instants only. When the momentary surprise had passed, his expression changed to a silencing imperious gaze.

"I will not kiss you!" he said pushing her away.

Had the wife now but gone no further. Yet, perhaps, under the harrowing circumstances, to speak out was the one wrong act which can be better understood, if not forgiven in her, than the right and politic one, her rival being now but a corpse. All the feeling she had been betrayed into showing she drew back to herself again by a strenuous effort of self-command.

"What have you to say as your reason?" she asked, her bitter voice being strangely low—quite that of another woman now.

"I have to say that I have been a bad, black-hearted man," he answered.

"And that this woman is your victim; and I not less than she."

"Ah! don't taunt me, madam. This woman is more to me, dead as she is, than ever you were, or are, or can be. If Satan had not tempted me with that face of yours, and those cursed coquetries, I should have married her. I never had another thought till you came in my way. Would to God that I had; but it is all too late!" He turned to Fanny then. "But never mind, darling," he said; "in the sight of Heaven you are my very, very wife!"

At these words there arose from Bathsheba's lips a long, low cry of measureless despair and indignation, such a wail of anguish as had never before been heard within those old-inhabited walls. It was the Τετελεσται **[b]** of her union with Troy.

"If she's—that,—what—am I?" she added, as a continuation of the same cry, and sobbing pitifully: and the rarity with her of such abandonment only made the condition more dire.

"You are nothing to me—nothing," said Troy, heartlessly. "A ceremony before a priest doesn't make a marriage. I am not morally yours."

A vehement impulse to flee from him, to run from this place, hide, and escape his words at any price, not stopping short of death itself, mastered Bathsheba now. She waited not an instant, but turned to the door and ran out.

Analysis: For me, this is the climatic point of the novel. Forget the melodramatic climax: the painful heart of the novel exists in this scene. This is one of the rare moments when Troy transcends the stereotype of the selfish cad and becomes a genuinely tortured individual as he gazes down upon his dead lover and child: he finally admits to himself what he has known all along that Fanny is his true wife. This operates on many levels: a psychological and a symbolic. Psychologically, he can't cope with Bathsheba's superior intelligence, her superior social position. Symbolically, Troy is the soldier who belongs with his maiden. But the times are out of kilter: something has gone wrong in this idyllic society and partners have become mismatched.

Even more subtly drawn is Bathsheba's response to this news. Hardy itemises her changing emotions very precisely: her jealousy of the dead Fanny, her anger and sense of betrayal, her thirst for approval, her desperate desire for things to be right. As Hardy notes: her psychological agony is far greater than Fanny's physical suffering.

Discussion point: Why is this a powerful and painful scene in the novel?

Questions

What rumour does Liddy tell Bathsheba about?

Who does Bathsheba want advice from and why does she not seek it?

What does Bathsheba realise when she opens the coffin?

How does she stop her jealous feelings from overwhelming her?

What does Troy learn about when he returns?

What does Bathsheba beg him to do and what is his response?

What does Bathsheba do?

GCSE style question: how does Hardy make the opening of the coffin such a shocking and suspenseful moment?

A Level style question: explore the role of illegitimate children in this text and another text of your choice.

Creative response: write Bathsheba's diary for this chapter, exploring her feelings for Fanny, Troy and Oak.

CHAPTER XLIV
UNDER A TREE—REACTION

Bathsheba went along the dark road, neither knowing nor caring about the direction or issue of her flight. The first time that she definitely noticed her position was when she reached a gate leading into a thicket overhung by some large oak and beech trees. On looking into the place, it occurred to her that she had seen it by daylight on some previous occasion, and that what appeared like an impassable thicket was in reality a brake of fern now withering fast. She could think of nothing better to do with her palpitating self than to go in here and hide; and entering, she lighted on a spot sheltered from the damp fog by a reclining trunk, where she sank down upon a tangled couch of fronds and stems. She mechanically pulled some armfuls round her to keep off the breezes, and closed her eyes.

Whether she slept or not that night Bathsheba was not clearly aware. But it was with a freshened existence and a cooler brain that, a long time afterwards, she became conscious of some interesting proceedings which were going on in the trees above her head and around.

A coarse-throated chatter was the first sound.

It was a sparrow just waking.

Next: "Chee-weeze-weeze-weeze!" from another retreat.

It was a finch.

Third: "Tink-tink-tink-tink-a-chink!" from the hedge.

It was a robin.

"Chuck-chuck-chuck!" overhead.

A squirrel.

Then, from the road, "With my ra-ta-ta, and my rum-tum-tum!"

It was a ploughboy. Presently he came opposite, and she believed from his voice that he was one of the boys on her own farm. He was followed by a shambling tramp of heavy feet, and looking through the ferns Bathsheba could just discern in the wan light of daybreak a team of her own horses. They stopped to drink at a pond on the other side of the way. She watched them flouncing into the pool, drinking, tossing up their heads, drinking again, the water dribbling from their lips in silver threads. There was another flounce, and they came out of the pond, and turned back again towards the farm.

She looked further around. Day was just dawning, and beside its cool air and colours her heated actions and resolves of the night stood out in lurid contrast. She perceived that in her lap, and clinging to her hair, were red and yellow leaves which had come down from the tree and settled silently upon her during her partial sleep. Bathsheba shook her dress to get rid of them, when multitudes of the same family lying round about her rose and fluttered away in the breeze thus created, "like ghosts from an enchanter fleeing."

There was an opening towards the east, and the glow from the as yet unrisen sun attracted her eyes thither. From her feet, and between the beautiful yellowing ferns with their feathery arms, the ground sloped downwards to a hollow, in which was a species of swamp, dotted with fungi. A morning mist hung over it now—a fulsome yet magnificent silvery veil, full of light from the sun, yet semi-opaque—the hedge behind it being in some measure hidden by its hazy luminousness. Up the sides of this depression grew sheaves of the common rush, and here and there a peculiar species of flag, the blades of which glistened in the emerging sun, like scythes. But the general aspect of the swamp was malignant. From its moist and poisonous coat seemed to be exhaled the essences of evil things in the earth, and in the waters under the earth. The fungi grew in all manner of positions from rotting leaves and tree stumps, some exhibiting to her listless gaze their clammy tops, others their oozing gills. Some were marked with great splotches, red as arterial blood, others were saffron yellow, and others tall and attenuated, with stems like macaroni. Some were leathery and of richest browns. The hollow seemed a nursery of pestilences small and great, in the immediate neighbourhood of comfort and health, and Bathsheba arose with a tremor at the thought of having passed the night on the brink of so dismal a place.

There were now other footsteps to be heard along the road. Bathsheba's nerves were still unstrung: she crouched down out of sight again, and the pedestrian came into view. He was a schoolboy, with a bag slung over his shoulder containing his dinner, and a book in his hand. He paused by the gate, and, without looking up, continued murmuring words in tones quite loud enough to reach her ears.

"'O Lord, O Lord, O Lord, O Lord, O Lord':—that I know out o' book. 'Give us, give us, give us, give us, give us':—that I know. 'Grace that, grace that, grace that, grace that':—that I know." Other words followed to the same effect. The boy was of the dunce class apparently; the book was a psalter, and this was his way of learning the collect. In the worst attacks of trouble there appears to be always a superficial film of consciousness which is left disengaged and open to the notice of trifles, and Bathsheba was faintly amused at the boy's method, till he too passed on.

By this time stupor had given place to anxiety, and anxiety began to make room for hunger and thirst. A form now appeared upon the rise on the other side of the swamp, half-hidden by the mist, and came towards Bathsheba. The woman—for it was a woman—approached with her face askance, as if looking earnestly on all sides of her. When she got a little further round to the left, and drew nearer, Bathsheba could see the newcomer's profile against the sunny sky, and knew the wavy sweep from forehead to chin, with neither angle nor decisive line anywhere about it, to be the familiar contour of Liddy Smallbury.

Bathsheba's heart bounded with gratitude in the thought that she was not altogether deserted, and she jumped up. "Oh, Liddy!" she said, or attempted to say; but the words had only been framed by her lips; there came no sound. She had lost her voice by exposure to the clogged atmosphere all these hours of night.

"Oh, ma'am! I am so glad I have found you," said the girl, as soon as she saw Bathsheba.

"You can't come across," Bathsheba said in a whisper, which she vainly endeavoured to make loud enough to reach Liddy's ears. Liddy, not knowing this, stepped down upon the swamp, saying, as she did so, "It will bear me up, I think."

Bathsheba never forgot that transient little picture of Liddy crossing the swamp to her there in the morning light. Iridescent bubbles of dank subterranean breath rose from the sweating sod beside the waiting-maid's feet as she trod, hissing as they burst and expanded away to join the vapoury firmament above. Liddy did not sink, as Bathsheba had anticipated.

She landed safely on the other side, and looked up at the beautiful though pale and weary face of her young mistress.

"Poor thing!" said Liddy, with tears in her eyes, "Do hearten yourself up a little, ma'am. However did—"

"I can't speak above a whisper—my voice is gone for the present," said Bathsheba, hurriedly. "I suppose the damp air from that hollow has taken it away. Liddy, don't question me, mind. Who sent you—anybody?"

"Nobody. I thought, when I found you were not at home, that something cruel had happened. I fancy I heard his voice late last night; and so, knowing something was wrong—"

"Is he at home?"

"No; he left just before I came out."

"Is Fanny taken away?"

"Not yet. She will soon be—at nine o'clock."

"We won't go home at present, then. Suppose we walk about in this wood?"

Liddy, without exactly understanding everything, or anything, in this episode, assented, and they walked together further among the trees.

"But you had better come in, ma'am, and have something to eat. You will die of a chill!"

"I shall not come indoors yet—perhaps never."

"Shall I get you something to eat, and something else to put over your head besides that little shawl?"

"If you will, Liddy."

Liddy vanished, and at the end of twenty minutes returned with a cloak, hat, some slices of bread and butter, a tea-cup, and some hot tea in a little china jug.

Analysis: The developing friendship between Liddy and Bathsheba is poignant here: the mistress having to turn to her servant for comfort in a humiliating admission of defeat. Movingly, Liddy accepts her position as parent to Bathsheba's broken child and comforts her. Like Troy in the previous scene, we see Liddy stepping out of being the stereotype of the gossiping servant and becoming a fully rounded human being.

Discussion point: What you think of the way Hardy presents Liddy?

"Is Fanny gone?" said Bathsheba.

"No," said her companion, pouring out the tea.

Bathsheba wrapped herself up and ate and drank sparingly. Her voice was then a little clearer, and trifling colour returned to her face. "Now we'll walk about again," she said.

They wandered about the wood for nearly two hours, Bathsheba replying in monosyllables to Liddy's prattle, for her mind ran on one subject, and one only. She interrupted with—

"I wonder if Fanny is gone by this time?"

"I will go and see."

She came back with the information that the men were just taking away the corpse; that Bathsheba had been inquired for; that she had replied to the effect that her mistress was unwell and could not be seen.

"Then they think I am in my bedroom?"

"Yes." Liddy then ventured to add: "You said when I first found you that you might never go home again—you didn't mean it, ma'am?"

"No; I've altered my mind. It is only women with no pride in them who run away from their husbands. There is one position worse than that of being found dead in your husband's house from his ill usage, and that is, to be found alive through having gone away to the house of somebody else. I've thought of it all this morning, and I've chosen my course. A runaway wife is an encumbrance to everybody, a burden to herself and a byword—all of which make up a heap of misery greater than any that comes by staying at home—though this may include the trifling items of insult, beating, and starvation. Liddy, if ever you marry—God forbid that you ever should!—

you'll find yourself in a fearful situation; but mind this, don't you flinch. Stand your ground, and be cut to pieces. That's what I'm going to do."

"Oh, mistress, don't talk so!" said Liddy, taking her hand; "but I knew you had too much sense to bide away. May I ask what dreadful thing it is that has happened between you and him?"

"You may ask; but I may not tell."

In about ten minutes they returned to the house by a circuitous route, entering at the rear. Bathsheba glided up the back stairs to a disused attic, and her companion followed.

"Liddy," she said, with a lighter heart, for youth and hope had begun to reassert themselves; "you are to be my confidante for the present— somebody must be—and I choose you. Well, I shall take up my abode here for a while. Will you get a fire lighted, put down a piece of carpet, and help me to make the place comfortable. Afterwards, I want you and Maryann to bring up that little stump bedstead in the small room, and the bed belonging to it, and a table, and some other things... What shall I do to pass the heavy time away?"

"Hemming handkerchiefs is a very good thing," said Liddy.

"Oh no, no! I hate needlework—I always did."

"Knitting?"

"And that, too."

"You might finish your sampler. Only the carnations and peacocks want filling in; and then it could be framed and glazed, and hung beside your aunt's ma'am."

"Samplers are out of date—horribly countrified. No Liddy, I'll read. Bring up some books—not new ones. I haven't heart to read anything new."

"Some of your uncle's old ones, ma'am?"

"Yes. Some of those we stowed away in boxes." A faint gleam of humour passed over her face as she said: "Bring Beaumont and Fletcher's Maid's Tragedy, and the Mourning Bride, and—let me see—Night Thoughts, and the Vanity of Human Wishes."

"And that story of the black man, who murdered his wife Desdemona? It is a nice dismal one that would suit you excellent just now."

"Now, Liddy, you've been looking into my books without telling me; and I said you were not to! How do you know it would suit me? It wouldn't suit me at all."

"But if the others do—"

"No, they don't; and I won't read dismal books. Why should I read dismal books, indeed? Bring me Love in a Village, and Maid of the Mill, and Doctor Syntax, and some volumes of theSpectator."

All that day Bathsheba and Liddy lived in the attic in a state of barricade; a precaution which proved to be needless as against Troy, for he did not appear in the neighbourhood or trouble them at all.

Analysis: Bathsheba, who has contemplated suicide, now becomes a recluse, barricading herself away. We see that the once vivacious, outgoing girl who was able to pronounce herself bailiff is now utterly defeated by the betrayal of her husband.

Discussion point: What does the reader feel for Bathsheba at this point in the novel?

Bathsheba sat at the window till sunset, sometimes attempting to read, at other times watching every movement outside without much purpose, and listening without much interest to every sound.

The sun went down almost blood-red that night, and a livid cloud received its rays in the east. Up against this dark background the west front of the church tower—the only part of the edifice visible from the farm-house windows—rose distinct and lustrous, the vane upon the summit bristling with rays. Hereabouts, at six o'clock, the young men of the village gathered, as was their custom, for a game of Prisoners' base. The spot had been consecrated to this ancient diversion from time immemorial, the old stocks conveniently forming a base facing the boundary of the churchyard, in front of which the ground was trodden hard and bare as a pavement by the players. She could see the brown and black heads of the young lads darting about right and left, their white shirt-sleeves gleaming in the sun; whilst occasionally a shout and a peal of hearty laughter varied the stillness of the evening air. They continued playing for a quarter of an hour or so, when the game concluded abruptly, and the players leapt over the wall and vanished round to the other side behind a yew-tree, which was also half behind a beech, now spreading in one mass of golden foliage, on which the branches traced black lines.

"Why did the base-players finish their game so suddenly?" Bathsheba inquired, the next time that Liddy entered the room.

"I think 'twas because two men came just then from Casterbridge and began putting up a grand carved tombstone," said Liddy. "The lads went to see whose it was."

"Do you know?" Bathsheba asked.

"I don't," said Liddy.

Questions

Where does Bathsheba sleep?

What does Liddy tell her?

When does Bathsheba return to the house?

Where do Liddy and Bathsheba stay for that day while they wait for Troy's return?

What do they see happening at sunset in the churchyard?

GCSE style question: how does Hardy present Bathsheba in this chapter?

Creative response: write Liddy's diary, exploring what she feels towards her mistress, Troy and the events so far.

CHAPTER XLV
TROY'S ROMANTICISM

When Troy's wife had left the house at the previous midnight his first act was to cover the dead from sight. This done he ascended the stairs, and throwing himself down upon the bed dressed as he was, he waited miserably for the morning.

Fate had dealt grimly with him through the last four-and-twenty hours. His day had been spent in a way which varied very materially from his intentions regarding it. There is always an inertia to be overcome in striking out a new line of conduct—not more in ourselves, it seems, than in circumscribing events, which appear as if leagued together to allow no novelties in the way of amelioration.

Twenty pounds having been secured from Bathsheba, he had managed to add to the sum every farthing he could muster on his own account, which had been seven pounds ten. With this money, twenty-seven pounds ten in all, he had hastily driven from the gate that morning to keep his appointment with Fanny Robin.

On reaching Casterbridge he left the horse and trap at an inn, and at five minutes before ten came back to the bridge at the lower end of the town, and sat himself upon the parapet. The clocks struck the hour, and no Fanny appeared. In fact, at that moment she was being robed in her grave-clothes by two attendants at the Union poorhouse—the first and last tiring-women the gentle creature had ever been honoured with. The quarter went, the half hour. A rush of recollection came upon Troy as he waited: this was the second time she had broken a serious engagement with him. In anger he vowed it should be the last, and at eleven o'clock, when he had lingered and watched the stone of the bridge till he knew every lichen upon their face and heard the chink of the ripples underneath till they oppressed him, he jumped from his seat, went to the inn for his gig, and in a bitter mood of indifference concerning the past, and recklessness about the future, drove on to Budmouth races.

He reached the race-course at two o'clock, and remained either there or in the town till nine. But Fanny's image, as it had appeared to him in the sombre shadows of that Saturday evening, returned to his mind, backed up by Bathsheba's reproaches. He vowed he would not bet, and he kept his vow, for on leaving the town at nine o'clock in the evening he had diminished his cash only to the extent of a few shillings.

He trotted slowly homeward, and it was now that he was struck for the first time with a thought that Fanny had been really prevented by illness from keeping her promise. This time she could have made no mistake. He regretted that he had not remained in Casterbridge and made inquiries. Reaching home he quietly unharnessed the horse and came indoors, as we have seen, to the fearful shock that awaited him.

As soon as it grew light enough to distinguish objects, Troy arose from the coverlet of the bed, and in a mood of absolute indifference to Bathsheba's whereabouts, and almost oblivious of her existence, he stalked downstairs and left the house by the back door. His walk was towards the churchyard, entering which he searched around till he found a newly dug unoccupied grave—the grave dug the day before for Fanny. The position of this having been marked, he hastened on to Casterbridge, only pausing and musing for a while at the hill whereon he had last seen Fanny alive.

Reaching the town, Troy descended into a side street and entered a pair of gates surmounted by a board bearing the words, "Lester, stone and marble mason." Within were lying about stones of all sizes and designs, inscribed as being sacred to the memory of unnamed persons who had not yet died.

Troy was so unlike himself now in look, word, and deed, that the want of likeness was perceptible even to his own consciousness. His method of engaging himself in this business of purchasing a tomb was that of an absolutely unpractised man. He could not bring himself to consider, calculate, or economize. He waywardly wished for something, and he set about obtaining it like a child in a nursery. "I want a good tomb," he said to the man who stood in a little office within the yard. "I want as good a one as you can give me for twenty-seven pounds."

It was all the money he possessed.

"That sum to include everything?"

"Everything. Cutting the name, carriage to Weatherbury, and erection. And I want it now, at once."

"We could not get anything special worked this week."

"I must have it now."

"If you would like one of these in stock it could be got ready immediately."

"Very well," said Troy, impatiently. "Let's see what you have."

"The best I have in stock is this one," said the stone-cutter, going into a shed. "Here's a marble headstone beautifully crocketed, with medallions beneath of typical subjects; here's the footstone after the same pattern, and here's the coping to enclose the grave. The polishing alone of the set cost me eleven pounds—the slabs are the best of their kind, and I can warrant them to resist rain and frost for a hundred years without flying."

"And how much?"

"Well, I could add the name, and put it up at Weatherbury for the sum you mention."

"Get it done to-day, and I'll pay the money now."

The man agreed, and wondered at such a mood in a visitor who wore not a shred of mourning. Troy then wrote the words which were to form the inscription, settled the account and went away. In the afternoon he came back again, and found that the lettering was almost done. He waited in the yard till the tomb was packed, and saw it placed in the cart and starting on its way to Weatherbury, giving directions to the two men who were to accompany it to inquire of the sexton for the grave of the person named in the inscription.

It was quite dark when Troy came out of Casterbridge. He carried rather a heavy basket upon his arm, with which he strode moodily along the road, resting occasionally at bridges and gates, whereon he deposited his burden for a time. Midway on his journey he met, returning in the darkness, the men and the waggon which had conveyed the tomb. He merely inquired if the work was done, and, on being assured that it was, passed on again.

Troy entered Weatherbury churchyard about ten o'clock and went immediately to the corner where he had marked the vacant grave early in the morning. It was on the obscure side of the tower, screened to a great extent from the view of passers along the road—a spot which until lately had been abandoned to heaps of stones and bushes of alder, but now it was cleared and made orderly for interments, by reason of the rapid filling of the ground elsewhere.

Here now stood the tomb as the men had stated, snow-white and shapely in the gloom, consisting of head and foot-stone, and enclosing border of marble-work uniting them. In the midst was mould, suitable for plants.

Troy deposited his basket beside the tomb, and vanished for a few minutes. When he returned he carried a spade and a lantern, the light of which he directed for a few moments upon the marble, whilst he read the inscription. He hung his lantern on the lowest bough of the yew-tree, and took from his basket flower-roots of several varieties. There were bundles of snow-drop, hyacinth and crocus bulbs, violets and double daisies, which were to bloom in early spring, and of carnations, pinks, picotees, lilies of the valley, forget-me-not, summer's farewell, meadow-saffron and others, for the later seasons of the year.

Troy laid these out upon the grass, and with an impassive face set to work to plant them. The snowdrops were arranged in a line on the outside of the coping, the remainder within the enclosure of the grave. The crocuses and hyacinths were to grow in rows; some of the summer flowers he placed over her head and feet, the lilies and forget-me-nots over her heart. The remainder were dispersed in the spaces between these.

Troy, in his prostration at this time, had no perception that in the futility of these romantic doings, dictated by a remorseful reaction from previous indifference, there was any element of absurdity. Deriving his idiosyncrasies from both sides of the Channel, he showed at such junctures as the present the inelasticity of the Englishman, together with that blindness to the line where sentiment verges on mawkishness, characteristic of the French.

It was a cloudy, muggy, and very dark night, and the rays from Troy's lantern spread into the two old yews with a strange illuminating power, flickering, as it seemed, up to the black ceiling of cloud above. He felt a large drop of rain upon the back of his hand, and presently one came and entered one of the holes of the lantern, whereupon the candle sputtered and went out. Troy was weary and it being now not far from midnight, and the rain threatening to increase, he resolved to leave the finishing touches of his labour until the day should break. He groped along the wall and over the graves in the dark till he found himself round at the north side. Here he entered the porch, and, reclining upon the bench within, fell asleep.

Analysis: Troy, in a desperate bid to redeem himself puts flowers by the tomb, taking refuge in the porch of the church, the place which he has shunned previously -- though lied to Bathsheba about going to.

Discussion point: Why is Troy so intent upon tending to Fanny's tomb?

Questions

What did Troy do when Bathsheba left?
What happened the previous day when he was supposed to meet Fanny?
What does Troy insist is made for the dead Fanny?
What does he do around Fanny's grave?
Where does he stay that night?
GCSE style question: how does Hardy present Troy in this chapter?
A Level style question: explore the way Hardy presents Troy's 'romanticism' in this chapter.
Creative response: write Troy's diary for this chapter, exploring his feelings for Fanny and his dead child.

CHAPTER XLVI
THE GURGOYLE: ITS DOINGS

The tower of Weatherbury Church was a square erection of fourteenth-century date, having two stone gurgoyles on each of the four faces of its parapet. Of these eight carved protuberances only two at this time continued to serve the purpose of their erection—that of spouting the water from the lead roof within. One mouth in each front had been closed by bygone church-wardens as superfluous, and two others were broken away and choked—a matter not of much consequence to the wellbeing of the tower, for the two mouths which still remained open and active were gaping enough to do all the work.

It has been sometimes argued that there is no truer criterion of the vitality of any given art-period than the power of the master-spirits of that time in grotesque; and certainly in the instance of Gothic art there is no disputing the proposition. Weatherbury tower was a somewhat early instance of the use of an ornamental parapet in parish as distinct from cathedral churches, and the gurgoyles, which are the necessary correlatives of a parapet, were exceptionally prominent—of the boldest cut that the hand could shape, and of the most original design that a human brain could conceive. There was, so to speak, that symmetry in their distortion which is less the characteristic of British than of Continental grotesques of the period. All the eight were different from each other. A beholder was convinced that nothing on earth could be more hideous than those he saw on the north side until he went round to the south. Of the two on this latter face, only that at the south-eastern corner concerns the story. It was too human to be called like a dragon, too impish to be like a man, too animal to be like a fiend, and not enough like a bird to be called a griffin. This horrible stone entity was fashioned as if covered with a wrinkled hide; it had short, erect ears, eyes starting from their sockets, and its fingers and hands were seizing the corners of its mouth, which they thus seemed to pull open to give free passage to the water it vomited. The lower row of teeth was quite washed away, though the upper still remained. Here and thus, jutting a couple of feet from the wall against which its feet rested as a support, the creature had for four hundred years laughed at the surrounding landscape, voicelessly in dry weather, and in wet with a gurgling and snorting sound.

Troy slept on in the porch, and the rain increased outside. Presently the gurgoyle spat. In due time a small stream began to trickle through the seventy feet of aerial space between its mouth and the ground, which the water-drops smote like duckshot in their accelerated velocity. The stream thickened in substance, and increased in power, gradually spouting further and yet further from the side of the tower. When the rain fell in a steady and ceaseless torrent the stream dashed downward in volumes.

We follow its course to the ground at this point of time. The end of the liquid parabola has come forward from the wall, has advanced over the plinth mouldings, over a heap of stones, over the marble border, into the midst of Fanny Robin's grave.

The force of the stream had, until very lately, been received upon some loose stones spread thereabout, which had acted as a shield to the soil under the onset. These during the summer had been cleared from the ground, and there was now nothing to resist the down-fall but the bare earth. For several years the stream had not spouted so far from the tower as it was doing on this night, and such a contingency had been over-looked. Sometimes this obscure corner received no inhabitant for the space of two or three years, and then it was usually but a pauper, a poacher, or other sinner of undignified sins.

The persistent torrent from the gurgoyle's jaws directed all its vengeance into the grave. The rich tawny mould was stirred into motion, and boiled like chocolate. The water accumulated and washed deeper down, and the roar of the pool thus formed spread into the night as the head and chief among other noises of the kind created by the deluging rain. The flowers so carefully planted by Fanny's repentant lover began to move and writhe in their bed. The winter-violets turned slowly upside down, and became a mere mat of mud. Soon the snowdrop and other bulbs danced in the boiling mass like ingredients in a cauldron. Plants of the tufted species were loosened, rose to the surface, and floated off.

Troy did not awake from his comfortless sleep till it was broad day. Not having been in bed for two nights his shoulders felt stiff, his feet tender, and his head heavy. He remembered his position, arose, shivered, took the spade, and again went out.

The rain had quite ceased, and the sun was shining through the green, brown, and yellow leaves, now sparkling and varnished by the raindrops to the brightness of similar effects in the landscapes of Ruysdael and Hobbema, and full of all those infinite beauties that arise from the union of water and colour with high lights. The air was rendered so transparent by the heavy fall of rain that the autumn hues of the middle distance were as rich as those near at hand, and the remote fields intercepted by the angle of the tower appeared in the same plane as the tower itself.

He entered the gravel path which would take him behind the tower. The path, instead of being stony as it had been the night before, was browned over with a thin coating of mud. At one place in the path he saw a tuft of stringy roots washed white and clean as a bundle of tendons. He picked it up—surely it could not be one of the primroses he had planted? He saw a bulb, another, and another as he advanced. Beyond doubt they were the crocuses. With a face of perplexed dismay Troy turned the corner and then beheld the wreck the stream had made.

The pool upon the grave had soaked away into the ground, and in its place was a hollow. The disturbed earth was washed over the grass and pathway in the guise of the brown mud he had already seen, and it spotted the marble tombstone with the same stains. Nearly all the flowers were washed clean out of the ground, and they lay, roots upwards, on the spots whither they had been splashed by the stream.

Troy's brow became heavily contracted. He set his teeth closely, and his compressed lips moved as those of one in great pain. This singular accident, by a strange confluence of emotions in him, was felt as the sharpest sting of all. Troy's face was very expressive, and any observer who had seen him now would hardly have believed him to be a man who had laughed, and sung, and poured love-trifles into a woman's ear. To curse his miserable lot was at first his impulse, but even that lowest stage of rebellion needed an activity whose absence was necessarily antecedent to the existence of the morbid misery which wrung him. The sight, coming as it did, superimposed upon the other dark scenery of the previous days, formed a sort of climax to the whole panorama, and it was more than he could endure. Sanguine by nature, Troy had a power of eluding grief by simply adjourning it. He could put off the consideration of any particular spectre till the matter had become old and softened by time. The planting of flowers on Fanny's grave had been perhaps but a species of elusion of the primary grief, and now it was as if his intention had been known and circumvented.

Almost for the first time in his life, Troy, as he stood by this dismantled grave, wished himself another man. It is seldom that a person with much animal spirit does not feel that the fact of his life being his own is the one qualification which singles it out as a more hopeful life than that of others who may actually resemble him in every particular. Troy had felt, in his transient way, hundreds of times, that he could not envy other people their condition, because the possession of that condition would have necessitated a different personality, when he desired no other than his own. He had not minded the peculiarities of his birth, the vicissitudes of his life, the meteor-like uncertainty of all that related to him, because these appertained to the hero of his story, without whom there would have been no story at all for him; and it seemed to be only in the nature of things that matters would right themselves at some proper date and wind up well. This very morning the illusion completed its disappearance, and, as it were, all of a sudden, Troy hated himself. The suddenness was probably more apparent than real. A coral reef which just comes short of the ocean surface is no more to the horizon than if it had never been begun, and the mere finishing stroke is what often appears to create an event which has long been potentially an accomplished thing.

He stood and meditated—a miserable man. Whither should he go? "He that is accursed, let him be accursed still," was the pitiless anathema written in this spoliated effort of his new-born solicitousness. A man who has spent his primal strength in journeying in one direction has not much spirit left for reversing his course. Troy had, since yesterday, faintly reversed his; but the merest opposition had disheartened him. To turn about would have been hard enough under the greatest providential encouragement; but to find that Providence, far from helping him into a new course, or showing any wish that he might adopt one, actually jeered his first trembling and critical attempt in that kind, was more than nature could bear.

He slowly withdrew from the grave. He did not attempt to fill up the hole, replace the flowers, or do anything at all. He simply threw up his cards and forswore his game for that time and always. Going out of the churchyard silently and unobserved—none of the villagers having yet risen—he passed down some fields at the back, and emerged just as secretly upon the high road. Shortly afterwards he had gone from the village.

Meanwhile, Bathsheba remained a voluntary prisoner in the attic. The door was kept locked, except during the entries and exits of Liddy, for whom a bed had been arranged in a small adjoining room. The light of Troy's lantern in the churchyard was noticed about ten o'clock by the maid-servant, who casually glanced from the window in that direction whilst taking her supper, and she called Bathsheba's attention to it. They looked curiously at the phenomenon for a time, until Liddy was sent to bed.

Bathsheba did not sleep very heavily that night. When her attendant was unconscious and softly breathing in the next room, the mistress of the house was still looking out of the window at the faint gleam spreading from among the trees—not in a steady shine, but blinking like a revolving coast-light, though this appearance failed to suggest to her that a person was passing and repassing in front of it. Bathsheba sat here till it began to rain, and the light vanished, when she withdrew to lie restlessly in her bed and re-enact in a worn mind the lurid scene of yesternight.

Almost before the first faint sign of dawn appeared she arose again, and opened the window to obtain a full breathing of the new morning air, the panes being now wet with trembling tears left by the night rain, each one rounded with a pale lustre caught from primrose-hued slashes through a cloud low down in the awakening sky. From the trees came the sound of steady dripping upon the drifted leaves under them, and from the direction of the church she could hear another noise—peculiar, and not intermittent like the rest, the purl of water falling into a pool.

Liddy knocked at eight o'clock, and Bathsheba un-locked the door.

"What a heavy rain we've had in the night, ma'am!" said Liddy, when her inquiries about breakfast had been made.

"Yes, very heavy."

"Did you hear the strange noise from the churchyard?"

"I heard one strange noise. I've been thinking it must have been the water from the tower spouts."

"Well, that's what the shepherd was saying, ma'am. He's now gone on to see."

"Oh! Gabriel has been here this morning!"

"Only just looked in in passing—quite in his old way, which I thought he had left off lately. But the tower spouts used to spatter on the stones, and we are puzzled, for this was like the boiling of a pot."

Not being able to read, think, or work, Bathsheba asked Liddy to stay and breakfast with her. The tongue of the more childish woman still ran upon recent events. "Are you going across to the church, ma'am?" she asked.

"Not that I know of," said Bathsheba.

"I thought you might like to go and see where they have put Fanny. The trees hide the place from your window."

Bathsheba had all sorts of dreads about meeting her husband. "Has Mr. Troy been in to-night?" she said.

"No, ma'am; I think he's gone to Budmouth."

Budmouth! The sound of the word carried with it a much diminished perspective of him and his deeds; there were thirteen miles interval betwixt them now. She hated questioning Liddy about her husband's movements, and indeed had hitherto sedulously avoided doing so; but now all the house knew that there had been some dreadful disagreement between them, and it was futile to attempt disguise. Bathsheba had reached a stage at which people cease to have any appreciative regard for public opinion.

"What makes you think he has gone there?" she said.

"Laban Tall saw him on the Budmouth road this morning before breakfast."

Bathsheba was momentarily relieved of that wayward heaviness of the past twenty-four hours which had quenched the vitality of youth in her without substituting the philosophy of maturer years, and she resolved to go out and walk a little way. So when breakfast was over, she put on her bonnet, and took a direction towards the church. It was nine o'clock, and the men having returned to work again from their first meal, she was not likely to meet many of them in the road. Knowing that Fanny had been laid in the reprobates' quarter of the graveyard, called in the parish "behind church," which was invisible from the road, it was impossible to resist the impulse to enter and look upon a spot which, from nameless feelings, she at the same time dreaded to see. She had been unable to overcome an impression that some connection existed between her rival and the light through the trees.

Bathsheba skirted the buttress, and beheld the hole and the tomb, its delicately veined surface splashed and stained just as Troy had seen it and left it two hours earlier. On the other side of the scene stood Gabriel. His eyes, too, were fixed on the tomb, and her arrival having been noiseless, she had not as yet attracted his attention. Bathsheba did not at once perceive that the grand tomb and the disturbed grave were Fanny's, and she looked on both sides and around for some humbler mound, earthed up and clodded in the usual way. Then her eye followed Oak's, and she read the words with which the inscription opened:—

Erected by Francis Troy
In Beloved Memory of
Fanny Robin

Oak saw her, and his first act was to gaze inquiringly and learn how she received this knowledge of the authorship of the work, which to himself had caused considerable astonishment. But such discoveries did not much affect her now. Emotional convulsions seemed to have become the commonplaces of her history, and she bade him good morning, and asked him to fill in the hole with the spade which was standing by. Whilst Oak was doing as she desired, Bathsheba collected the flowers, and began planting them with that sympathetic manipulation of roots and leaves which is so conspicuous in a woman's gardening, and which flowers seem to understand and thrive upon. She requested Oak to get the churchwardens to turn the leadwork at the mouth of the gurgoyle that hung gaping down upon them, that by this means the stream might be directed sideways, and a repetition of the accident prevented. Finally, with the superfluous magnanimity of a woman whose narrower instincts have brought down bitterness upon her instead of love, she wiped the mud spots from the tomb as if she rather liked its words than otherwise, and went again home.

Questions

What happens to flowers on Fanny's grave?

What does Troy decide to do when he wakes?

What does Bathsheba do when she sees the ruined grave?

GCSE style question: how does Hardy present Bathsheba in this chapter?

A Level style question: compare and contrast the ways in which this text and another of your choice explore the theme of compassion.

Creative response: write a poem/story/description called 'The Tombstone' or write Bathsheba's diary for this chapter.

CHAPTER XLVII
ADVENTURES BY THE SHORE

Troy wandered along towards the south. A composite feeling, made up of disgust with the, to him, humdrum tediousness of a farmer's life, gloomy images of her who lay in the churchyard, remorse, and a general averseness to his wife's society, impelled him to seek a home in any place on earth save Weatherbury. The sad accessories of Fanny's end confronted him as vivid pictures which threatened to be indelible, and made life in Bathsheba's house intolerable. At three in the afternoon he found himself at the foot of a slope more than a mile in length, which ran to the ridge of a range of hills lying parallel with the shore, and forming a monotonous barrier between the basin of cultivated country inland and the wilder scenery of the coast. Up the hill stretched a road nearly straight and perfectly white, the two sides approaching each other in a gradual taper till they met the sky at the top about two miles off. Throughout the length of this narrow and irksome inclined plane not a sign of life was visible on this garish afternoon. Troy toiled up the road with a languor and depression greater than any he had experienced for many a day and year before. The air was warm and muggy, and the top seemed to recede as he approached.

At last he reached the summit, and a wide and novel prospect burst upon him with an effect almost like that of the Pacific upon Balboa's gaze. The broad steely sea, marked only by faint lines, which had a semblance of being etched thereon to a degree not deep enough to disturb its general evenness, stretched the whole width of his front and round to the right, where, near the town and port of Budmouth, the sun bristled down upon it, and banished all colour, to substitute in its place a clear oily polish. Nothing moved in sky, land, or sea, except a frill of milkwhite foam along the nearer angles of the shore, shreds of which licked the contiguous stones like tongues.

He descended and came to a small basin of sea enclosed by the cliffs. Troy's nature freshened within him; he thought he would rest and bathe here before going farther. He undressed and plunged in. Inside the cove the water was uninteresting to a swimmer, being smooth as a pond, and to get a little of the ocean swell, Troy presently swam between the two projecting spurs of rock which formed the pillars of Hercules to this miniature Mediterranean. Unfortunately for Troy a current unknown to him existed outside, which, unimportant to craft of any burden, was awkward for a swimmer who might be taken in it unawares. Troy found himself carried to the left and then round in a swoop out to sea.

He now recollected the place and its sinister character. Many bathers had there prayed for a dry death from time to time, and, like Gonzalo also, had been unanswered; and Troy began to deem it possible that he might be added to their number. Not a boat of any kind was at present within sight, but far in the distance Budmouth lay upon the sea, as it were quietly regarding his efforts, and beside the town the harbour showed its position by a dim meshwork of ropes and spars. After well-nigh exhausting himself in attempts to get back to the mouth of the cove, in his weakness swimming several inches deeper than was his wont, keeping up his breathing entirely by his nostrils, turning upon his back a dozen times over, swimming en papillon, and so on, Troy resolved as a last resource to tread water at a slight incline, and so endeavour to reach the shore at any point, merely giving himself a gentle impetus inwards whilst carried on in the general direction of the tide. This, necessarily a slow process, he found to be not altogether so difficult, and though there was no choice of a landing-place— the objects on shore passing by him in a sad and slow procession—he perceptibly approached the extremity of a spit of land yet further to the right, now well defined against the sunny portion of the horizon. While the swimmer's eyes were fixed upon the spit as his only means of salvation on this side of the Unknown, a moving object broke the outline of the extremity, and immediately a ship's boat appeared manned with several sailor lads, her bows towards the sea.

All Troy's vigour spasmodically revived to prolong the struggle yet a little further. Swimming with his right arm, he held up his left to hail them, splashing upon the waves, and shouting with all his might. From the position of the setting sun his white form was distinctly visible upon the now deep-hued bosom of the sea to the east of the boat, and the men saw him at once. Backing their oars and putting the boat about, they pulled towards him with a will, and in five or six minutes from the time of his first halloo, two of the sailors hauled him in over the stern.

They formed part of a brig's crew, and had come ashore for sand. Lending him what little clothing they could spare among them as a slight protection against the rapidly cooling air, they agreed to land him in the morning; and without further delay, for it was growing late, they made again towards the roadstead where their vessel lay.

Analysis: It's clear here that Troy is not intending to commit suicide or to fake his own suicide but being the opportunist that he is, he grasps at the chance to disappear. There is a sense that he wants to fade into nothingness. Hardy creates mystery and suspense here because we know at some point he will return.

Discussion point: Why does Troy's faked death create suspense?

And now night drooped slowly upon the wide watery levels in front; and at no great distance from them, where the shoreline curved round, and formed a long riband of shade upon the horizon, a series of points of yellow light began to start into existence, denoting the spot to be the site of Budmouth, where the lamps were being lighted along the parade. The cluck of their oars was the only sound of any distinctness upon the sea, and as they laboured amid the thickening shades the lamp-lights grew larger, each appearing to send a flaming sword deep down into the waves before it, until there arose, among other dim shapes of the kind, the form of the vessel for which they were bound.

Questions

Where does Troy take a swim?
What happens to him while swimming?
GCSE style question: how does Hardy make Troy's disappearance suspenseful?
Creative response: write a poem/story about swimming.

CHAPTER XLVIII
DOUBTS ARISE—DOUBTS LINGER

Bathsheba underwent the enlargement of her husband's absence from hours to days with a slight feeling of surprise, and a slight feeling of relief; yet neither sensation rose at any time far above the level commonly designated as indifference. She belonged to him: the certainties of that position were so well defined, and the reasonable probabilities of its issue so bounded that she could not speculate on contingencies. Taking no further interest in herself as a splendid woman, she acquired the indifferent feelings of an outsider in contemplating her probable fate as a singular wretch; for Bathsheba drew herself and her future in colours that no reality could exceed for darkness. Her original vigorous pride of youth had sickened, and with it had declined all her anxieties about coming years, since anxiety recognizes a better and a worse alternative, and Bathsheba had made up her mind that alternatives on any noteworthy scale had ceased for her. Soon, or later—and that not very late—her husband would be home again. And then the days of their tenancy of the Upper Farm would be numbered. There had originally been shown by the agent to the estate some distrust of Bathsheba's tenure as James Everdene's successor, on the score of her sex, and her youth, and her beauty; but the peculiar nature of her uncle's will, his own frequent testimony before his death to her cleverness in such a pursuit, and her vigorous marshalling of the numerous flocks and herds which came suddenly into her hands before negotiations were concluded, had won confidence in her powers, and no further objections had been raised. She had latterly been in great doubt as to what the legal effects of her marriage would be upon her position; but no notice had been taken as yet of her change of name, and only one point was clear—that in the event of her own or her husband's inability to meet the agent at the forthcoming January rent-day, very little consideration would be shown, and, for that matter, very little would be deserved. Once out of the farm, the approach of poverty would be sure.

Hence Bathsheba lived in a perception that her purposes were broken off. She was not a woman who could hope on without good materials for the process, differing thus from the less far-sighted and energetic, though more petted ones of the sex, with whom hope goes on as a sort of clockwork which the merest food and shelter are sufficient to wind up; and perceiving clearly that her mistake had been a fatal one, she accepted her position, and waited coldly for the end.

The first Saturday after Troy's departure she went to Casterbridge alone, a journey she had not before taken since her marriage. On this Saturday Bathsheba was passing slowly on foot through the crowd of rural business-men gathered as usual in front of the market-house, who were as usual gazed upon by the burghers with feelings that those healthy lives were dearly paid for by exclusion from possible aldermanship, when a man, who had apparently been following her, said some words to another on her left hand. Bathsheba's ears were keen as those of any wild animal, and she distinctly heard what the speaker said, though her back was towards him.

"I am looking for Mrs. Troy. Is that she there?"

"Yes; that's the young lady, I believe," said the the person addressed.

"I have some awkward news to break to her. Her husband is drowned."

As if endowed with the spirit of prophecy, Bathsheba gasped out, "No, it is not true; it cannot be true!" Then she said and heard no more. The ice of self-command which had latterly gathered over her was broken, and the currents burst forth again, and overwhelmed her. A darkness came into her eyes, and she fell.

But not to the ground. A gloomy man, who had been observing her from under the portico of the old corn-exchange when she passed through the group without, stepped quickly to her side at the moment of her exclamation, and caught her in his arms as she sank down.

"What is it?" said Boldwood, looking up at the bringer of the big news, as he supported her.

"Her husband was drowned this week while bathing in Lulwind Cove. A coastguardsman found his clothes, and brought them into Budmouth yesterday."

Thereupon a strange fire lighted up Boldwood's eye, and his face flushed with the suppressed excitement of an unutterable thought.

Analysis: With the announcement of Troy's death, Boldwood once again gets his hopes up. A "strange fire" lights his eye. At this latter end of the novel, Boldwood is definitely presented by Hardy as mad: during the storm he has neglected his crops because he feels so woebegone in love and now there is a crazed eagerness about him. Some critics have noted that he is too much of a caricatured crazy person at this point. I think this is unfair; Hardy presents him as a man who thinks he can redeem his life by reclaiming Bathsheba. Hardy's description of how Boldwood feels about the thought of being with his loved one suggests he is still in the grip of his sexual frenzy about her.

Discussion point: What do you think about the presentation of Boldwood here?

Everybody's glance was now centred upon him and the unconscious

Bathsheba. He lifted her bodily off the ground, and smoothed down the folds of her dress as a child might have taken a storm-beaten bird and arranged its ruffled plumes, and bore her along the pavement to the King's Arms Inn. Here he passed with her under the archway into a private room; and by the time he had deposited—so lothly—the precious burden upon a sofa, Bathsheba had opened her eyes. Remembering all that had occurred, she murmured, "I want to go home!"

Boldwood left the room. He stood for a moment in the passage to recover his senses. The experience had been too much for his consciousness to keep up with, and now that he had grasped it it had gone again. For those few heavenly, golden moments she had been in his arms. What did it matter about her not knowing it? She had been close to his breast; he had been close to hers.

He started onward again, and sending a woman to her, went out to ascertain all the facts of the case. These appeared to be limited to what he had already heard. He then ordered her horse to be put into the gig, and when all was ready returned to inform her. He found that, though still pale and unwell, she had in the meantime sent for the Budmouth man who brought the tidings, and learnt from him all there was to know.

Being hardly in a condition to drive home as she had driven to town, Boldwood, with every delicacy of manner and feeling, offered to get her a driver, or to give her a seat in his phaeton, which was more comfortable than her own conveyance. These proposals Bathsheba gently declined, and the farmer at once departed.

About half-an-hour later she invigorated herself by an effort, and took her seat and the reins as usual—in external appearance much as if nothing had happened. She went out of the town by a tortuous back street, and drove slowly along, unconscious of the road and the scene. The first shades of evening were showing themselves when Bathsheba reached home, where, silently alighting and leaving the horse in the hands of the boy, she proceeded at once upstairs. Liddy met her on the landing. The news had preceded Bathsheba to Weatherbury by half-an-hour, and Liddy looked inquiringly into her mistress's face. Bathsheba had nothing to say.

She entered her bedroom and sat by the window, and thought and thought till night enveloped her, and the extreme lines only of her shape were visible. Somebody came to the door, knocked, and opened it.

"Well, what is it, Liddy?" she said.

"I was thinking there must be something got for you to wear," said Liddy, with hesitation.

"What do you mean?"

"Mourning."

"No, no, no," said Bathsheba, hurriedly.

"But I suppose there must be something done for poor—"

"Not at present, I think. It is not necessary."

"Why not, ma'am?"

"Because he's still alive."

"How do you know that?" said Liddy, amazed.

"I don't know it. But wouldn't it have been different, or shouldn't I have heard more, or wouldn't they have found him, Liddy?—or—I don't know how it is, but death would have been different from how this is. I am perfectly convinced that he is still alive!"

Bathsheba remained firm in this opinion till Monday, when two circumstances conjoined to shake it. The first was a short paragraph in the local newspaper, which, beyond making by a methodizing pen formidable presumptive evidence of Troy's death by drowning, contained the important testimony of a young Mr. Barker, M.D., of Budmouth, who spoke to being an eyewitness of the accident, in a letter to the editor. In this he stated that he was passing over the cliff on the remoter side of the cove just as the sun was setting. At that time he saw a bather carried along in the current outside the mouth of the cove, and guessed in an instant that there was but a poor chance for him unless he should be possessed of unusual muscular powers. He drifted behind a projection of the coast, and Mr. Barker followed along the shore in the same direction. But by the time that he could reach an elevation sufficiently great to command a view of the sea beyond, dusk had set in, and nothing further was to be seen.

The other circumstance was the arrival of his clothes, when it became necessary for her to examine and identify them—though this had virtually been done long before by those who inspected the letters in his pockets. It was so evident to her in the midst of her agitation that Troy had undressed in the full conviction of dressing again almost immediately, that the notion that anything but death could have prevented him was a perverse one to entertain.

Then Bathsheba said to herself that others were assured in their opinion; strange that she should not be. A strange reflection occurred to her, causing her face to flush. Suppose that Troy had followed Fanny into another world. Had he done this intentionally, yet contrived to make his death appear like an accident? Nevertheless, this thought of how the apparent might differ from the real—made vivid by her bygone jealousy of Fanny, and the remorse he had shown that night—did not blind her to the perception of a likelier difference, less tragic, but to herself far more disastrous.

When alone late that evening beside a small fire, and much calmed down, Bathsheba took Troy's watch into her hand, which had been restored to her with the rest of the articles belonging to him. She opened the case as he had opened it before her a week ago. There was the little coil of pale hair which had been as the fuze to this great explosion.

"He was hers and she was his; they should be gone together," she said. "I am nothing to either of them, and why should I keep her hair?" She took it in her hand, and held it over the fire. "No—I'll not burn it—I'll keep it in memory of her, poor thing!" she added, snatching back her hand.

Questions

What does Bathsheba think will happen when Troy returns?

What happens when she is informed that Troy has drowned?

What does she really think has happened?

What helps convince her that he probably is dead?

Who is now very hopeful things will be better for him?

GCSE question: how does Hardy maintain the suspense and momentum of the story in this chapter?

Creative response: write a story called 'Missing' about a missing person. Or write Bathsheba's diary in which she reflects upon Troy's 'death'.

CHAPTER XLIX
OAK'S ADVANCEMENT—A GREAT HOPE

The later autumn and the winter drew on apace, and the leaves lay thick upon the turf of the glades and the mosses of the woods. Bathsheba, having previously been living in a state of suspended feeling which was not suspense, now lived in a mood of quietude which was not precisely peacefulness. While she had known him to be alive she could have thought of his death with equanimity; but now that it might be she had lost him, she regretted that he was not hers still. She kept the farm going, raked in her profits without caring keenly about them, and expended money on ventures because she had done so in bygone days, which, though not long gone by, seemed infinitely removed from her present. She looked back upon that past over a great gulf, as if she were now a dead person, having the faculty of meditation still left in her, by means of which, like the mouldering gentlefolk of the poet's story, she could sit and ponder what a gift life used to be.

However, one excellent result of her general apathy was the long-delayed installation of Oak as bailiff; but he having virtually exercised that function for a long time already, the change, beyond the substantial increase of wages it brought, was little more than a nominal one addressed to the outside world.

Boldwood lived secluded and inactive. Much of his wheat and all his barley of that season had been spoilt by the rain. It sprouted, grew into intricate mats, and was ultimately thrown to the pigs in armfuls. The strange neglect which had produced this ruin and waste became the subject of whispered talk among all the people round; and it was elicited from one of Boldwood's men that forgetfulness had nothing to do with it, for he had been reminded of the danger to his corn as many times and as persistently as inferiors dared to do. The sight of the pigs turning in disgust from the rotten ears seemed to arouse Boldwood, and he one evening sent for Oak. Whether it was suggested by Bathsheba's recent act of promotion or not, the farmer proposed at the interview that Gabriel should undertake the superintendence of the Lower Farm as well as of Bathsheba's, because of the necessity Boldwood felt for such aid, and the impossibility of discovering a more trustworthy man. Gabriel's malignant star was assuredly setting fast.

Bathsheba, when she learnt of this proposal—for Oak was obliged to consult her—at first languidly objected. She considered that the two farms together were too extensive for the observation of one man. Boldwood, who was apparently determined by personal rather than commercial reasons, suggested that Oak should be furnished with a horse for his sole use, when the plan would present no difficulty, the two farms lying side by side. Boldwood did not directly communicate with her during these negotiations, only speaking to Oak, who was the go-between throughout. All was harmoniously arranged at last, and we now see Oak mounted on a strong cob, and daily trotting the length and breadth of about two thousand acres in a cheerful spirit of surveillance, as if the crops all belonged to him—the actual mistress of the one-half and the master of the other, sitting in their respective homes in gloomy and sad seclusion.

Out of this there arose, during the spring succeeding, a talk in the parish that Gabriel Oak was feathering his nest fast.

"Whatever d'ye think," said Susan Tall, "Gable Oak is coming it quite the dand. He now wears shining boots with hardly a hob in 'em, two or three times a-week, and a tall hat a-Sundays, and 'a hardly knows the name of smockfrock. When I see people strut enough to be cut up into bantam cocks, I stand dormant with wonder, and says no more!"

It was eventually known that Gabriel, though paid a fixed wage by Bathsheba independent of the fluctuations of agricultural profits, had made an engagement with Boldwood by which Oak was to receive a share of the receipts—a small share certainly, yet it was money of a higher quality than mere wages, and capable of expansion in a way that wages were not. Some were beginning to consider Oak a "near" man, for though his condition had thus far improved, he lived in no better style than before, occupying the same cottage, paring his own potatoes, mending his stockings, and sometimes even making his bed with his own hands. But as Oak was not only provokingly indifferent to public opinion, but a man who clung persistently to old habits and usages, simply because they were old, there was room for doubt as to his motives.

Analysis: How Oak's fate has reversed! Here we see him triumphing materially but still living his modest life. Interestingly, while Oak has been throughout most of the novel an embodiment of the old country values of believing that community should be put ahead of profit, his embracing of the new technologies to harvest the crops, his ability to manage both Bathsheba and Boldwood's farms, suggest someone who now is a symbol for the new world order: the efficient, thrifty world order of the modern businessman.

Discussion point: What do you think of Hardy's presentation of Oak here?

A great hope had latterly germinated in Boldwood, whose unreasoning devotion to Bathsheba could only be characterized as a fond madness which neither time nor circumstance, evil nor good report, could weaken or destroy. This fevered hope had grown up again like a grain of mustard-seed during the quiet which followed the hasty conjecture that Troy was drowned. He nourished it fearfully, and almost shunned the contemplation of it in earnest, lest facts should reveal the wildness of the dream. Bathsheba having at last been persuaded to wear mourning, her appearance as she entered the church in that guise was in itself a weekly addition to his faith that a time was coming—very far off perhaps, yet surely nearing—when his waiting on events should have its reward. How long he might have to wait he had not yet closely considered. What he would try to recognize was that the severe schooling she had been subjected to had made Bathsheba much more considerate than she had formerly been of the feelings of others, and he trusted that, should she be willing at any time in the future to marry any man at all, that man would be himself. There was a substratum of good feeling in her: her self-reproach for the injury she had thoughtlessly done him might be depended upon now to a much greater extent than before her infatuation and disappointment. It would be possible to approach her by the channel of her good nature, and to suggest a friendly businesslike compact between them for fulfilment at some future day, keeping the passionate side of his desire entirely out of her sight. Such was Boldwood's hope.

To the eyes of the middle-aged, Bathsheba was perhaps additionally charming just now. Her exuberance of spirit was pruned down; the original phantom of delight had shown herself to be not too bright for human nature's daily food, and she had been able to enter this second poetical phase without losing much of the first in the process.

Bathsheba's return from a two months' visit to her old aunt at Norcombe afforded the impassioned and yearning farmer a pretext for inquiring directly after her—now possibly in the ninth month of her widowhood—and endeavouring to get a notion of her state of mind regarding him. This occurred in the middle of the haymaking, and Boldwood contrived to be near Liddy, who was assisting in the fields.

"I am glad to see you out of doors, Lydia," he said pleasantly.

She simpered, and wondered in her heart why he should speak so frankly to her.

"I hope Mrs. Troy is quite well after her long absence," he continued, in a manner expressing that the coldest-hearted neighbour could scarcely say less about her.

"She is quite well, sir."

"And cheerful, I suppose."

"Yes, cheerful."

"Fearful, did you say?"

"Oh no. I merely said she was cheerful."

"Tells you all her affairs?"

"No, sir."

"Some of them?"

"Yes, sir."

"Mrs. Troy puts much confidence in you, Lydia, and very wisely, perhaps."

"She do, sir. I've been with her all through her troubles, and was with her at the time of Mr. Troy's going and all. And if she were to marry again I expect I should bide with her."

"She promises that you shall—quite natural," said the strategic lover, throbbing throughout him at the presumption which Liddy's words appeared to warrant—that his darling had thought of re-marriage.

"No—she doesn't promise it exactly. I merely judge on my own account."

"Yes, yes, I understand. When she alludes to the possibility of marrying again, you conclude—"

"She never do allude to it, sir," said Liddy, thinking how very stupid Mr. Boldwood was getting.

"Of course not," he returned hastily, his hope falling again. "You needn't take quite such long reaches with your rake, Lydia—short and quick ones are best. Well, perhaps, as she is absolute mistress again now, it is wise of her to resolve never to give up her freedom."

"My mistress did certainly once say, though not seriously, that she supposed she might marry again at the end of seven years from last year, if she cared to risk Mr. Troy's coming back and claiming her."

"Ah, six years from the present time. Said that she might. She might marry at once in every reasonable person's opinion, whatever the lawyers may say to the contrary."

"Have you been to ask them?" said Liddy, innocently.

"Not I," said Boldwood, growing red. "Liddy, you needn't stay here a minute later than you wish, so Mr. Oak says. I am now going on a little farther. Good-afternoon."

He went away vexed with himself, and ashamed of having for this one time in his life done anything which could be called underhand. Poor Boldwood had no more skill in finesse than a battering-ram, and he was uneasy with a sense of having made himself to appear stupid and, what was worse, mean. But he had, after all, lighted upon one fact by way of repayment. It was a singularly fresh and fascinating fact, and though not without its sadness it was pertinent and real. In little more than six years from this time Bathsheba might certainly marry him. There was something definite in that hope, for admitting that there might have been no deep thought in her words to Liddy about marriage, they showed at least her creed on the matter.

This pleasant notion was now continually in his mind. Six years were a long time, but how much shorter than never, the idea he had for so long been obliged to endure! Jacob had served twice seven years for Rachel: what were six for such a woman as this? He tried to like the notion of waiting for her better than that of winning her at once. Boldwood felt his love to be so deep and strong and eternal, that it was possible she had never yet known its full volume, and this patience in delay would afford him an opportunity of giving sweet proof on the point. He would annihilate the six years of his life as if they were minutes—so little did he value his time on earth beside her love. He would let her see, all those six years of intangible ethereal courtship, how little care he had for anything but as it bore upon the consummation.

Meanwhile the early and the late summer brought round the week in which Greenhill Fair was held. This fair was frequently attended by the folk of Weatherbury.

Analysis: Hardy carefully ratchets up the suspense by having Liddy inform Boldwood that there is a chance Bathsheba will marry in six years' time. We sense his desperation in his red face, his searching questions. He never would normally speak to someone as insignificant as Liddy but he does now because he needs to know the truth.

Discussion point: How does Hardy generate suspense here?

Questions

Who does Bathsheba appoint as bailiff?
What happens to Boldwood's crops?
Why does Oak agree to look after Boldwood's farm?
What do the villagers think of Gabriel?
What does Bathsheba wear and why?
What does Boldwood learn from Liddy?
What does Boldwood convince himself of?
GCSE style question: how does Hardy present Boldwood in this chapter?
A Level style question: compare and contrast Boldwood's obsessive nature with another similar obsessive person in another text of your choice.
Creative response: write Boldwood's diary for this chapter.

CHAPTER L
THE SHEEP FAIR—TROY
TOUCHES HIS WIFE'S HAND

Greenhill was the Nijni Novgorod of South Wessex; and the busiest, merriest, noisiest day of the whole statute number was the day of the sheep fair. This yearly gathering was upon the summit of a hill which retained in good preservation the remains of an ancient earthwork, consisting of a huge rampart and entrenchment of an oval form encircling the top of the hill, though somewhat broken down here and there. To each of the two chief openings on opposite sides a winding road ascended, and the level green space of ten or fifteen acres enclosed by the bank was the site of the fair. A few permanent erections dotted the spot, but the majority of visitors patronized canvas alone for resting and feeding under during the time of their sojourn here.

Shepherds who attended with their flocks from long distances started from home two or three days, or even a week, before the fair, driving their charges a few miles each day—not more than ten or twelve—and resting them at night in hired fields by the wayside at previously chosen points, where they fed, having fasted since morning. The shepherd of each flock marched behind, a bundle containing his kit for the week strapped upon his shoulders, and in his hand his crook, which he used as the staff of his pilgrimage. Several of the sheep would get worn and lame, and occasionally a lambing occurred on the road. To meet these contingencies, there was frequently provided, to accompany the flocks from the remoter points, a pony and waggon into which the weakly ones were taken for the remainder of the journey.

The Weatherbury Farms, however, were no such long distance from the hill, and those arrangements were not necessary in their case. But the large united flocks of Bathsheba and Farmer Boldwood formed a valuable and imposing multitude which demanded much attention, and on this account Gabriel, in addition to Boldwood's shepherd and Cain Ball, accompanied them along the way, through the decayed old town of Kingsbere, and upward to the plateau,—old George the dog of course behind them.

When the autumn sun slanted over Greenhill this morning and lighted the dewy flat upon its crest, nebulous clouds of dust were to be seen floating between the pairs of hedges which streaked the wide prospect around in all directions. These gradually converged upon the base of the hill, and the flocks became individually visible, climbing the serpentine ways which led to the top. Thus, in a slow procession, they entered the opening to which the roads tended, multitude after multitude, horned and hornless—blue flocks and red flocks, buff flocks and brown flocks, even green and salmon-tinted flocks, according to the fancy of the colourist and custom of the farm. Men were shouting, dogs were barking, with greatest animation, but the thronging travellers in so long a journey had grown nearly indifferent to such terrors, though they still bleated piteously at the unwontedness of their experiences, a tall shepherd rising here and there in the midst of them, like a gigantic idol amid a crowd of prostrate devotees.

The great mass of sheep in the fair consisted of South Downs and the old Wessex horned breeds; to the latter class Bathsheba's and Farmer Boldwood's mainly belonged. These filed in about nine o'clock, their vermiculated horns lopping gracefully on each side of their cheeks in geometrically perfect spirals, a small pink and white ear nestling under each horn. Before and behind came other varieties, perfect leopards as to the full rich substance of their coats, and only lacking the spots. There were also a few of the Oxfordshire breed, whose wool was beginning to curl like a child's flaxen hair, though surpassed in this respect by the effeminate

Leicesters, which were in turn less curly than the Cotswolds. But the most picturesque by far was a small flock of Exmoors, which chanced to be there this year. Their pied faces and legs, dark and heavy horns, tresses of wool hanging round their swarthy foreheads, quite relieved the monotony of the flocks in that quarter.

All these bleating, panting, and weary thousands had entered and were penned before the morning had far advanced, the dog belonging to each flock being tied to the corner of the pen containing it. Alleys for pedestrians intersected the pens, which soon became crowded with buyers and sellers from far and near.

In another part of the hill an altogether different scene began to force itself upon the eye towards midday. A circular tent, of exceptional newness and size, was in course of erection here. As the day drew on, the flocks began to change hands, lightening the shepherd's responsibilities; and they turned their attention to this tent and inquired of a man at work there, whose soul seemed concentrated on tying a bothering knot in no time, what was going on.

"The Royal Hippodrome Performance of Turpin's Ride to York and the Death of Black Bess," replied the man promptly, without turning his eyes or leaving off tying.

As soon as the tent was completed the band struck up highly stimulating harmonies, and the announcement was publicly made, Black Bess standing in a conspicuous position on the outside, as a living proof, if proof were wanted, of the truth of the oracular utterances from the stage over which the people were to enter. These were so convinced by such genuine appeals to heart and understanding both that they soon began to crowd in abundantly, among the foremost being visible Jan Coggan and Joseph Poorgrass, who were holiday keeping here to-day.

"That's the great ruffen pushing me!" screamed a woman in front of Jan over her shoulder at him when the rush was at its fiercest.

"How can I help pushing ye when the folk behind push me?" said Coggan, in a deprecating tone, turning his head towards the aforesaid folk as far as he could without turning his body, which was jammed as in a vice.

There was a silence; then the drums and trumpets again sent forth their echoing notes. The crowd was again ecstasied, and gave another lurch in which Coggan and Poorgrass were again thrust by those behind upon the women in front.

"Oh that helpless feymels should be at the mercy of such ruffens!" exclaimed one of these ladies again, as she swayed like a reed shaken by the wind.

"Now," said Coggan, appealing in an earnest voice to the public at large as it stood clustered about his shoulder-blades, "did ye ever hear such onreasonable woman as that? Upon my carcase, neighbours, if I could only get out of this cheese-wring, the damn women might eat the show for me!"

"Don't ye lose yer temper, Jan!" implored Joseph Poorgrass, in a whisper. "They might get their men to murder us, for I think by the shine of their eyes that they be a sinful form of womankind."

Jan held his tongue, as if he had no objection to be pacified to please a friend, and they gradually reached the foot of the ladder, Poorgrass being flattened like a jumping-jack, and the sixpence, for admission, which he had got ready half-an-hour earlier, having become so reeking hot in the tight squeeze of his excited hand that the woman in spangles, brazen rings set with glass diamonds, and with chalked face and shoulders, who took the money of him, hastily dropped it again from a fear that some trick had been played to burn her fingers. So they all entered, and the cloth of the tent, to the eyes of an observer on the outside, became bulged into innumerable pimples such as we observe on a sack of potatoes, caused by the various human heads, backs, and elbows at high pressure within.

At the rear of the large tent there were two small dressing-tents. One of these, alloted to the male performers, was partitioned into halves by a cloth; and in one of the divisions there was sitting on the grass, pulling on a pair of jack-boots, a young man whom we instantly recognise as Sergeant Troy.

Troy's appearance in this position may be briefly accounted for. The brig aboard which he was taken in Budmouth Roads was about to start on a voyage, though somewhat short of hands. Troy read the articles and joined, but before they sailed a boat was despatched across the bay to Lulwind cove; as he had half expected, his clothes were gone. He ultimately worked his passage to the United States, where he made a precarious living in various towns as Professor of Gymnastics, Sword Exercise, Fencing, and Pugilism. A few months were sufficient to give him a distaste for this kind of life. There was a certain animal form of refinement in his nature; and however pleasant a strange condition might be whilst privations were easily warded off, it was disadvantageously coarse when money was short. There was ever present, too, the idea that he could claim a home and its comforts did he but chose to return to England and Weatherbury Farm. Whether Bathsheba thought him dead was a frequent subject of curious conjecture. To England he did return at last; but the fact of drawing nearer to Weatherbury abstracted its fascinations, and his intention to enter his old groove at the place became modified. It was with gloom he considered on landing at Liverpool that if he were to go home his reception would be of a kind very unpleasant to contemplate; for what Troy had in the way of emotion was an occasional fitful sentiment which sometimes caused him as much inconvenience as emotion of a strong and healthy kind. Bathsheba was not a woman to be made a fool of, or a woman to suffer in silence; and how could he endure existence with a spirited wife to whom at first entering he would be beholden for food and lodging? Moreover, it was not at all unlikely that his wife would fail at her farming, if she had not already done so; and he would then become liable for her maintenance: and what a life such a future of poverty with her would be, the spectre of Fanny constantly between them, harrowing his temper and embittering her words! Thus, for reasons touching on distaste, regret, and shame commingled, he put off his return from day to day, and would have decided to put it off altogether if he could have found anywhere else the ready-made establishment which existed for him there.

At this time—the July preceding the September in which we find at Greenhill Fair—he fell in with a travelling circus which was performing in the outskirts of a northern town. Troy introduced himself to the manager by taming a restive horse of the troupe, hitting a suspended apple with a pistol-bullet fired from the animal's back when in full gallop, and other feats. For his merits in these—all more or less based upon his experiences as a dragoon-guardsman—Troy was taken into the company, and the play of Turpin was prepared with a view to his personation of the chief character. Troy was not greatly elated by the appreciative spirit in which he was undoubtedly treated, but he thought the engagement might afford him a few weeks for consideration. It was thus carelessly, and without having formed any definite plan for the future, that Troy found himself at Greenhill Fair with the rest of the company on this day.

And now the mild autumn sun got lower, and in front of the pavilion the following incident had taken place. Bathsheba—who was driven to the fair that day by her odd man Poorgrass—had, like every one else, read or heard the announcement that Mr. Francis, the Great Cosmopolitan Equestrian and Roughrider, would enact the part of Turpin, and she was not yet too old and careworn to be without a little curiosity to see him. This particular show was by far the largest and grandest in the fair, a horde of little shows grouping themselves under its shade like chickens around a hen. The crowd had passed in, and Boldwood, who had been watching all the day for an opportunity of speaking to her, seeing her comparatively isolated, came up to her side.

"I hope the sheep have done well to-day, Mrs. Troy?" he said, nervously.

"Oh yes, thank you," said Bathsheba, colour springing up in the centre of her cheeks. "I was fortunate enough to sell them all just as we got upon the hill, so we hadn't to pen at all."

"And now you are entirely at leisure?"

"Yes, except that I have to see one more dealer in two hours' time: otherwise I should be going home. He was looking at this large tent and the announcement. Have you ever seen the play of 'Turpin's Ride to York'? Turpin was a real man, was he not?"

"Oh yes, perfectly true—all of it. Indeed, I think I've heard Jan Coggan say that a relation of his knew Tom King, Turpin's friend, quite well."

"Coggan is rather given to strange stories connected with his relations, we must remember. I hope they can all be believed."

"Yes, yes; we know Coggan. But Turpin is true enough. You have never seen it played, I suppose?"

"Never. I was not allowed to go into these places when I was young. Hark! What's that prancing? How they shout!"

"Black Bess just started off, I suppose. Am I right in supposing you would like to see the performance, Mrs. Troy? Please excuse my mistake, if it is one; but if you would like to, I'll get a seat for you with pleasure." Perceiving that she hesitated, he added, "I myself shall not stay to see it: I've seen it before."

Now Bathsheba did care a little to see the show, and had only withheld her feet from the ladder because she feared to go in alone. She had been hoping that Oak might appear, whose assistance in such cases was always accepted as an inalienable right, but Oak was nowhere to be seen; and hence it was that she said, "Then if you will just look in first, to see if there's room, I think I will go in for a minute or two."

And so a short time after this Bathsheba appeared in the tent with Boldwood at her elbow, who, taking her to a "reserved" seat, again withdrew.

This feature consisted of one raised bench in a very conspicuous part of the circle, covered with red cloth, and floored with a piece of carpet, and Bathsheba immediately found, to her confusion, that she was the single reserved individual in the tent, the rest of the crowded spectators, one and all, standing on their legs on the borders of the arena, where they got twice as good a view of the performance for half the money. Hence as many eyes were turned upon her, enthroned alone in this place of honour, against a scarlet background, as upon the ponies and clown who were engaged in preliminary exploits in the centre, Turpin not having yet appeared. Once there, Bathsheba was forced to make the best of it and remain: she sat down, spreading her skirts with some dignity over the unoccupied space on each side of her, and giving a new and feminine aspect to the pavilion. In a few minutes she noticed the fat red nape of Coggan's neck among those standing just below her, and Joseph Poorgrass's saintly profile a little further on.

The interior was shadowy with a peculiar shade. The strange luminous semi-opacities of fine autumn afternoons and eves intensified into Rembrandt effects the few yellow sunbeams which came through holes and divisions in the canvas, and spirted like jets of gold-dust across the dusky blue atmosphere of haze pervading the tent, until they alighted on inner surfaces of cloth opposite, and shone like little lamps suspended there.

Troy, on peeping from his dressing-tent through a slit for a reconnoitre before entering, saw his unconscious wife on high before him as described, sitting as queen of the tournament. He started back in utter confusion, for although his disguise effectually concealed his personality, he instantly felt that she would be sure to recognize his voice. He had several times during the day thought of the possibility of some Weatherbury person or other appearing and recognizing him; but he had taken the risk carelessly. If they see me, let them, he had said. But here was Bathsheba in her own person; and the reality of the scene was so much intenser than any of his prefigurings that he felt he had not half enough considered the point.

She looked so charming and fair that his cool mood about Weatherbury people was changed. He had not expected her to exercise this power over him in the twinkling of an eye. Should he go on, and care nothing? He could not bring himself to do that. Beyond a politic wish to remain unknown, there suddenly arose in him now a sense of shame at the possibility that his attractive young wife, who already despised him, should despise him more by discovering him in so mean a condition after so long a time. He actually blushed at the thought, and was vexed beyond measure that his sentiments of dislike towards Weatherbury should have led him to dally about the country in this way.

But Troy was never more clever than when absolutely at his wit's end. He hastily thrust aside the curtain dividing his own little dressing space from that of the manager and proprietor, who now appeared as the individual called Tom King as far down as his waist, and as the aforesaid respectable manager thence to his toes.

"Here's the devil to pay!" said Troy.

"How's that?"

"Why, there's a blackguard creditor in the tent I don't want to see, who'll discover me and nab me as sure as Satan if I open my mouth. What's to be done?"

"You must appear now, I think."

"I can't."

"But the play must proceed."

"Do you give out that Turpin has got a bad cold, and can't speak his part, but that he'll perform it just the same without speaking."

The proprietor shook his head.

"Anyhow, play or no play, I won't open my mouth," said Troy, firmly.

"Very well, then let me see. I tell you how we'll manage," said the other, who perhaps felt it would be extremely awkward to offend his leading man just at this time. "I won't tell 'em anything about your keeping silence; go on with the piece and say nothing, doing what you can by a judicious wink now and then, and a few indomitable nods in the heroic places, you know. They'll never find out that the speeches are omitted."

This seemed feasible enough, for Turpin's speeches were not many or long, the fascination of the piece lying entirely in the action; and accordingly the play began, and at the appointed time Black Bess leapt into the grassy circle amid the plaudits of the spectators. At the turnpike scene, where Bess and Turpin are hotly pursued at midnight by the officers, and the half-awake gatekeeper in his tasselled nightcap denies that any horseman has passed, Coggan uttered a broad-chested "Well done!" which could be heard all over the fair above the bleating, and Poorgrass smiled delightedly with a nice sense of dramatic contrast between our hero, who coolly leaps the gate, and halting justice in the form of his enemies, who must needs pull up cumbersomely and wait to be let through. At the death of Tom King, he could not refrain from seizing Coggan by the hand, and whispering, with tears in his eyes, "Of course he's not really shot, Jan—only seemingly!" And when the last sad scene came on, and the body of the gallant and faithful Bess had to be carried out on a shutter by twelve volunteers from among the spectators, nothing could restrain Poorgrass from lending a hand, exclaiming, as he asked Jan to join him, "Twill be something to tell of at Warren's in future years, Jan, and hand down to our children." For many a year in Weatherbury, Joseph told, with the air of a man who had had experiences in his time, that he touched with his own hand the hoof of Bess as she lay upon the board upon his shoulder. If, as some thinkers hold, immortality consists in being enshrined in others' memories, then did Black Bess become immortal that day if she never had done so before.

Meanwhile Troy had added a few touches to his ordinary make-up for the character, the more effectually to disguise himself, and though he had felt faint qualms on first entering, the metamorphosis effected by judiciously "lining" his face with a wire rendered him safe from the eyes of Bathsheba and her men. Nevertheless, he was relieved when it was got through.

Analysis: Fate brings Troy back to Bathsheba. He has been away in the States scraping a living as a circus performer and now returned with the fayre, profiting from his skill with a horse and sword. Dressed as the villain, he now becomes a villain, plotting his evil return, heedless of Bathsheba's welfare and intent only on bettering himself. He is ashamed that she should find out about his being in the circus because in those days being in a circus was not the thing a respectable soldier like Troy would do. The plot becomes rather contrived here: together with the evil Pennyways, who has seen him at the fayre and threatens to 'out' him, he plans to go back to Bathsheba and claim what is his. It is important to note that he is fully within his rights to do this; in those days, a husband owned his wife as if she was a piece of his property. Now Troy decides to exercise those rights.

Discussion point: What do you think of Hardy's presentation of Troy at this point?

There was a second performance in the evening, and the tent was lighted up. Troy had taken his part very quietly this time, venturing to introduce a few speeches on occasion; and was just concluding it when, whilst standing at the edge of the circle contiguous to the first row of spectators, he observed within a yard of him the eye of a man darted keenly into his side features. Troy hastily shifted his position, after having recognized in the scrutineer the knavish bailiff Pennyways, his wife's sworn enemy, who still hung about the outskirts of Weatherbury.

At first Troy resolved to take no notice and abide by circumstances. That he had been recognized by this man was highly probable; yet there was room for a doubt. Then the great objection he had felt to allowing news of his proximity to precede him to Weatherbury in the event of his return, based on a feeling that knowledge of his present occupation would discredit him still further in his wife's eyes, returned in full force. Moreover, should he resolve not to return at all, a tale of his being alive and being in the neighbourhood would be awkward; and he was anxious to acquire a knowledge of his wife's temporal affairs before deciding which to do.

In this dilemma Troy at once went out to reconnoitre. It occurred to him that to find Pennyways, and make a friend of him if possible, would be a very wise act. He had put on a thick beard borrowed from the establishment, and in this he wandered about the fair-field. It was now almost dark, and respectable people were getting their carts and gigs ready to go home.

The largest refreshment booth in the fair was provided by an innkeeper from a neighbouring town. This was considered an unexceptional place for obtaining the necessary food and rest: Host Trencher (as he was jauntily called by the local newspaper) being a substantial man of high repute for catering through all the country round. The tent was divided into first and second-class compartments, and at the end of the first-class division was a yet further enclosure for the most exclusive, fenced off from the body of the tent by a luncheon-bar, behind which the host himself stood bustling about in white apron and shirt-sleeves, and looking as if he had never lived anywhere but under canvas all his life. In these penetralia were chairs and a table, which, on candles being lighted, made quite a cozy and luxurious show, with an urn, plated tea and coffee pots, china teacups, and plum cakes.

Troy stood at the entrance to the booth, where a gipsy-woman was frying pancakes over a little fire of sticks and selling them at a penny a-piece, and looked over the heads of the people within. He could see nothing of Pennyways, but he soon discerned Bathsheba through an opening into the reserved space at the further end. Troy thereupon retreated, went round the tent into the darkness, and listened. He could hear Bathsheba's voice immediately inside the canvas; she was conversing with a man. A warmth overspread his face: surely she was not so unprincipled as to flirt in a fair! He wondered if, then, she reckoned upon his death as an absolute certainty. To get at the root of the matter, Troy took a penknife from his pocket and softly made two little cuts crosswise in the cloth, which, by folding back the corners left a hole the size of a wafer. Close to this he placed his face, withdrawing it again in a movement of surprise; for his eye had been within twelve inches of the top of Bathsheba's head. It was too near to be convenient. He made another hole a little to one side and lower down, in a shaded place beside her chair, from which it was easy and safe to survey her by looking horizontally.

Troy took in the scene completely now. She was leaning back, sipping a cup of tea that she held in her hand, and the owner of the male voice was Boldwood, who had apparently just brought the cup to her, Bathsheba, being in a negligent mood, leant so idly against the canvas that it was pressed to the shape of her shoulder, and she was, in fact, as good as in Troy's arms; and he was obliged to keep his breast carefully backward that she might not feel its warmth through the cloth as he gazed in.

Troy found unexpected chords of feeling to be stirred again within him as they had been stirred earlier in the day. She was handsome as ever, and she was his. It was some minutes before he could counteract his sudden wish to go in, and claim her. Then he thought how the proud girl who had always looked down upon him even whilst it was to love him, would hate him on discovering him to be a strolling player. Were he to make himself known, that chapter of his life must at all risks be kept for ever from her and from the Weatherbury people, or his name would be a byword throughout the parish. He would be nicknamed "Turpin" as long as he lived. Assuredly before he could claim her these few past months of his existence must be entirely blotted out.

"Shall I get you another cup before you start, ma'am?" said Farmer Boldwood.

"Thank you," said Bathsheba. "But I must be going at once. It was great neglect in that man to keep me waiting here till so late. I should have gone two hours ago, if it had not been for him. I had no idea of coming in here; but there's nothing so refreshing as a cup of tea, though I should never have got one if you hadn't helped me."

Troy scrutinized her cheek as lit by the candles, and watched each varying shade thereon, and the white shell-like sinuosities of her little ear. She took out her purse and was insisting to Boldwood on paying for her tea for herself, when at this moment Pennyways entered the tent. Troy trembled: here was his scheme for respectability endangered at once. He was about to leave his hole of espial, attempt to follow Pennyways, and find out if the ex-bailiff had recognized him, when he was arrested by the conversation, and found he was too late.

"Excuse me, ma'am," said Pennyways; "I've some private information for your ear alone."

"I cannot hear it now," she said, coldly. That Bathsheba could not endure this man was evident; in fact, he was continually coming to her with some tale or other, by which he might creep into favour at the expense of persons maligned.

"I'll write it down," said Pennyways, confidently. He stooped over the table, pulled a leaf from a warped pocket-book, and wrote upon the paper, in a round hand—

"Your husband is here. I've seen him. Who's the fool now?"

This he folded small, and handed towards her. Bathsheba would not read it; she would not even put out her hand to take it. Pennyways, then, with a laugh of derision, tossed it into her lap, and, turning away, left her.

From the words and action of Pennyways, Troy, though he had not been able to see what the ex-bailiff wrote, had not a moment's doubt that the note referred to him. Nothing that he could think of could be done to check the exposure. "Curse my luck!" he whispered, and added imprecations which rustled in the gloom like a pestilent wind. Meanwhile Boldwood said, taking up the note from her lap—

"Don't you wish to read it, Mrs. Troy? If not, I'll destroy it."

"Oh, well," said Bathsheba, carelessly, "perhaps it is unjust not to read it; but I can guess what it is about. He wants me to recommend him, or it is to tell me of some little scandal or another connected with my work-people. He's always doing that."

Bathsheba held the note in her right hand. Boldwood handed towards her a plate of cut bread-and-butter; when, in order to take a slice, she put the note into her left hand, where she was still holding the purse, and then allowed her hand to drop beside her close to the canvas. The moment had come for saving his game, and Troy impulsively felt that he would play the card. For yet another time he looked at the fair hand, and saw the pink finger-tips, and the blue veins of the wrist, encircled by a bracelet of coral chippings which she wore: how familiar it all was to him! Then, with the lightning action in which he was such an adept, he noiselessly slipped his hand under the bottom of the tent-cloth, which was far from being pinned tightly down, lifted it a little way, keeping his eye to the hole, snatched the note from her fingers, dropped the canvas, and ran away in the gloom towards the bank and ditch, smiling at the scream of astonishment which burst from her. Troy then slid down on the outside of the rampart, hastened round in the bottom of the entrenchment to a distance of a hundred yards, ascended again, and crossed boldly in a slow walk towards the front entrance of the tent. His object was now to get to Pennyways, and prevent a repetition of the announcement until such time as he should choose.

Troy reached the tent door, and standing among the groups there gathered, looked anxiously for Pennyways, evidently not wishing to make himself prominent by inquiring for him. One or two men were speaking of a daring attempt that had just been made to rob a young lady by lifting the canvas of the tent beside her. It was supposed that the rogue had imagined a slip of paper which she held in her hand to be a bank note, for he had seized it, and made off with it, leaving her purse behind. His chagrin and disappointment at discovering its worthlessness would be a good joke, it was said. However, the occurrence seemed to have become known to few, for it had not interrupted a fiddler, who had lately begun playing by the door of the tent, nor the four bowed old men with grim countenances and walking-sticks in hand, who were dancing "Major Malley's Reel" to the tune. Behind these stood Pennyways. Troy glided up to him, beckoned, and whispered a few words; and with a mutual glance of concurrence the two men went into the night together.

Questions

What does Oak take to Greenhill Fair?
What is Troy doing there?
What has Troy been doing for the intervening time?
How does he avoid being recognised by Bathsheba?
Who recognises him?
What does Pennyways try to do when he realizes who is at the fair?
How does Troy stop Pennyways communicating with Bathsheba?
GCSE style question: how does Hardy present Troy in this chapter?
Creative response: write Troy's diary for this chapter, outlining his thoughts about seeing Bathsheba again.

CHAPTER LI
BATHSHEBA TALKS WITH HER OUTRIDER

The arrangement for getting back again to Weatherbury had been that Oak should take the place of Poorgrass in Bathsheba's conveyance and drive her home, it being discovered late in the afternoon that Joseph was suffering from his old complaint, a multiplying eye, and was, therefore, hardly trustworthy as coachman and protector to a woman. But Oak had found himself so occupied, and was full of so many cares relative to those portions of Boldwood's flocks that were not disposed of, that Bathsheba, without telling Oak or anybody, resolved to drive home herself, as she had many times done from Casterbridge Market, and trust to her good angel for performing the journey unmolested. But having fallen in with Farmer Boldwood accidentally (on her part at least) at the refreshment-tent, she found it impossible to refuse his offer to ride on horseback beside her as escort. It had grown twilight before she was aware, but Boldwood assured her that there was no cause for uneasiness, as the moon would be up in half-an-hour.

Immediately after the incident in the tent, she had risen to go—now absolutely alarmed and really grateful for her old lover's protection— though regretting Gabriel's absence, whose company she would have much preferred, as being more proper as well as more pleasant, since he was her own managing-man and servant. This, however, could not be helped; she would not, on any consideration, treat Boldwood harshly, having once already ill-used him, and the moon having risen, and the gig being ready, she drove across the hilltop in the wending way's which led downwards—to oblivious obscurity, as it seemed, for the moon and the hill it flooded with light were in appearance on a level, the rest of the world lying as a vast shady concave between them. Boldwood mounted his horse, and followed in close attendance behind. Thus they descended into the lowlands, and the sounds of those left on the hill came like voices from the sky, and the lights were as those of a camp in heaven. They soon passed the merry stragglers in the immediate vicinity of the hill, traversed Kingsbere, and got upon the high road.

The keen instincts of Bathsheba had perceived that the farmer's staunch devotion to herself was still undiminished, and she sympathized deeply. The sight had quite depressed her this evening; had reminded her of her folly; she wished anew, as she had wished many months ago, for some means of making reparation for her fault. Hence her pity for the man who so persistently loved on to his own injury and permanent gloom had betrayed Bathsheba into an injudicious considerateness of manner, which appeared almost like tenderness, and gave new vigour to the exquisite dream of a Jacob's seven years service in poor Boldwood's mind.

He soon found an excuse for advancing from his position in the rear, and rode close by her side. They had gone two or three miles in the moonlight, speaking desultorily across the wheel of her gig concerning the fair, farming, Oak's usefulness to them both, and other indifferent subjects, when Boldwood said suddenly and simply—

"Mrs. Troy, you will marry again some day?"

This point-blank query unmistakably confused her, and it was not till a minute or more had elapsed that she said, "I have not seriously thought of any such subject."

"I quite understand that. Yet your late husband has been dead nearly one year, and—"

"You forget that his death was never absolutely proved, and may not have taken place; so that I may not be really a widow," she said, catching at the straw of escape that the fact afforded.

"Not absolutely proved, perhaps, but it was proved circumstantially. A man saw him drowning, too. No reasonable person has any doubt of his death; nor have you, ma'am, I should imagine."

"I have none now, or I should have acted differently," she said, gently. "I certainly, at first, had a strange unaccountable feeling that he could not have perished, but I have been able to explain that in several ways since. But though I am fully persuaded that I shall see him no more, I am far from thinking of marriage with another. I should be very contemptible to indulge in such a thought."

They were silent now awhile, and having struck into an unfrequented track across a common, the creaks of Boldwood's saddle and her gig springs were all the sounds to be heard. Boldwood ended the pause.

"Do you remember when I carried you fainting in my arms into the King's Arms, in Casterbridge? Every dog has his day: that was mine."

"I know—I know it all," she said, hurriedly.

"I, for one, shall never cease regretting that events so fell out as to deny you to me."

"I, too, am very sorry," she said, and then checked herself. "I mean, you know, I am sorry you thought I—"

"I have always this dreary pleasure in thinking over those past times with you—that I was something to you before he was anything, and that you belonged almost to me. But, of course, that's nothing. You never liked me."

"I did; and respected you, too."

"Do you now?"

"Yes."

"Which?"

"How do you mean which?"

"Do you like me, or do you respect me?"

"I don't know—at least, I cannot tell you. It is difficult for a woman to define her feelings in language which is chiefly made by men to express theirs. My treatment of you was thoughtless, inexcusable, wicked! I shall eternally regret it. If there had been anything I could have done to make amends I would most gladly have done it—there was nothing on earth I so longed to do as to repair the error. But that was not possible."

"Don't blame yourself—you were not so far in the wrong as you suppose. Bathsheba, suppose you had real complete proof that you are what, in fact, you are—a widow—would you repair the old wrong to me by marrying me?"

"I cannot say. I shouldn't yet, at any rate."

"But you might at some future time of your life?"

"Oh yes, I might at some time."

"Well, then, do you know that without further proof of any kind you may marry again in about six years from the present—subject to nobody's objection or blame?"

"Oh yes," she said, quickly. "I know all that. But don't talk of it—seven or six years—where may we all be by that time?"

"They will soon glide by, and it will seem an astonishingly short time to look back upon when they are past—much less than to look forward to now."

"Yes, yes; I have found that in my own experience."

"Now listen once more," Boldwood pleaded. "If I wait that time, will you marry me? You own that you owe me amends—let that be your way of making them."

"But, Mr. Boldwood—six years—"

"Do you want to be the wife of any other man?"

"No indeed! I mean, that I don't like to talk about this matter now. Perhaps it is not proper, and I ought not to allow it. Let us drop it. My husband may be living, as I said."

"Of course, I'll drop the subject if you wish. But propriety has nothing to do with reasons. I am a middle-aged man, willing to protect you for the remainder of our lives. On your side, at least, there is no passion or blamable haste—on mine, perhaps, there is. But I can't help seeing that if you choose from a feeling of pity, and, as you say, a wish to make amends, to make a bargain with me for a far-ahead time—an agreement which will set all things right and make me happy, late though it may be—there is no fault to be found with you as a woman. Hadn't I the first place beside you? Haven't you been almost mine once already? Surely you can say to me as much as this, you will have me back again should circumstances permit? Now, pray speak! O Bathsheba, promise—it is only a little promise—that if you marry again, you will marry me!"

His tone was so excited that she almost feared him at this moment, even whilst she sympathized. It was a simple physical fear—the weak of the strong; there was no emotional aversion or inner repugnance. She said, with some distress in her voice, for she remembered vividly his outburst on the Yalbury Road, and shrank from a repetition of his anger:—

"I will never marry another man whilst you wish me to be your wife, whatever comes—but to say more—you have taken me so by surprise—"

"But let it stand in these simple words—that in six years' time you will be my wife? Unexpected accidents we'll not mention, because those, of course, must be given way to. Now, this time I know you will keep your word."

"That's why I hesitate to give it."

"But do give it! Remember the past, and be kind."

She breathed; and then said mournfully: "Oh what shall I do? I don't love you, and I much fear that I never shall love you as much as a woman ought to love a husband. If you, sir, know that, and I can yet give you happiness by a mere promise to marry at the end of six years, if my husband should not come back, it is a great honour to me. And if you value such an act of friendship from a woman who doesn't esteem herself as she did, and has little love left, why I—I will—"

"Promise!"

"—Consider, if I cannot promise soon."

"But soon is perhaps never?"

"Oh no, it is not! I mean soon. Christmas, we'll say."

"Christmas!" He said nothing further till he added: "Well, I'll say no more to you about it till that time."

Analysis:
Boldwood has honed his skills of emotional blackmail, crushing Bathsheba with his insistent pleas and reminders of her past conduct. Notice how he manages to extract from inch by inch a promise that she will consider marrying him at Christmas. Thus Hardy sets up the dramatic climax of the novel, choosing to make it occur in the chill of winter time, rather the heat of summer.

Discussion point:
How does Hardy make the conversation between Bathsheba and Boldwood so dramatic here?

Bathsheba was in a very peculiar state of mind, which showed how entirely the soul is the slave of the body, the ethereal spirit dependent for its quality upon the tangible flesh and blood. It is hardly too much to say that she felt coerced by a force stronger than her own will, not only into the act of promising upon this singularly remote and vague matter, but into the emotion of fancying that she ought to promise. When the weeks intervening between the night of this conversation and Christmas day began perceptibly to diminish, her anxiety and perplexity increased.

One day she was led by an accident into an oddly confidential dialogue with Gabriel about her difficulty. It afforded her a little relief—of a dull and cheerless kind. They were auditing accounts, and something occurred in the course of their labours which led Oak to say, speaking of Boldwood, "He'll never forget you, ma'am, never."

Then out came her trouble before she was aware; and she told him how she had again got into the toils; what Boldwood had asked her, and how he was expecting her assent. "The most mournful reason of all for my agreeing to it," she said sadly, "and the true reason why I think to do so for good or for evil, is this—it is a thing I have not breathed to a living soul as yet—I believe that if I don't give my word, he'll go out of his mind."

"Really, do ye?" said Gabriel, gravely.

"I believe this," she continued, with reckless frankness; "and Heaven knows I say it in a spirit the very reverse of vain, for I am grieved and troubled to my soul about it—I believe I hold that man's future in my hand. His career depends entirely upon my treatment of him. O Gabriel, I tremble at my responsibility, for it is terrible!"

"Well, I think this much, ma'am, as I told you years ago," said Oak, "that his life is a total blank whenever he isn't hoping for 'ee; but I can't suppose—I hope that nothing so dreadful hangs on to it as you fancy. His natural manner has always been dark and strange, you know. But since the case is so sad and odd-like, why don't ye give the conditional promise? I think I would."

"But is it right? Some rash acts of my past life have taught me that a watched woman must have very much circumspection to retain only a very little credit, and I do want and long to be discreet in this! And six years— why we may all be in our graves by that time, even if Mr. Troy does not come back again, which he may not impossibly do! Such thoughts give a sort of absurdity to the scheme. Now, isn't it preposterous, Gabriel? However he came to dream of it, I cannot think. But is it wrong? You know—you are older than I."

"Eight years older, ma'am."

"Yes, eight years—and is it wrong?"

"Perhaps it would be an uncommon agreement for a man and woman to make: I don't see anything really wrong about it," said Oak, slowly. "In fact the very thing that makes it doubtful if you ought to marry en under any condition, that is, your not caring about him—for I may suppose—"

"Yes, you may suppose that love is wanting," she said shortly. "Love is an utterly bygone, sorry, worn-out, miserable thing with me—for him or any one else."

"Well, your want of love seems to me the one thing that takes away harm from such an agreement with him. If wild heat had to do wi' it, making ye long to over-come the awkwardness about your husband's vanishing, it mid be wrong; but a cold-hearted agreement to oblige a man seems different, somehow. The real sin, ma'am in my mind, lies in thinking of ever wedding wi' a man you don't love honest and true."

"That I'm willing to pay the penalty of," said Bathsheba, firmly. "You know, Gabriel, this is what I cannot get off my conscience—that I once seriously injured him in sheer idleness. If I had never played a trick upon him, he would never have wanted to marry me. Oh if I could only pay some heavy damages in money to him for the harm I did, and so get the sin off my soul that way! ... Well, there's the debt, which can only be discharged in one way, and I believe I am bound to do it if it honestly lies in my power, without any consideration of my own future at all. When a rake gambles away his expectations, the fact that it is an inconvenient debt doesn't make him the less liable. I've been a rake, and the single point I ask you is, considering that my own scruples, and the fact that in the eye of the law my husband is only missing, will keep any man from marrying me until seven years have passed—am I free to entertain such an idea, even though 'tis a sort of penance—for it will be that? I hatethe act of marriage under such circumstances, and the class of women I should seem to belong to by doing it!"

"It seems to me that all depends upon whe'r you think, as everybody else do, that your husband is dead."

"Yes—I've long ceased to doubt that. I well know what would have brought him back long before this time if he had lived."

"Well, then, in a religious sense you will be as free to think o' marrying again as any real widow of one year's standing. But why don't ye ask Mr. Thirdly's advice on how to treat Mr. Boldwood?"

"No. When I want a broad-minded opinion for general cnlightenment, distinct from special advice, I never go to a man who deals in the subject professionally. So I like the parson's opinion on law, the lawyer's on doctoring, the doctor's on business, and my business-man's—that is, yours—on morals."

"And on love—"

"My own."

"I'm afraid there's a hitch in that argument," said Oak, with a grave smile.

She did not reply at once, and then saying, "Good evening, Mr. Oak." went away.

She had spoken frankly, and neither asked nor expected any reply from Gabriel more satisfactory than that she had obtained. Yet in the centremost parts of her complicated heart there existed at this minute a little pang of disappointment, for a reason she would not allow herself to recognize. Oak had not once wished her free that he might marry her himself—had not once said, "I could wait for you as well as he." That was the insect sting. Not that she would have listened to any such hypothesis. O no—for wasn't she saying all the time that such thoughts of the future were improper, and wasn't Gabriel far too poor a man to speak sentiment to her? Yet he might have just hinted about that old love of his, and asked, in a playful off-hand way, if he might speak of it. It would have seemed pretty and sweet, if no more; and then she would have shown how kind and inoffensive a woman's "No" can sometimes be. But to give such cool advice—the very advice she had asked for—it ruffled our heroine all the afternoon.

Questions

What does Boldwood do when they return back to Weatherbury?

How does Bathsheba try and stall him?

What does Boldwood argue?

What does Bathsheba promise him? Not to marry anyone else, but that she will give her final word at Christmas.

What does Bathsheba confide to Oak?

Why does Bathsheba take Boldwood's proposal seriously?

GCSE style question: how does Hardy present Oak and Bathsheba's deepening relationship in this chapter?

Creative response: write Bathsheba's diary for this chapter, exploring her feelings towards Oak, Boldwood and Troy.

CHAPTER LII
CONVERGING COURSES

I

Christmas-eve came, and a party that Boldwood was to give in the evening was the great subject of talk in Weatherbury. It was not that the rarity of Christmas parties in the parish made this one a wonder, but that Boldwood should be the giver. The announcement had had an abnormal and incongruous sound, as if one should hear of croquet-playing in a cathedral aisle, or that some much-respected judge was going upon the stage. That the party was intended to be a truly jovial one there was no room for doubt. A large bough of mistletoe had been brought from the woods that day, and suspended in the hall of the bachelor's home. Holly and ivy had followed in armfuls. From six that morning till past noon the huge wood fire in the kitchen roared and sparkled at its highest, the kettle, the saucepan, and the three-legged pot appearing in the midst of the flames like Shadrach, Meshach, and Abednego; moreover, roasting and basting operations were continually carried on in front of the genial blaze.

As it grew later the fire was made up in the large long hall into which the staircase descended, and all encumbrances were cleared out for dancing. The log which was to form the back-brand of the evening fire was the uncleft trunk of a tree, so unwieldy that it could be neither brought nor rolled to its place; and accordingly two men were to be observed dragging and heaving it in by chains and levers as the hour of assembly drew near.

In spite of all this, the spirit of revelry was wanting in the atmosphere of the house. Such a thing had never been attempted before by its owner, and it was now done as by a wrench. Intended gaieties would insist upon appearing like solemn grandeurs, the organization of the whole effort was carried out coldly, by hirelings, and a shadow seemed to move about the rooms, saying that the proceedings were unnatural to the place and the lone man who lived therein, and hence not good.

II

Bathsheba was at this time in her room, dressing for the event. She had called for candles, and Liddy entered and placed one on each side of her mistress's glass.

"Don't go away, Liddy," said Bathsheba, almost timidly. "I am foolishly agitated—I cannot tell why. I wish I had not been obliged to go to this dance; but there's no escaping now. I have not spoken to Mr. Boldwood since the autumn, when I promised to see him at Christmas on business, but I had no idea there was to be anything of this kind."

"But I would go now," said Liddy, who was going with her; for Boldwood had been indiscriminate in his invitations.

"Yes, I shall make my appearance, of course," said Bathsheba. "But I am the cause of the party, and that upsets me!—Don't tell, Liddy."

"Oh no, ma'am. You the cause of it, ma'am?"

"Yes. I am the reason of the party—I. If it had not been for me, there would never have been one. I can't explain any more—there's no more to be explained. I wish I had never seen Weatherbury."

"That's wicked of you—to wish to be worse off than you are."

"No, Liddy. I have never been free from trouble since I have lived here, and this party is likely to bring me more. Now, fetch my black silk dress, and see how it sits upon me."

"But you will leave off that, surely, ma'am? You have been a widow-lady fourteen months, and ought to brighten up a little on such a night as this."

"Is it necessary? No; I will appear as usual, for if I were to wear any light dress people would say things about me, and I should seem to be rejoicing when I am solemn all the time. The party doesn't suit me a bit; but never mind, stay and help to finish me off."

III

Boldwood was dressing also at this hour. A tailor from Casterbridge was with him, assisting him in the operation of trying on a new coat that had just been brought home.

Never had Boldwood been so fastidious, unreasonable about the fit, and generally difficult to please. The tailor walked round and round him, tugged at the waist, pulled the sleeve, pressed out the collar, and for the first time in his experience Boldwood was not bored. Times had been when the farmer had exclaimed against all such niceties as childish, but now no philosophic or hasty rebuke whatever was provoked by this man for attaching as much importance to a crease in the coat as to an earthquake in South America. Boldwood at last expressed himself nearly satisfied, and paid the bill, the tailor passing out of the door just as Oak came in to report progress for the day.

"Oh, Oak," said Boldwood. "I shall of course see you here to-night. Make yourself merry. I am determined that neither expense nor trouble shall be spared."

"I'll try to be here, sir, though perhaps it may not be very early," said Gabriel, quietly. "I am glad indeed to see such a change in 'ee from what it used to be."

"Yes—I must own it—I am bright to-night: cheerful and more than cheerful—so much so that I am almost sad again with the sense that all of it is passing away. And sometimes, when I am excessively hopeful and blithe, a trouble is looming in the distance: so that I often get to look upon gloom in me with content, and to fear a happy mood. Still this may be absurd—I feel that it is absurd. Perhaps my day is dawning at last."

"I hope it 'ill be a long and a fair one."

Far From The Madding Crowd: The Study Guide Edition

"Thank you—thank you. Yet perhaps my cheerfulness rests on a slender hope. And yet I trust my hope. It is faith, not hope. I think this time I reckon with my host.—Oak, my hands are a little shaky, or something; I can't tie this neckerchief properly. Perhaps you will tie it for me. The fact is, I have not been well lately, you know."

"I am sorry to hear that, sir."

"Oh, it's nothing. I want it done as well as you can, please. Is there any late knot in fashion, Oak?"

"I don't know, sir," said Oak. His tone had sunk to sadness.

Boldwood approached Gabriel, and as Oak tied the neckerchief the farmer went on feverishly—

"Does a woman keep her promise, Gabriel?"

"If it is not inconvenient to her she may."

"—Or rather an implied promise."

"I won't answer for her implying," said Oak, with faint bitterness. "That's a word as full o' holes as a sieve with them."

"Oak, don't talk like that. You have got quite cynical lately—how is it? We seem to have shifted our positions: I have become the young and hopeful man, and you the old and unbelieving one. However, does a woman keep a promise, not to marry, but to enter on an engagement to marry at some time? Now you know women better than I—tell me."

"I am afeard you honour my understanding too much. However, she may keep such a promise, if it is made with an honest meaning to repair a wrong."

"It has not gone far yet, but I think it will soon—yes, I know it will," he said, in an impulsive whisper. "I have pressed her upon the subject, and she inclines to be kind to me, and to think of me as a husband at a long future time, and that's enough for me. How can I expect more? She has a notion that a woman should not marry within seven years of her husband's disappearance—that her own self shouldn't, I mean—because his body was not found. It may be merely this legal reason which influences her, or it may be a religious one, but she is reluctant to talk on the point. Yet she has promised—implied—that she will ratify an engagement to-night."

"Seven years," murmured Oak.

"No, no—it's no such thing!" he said, with impatience. "Five years, nine months, and a few days. Fifteen months nearly have passed since he vanished, and is there anything so wonderful in an engagement of little more than five years?"

"It seems long in a forward view. Don't build too much upon such promises, sir. Remember, you have once be'n deceived. Her meaning may be good; but there—she's young yet."

"Deceived? Never!" said Boldwood, vehemently. "She never promised me at that first time, and hence she did not break her promise! If she promises me, she'll marry me. Bathsheba is a woman to her word."

IV

305

Troy was sitting in a corner of The White Hart tavern at Casterbridge, smoking and drinking a steaming mixture from a glass. A knock was given at the door, and Pennyways entered.

"Well, have you seen him?" Troy inquired, pointing to a chair.

"Boldwood?"

"No—Lawyer Long."

"He wadn' at home. I went there first, too."

"That's a nuisance."

"'Tis rather, I suppose."

"Yet I don't see that, because a man appears to be drowned and was not, he should be liable for anything. I shan't ask any lawyer—not I."

"But that's not it, exactly. If a man changes his name and so forth, and takes steps to deceive the world and his own wife, he's a cheat, and that in the eye of the law is ayless a rogue, and that is ayless a lammocken vagabond; and that's a punishable situation."

"Ha-ha! Well done, Pennyways," Troy had laughed, but it was with some anxiety that he said, "Now, what I want to know is this, do you think there's really anything going on between her and Boldwood? Upon my soul, I should never have believed it! How she must detest me! Have you found out whether she has encouraged him?"

"I haen't been able to learn. There's a deal of feeling on his side seemingly, but I don't answer for her. I didn't know a word about any such thing till yesterday, and all I heard then was that she was gwine to the party at his house to-night. This is the first time she has ever gone there, they say. And they say that she've not so much as spoke to him since they were at Greenhill Fair: but what can folk believe o't? However, she's not fond of him—quite offish and quite careless, I know."

"I'm not so sure of that... She's a handsome woman, Pennyways, is she not? Own that you never saw a finer or more splendid creature in your life. Upon my honour, when I set eyes upon her that day I wondered what I could have been made of to be able to leave her by herself so long. And then I was hampered with that bothering show, which I'm free of at last, thank the stars." He smoked on awhile, and then added, "How did she look when you passed by yesterday?"

"Oh, she took no great heed of me, ye may well fancy; but she looked well enough, far's I know. Just flashed her haughty eyes upon my poor scram body, and then let them go past me to what was yond, much as if I'd been no more than a leafless tree. She had just got off her mare to look at the last wring-down of cider for the year; she had been riding, and so her colours were up and her breath rather quick, so that her bosom plimmed and fell— plimmed and fell—every time plain to my eye. Ay, and there were the fellers round her wringing down the cheese and bustling about and saying, 'Ware o' the pommy, ma'am: 'twill spoil yer gown.' 'Never mind me,' says she. Then Gabe brought her some of the new cider, and she must needs go drinking it through a strawmote, and not in a nateral way at all. 'Liddy,' says she, 'bring indoors a few gallons, and I'll make some cider-wine.' Sergeant, I was no more to her than a morsel of scroff in the fuel-house!"

"I must go and find her out at once—O yes, I see that—I must go. Oak is head man still, isn't he?"

"Yes, 'a b'lieve. And at Little Weatherbury Farm too. He manages everything."

"'Twill puzzle him to manage her, or any other man of his compass!"

"I don't know about that. She can't do without him, and knowing it well he's pretty independent. And she've a few soft corners to her mind, though I've never been able to get into one, the devil's in't!"

"Ah, baily, she's a notch above you, and you must own it: a higher class of animal—a finer tissue. However, stick to me, and neither this haughty goddess, dashing piece of womanhood, Juno-wife of mine (Juno was a goddess, you know), nor anybody else shall hurt you. But all this wants looking into, I perceive. What with one thing and another, I see that my work is well cut out for me."

V

"How do I look to-night, Liddy?" said Bathsheba, giving a final adjustment to her dress before leaving the glass.

"I never saw you look so well before. Yes—I'll tell you when you looked like it—that night, a year and a half ago, when you came in so wildlike, and scolded us for making remarks about you and Mr. Troy."

"Everybody will think that I am setting myself to captivate Mr. Boldwood, I suppose," she murmured. "At least they'll say so. Can't my hair be brushed down a little flatter? I dread going—yet I dread the risk of wounding him by staying away."

"Anyhow, ma'am, you can't well be dressed plainer than you are, unless you go in sackcloth at once. 'Tis your excitement is what makes you look so noticeable to-night."

"I don't know what's the matter, I feel wretched at one time, and buoyant at another. I wish I could have continued quite alone as I have been for the last year or so, with no hopes and no fears, and no pleasure and no grief."

"Now just suppose Mr. Boldwood should ask you—only just suppose it—to run away with him, what would you do, ma'am?"

"Liddy—none of that," said Bathsheba, gravely. "Mind, I won't hear joking on any such matter. Do you hear?"

"I beg pardon, ma'am. But knowing what rum things we women be, I just said—however, I won't speak of it again."

"No marrying for me yet for many a year; if ever, 'twill be for reasons very, very different from those you think, or others will believe! Now get my cloak, for it is time to go."

VI

"Oak," said Boldwood, "before you go I want to mention what has been passing in my mind lately—that little arrangement we made about your share in the farm I mean. That share is small, too small, considering how little I attend to business now, and how much time and thought you give to it. Well, since the world is brightening for me, I want to show my sense of it by increasing your proportion in the partnership. I'll make a memorandum of the arrangement which struck me as likely to be convenient, for I haven't time to talk about it now; and then we'll discuss it at our leisure. My intention is ultimately to retire from the management altogether, and until you can take all the expenditure upon your shoulders, I'll be a sleeping partner in the stock. Then, if I marry her—and I hope—I feel I shall, why—"

"Pray don't speak of it, sir," said Oak, hastily. "We don't know what may happen. So many upsets may befall 'ee. There's many a slip, as they say—and I would advise you—I know you'll pardon me this once—not to be too sure."

Analysis: It is now just before the Christmas party and Boldwood is very nervous but almost delirious with the possibility that he might finally be attaining his loved one. Notice that he has lost his previous interest in the properties of his farm and only wishes to possess the property of Bathsheba. Thus Hardy presents him as an essentially acquisitive mind, whose passion is fuelled by a desire to possess and control his loved one. There is huge irony in the way in which Oak replies to him: we are aware of course that he has own reasons for not wanting Bathsheba to marry Boldwood -- reasons that Boldwood is entirely unaware of.

Discussion point: Why does Hardy present Boldwood as so fevered and desperate here?

"I know, I know. But the feeling I have about increasing your share is on account of what I know of you. Oak, I have learnt a little about your secret: your interest in her is more than that of bailiff for an employer. But you have behaved like a man, and I, as a sort of successful rival—successful partly through your goodness of heart—should like definitely to show my sense of your friendship under what must have been a great pain to you."

"O that's not necessary, thank 'ee," said Oak, hurriedly. "I must get used to such as that; other men have, and so shall I."

Oak then left him. He was uneasy on Boldwood's account, for he saw anew that this constant passion of the farmer made him not the man he once had been.

As Boldwood continued awhile in his room alone—ready and dressed to receive his company—the mood of anxiety about his appearance seemed to pass away, and to be succeeded by a deep solemnity. He looked out of the window, and regarded the dim outline of the trees upon the sky, and the twilight deepening to darkness.

Then he went to a locked closet, and took from a locked drawer therein a small circular case the size of a pillbox, and was about to put it into his pocket. But he lingered to open the cover and take a momentary glance inside. It contained a woman's finger-ring, set all the way round with small diamonds, and from its appearance had evidently been recently purchased.

Boldwood's eyes dwelt upon its many sparkles a long time, though that its material aspect concerned him little was plain from his manner and mien, which were those of a mind following out the presumed thread of that jewel's future history.

The noise of wheels at the front of the house became audible. Boldwood closed the box, stowed it away carefully in his pocket, and went out upon the landing. The old man who was his indoor factotum came at the same moment to the foot of the stairs.

"They be coming, sir—lots of 'em—a-foot and a-driving!"

"I was coming down this moment. Those wheels I heard—is it Mrs. Troy?"

"No, sir—'tis not she yet."

A reserved and sombre expression had returned to Boldwood's face again, but it poorly cloaked his feelings when he pronounced Bathsheba's name; and his feverish anxiety continued to show its existence by a galloping motion of his fingers upon the side of his thigh as he went down the stairs.

VII

"How does this cover me?" said Troy to Pennyways. "Nobody would recognize me now, I'm sure."

He was buttoning on a heavy grey overcoat of Noachian cut, with cape and high collar, the latter being erect and rigid, like a girdling wall, and nearly reaching to the verge of a travelling cap which was pulled down over his ears.

Pennyways snuffed the candle, and then looked up and deliberately inspected Troy.

"You've made up your mind to go then?" he said.

"Made up my mind? Yes; of course I have."

"Why not write to her? 'Tis a very queer corner that you have got into, sergeant. You see all these things will come to light if you go back, and they won't sound well at all. Faith, if I was you I'd even bide as you be—a single man of the name of Francis. A good wife is good, but the best wife is not so good as no wife at all. Now that's my outspoke mind, and I've been called a long-headed feller here and there."

"All nonsense!" said Troy, angrily. "There she is with plenty of money, and a house and farm, and horses, and comfort, and here am I living from hand to mouth—a needy adventurer. Besides, it is no use talking now; it is too late, and I am glad of it; I've been seen and recognized here this very afternoon. I should have gone back to her the day after the fair, if it hadn't been for you talking about the law, and rubbish about getting a separation; and I don't put it off any longer. What the deuce put it into my head to run away at all, I can't think! Humbugging sentiment—that's what it was. But what man on earth was to know that his wife would be in such a hurry to get rid of his name!"

"I should have known it. She's bad enough for anything."

"Pennyways, mind who you are talking to."

"Well, sergeant, all I say is this, that if I were you I'd go abroad again where I came from—'tisn't too late to do it now. I wouldn't stir up the business and get a bad name for the sake of living with her—for all that about your play-acting is sure to come out, you know, although you think otherwise. My eyes and limbs, there'll be a racket if you go back just now—in the middle of Boldwood's Christmasing!"

"H'm, yes. I expect I shall not be a very welcome guest if he has her there," said the sergeant, with a slight laugh. "A sort of Alonzo the Brave; and when I go in the guests will sit in silence and fear, and all laughter and pleasure will be hushed, and the lights in the chamber burn blue, and the worms—Ugh, horrible!—Ring for some more brandy, Pennyways, I felt an awful shudder just then! Well, what is there besides? A stick—I must have a walking-stick."

Pennyways now felt himself to be in something of a difficulty, for should Bathsheba and Troy become reconciled it would be necessary to regain her good opinion if he would secure the patronage of her husband. "I sometimes think she likes you yet, and is a good woman at bottom," he said, as a saving sentence. "But there's no telling to a certainty from a body's outside. Well, you'll do as you like about going, of course, sergeant, and as for me, I'll do as you tell me."

"Now, let me see what the time is," said Troy, after emptying his glass in one draught as he stood. "Half-past six o'clock. I shall not hurry along the road, and shall be there then before nine."

Questions

What clothes does Bathsheba dress in for the Christmas Party, and what does Boldwood dress in?

What does Boldwood confide in to Gabriel?

What does Troy plan to do in Casterbridge?

What does Boldwood put in his pocket?

What does Gabriel repeatedly try to tell Boldwood?

What does Troy do?

GCSE style question: how does Hardy create an impending sense of doom and disaster in this chapter?

A Level style question: compare and contrast the ways in which Hardy presents the theme of hope in this novel with another text of your choice.

Creative response: write Boldwood's diary for this chapter or write a story/poem called 'The Great Hope'.

CHAPTER LIII
CONCURRITUR—HORAE
MOMENTO

Outside the front of Boldwood's house a group of men stood in the dark, with their faces towards the door, which occasionally opened and closed for the passage of some guest or servant, when a golden rod of light would stripe the ground for the moment and vanish again, leaving nothing outside but the glowworm shine of the pale lamp amid the evergreens over the door.

"He was seen in Casterbridge this afternoon—so the boy said," one of them remarked in a whisper. "And I for one believe it. His body was never found, you know."

"'Tis a strange story," said the next. "You may depend upon't that she knows nothing about it."

"Not a word."

"Perhaps he don't mean that she shall," said another man.

"If he's alive and here in the neighbourhood, he means mischief," said the first. "Poor young thing: I do pity her, if 'tis true. He'll drag her to the dogs."

"O no; he'll settle down quiet enough," said one disposed to take a more hopeful view of the case.

"What a fool she must have been ever to have had anything to do with the man! She is so self-willed and independent too, that one is more minded to say it serves her right than pity her."

"No, no. I don't hold with 'ee there. She was no otherwise than a girl mind, and how could she tell what the man was made of? If 'tis really true, 'tis too hard a punishment, and more than she ought to hae.—Hullo, who's that?" This was to some footsteps that were heard approaching.

"William Smallbury," said a dim figure in the shades, coming up and joining them. "Dark as a hedge, to-night, isn't it? I all but missed the plank over the river ath'art there in the bottom—never did such a thing before in my life. Be ye any of Boldwood's workfolk?" He peered into their faces.

"Yes—all o' us. We met here a few minutes ago."

"Oh, I hear now—that's Sam Samway: thought I knowed the voice, too. Going in?"

"Presently. But I say, William," Samway whispered, "have ye heard this strange tale?"

"What—that about Sergeant Troy being seen, d'ye mean, souls?" said Smallbury, also lowering his voice.

"Ay: in Casterbridge."

"Yes, I have. Laban Tall named a hint of it to me but now—but I don't think it. Hark, here Laban comes himself, 'a b'lieve." A footstep drew near.

"Laban?"

"Yes, 'tis I," said Tall.

"Have ye heard any more about that?"

"No," said Tall, joining the group. "And I'm inclined to think we'd better keep quiet. If so be 'tis not true, 'twill flurry her, and do her much harm to repeat it; and if so be 'tis true, 'twill do no good to forestall her time o' trouble. God send that it mid be a lie, for though Henery Fray and some of 'em do speak against her, she's never been anything but fair to me. She's hot and hasty, but she's a brave girl who'll never tell a lie however much the truth may harm her, and I've no cause to wish her evil."

"She never do tell women's little lies, that's true; and 'tis a thing that can be said of very few. Ay, all the harm she thinks she says to yer face: there's nothing underhand wi' her."

They stood silent then, every man busied with his own thoughts, during which interval sounds of merriment could be heard within. Then the front door again opened, the rays streamed out, the well-known form of Boldwood was seen in the rectangular area of light, the door closed, and Boldwood walked slowly down the path.

"'Tis master," one of the men whispered, as he neared them. "We'd better stand quiet—he'll go in again directly. He would think it unseemly o' us to be loitering here."

Boldwood came on, and passed by the men without seeing them, they being under the bushes on the grass. He paused, leant over the gate, and breathed a long breath. They heard low words come from him.

"I hope to God she'll come, or this night will be nothing but misery to me! Oh my darling, my darling, why do you keep me in suspense like this?"

He said this to himself, and they all distinctly heard it.

Analysis: Here we find the locals gossiping about the reappearance of Troy while Boldwood is so fevered in his desperation to have Bathsheba that he is now talking to himself. Notice how Hardy seems to be suggesting that the poor, ill-educated locals are far wiser than the land-owning, well-educated Boldwood.

Discussion point: What do you think of the contrasting pictures that Hardy paints of the locals and Boldwood here? How is the writer building suspense here?

Boldwood remained silent after that, and the noise from indoors was again just audible, until, a few minutes later, light wheels could be distinguished coming down the hill. They drew nearer, and ceased at the gate. Boldwood hastened back to the door, and opened it; and the light shone upon Bathsheba coming up the path.

Boldwood compressed his emotion to mere welcome: the men marked her light laugh and apology as she met him: he took her into the house; and the door closed again.

"Gracious heaven, I didn't know it was like that with him!" said one of the men. "I thought that fancy of his was over long ago."

"You don't know much of master, if you thought that," said Samway.

"I wouldn't he should know we heard what 'a said for the world," remarked a third.

"I wish we had told of the report at once," the first uneasily continued. "More harm may come of this than we know of. Poor Mr. Boldwood, it will be hard upon en. I wish Troy was in—Well, God forgive me for such a wish! A scoundrel to play a poor wife such tricks. Nothing has prospered in Weatherbury since he came here. And now I've no heart to go in. Let's look into Warren's for a few minutes first, shall us, neighbours?"

Samway, Tall, and Smallbury agreed to go to Warren's, and went out at the gate, the remaining ones entering the house. The three soon drew near the malt-house, approaching it from the adjoining orchard, and not by way of the street. The pane of glass was illuminated as usual. Smallbury was a little in advance of the rest when, pausing, he turned suddenly to his companions and said, "Hist! See there."

The light from the pane was now perceived to be shining not upon the ivied wall as usual, but upon some object close to the glass. It was a human face.

"Let's come closer," whispered Samway; and they approached on tiptoe. There was no disbelieving the report any longer. Troy's face was almost close to the pane, and he was looking in. Not only was he looking in, but he appeared to have been arrested by a conversation which was in progress in the malt-house, the voices of the interlocutors being those of Oak and the maltster.

"The spree is all in her honour, isn't it—hey?" said the old man. "Although he made believe 'tis only keeping up o' Christmas?"

"I cannot say," replied Oak.

"Oh 'tis true enough, faith. I cannot understand Farmer Boldwood being such a fool at his time of life as to ho and hanker after this woman in the way 'a do, and she not care a bit about en."

The men, after recognizing Troy's features, withdrew across the orchard as quietly as they had come. The air was big with Bathsheba's fortunes to-night: every word everywhere concerned her. When they were quite out of earshot all by one instinct paused.

"It gave me quite a turn—his face," said Tall, breathing.

"And so it did me," said Samway. "What's to be done?"

"I don't see that 'tis any business of ours," Smallbury murmured dubiously.

"But it is! 'Tis a thing which is everybody's business," said Samway. "We know very well that master's on a wrong tack, and that she's quite in the dark, and we should let 'em know at once. Laban, you know her best—you'd better go and ask to speak to her."

"I bain't fit for any such thing," said Laban, nervously. "I should think William ought to do it if anybody. He's oldest."

"I shall have nothing to do with it," said Smallbury. "'Tis a ticklish business altogether. Why, he'll go on to her himself in a few minutes, ye'll see."

"We don't know that he will. Come, Laban."

"Very well, if I must I must, I suppose," Tall reluctantly answered. "What must I say?"

"Just ask to see master."

"Oh no; I shan't speak to Mr. Boldwood. If I tell anybody, 'twill be mistress."

"Very well," said Samway.

Laban then went to the door. When he opened it the hum of bustle rolled out as a wave upon a still strand—the assemblage being immediatcly inside the hall—and was deadened to a murmur as he closed it again. Each man waited intently, and looked around at the dark tree tops gently rocking against the sky and occasionally shivering in a slight wind, as if he took interest in the scene, which neither did. One of them began walking up and down, and then came to where he started from and stopped again, with a sense that walking was a thing not worth doing now.

"I should think Laban must have seen mistress by this time," said Smallbury, breaking the silence. "Perhaps she won't come and speak to him."

The door opened. Tall appeared, and joined them.

"Well?" said both.

"I didn't like to ask for her after all," Laban faltered out. "They were all in such a stir, trying to put a little spirit into the party. Somehow the fun seems to hang fire, though everything's there that a heart can desire, and I couldn't for my soul interfere and throw damp upon it—if 'twas to save my life, I couldn't!"

"I suppose we had better all go in together," said Samway, gloomily. "Perhaps I may have a chance of saying a word to master."

So the men entered the hall, which was the room selected and arranged for the gathering because of its size. The younger men and maids were at last just beginning to dance. Bathsheba had been perplexed how to act, for she was not much more than a slim young maid herself, and the weight of stateliness sat heavy upon her. Sometimes she thought she ought not to have come under any circumstances; then she considered what cold unkindness that would have been, and finally resolved upon the middle course of staying for about an hour only, and gliding off unobserved, having from the first made up her mind that she could on no account dance, sing, or take any active part in the proceedings.

Her allotted hour having been passed in chatting and looking on, Bathsheba told Liddy not to hurry herself, and went to the small parlour to prepare for departure, which, like the hall, was decorated with holly and ivy, and well lighted up.

Nobody was in the room, but she had hardly been there a moment when the master of the house entered.

"Mrs. Troy—you are not going?" he said. "We've hardly begun!"

"If you'll excuse me, I should like to go now." Her manner was restive, for she remembered her promise, and imagined what he was about to say. "But as it is not late," she added, "I can walk home, and leave my man and Liddy to come when they choose."

"I've been trying to get an opportunity of speaking to you," said

Boldwood. "You know perhaps what I long to say?"

Bathsheba silently looked on the floor.

"You do give it?" he said, eagerly.

"What?" she whispered.

"Now, that's evasion! Why, the promise. I don't want to intrude upon you at all, or to let it become known to anybody. But do give your word! A mere business compact, you know, between two people who are beyond the influence of passion." Boldwood knew how false this picture was as regarded himself; but he had proved that it was the only tone in which she would allow him to approach her. "A promise to marry me at the end of five years and three-quarters. You owe it to me!"

"I feel that I do," said Bathsheba; "that is, if you demand it. But I am a changed woman—an unhappy woman—and not—not—"

"You are still a very beautiful woman," said Boldwood. Honesty and pure conviction suggested the remark, unaccompanied by any perception that it might have been adopted by blunt flattery to soothe and win her.

However, it had not much effect now, for she said, in a passionless murmur which was in itself a proof of her words: "I have no feeling in the matter at all. And I don't at all know what is right to do in my difficult position, and I have nobody to advise me. But I give my promise, if I must. I give it as the rendering of a debt, conditionally, of course, on my being a widow."

"You'll marry me between five and six years hence?"

"Don't press me too hard. I'll marry nobody else."

"But surely you will name the time, or there's nothing in the promise at all?"

"Oh, I don't know, pray let me go!" she said, her bosom beginning to rise. "I am afraid what to do! I want to be just to you, and to be that seems to be wronging myself, and perhaps it is breaking the commandments. There is considerable doubt of his death, and then it is dreadful; let me ask a solicitor, Mr. Boldwood, if I ought or no!"

"Say the words, dear one, and the subject shall be dismissed; a blissful loving intimacy of six years, and then marriage—O Bathsheba, say them!" he begged in a husky voice, unable to sustain the forms of mere friendship any longer. "Promise yourself to me; I deserve it, indeed I do, for I have loved you more than anybody in the world! And if I said hasty words and showed uncalled-for heat of manner towards you, believe me, dear, I did not mean to distress you; I was in agony, Bathsheba, and I did not know what I said. You wouldn't let a dog suffer what I have suffered, could you but know it! Sometimes I shrink from your knowing what I have felt for you, and sometimes I am distressed that all of it you never will know. Be gracious, and give up a little to me, when I would give up my life for you!"

The trimmings of her dress, as they quivered against the light, showed how agitated she was, and at last she burst out crying. "And you'll not—press me—about anything more—if I say in five or six years?" she sobbed, when she had power to frame the words.

"Yes, then I'll leave it to time."

She waited a moment. "Very well. I'll marry you in six years from this day, if we both live," she said solemnly.

"And you'll take this as a token from me."

Boldwood had come close to her side, and now he clasped one of her hands in both his own, and lifted it to his breast.

"What is it? Oh I cannot wear a ring!" she exclaimed, on seeing what he held; "besides, I wouldn't have a soul know that it's an engagement! Perhaps it is improper? Besides, we are not engaged in the usual sense, are we? Don't insist, Mr. Boldwood—don't!" In her trouble at not being able to get her hand away from him at once, she stamped passionately on the floor with one foot, and tears crowded to her eyes again.

"It means simply a pledge—no sentiment—the seal of a practical compact," he said more quietly, but still retaining her hand in his firm grasp. "Come, now!" And Boldwood slipped the ring on her finger.

"I cannot wear it," she said, weeping as if her heart would break. "You frighten me, almost. So wild a scheme! Please let me go home!"

"Only to-night: wear it just to-night, to please me!"

Bathsheba sat down in a chair, and buried her face in her handkerchief, though Boldwood kept her hand yet. At length she said, in a sort of hopeless whisper—

"Very well, then, I will to-night, if you wish it so earnestly. Now loosen my hand; I will, indeed I will wear it to-night."

"And it shall be the beginning of a pleasant secret courtship of six years, with a wedding at the end?"

"It must be, I suppose, since you will have it so!" she said, fairly beaten into non-resistance.

Boldwood pressed her hand, and allowed it to drop in her lap. "I am happy now," he said. "God bless you!"

He left the room, and when he thought she might be sufficiently composed sent one of the maids to her. Bathsheba cloaked the effects of the late scene as she best could, followed the girl, and in a few moments came downstairs with her hat and cloak on, ready to go.

Analysis: Finally, Bathsheba is crushed into submission. Having been broken by her marriage to Troy, she gives up protesting, just wanting the insidiously insistent Boldwood to leave her alone.

Discussion point: What do we feel for Bathsheba at this point?

To get to the door it was necessary to pass through the hall, and before doing so she paused on the bottom of the staircase which descended into one corner, to take a last look at the gathering.

There was no music or dancing in progress just now. At the lower end, which had been arranged for the work-folk specially, a group conversed in whispers, and with clouded looks. Boldwood was standing by the fireplace, and he, too, though so absorbed in visions arising from her promise that he scarcely saw anything, seemed at that moment to have observed their peculiar manner, and their looks askance.

"What is it you are in doubt about, men?" he said.

One of them turned and replied uneasily: "It was something Laban heard of, that's all, sir."

"News? Anybody married or engaged, born or dead?" inquired the farmer, gaily. "Tell it to us, Tall. One would think from your looks and mysterious ways that it was something very dreadful indeed."

"Oh no, sir, nobody is dead," said Tall.

"I wish somebody was," said Samway, in a whisper.

"What do you say, Samway?" asked Boldwood, somewhat sharply. "If you have anything to say, speak out; if not, get up another dance."

"Mrs. Troy has come downstairs," said Samway to Tall. "If you want to tell her, you had better do it now."

"Do you know what they mean?" the farmer asked Bathsheba, across the room.

"I don't in the least," said Bathsheba.

There was a smart rapping at the door. One of the men opened it instantly, and went outside.

"Mrs. Troy is wanted," he said, on returning.

"Quite ready," said Bathsheba. "Though I didn't tell them to send."

"It is a stranger, ma'am," said the man by the door.

"A stranger?" she said.

"Ask him to come in," said Boldwood.

The message was given, and Troy, wrapped up to his eyes as we have seen him, stood in the doorway.

There was an unearthly silence, all looking towards the newcomer. Those who had just learnt that he was in the neighbourhood recognized him instantly; those who did not were perplexed. Nobody noted Bathsheba. She was leaning on the stairs. Her brow had heavily contracted; her whole face was pallid, her lips apart, her eyes rigidly staring at their visitor.

Boldwood was among those who did not notice that he was Troy. "Come in, come in!" he repeated, cheerfully, "and drain a Christmas beaker with us, stranger!"

Troy next advanced into the middle of the room, took off his cap, turned down his coat-collar, and looked Boldwood in the face. Even then Boldwood did not recognize that the impersonator of Heaven's persistent irony towards him, who had once before broken in upon his bliss, scourged him, and snatched his delight away, had come to do these things a second time. Troy began to laugh a mechanical laugh: Boldwood recognized him now.

Troy turned to Bathsheba. The poor girl's wretchedness at this time was beyond all fancy or narration. She had sunk down on the lowest stair; and there she sat, her mouth blue and dry, and her dark eyes fixed vacantly upon him, as if she wondered whether it were not all a terrible illusion.

Then Troy spoke. "Bathsheba, I come here for you!"

She made no reply.

"Come home with me: come!"

Bathsheba moved her feet a little, but did not rise. Troy went across to her.

"Come, madam, do you hear what I say?" he said, peremptorily.

A strange voice came from the fireplace—a voice sounding far off and confined, as if from a dungeon. Hardly a soul in the assembly recognized the thin tones to be those of Boldwood. Sudden despair had transformed him.

"Bathsheba, go with your husband!"

Nevertheless, she did not move. The truth was that Bathsheba was beyond the pale of activity—and yet not in a swoon. She was in a state of mental gutta serena; her mind was for the minute totally deprived of light at the same time no obscuration was apparent from without.

Troy stretched out his hand to pull her her towards him, when she quickly shrank back. This visible dread of him seemed to irritate Troy, and he seized her arm and pulled it sharply. Whether his grasp pinched her, or whether his mere touch was the cause, was never known, but at the moment of his seizure she writhed, and gave a quick, low scream.

The scream had been heard but a few seconds when it was followed by sudden deafening report that echoed through the room and stupefied them all. The oak partition shook with the concussion, and the place was filled with grey smoke.

In bewilderment they turned their eyes to Boldwood. At his back, as stood before the fireplace, was a gun-rack, as is usual in farmhouses, constructed to hold two guns. When Bathsheba had cried out in her husband's grasp, Boldwood's face of gnashing despair had changed. The veins had swollen, and a frenzied look had gleamed in his eye. He had turned quickly, taken one of the guns, cocked it, and at once discharged it at Troy.

Troy fell. The distance apart of the two men was so small that the charge of shot did not spread in the least, but passed like a bullet into his body. He uttered a long guttural sigh—there was a contraction—an extension—then his muscles relaxed, and he lay still.

Boldwood was seen through the smoke to be now again engaged with the gun. It was double-barrelled, and he had, meanwhile, in some way fastened his hand-kerchief to the trigger, and with his foot on the other end was in the act of turning the second barrel upon himself. Samway his man was the first to see this, and in the midst of the general horror darted up to him. Boldwood had already twitched the handkerchief, and the gun exploded a second time, sending its contents, by a timely blow from Samway, into the beam which crossed the ceiling.

"Well, it makes no difference!" Boldwood gasped. "There is another way for me to die."

Then he broke from Samway, crossed the room to Bathsheba, and kissed her hand. He put on his hat, opened the door, and went into the darkness, nobody thinking of preventing him.

Analysis: This is the climactic scene in the novel. It is superbly melodramatic. Hardy uses all his powers of description to evoke the desperate scene: sights, sounds, smells, textures are all evoked when he describes the appearance of Troy, Troy's brutal treatment of his wife and Boldwood's deadly response. The main threads of the narrative are brought together in the death of Troy.

Discussion point: Why did Hardy write this melodramatic climatic scene do you think? How successful is it as a climax to the novel?

Questions

What are the villagers discussing?
What happens when the villagers see Troy outside Warren's Malthouse?
How does Bathsheba behave at the party?
What does Boldwood manage to extract from Bathsheba?
Why does Bathsheba agree to wear his engagement ring?
What does Troy do when he enters the party?
What does Boldwood do?
GCSE style question: how does Hardy make this such a thrilling and possibly melodramatic climax to the novel?
A Level style question: compare and contrast this climactic moment with another climax from another text of your choice.
Creative response: write Bathsheba's diary for this chapter and/or a story/poem/description called 'The Showdown'.

CHAPTER LIV
AFTER THE SHOCK

Boldwood passed into the high road and turned in the direction of Casterbridge. Here he walked at an even, steady pace over Yalbury Hill, along the dead level beyond, mounted Mellstock Hill, and between eleven and twelve o'clock crossed the Moor into the town. The streets were nearly deserted now, and the waving lamp-flames only lighted up rows of grey shop-shutters, and strips of white paving upon which his step echoed as his passed along. He turned to the right, and halted before an archway of heavy stonework, which was closed by an iron studded pair of doors. This was the entrance to the gaol, and over it a lamp was fixed, the light enabling the wretched traveller to find a bell-pull.

The small wicket at last opened, and a porter appeared. Boldwood stepped forward, and said something in a low tone, when, after a delay, another man came. Boldwood entered, and the door was closed behind him, and he walked the world no more.

Long before this time Weatherbury had been thoroughly aroused, and the wild deed which had terminated Boldwood's merrymaking became known to all. Of those out of the house Oak was one of the first to hear of the catastrophe, and when he entered the room, which was about five minutes after Boldwood's exit, the scene was terrible. All the female guests were huddled aghast against the walls like sheep in a storm, and the men were bewildered as to what to do. As for Bathsheba, she had changed. She was sitting on the floor beside the body of Troy, his head pillowed in her lap, where she had herself lifted it. With one hand she held her handkerchief to his breast and covered the wound, though scarcely a single drop of blood had flowed, and with the other she tightly clasped one of his. The household convulsion had made her herself again. The temporary coma had ceased, and activity had come with the necessity for it. Deeds of endurance, which seem ordinary in philosophy, are rare in conduct, and Bathsheba was astonishing all around her now, for her philosophy was her conduct, and she seldom thought practicable what she did not practise. She was of the stuff of which great men's mothers are made. She was indispensable to high generation, hated at tea parties, feared in shops, and loved at crises. Troy recumbent in his wife's lap formed now the sole spectacle in the middle of the spacious room.

"Gabriel," she said, automatically, when he entered, turning up a face of which only the well-known lines remained to tell him it was hers, all else in the picture having faded quite. "Ride to Casterbridge instantly for a surgeon. It is, I believe, useless, but go. Mr. Boldwood has shot my husband."

Her statement of the fact in such quiet and simple words came with more force than a tragic declamation, and had somewhat the effect of setting the distorted images in each mind present into proper focus. Oak, almost before he had comprehended anything beyond the briefest abstract of the event, hurried out of the room, saddled a horse and rode away. Not till he had ridden more than a mile did it occur to him that he would have done better by sending some other man on this errand, remaining himself in the house. What had become of Boldwood? He should have been looked after. Was he mad—had there been a quarrel? Then how had Troy got there? Where had he come from? How did this remarkable reappearance effect itself when he was supposed by many to be at the bottom of the sea? Oak had in some slight measure been prepared for the presence of Troy by hearing a rumour of his return just before entering Boldwood's house; but before he had weighed that information, this fatal event had been superimposed. However, it was too late now to think of sending another messenger, and he rode on, in the excitement of these self-inquiries not discerning, when about three miles from Casterbridge, a square-figured pedestrian passing along under the dark hedge in the same direction as his own.

The miles necessary to be traversed, and other hindrances incidental to the lateness of the hour and the darkness of the night, delayed the arrival of Mr. Aldritch, the surgeon; and more than three hours passed between the time at which the shot was fired and that of his entering the house. Oak was additionally detained in Casterbridge through having to give notice to the authorities of what had happened; and he then found that Boldwood had also entered the town, and delivered himself up.

In the meantime the surgeon, having hastened into the hall at Boldwood's, found it in darkness and quite deserted. He went on to the back of the house, where he discovered in the kitchen an old man, of whom he made inquiries.

"She's had him took away to her own house, sir," said his informant.

"Who has?" said the doctor.

"Mrs. Troy. 'A was quite dead, sir."

This was astonishing information. "She had no right to do that," said the doctor. "There will have to be an inquest, and she should have waited to know what to do."

"Yes, sir; it was hinted to her that she had better wait till the law was known. But she said law was nothing to her, and she wouldn't let her dear husband's corpse bide neglected for folks to stare at for all the crowners in England."

Mr. Aldritch drove at once back again up the hill to Bathsheba's. The first person he met was poor Liddy, who seemed literally to have dwindled smaller in these few latter hours. "What has been done?" he said.

"I don't know, sir," said Liddy, with suspended breath. "My mistress has done it all."

"Where is she?"

"Upstairs with him, sir. When he was brought home and taken upstairs, she said she wanted no further help from the men. And then she called me, and made me fill the bath, and after that told me I had better go and lie down because I looked so ill. Then she locked herself into the room alone with him, and would not let a nurse come in, or anybody at all. But I thought I'd wait in the next room in case she should want me. I heard her moving about inside for more than an hour, but she only came out once, and that was for more candles, because hers had burnt down into the socket. She said we were to let her know when you or Mr. Thirdly came, sir."

Oak entered with the parson at this moment, and they all went upstairs together, preceded by Liddy Smallbury. Everything was silent as the grave when they paused on the landing. Liddy knocked, and Bathsheba's dress was heard rustling across the room: the key turned in the lock, and she opened the door. Her looks were calm and nearly rigid, like a slightly animated bust of Melpomene.

"Oh, Mr. Aldritch, you have come at last," she murmured from her lips merely, and threw back the door. "Ah, and Mr. Thirdly. Well, all is done, and anybody in the world may see him now." She then passed by him, crossed the landing, and entered another room.

Looking into the chamber of death she had vacated they saw by the light of the candles which were on the drawers a tall straight shape lying at the further end of the bedroom, wrapped in white. Everything around was quite orderly. The doctor went in, and after a few minutes returned to the landing again, where Oak and the parson still waited.

"It is all done, indeed, as she says," remarked Mr. Aldritch, in a subdued voice. "The body has been undressed and properly laid out in grave clothes. Gracious Heaven—this mere girl! She must have the nerve of a stoic!"

"The heart of a wife merely," floated in a whisper about the ears of the three, and turning they saw Bathsheba in the midst of them. Then, as if at that instant to prove that her fortitude had been more of will than of spontaneity, she silently sank down between them and was a shapeless heap of drapery on the floor. The simple consciousness that superhuman strain was no longer required had at once put a period to her power to continue it.

They took her away into a further room, and the medical attendance which had been useless in Troy's case was invaluable in Bathsheba's, who fell into a series of fainting-fits that had a serious aspect for a time. The sufferer was got to bed, and Oak, finding from the bulletins that nothing really dreadful was to be apprehended on her score, left the house. Liddy kept watch in Bathsheba's chamber, where she heard her mistress, moaning in whispers through the dull slow hours of that wretched night: "Oh it is my fault—how can I live! O Heaven, how can I live!"

Questions

Where does Boldwood go?
What does Bathsheba do?
What does Bathsheba ask to happen to Troy's body?
Why is the surgeon angry when he arrives?
What does Bathsheba do?
GCSE style question: how does Hardy present Bathsheba in this chapter?
Creative response: write Bathsheba's diary for this chapter or write a story/poem/description called 'It's All Too Much'.

CHAPTER LV
THE MARCH FOLLOWING—
"BATHSHEBA BOLDWOOD"

We pass rapidly on into the month of March, to a breezy day without sunshine, frost, or dew. On Yalbury Hill, about midway between Weatherbury and Casterbridge, where the turnpike road passes over the crest, a numerous concourse of people had gathered, the eyes of the greater number being frequently stretched afar in a northerly direction. The groups consisted of a throng of idlers, a party of javelin-men, and two trumpeters, and in the midst were carriages, one of which contained the high sheriff. With the idlers, many of whom had mounted to the top of a cutting formed for the road, were several Weatherbury men and boys—among others Poorgrass, Coggan, and Cain Ball.

At the end of half-an-hour a faint dust was seen in the expected quarter, and shortly after a travelling-carriage, bringing one of the two judges on the Western Circuit, came up the hill and halted on the top. The judge changed carriages whilst a flourish was blown by the big-cheeked trumpeters, and a procession being formed of the vehicles and javelin-men, they all proceeded towards the town, excepting the Weatherbury men, who as soon as they had seen the judge move off returned home again to their work.

"Joseph, I seed you squeezing close to the carriage," said Coggan, as they walked. "Did ye notice my lord judge's face?"

"I did," said Poorgrass. "I looked hard at en, as if I would read his very soul; and there was mercy in his eyes—or to speak with the exact truth required of us at this solemn time, in the eye that was towards me."

"Well, I hope for the best," said Coggan, "though bad that must be. However, I shan't go to the trial, and I'd advise the rest of ye that bain't wanted to bide away. 'Twill disturb his mind more than anything to see us there staring at him as if he were a show."

"The very thing I said this morning," observed Joseph, "'Justice is come to weigh him in the balances,' I said in my reflectious way, 'and if he's found wanting, so be it unto him,' and a bystander said 'Hear, hear! A man who can talk like that ought to be heard.' But I don't like dwelling upon it, for my few words are my few words, and not much; though the speech of some men is rumoured abroad as though by nature formed for such."

"So 'tis, Joseph. And now, neighbours, as I said, every man bide at home."

The resolution was adhered to; and all waited anxiously for the news next day. Their suspense was diverted, however, by a discovery which was made in the afternoon, throwing more light on Boldwood's conduct and condition than any details which had preceded it.

That he had been from the time of Greenhill Fair until the fatal Christmas Eve in excited and unusual moods was known to those who had been intimate with him; but nobody imagined that there had shown in him unequivocal symptoms of the mental derangement which Bathsheba and Oak, alone of all others and at different times, had momentarily suspected. In a locked closet was now discovered an extraordinary collection of articles. There were several sets of ladies' dresses in the piece, of sundry expensive materials; silks and satins, poplins and velvets, all of colours which from Bathsheba's style of dress might have been judged to be her favourites. There were two muffs, sable and ermine. Above all there was a case of jewellery, containing four heavy gold bracelets and several lockets and rings, all of fine quality and manufacture. These things had been bought in Bath and other towns from time to time, and brought home by stealth. They were all carefully packed in paper, and each package was labelled "Bathsheba Boldwood," a date being subjoined six years in advance in every instance.

Analysis: The true extent of Boldwood's madness is revealed when it is found out that he has been buying items for Bathsheba and labelling them 'Bathsheba Boldwood'. Some critics have felt this is evidence of his sexually perverse nature. The clothes have a sensual quality, being ladies' dresses, "silks and satins, poplins and velvets". This detail is marvellous because we have a sense that Boldwood has had a sensual relationship with the clothes in an attempt to get close to his loved one.

Discussion point: What does the discovery of the clothes tell us about Boldwood?

These somewhat pathetic evidences of a mind crazed with care and love were the subject of discourse in Warren's malt-house when Oak entered from Casterbridge with tidings of sentence. He came in the afternoon, and his face, as the kiln glow shone upon it, told the tale sufficiently well. Boldwood, as every one supposed he would do, had pleaded guilty, and had been sentenced to death.

Analysis: Wanting the oblivion of death, Boldwood is reprieved because he is judged to be mad.

Discussion point: Why does Hardy not describe Boldwood's execution but instead decides to put him a mad house? What is Hardy trying to say here?

The conviction that Boldwood had not been morally responsible for his later acts now became general. Facts elicited previous to the trial had pointed strongly in the same direction, but they had not been of sufficient weight to lead to an order for an examination into the state of Boldwood's mind. It was astonishing, now that a presumption of insanity was raised, how many collateral circumstances were remembered to which a condition of mental disease seemed to afford the only explanation—among others, the unprecedented neglect of his corn stacks in the previous summer.

A petition was addressed to the Home Secretary, advancing the circumstances which appeared to justify a request for a reconsideration of the sentence. It was not "numerously signed" by the inhabitants of Casterbridge, as is usual in such cases, for Boldwood had never made many friends over the counter. The shops thought it very natural that a man who, by importing direct from the producer, had daringly set aside the first great principle of provincial existence, namely that God made country villages to supply customers to county towns, should have confused ideas about the Decalogue. The prompters were a few merciful men who had perhaps too feelingly considered the facts latterly unearthed, and the result was that evidence was taken which it was hoped might remove the crime in a moral point of view, out of the category of wilful murder, and lead it to be regarded as a sheer outcome of madness.

The upshot of the petition was waited for in Weatherbury with solicitous interest. The execution had been fixed for eight o'clock on a Saturday morning about a fortnight after the sentence was passed, and up to Friday afternoon no answer had been received. At that time Gabriel came from Casterbridge Gaol, whither he had been to wish Boldwood good-bye, and turned down a by-street to avoid the town. When past the last house he heard a hammering, and lifting his bowed head he looked back for a moment. Over the chimneys he could see the upper part of the gaol entrance, rich and glowing in the afternoon sun, and some moving figures were there. They were carpenters lifting a post into a vertical position within the parapet. He withdrew his eyes quickly, and hastened on.

It was dark when he reached home, and half the village was out to meet him.

"No tidings," Gabriel said, wearily. "And I'm afraid there's no hope. I've been with him more than two hours."

"Do ye think he really was out of his mind when he did it?" said Smallbury.

"I can't honestly say that I do," Oak replied. "However, that we can talk of another time. Has there been any change in mistress this afternoon?"

"None at all."

"Is she downstairs?"

"No. And getting on so nicely as she was too. She's but very little better now again than she was at Christmas. She keeps on asking if you be come, and if there's news, till one's wearied out wi' answering her. Shall I go and say you've come?"

"No," said Oak. "There's a chance yet; but I couldn't stay in town any longer—after seeing him too. So Laban—Laban is here, isn't he?"

"Yes," said Tall.

"What I've arranged is, that you shall ride to town the last thing to-night; leave here about nine, and wait a while there, getting home about twelve. If nothing has been received by eleven to-night, they say there's no chance at all."

"I do so hope his life will be spared," said Liddy. "If it is not, she'll go out of her mind too. Poor thing; her sufferings have been dreadful; she deserves anybody's pity."

"Is she altered much?" said Coggan.

"If you haven't seen poor mistress since Christmas, you wouldn't know her," said Liddy. "Her eyes are so miserable that she's not the same woman. Only two years ago she was a romping girl, and now she's this!"

Laban departed as directed, and at eleven o'clock that night several of the villagers strolled along the road to Casterbridge and awaited his arrival—among them Oak, and nearly all the rest of Bathsheba's men. Gabriel's anxiety was great that Boldwood might be saved, even though in his conscience he felt that he ought to die; for there had been qualities in the farmer which Oak loved. At last, when they all were weary the tramp of a horse was heard in the distance—

First dead, as if on turf it trode,
Then, clattering on the village road
In other pace than forth he yode.

"We shall soon know now, one way or other." said Coggan, and they all stepped down from the bank on which they had been standing into the road, and the rider pranced into the midst of them.

"Is that you, Laban?" said Gabriel.

"Yes—'tis come. He's not to die. 'Tis confinement during Her Majesty's pleasure."

"Hurrah!" said Coggan, with a swelling heart. "God's above the devil yet!"

Questions

Why is there a plea for mercy at Boldwood's trial?

What sentence does Boldwood receive?

What is discovered in Boldwood's house?

Who spends time with Boldwood as the scaffold is prepared?

GCSE style question: how does Hardy build suspense in this chapter?

A Level style question: compare and contrast Boldwood's trial with another courtroom drama in another relevant text.

Creative response: write Oak's diary for this chapter, reflecting upon his feelings for Boldwood; or write a newspaper article about the trial.

CHAPTER LVI
BEAUTY IN LONELINESS—AFTER ALL

Bathsheba revived with the spring. The utter prostration that had followed the low fever from which she had suffered diminished perceptibly when all uncertainty upon every subject had come to an end.

But she remained alone now for the greater part of her time, and stayed in the house, or at furthest went into the garden. She shunned every one, even Liddy, and could be brought to make no confidences, and to ask for no sympathy.

As the summer drew on she passed more of her time in the open air, and began to examine into farming matters from sheer necessity, though she never rode out or personally superintended as at former times. One Friday evening in August she walked a little way along the road and entered the village for the first time since the sombre event of the preceding Christmas. None of the old colour had as yet come to her cheek, and its absolute paleness was heightened by the jet black of her gown, till it appeared preternatural. When she reached a little shop at the other end of the place, which stood nearly opposite to the churchyard, Bathsheba heard singing inside the church, and she knew that the singers were practising. She crossed the road, opened the gate, and entered the graveyard, the high sills of the church windows effectually screening her from the eyes of those gathered within. Her stealthy walk was to the nook wherein Troy had worked at planting flowers upon Fanny Robin's grave, and she came to the marble tombstone.

A motion of satisfaction enlivened her face as she read the complete inscription. First came the words of Troy himself:—

Erected by Francis Troy
In Beloved Memory of
Fanny Robin
Who died October 9, 18—,
Aged 20 years

Underneath this was now inscribed in new letters:—

In the Same Grave lie
The Remains of the aforesaid
Francis Troy,
Who died December 24th, 18—,
Aged 26 years

Whilst she stood and read and meditated the tones of the organ began again in the church, and she went with the same light step round to the porch and listened. The door was closed, and the choir was learning a new hymn. Bathsheba was stirred by emotions which latterly she had assumed to be altogether dead within her. The little attenuated voices of the children brought to her ear in distinct utterance the words they sang without thought or comprehension—

Lead, kindly Light, amid the encircling gloom,
Lead Thou me on.

Bathsheba's feeling was always to some extent dependent upon her whim, as is the case with many other women. Something big came into her throat and an uprising to her eyes—and she thought that she would allow the imminent tears to flow if they wished. They did flow and plenteously, and one fell upon the stone bench beside her. Once that she had begun to cry for she hardly knew what, she could not leave off for crowding thoughts she knew too well. She would have given anything in the world to be, as those children were, unconcerned at the meaning of their words, because too innocent to feel the necessity for any such expression. All the impassioned scenes of her brief experience seemed to revive with added emotion at that moment, and those scenes which had been without emotion during enactment had emotion then. Yet grief came to her rather as a luxury than as the scourge of former times.

Owing to Bathsheba's face being buried in her hands she did not notice a form which came quietly into the porch, and on seeing her, first moved as if to retreat, then paused and regarded her. Bathsheba did not raise her head for some time, and when she looked round her face was wet, and her eyes drowned and dim. "Mr. Oak," exclaimed she, disconcerted, "how long have you been here?"

"A few minutes, ma'am," said Oak, respectfully.

"Are you going in?" said Bathsheba; and there came from within the church as from a prompter—

I loved the garish day, and, spite of fears,
pride ruled my will: remember not past years.

"I was," said Gabriel. "I am one of the bass singers, you know. I have sung bass for several months."

"Indeed: I wasn't aware of that. I'll leave you, then."

Which I have loved long since, and lost awhile,

sang the children.

"Don't let me drive you away, mistress. I think I won't go in to-night."

"Oh no—you don't drive me away."

Then they stood in a state of some embarrassment, Bathsheba trying to wipe her dreadfully drenched and inflamed face without his noticing her. At length Oak said, "I've not seen you—I mean spoken to you—since ever so long, have I?" But he feared to bring distressing memories back, and interrupted himself with: "Were you going into church?"

"No," she said. "I came to see the tombstone privately—to see if they had cut the inscription as I wished. Mr. Oak, you needn't mind speaking to me, if you wish to, on the matter which is in both our minds at this moment."

"And have they done it as you wished?" said Oak.

"Yes. Come and see it, if you have not already."

So together they went and read the tomb. "Eight months ago!" Gabriel murmured when he saw the date. "It seems like yesterday to me."

"And to me as if it were years ago—long years, and I had been dead between. And now I am going home, Mr. Oak."

Oak walked after her. "I wanted to name a small matter to you as soon as I could," he said, with hesitation. "Merely about business, and I think I may just mention it now, if you'll allow me."

"Oh yes, certainly."

It is that I may soon have to give up the management of your farm, Mrs. Troy. The fact is, I am thinking of leaving England—not yet, you know—next spring."

"Leaving England!" she said, in surprise and genuine disappointment. "Why, Gabriel, what are you going to do that for?"

"Well, I've thought it best," Oak stammered out. "California is the spot I've had in my mind to try."

Analysis: Although we are told that Bathsheba has revived, we are aware that she is a changed woman. Now we learn that Oak is leaving her for California. Oak is no longer the man of the English soil, but intent upon leaving the rural idyll of Weatherbury Farm: events have changed the pastoral idyll into a place redolent of nightmares, woes, death, tragedies.

Discussion point: How does Hardy build suspense here?

"But it is understood everywhere that you are going to take poor Mr. Boldwood's farm on your own account."

"I've had the refusal o' it 'tis true; but nothing is settled yet, and I have reasons for giving up. I shall finish out my year there as manager for the trustees, but no more."

"And what shall I do without you? Oh, Gabriel, I don't think you ought to go away. You've been with me so long—through bright times and dark times—such old friends as we are—that it seems unkind almost. I had fancied that if you leased the other farm as master, you might still give a helping look across at mine. And now going away!"

"I would have willingly."

"Yet now that I am more helpless than ever you go away!"

"Yes, that's the ill fortune o' it," said Gabriel, in a distressed tone. "And it is because of that very helplessness that I feel bound to go. Good afternoon, ma'am" he concluded, in evident anxiety to get away, and at once went out of the churchyard by a path she could follow on no pretence whatever.

Bathsheba went home, her mind occupied with a new trouble, which being rather harassing than deadly was calculated to do good by diverting her from the chronic gloom of her life. She was set thinking a great deal about Oak and of his wish to shun her; and there occurred to Bathsheba several incidents of her latter intercourse with him, which, trivial when singly viewed, amounted together to a perceptible disinclination for her society. It broke upon her at length as a great pain that her last old disciple was about to forsake her and flee. He who had believed in her and argued on her side when all the rest of the world was against her, had at last like the others become weary and neglectful of the old cause, and was leaving her to fight her battles alone.

Three weeks went on, and more evidence of his want of interest in her was forthcoming. She noticed that instead of entering the small parlour or office where the farm accounts were kept, and waiting, or leaving a memorandum as he had hitherto done during her seclusion, Oak never came at all when she was likely to be there, only entering at unseasonable hours when her presence in that part of the house was least to be expected. Whenever he wanted directions he sent a message, or note with neither heading nor signature, to which she was obliged to reply in the same offhand style. Poor Bathsheba began to suffer now from the most torturing sting of all—a sensation that she was despised.

The autumn wore away gloomily enough amid these melancholy

conjectures, and Christmas-day came, completing a year of her legal widowhood, and two years and a quarter of her life alone. On examining her heart it appeared beyond measure strange that the subject of which the season might have been supposed suggestive—the event in the hall at Boldwood's—was not agitating her at all; but instead, an agonizing conviction that everybody abjured her—for what she could not tell—and that Oak was the ringleader of the recusants. Coming out of church that day she looked round in hope that Oak, whose bass voice she had heard rolling out from the gallery overhead in a most unconcerned manner, might chance to linger in her path in the old way. There he was, as usual, coming down the path behind her. But on seeing Bathsheba turn, he looked aside, and as soon as he got beyond the gate, and there was the barest excuse for a divergence, he made one, and vanished.

The next morning brought the culminating stroke; she had been expecting it long. It was a formal notice by letter from him that he should not renew his engagement with her for the following Lady-day.

Bathsheba actually sat and cried over this letter most bitterly. She was aggrieved and wounded that the possession of hopeless love from Gabriel, which she had grown to regard as her inalienable right for life, should have been withdrawn just at his own pleasure in this way. She was bewildered too by the prospect of having to rely on her own resources again: it seemed to herself that she never could again acquire energy sufficient to go to market, barter, and sell. Since Troy's death Oak had attended all sales and fairs for her, transacting her business at the same time with his own. What should she do now? Her life was becoming a desolation.

So desolate was Bathsheba this evening, that in an absolute hunger for pity and sympathy, and miserable in that she appeared to have outlived the only true friendship she had ever owned, she put on her bonnet and cloak and went down to Oak's house just after sunset, guided on her way by the pale primrose rays of a crescent moon a few days old.

A lively firelight shone from the window, but nobody was visible in the room. She tapped nervously, and then thought it doubtful if it were right for a single woman to call upon a bachelor who lived alone, although he was her manager, and she might be supposed to call on business without any real impropriety. Gabriel opened the door, and the moon shone upon his forehead.

"Mr. Oak," said Bathsheba, faintly.

"Yes; I am Mr. Oak," said Gabriel. "Who have I the honour—O how stupid of me, not to know you, mistress!"

"I shall not be your mistress much longer, shall I Gabriel?" she said, in pathetic tones.

"Well, no. I suppose—But come in, ma'am. Oh—and I'll get a light," Oak replied, with some awkwardness.

"No; not on my account."

"It is so seldom that I get a lady visitor that I'm afraid I haven't proper accommodation. Will you sit down, please? Here's a chair, and there's one, too. I am sorry that my chairs all have wood seats, and are rather hard, but

I—was thinking of getting some new ones." Oak placed two or three for her.

"They are quite easy enough for me."

So down she sat, and down sat he, the fire dancing in their faces, and upon the old furniture,

all a-sheenen
Wi' long years o' handlen,

that formed Oak's array of household possessions, which sent back a dancing reflection in reply. It was very odd to these two persons, who knew each other passing well, that the mere circumstance of their meeting in a new place and in a new way should make them so awkward and constrained. In the fields, or at her house, there had never been any embarrassment; but now that Oak had become the entertainer their lives seemed to be moved back again to the days when they were strangers.

"You'll think it strange that I have come, but—"

"Oh no; not at all."

"But I thought—Gabriel, I have been uneasy in the belief that I have offended you, and that you are going away on that account. It grieved me very much and I couldn't help coming."

Analysis: Here we gain a deep sense of Bathsheba and Oak's melancholy that everything is broken, that nothing can be fixed.

Discussion point: How does Hardy generate suspense here?

"Offended me! As if you could do that, Bathsheba!"

"Haven't I?" she asked, gladly. "But, what are you going away for else?"

"I am not going to emigrate, you know; I wasn't aware that you would wish me not to when I told 'ee or I shouldn't ha' thought of doing it," he said, simply. "I have arranged for Little Weatherbury Farm and shall have it in my own hands at Lady-day. You know I've had a share in it for some time. Still, that wouldn't prevent my attending to your business as before, hadn't it been that things have been said about us."

"What?" said Bathsheba, in surprise. "Things said about you and me! What are they?"

"I cannot tell you."

"It would be wiser if you were to, I think. You have played the part of mentor to me many times, and I don't see why you should fear to do it now."

"It is nothing that you have done, this time. The top and tail o't is this—that I am sniffing about here, and waiting for poor Boldwood's farm, with a thought of getting you some day."

"Getting me! What does that mean?"

"Marrying of 'ee, in plain British. You asked me to tell, so you mustn't blame me."

Bathsheba did not look quite so alarmed as if a cannon had been discharged by her ear, which was what Oak had expected. "Marrying me! I didn't know it was that you meant," she said, quietly. "Such a thing as that is too absurd—too soon—to think of, by far!"

"Yes; of course, it is too absurd. I don't desire any such thing; I should think that was plain enough by this time. Surely, surely you be the last person in the world I think of marrying. It is too absurd, as you say."

"'Too—s-s-soon' were the words I used."

"I must beg your pardon for correcting you, but you said, 'too absurd,' and so do I."

"I beg your pardon too!" she returned, with tears in her eyes. "'Too soon' was what I said. But it doesn't matter a bit—not at all—but I only meant, 'too soon.' Indeed, I didn't, Mr. Oak, and you must believe me!"

Gabriel looked her long in the face, but the firelight being faint there was not much to be seen. "Bathsheba," he said, tenderly and in surprise, and coming closer: "if I only knew one thing—whether you would allow me to love you and win you, and marry you after all—if I only knew that!"

"But you never will know," she murmured.

"Why?"

"Because you never ask."

"Oh—Oh!" said Gabriel, with a low laugh of joyousness. "My own dear—"

Analysis: Notice it is only when men try to leave her that Bathsheba really stirs herself to seek them out. With Oak wanting to leave and make a new life for himself in the States, she is stirred into action. Notice how this proposal scene is so different from the other ones. This scene is as much about what is not said as is stated.

Discussion point: How successful is this as a proposal scene? Why is it so much more unusual than the other proposal scenes in the novel?

"You ought not to have sent me that harsh letter this morning," she interrupted. "It shows you didn't care a bit about me, and were ready to desert me like all the rest of them! It was very cruel of you, considering I was the first sweetheart that you ever had, and you were the first I ever had; and I shall not forget it!"

"Now, Bathsheba, was ever anybody so provoking," he said, laughing. "You know it was purely that I, as an unmarried man, carrying on a business for you as a very taking young woman, had a proper hard part to play—more particular that people knew I had a sort of feeling for 'ee; and I fancied, from the way we were mentioned together, that it might injure your good name. Nobody knows the heat and fret I have been caused by it."

"And was that all?"

"All."

"Oh, how glad I am I came!" she exclaimed, thankfully, as she rose from her seat. "I have thought so much more of you since I fancied you did not want even to see me again. But I must be going now, or I shall be missed. Why Gabriel," she said, with a slight laugh, as they went to the door, "it seems exactly as if I had come courting you—how dreadful!"

"And quite right too," said Oak. "I've danced at your skittish heels, my beautiful Bathsheba, for many a long mile, and many a long day; and it is hard to begrudge me this one visit."

He accompanied her up the hill, explaining to her the details of his forthcoming tenure of the other farm. They spoke very little of their mutual feeling; pretty phrases and warm expressions being probably unnecessary between such tried friends. Theirs was that substantial affection which arises (if any arises at all) when the two who are thrown together begin first by knowing the rougher sides of each other's character, and not the best till further on, the romance growing up in the interstices of a mass of hard prosaic reality. This good-fellowship—camaraderie—usually occurring through similarity of pursuits, is unfortunately seldom superadded to love between the sexes, because men and women associate, not in their labours, but in their pleasures merely. Where, however, happy circumstance permits its development, the compounded feeling proves itself to be the only love which is strong as death—that love which many waters cannot quench, nor the floods drown, beside which the passion usually called by the name is evanescent as steam.

Questions

Who does Bathsheba leave the running of the farm to?

What does Gabriel tell Bathsheba as she is going to choir practice?

What is Bathsheba's response?

Why does Oak intend to resign his position as bailiff of Bathsheba's farm?

What does Bathsheba indicate he should do again?

What is Gabriel's response to Bathsheba's hint?

GCSE style question: how is this proposal scene similar and different to the first proposal scene between Gabriel and Bathsheba?

A Level style question: compare and contrast the resolution (the happy ending) with another similar resolution in a text of your choice.

Creative response: write a story/poem/description called 'Second Chance' or write either Bathsheba or Oak's diaries for this chapter.

CHAPTER LVII
A FOGGY NIGHT AND MORNING— CONCLUSION

"The most private, secret, plainest wedding that it is possible to have."

Those had been Bathsheba's words to Oak one evening, some time after the event of the preceding chapter, and he meditated a full hour by the clock upon how to carry out her wishes to the letter.

"A license—O yes, it must be a license," he said to himself at last. "Very well, then; first, a license."

On a dark night, a few days later, Oak came with mysterious steps from the surrogate's door, in Casterbridge. On the way home he heard a heavy tread in front of him, and, overtaking the man, found him to be Coggan. They walked together into the village until they came to a little lane behind the church, leading down to the cottage of Laban Tall, who had lately been installed as clerk of the parish, and was yet in mortal terror at church on Sundays when he heard his lone voice among certain hard words of the Psalms, whither no man ventured to follow him.

"Well, good-night, Coggan," said Oak, "I'm going down this way."

"Oh!" said Coggan, surprised; "what's going on to-night then, make so bold Mr. Oak?"

It seemed rather ungenerous not to tell Coggan, under the circumstances, for Coggan had been true as steel all through the time of Gabriel's unhappiness about Bathsheba, and Gabriel said, "You can keep a secret, Coggan?"

"You've proved me, and you know."

"Yes, I have, and I do know. Well, then, mistress and I mean to get married to-morrow morning."

"Heaven's high tower! And yet I've thought of such a thing from time to time; true, I have. But keeping it so close! Well, there, 'tis no consarn of of mine, and I wish 'ee joy o' her."

"Thank you, Coggan. But I assure 'ee that this great hush is not what I wished for at all, or what either of us would have wished if it hadn't been for certain things that would make a gay wedding seem hardly the thing. Bathsheba has a great wish that all the parish shall not be in church, looking at her—she's shy-like and nervous about it, in fact—so I be doing this to humour her."

"Ay, I see: quite right, too, I suppose I must say. And you be now going down to the clerk."

"Yes; you may as well come with me."

"I am afeard your labour in keeping it close will be throwed away," said Coggan, as they walked along. "Labe Tall's old woman will horn it all over parish in half-an-hour."

"So she will, upon my life; I never thought of that," said Oak, pausing. "Yet I must tell him to-night, I suppose, for he's working so far off, and leaves early."

"I'll tell 'ee how we could tackle her," said Coggan. "I'll knock and ask to speak to Laban outside the door, you standing in the background. Then he'll come out, and you can tell yer tale. She'll never guess what I want en for; and I'll make up a few words about the farm-work, as a blind."

This scheme was considered feasible; and Coggan advanced boldly, and rapped at Mrs. Tall's door. Mrs. Tall herself opened it.

"I wanted to have a word with Laban."

"He's not at home, and won't be this side of eleven o'clock. He've been forced to go over to Yalbury since shutting out work. I shall do quite as well."

"I hardly think you will. Stop a moment;" and Coggan stepped round the corner of the porch to consult Oak.

"Who's t'other man, then?" said Mrs. Tall.

"Only a friend," said Coggan.

"Say he's wanted to meet mistress near church-hatch to-morrow morning at ten," said Oak, in a whisper. "That he must come without fail, and wear his best clothes."

"The clothes will floor us as safe as houses!" said Coggan.

"It can't be helped," said Oak. "Tell her."

So Coggan delivered the message. "Mind, het or wet, blow or snow, he must come," added Jan. "'Tis very particular, indeed. The fact is, 'tis to witness her sign some law-work about taking shares wi' another farmer for a long span o' years. There, that's what 'tis, and now I've told 'ee, Mother Tall, in a way I shouldn't ha' done if I hadn't loved 'ee so hopeless well."

Coggan retired before she could ask any further; and next they called at the vicar's in a manner which excited no curiosity at all. Then Gabriel went home, and prepared for the morrow.

"Liddy," said Bathsheba, on going to bed that night, "I want you to call me at seven o'clock to-morrow, In case I shouldn't wake."

"But you always do wake afore then, ma'am."

"Yes, but I have something important to do, which I'll tell you of when the time comes, and it's best to make sure."

Bathsheba, however, awoke voluntarily at four, nor could she by any contrivance get to sleep again. About six, being quite positive that her watch had stopped during the night, she could wait no longer. She went and tapped at Liddy's door, and after some labour awoke her.

"But I thought it was I who had to call you?" said the bewildered Liddy. "And it isn't six yet."

"Indeed it is; how can you tell such a story, Liddy? I know it must be ever so much past seven. Come to my room as soon as you can; I want you to give my hair a good brushing."

When Liddy came to Bathsheba's room her mistress was already waiting. Liddy could not understand this extraordinary promptness. "Whatever is going on, ma'am?" she said.

"Well, I'll tell you," said Bathsheba, with a mischievous smile in her bright eyes. "Farmer Oak is coming here to dine with me to-day!"

"Farmer Oak—and nobody else?—you two alone?"

"Yes."

"But is it safe, ma'am, after what's been said?" asked her companion, dubiously. "A woman's good name is such a perishable article that—"

Bathsheba laughed with a flushed cheek, and whispered in Liddy's ear, although there was nobody present. Then Liddy stared and exclaimed, "Souls alive, what news! It makes my heart go quite bumpity-bump!"

"It makes mine rather furious, too," said Bathsheba. "However, there's no getting out of it now!"

It was a damp disagreeable morning. Nevertheless, at twenty minutes to ten o'clock, Oak came out of his house, and

> Went up the hill side
> With that sort of stride
> A man puts out when walking in search of a bride,

and knocked Bathsheba's door. Ten minutes later a large and a smaller umbrella might have been seen moving from the same door, and through the mist along the road to the church. The distance was not more than a quarter of a mile, and these two sensible persons deemed it unnecessary to drive. An observer must have been very close indeed to discover that the forms under the umbrellas were those of Oak and Bathsheba, arm-in-arm for the first time in their lives, Oak in a greatcoat extending to his knees, and Bathsheba in a cloak that reached her clogs. Yet, though so plainly dressed, there was a certain rejuvenated appearance about her:—

> As though a rose should shut and be a bud again.

Analysis: Events have tamed Bathsheba and she now marries Oak a different, more subdued woman, although she is only a few years old than the wild, beautiful girl at the beginning of the novel.

Discussion point: To what extent has Bathsheba changed in the novel?

Repose had again incarnadined her cheeks; and having, at Gabriel's request, arranged her hair this morning as she had worn it years ago on Norcombe Hill, she seemed in his eyes remarkably like a girl of that fascinating dream, which, considering that she was now only three or four-and-twenty, was perhaps not very wonderful. In the church were Tall, Liddy, and the parson, and in a remarkably short space of time the deed was done.

The two sat down very quietly to tea in Bathsheba's parlour in the evening of the same day, for it had been arranged that Farmer Oak should go there to live, since he had as yet neither money, house, nor furniture worthy of the name, though he was on a sure way towards them, whilst Bathsheba was, comparatively, in a plethora of all three.

Just as Bathsheba was pouring out a cup of tea, their ears were greeted by the firing of a cannon, followed by what seemed like a tremendous blowing of trumpets, in the front of the house.

"There!" said Oak, laughing, "I knew those fellows were up to something, by the look on their faces"

Oak took up the light and went into the porch, followed by Bathsheba with a shawl over her head. The rays fell upon a group of male figures gathered upon the gravel in front, who, when they saw the newly-married couple in the porch, set up a loud "Hurrah!" and at the same moment bang again went the cannon in the background, followed by a hideous clang of music from a drum, tambourine, clarionet, serpent, hautboy, tenor-viol, and double-bass—the only remaining relics of the true and original Weatherbury band—venerable worm-eaten instruments, which had celebrated in their own persons the victories of Marlborough, under the fingers of the forefathers of those who played them now. The performers came forward, and marched up to the front.

"Those bright boys, Mark Clark and Jan, are at the bottom of all this," said Oak. "Come in, souls, and have something to eat and drink wi' me and my wife."

"Not to-night," said Mr. Clark, with evident self-denial. "Thank ye all the same; but we'll call at a more seemly time. However, we couldn't think of letting the day pass without a note of admiration of some sort. If ye could send a drop of som'at down to Warren's, why so it is. Here's long life and happiness to neighbour Oak and his comely bride!"

"Thank ye; thank ye all," said Gabriel. "A bit and a drop shall be sent to Warren's for ye at once. I had a thought that we might very likely get a salute of some sort from our old friends, and I was saying so to my wife but now."

"Faith," said Coggan, in a critical tone, turning to his companions, "the man hev learnt to say 'my wife' in a wonderful naterel way, considering how very youthful he is in wedlock as yet—hey, neighbours all?"

"I never heerd a skilful old married feller of twenty years' standing pipe 'my wife' in a more used note than 'a did," said Jacob Smallbury. "It might have been a little more true to nater if't had been spoke a little chillier, but that wasn't to be expected just now."

"That improvement will come wi' time," said Jan, twirling his eye.

Then Oak laughed, and Bathsheba smiled (for she never laughed readily now), and their friends turned to go.

"Yes; I suppose that's the size o't," said Joseph Poorgrass with a cheerful sigh as they moved away; "and I wish him joy o' her; though I were once or twice upon saying to-day with holy Hosea, in my scripture manner, which is my second nature, 'Ephraim is joined to idols: let him alone.' But since 'tis as 'tis, why, it might have been worse, and I feel my thanks accordingly."

Questions

What is Gabriel and Bathsheba's wedding like?

Who are the witnesses?

What happens outside their house that night?

What does Gabriel send to Warren's Malthouse and why?

How has Bathsheba changed?

GCSE style question: how does the celebration of this wedding contrast with the celebrations after the 'Troy' wedding?

A Level style question: compare and contrast this ending with another ending of a relevant text of your choice.

Creative response: write Bathsheba's diary for this chapter, outlining her feelings for Oak and the villagers.

Answers to the questions

IMPORTANT NOTE: the answers to these questions are deliberately very brief; many of them could be much longer, particularly the GCSE style questions. In general, I have not attempted to answer the A Level questions because they really need independent and original thought. I have not reproduced any questions for which I have not provided an answer.

CHAPTER I
DESCRIPTION OF FARMER OAK – AN INCIDENT

How old Gabriel Oak? 28.

What time of year is it and what is the weather like? It is December and it is mild weather.

Who and what does Oak see in the wagon? He sees a pretty young woman with dark hair sitting on top of the wagon, surrounded by household goods.

What is the young woman doing when she thinks no one is looking? Admiring herself in the mirror.

What does Oak do to help the young woman and wagoner at the tollgate? He pays the two pence so that they can pass.

What thanks does he get from the young woman? None. She scarcely looks at him and then moves on.

What does Oak think her problem is? Vanity.

GCSE style question: how effective is this as an opening chapter to a novel? It is very cinematic; we see a vivid scene of the wagon, and it is revealing of Bathsheba's character in the way she seems mysterious, aloof and attractive. We learn about Oak – who is trying to make his own way in life – and the girl, who seems to be vain.

CHAPTER II
NIGHT—THE FLOCK—AN INTERIOR—ANOTHER INTERIOR

What instrument is Oak playing? A flute.

What is he caring for? A weak new born lamb.

Where does Oak live? In a shepherd's hut which is on wheels.

What do the stars tell Oak about his watch? That his watch is not working properly.

What does Oak spy through the roof of the farm? Two women tending to a cow, which is sick.

What does the young woman complain about? That there is no young man to do the difficult chores and that she has lost her hat.

Who is this young woman? The same young woman who Oak saw in the wagon.

CHAPTER III A GIRL ON HORSEBACK—CONVERSATION

What item of clothing does Gabriel get which belongs to the girl? Her hat.

What does Gabriel spy the girl doing on the horse? Lying on her back on the horse and passing underneath branches.

Why is the girl embarrassed when Gabriel gives her the hat? Because she realizes that Gabriel has been spying on her.

What does the girl do for the next five days? Tend to the cows.

Why is Gabriel nearly killed? Because he goes to sleep in his hut without lifting up the slide that lets the fumes from the fire out; this nearly suffocates him.

Why and how does the girl rescue him? She hears his dog howling; she enters the hut and throws warm milk over him.

What does she allow Gabriel to do and what will she not allow him to know? She allows him to hold her hand, suggesting that he can kiss it. She won't tell him her name.

GCSE style question: How does Hardy represent Bathsheba in this chapter? As unconventional (playing on the horse), as heroic (rescuing Gabriel), as flirtatious (letting him hold her hand), as mysterious (not telling him her name).

A Level style question: How does Hardy explore the theme of spying in these first three chapters of the book? Gabriel's spying on Bathsheba introduces the theme of spying/voyeurism. He represents the "male gaze"; viewing Bathsheba as an attractive female, as an object of desire, as mysterious and unobtainable.

Creative response: write a poem/short story called 'The Spy' about someone who enjoys spying on another person.

CHAPTER IV GABRIEL'S RESOLVE—THE VISIT—THE MISTAKE

Why is Gabriel upset that the cows have run dry? Because it means that the girl's visits to the dairy will end.

What does he decide to do? To ask the girl to marry him.

How does he prepare for his proposal? By dressing neatly, oiling his hair and calling on her aunt with the present of a lamb.

What does the aunt say when he states he wants to marry the girl? She says that Bathsheba is better educated than him and has many admirers.

What does Bathsheba do when Gabriel leaves? Runs after him, and assures him there are no rivals.

How does Gabriel try to tempt Bathsheba into marrying him? By saying that she will have a piano, a gig and babies.

What is Bathsheba's response? She is tempted by the idea of the cottage but put off by the thought of the babies. She refuses him.

What does Gabriel say he will do? He will remain faithful to her.

What does Bathsheba tell him to do? Not to propose again.

GCSE style question: How does Hardy make Gabriel's first proposal such a comic and touching moment? We gain a sense of Gabriel's hopeless love; he is a sympathetic figure, cast as the underdog in the situation.

A Level style question: compare and contrast this proposal scene with another one in a text of your choice.

Creative response: write a poem/story called 'The Proposal' which could be about a marriage proposal, or some other kind of proposal. Or write Bathsheba's diary for this chapter.

CHAPTER V
DEPARTURE OF BATHSHEBA—A PASTORAL TRAGEDY

What wakes Gabriel? Sheep bells.

What does he discover has happened to his pregnant ewes? All 200 of them have fallen off a precipice and died, having been chased by his younger dog.

Why is this a disaster for Gabriel? Because they were not insured; so he has lost everything.

What does he do with his sheep dog? He shoots him.

What is his financial situation after he sells off his stock and equipment? He has no money.

GCSE style question: how does Hardy make the death of the sheep such a shocking moment in the novel? The contrast with the previous comic chapter; the descriptions of the dying sheep at the bottom of the pit; Gabriel's realization that he has lost everything; his relief that he didn't marry.

A Level style question: compare and contrast this "disaster" scene with another representation of a disaster in a text of your choice.

Creative response: write a poem/story in which someone loses everything by an accident of fate.

CHAPTER VI
THE FAIR—THE JOURNEY—THE FIRE

What is a bailiff? A caretaker of a farm.

Why does Oak fail to get work as a shepherd or a bailiff? Because the farmers are suspicious that he was once a farmer himself. It's very odd that someone of a relatively "high" position would need to take such a "lowly" position.

Who is Joseph Poorgrass talking about? Joseph's new mistress, Bathsheba.

How does Gabriel help put out the fire in the hay ricks? He calms down the farmhands, gets them to bring the water in a sensible fashion, climbs the rick and puts out the fire with his crook.

Who does Gabriel discover is the mistress of the farm? Bathsheba.

How are the roles reversed between Bathsheba and Gabriel? She is the mistress of the farm, and he has no farm.

GCSE style question: how does Hardy make the fire in the hayricks such an exciting scene? By conveying the panic of the farmhands, Gabriel's thoughtful response and his heroism, and the appearance of Bathsheba on a horse at the end.

A Level style question: compare and contrast the representation of the fire with another scene in literature where there is a fire, e.g. Jane rescuing Rochester in his burning bed in *Jane Eyre*.

Creative response: write a story/poem/description called 'The Fire'.

CHAPTER VII
RECOGNITION—A TIMID GIRL

What job does Bathsheba give Oak? Shepherd.

Why is Gabriel amazed at Bathsheba? The way she has changed from an 'unpractised girl' to a 'supervising and cool woman'.

Who does he meet by the churchyard and what does he give her? He meets a poorly dressed girl, Fanny Robin, and gives her all his money.

Why does the girl shock him and what does he promise to do? She shocks him because of her fast pulse; he promises to give her all his money.

GCSE style question: how does Hardy make Fanny Robin a mysterious and poignant figure? By the fact that she is pretty, poorly dressed, and mysterious.

A Level style question: compare and contrast the representation of Bathsheba with Fanny.

Creative response: write a poem/story/description of a person who is suffering from poverty.

CHAPTER VIII
THE MALTHOUSE—THE CHAT— NEWS

How do the villagers feel about Gabriel and how do we know this? He is easily accepted and is invited to drink from the communal drinking cup.

What is a malster and a Malthouse? Someone who makes beer, and a place where beer is drank.

Who did the malster know of Gabriel's family? His father and grandfather.

Where does Gabriel stay? In Jan Coggan's lodgings.

What news is there in Warren's Malthouse? Pennyways, the bailiff, has been caught stealing and Fanny Robin has gone missing.

What does Bathsheba do about Fanny Robin? She asks the men to find out about her soldier lover in Casterbridge.

GCSE style question: how does Hardy represent the local people in this chapter? They are represented as a loving, kind community, full of humour and generosity; they are also poor and frugal. Hardy uses his knowledge of the Dorset dialect to represent their speech in a lively fashion; contrary to many writers, he represents the locals as intelligent and knowing.

A Level style question: compare and contrast the representation of drinking alcohol in *FFMC* with another text of your choice.

Creative response: write a description/poem of a bar/café or place where people gather to socialize.

CHAPTER IX
THE HOMESTEAD—A VISITOR— HALF-CONFIDENCES

Why does Bathsheba refuse to see Boldwood? Because she is dusty and untidy from sorting out her uncle's goods.

Why has Boldwood called? To find out news of Fanny.

What does she learn about Boldwood from Liddy? That he is handsome, rich and single.

What did Boldwood do for Fanny? He became friends with her as a child, paid for her education and found her a job as a servant to Bathsheba's uncle.

Why is Bathsheba cross with Coggan's son? Because he did not stop Boldwood from thinking that she was old and boring.

What does she tell Liddy about her love life? That someone had already made a proposal of marriage to her.

GCSE style question: how does Hardy represent the relationship between Liddy and Bathsheba here? As a relationship which is both about a mistress and a servant, but also one which has the potential for genuine female friendship. They share information about who they love.

A Level style question: compare and contrast the representation of female friendship in the novel with another important female friendship in another text.

Creative response: write a poem/description of a friendship.

CHAPTER X
MISTRESS AND MEN

How does Bathsheba pay her workmen? She gives them their wages, plus a generous bonus.

What is she going to do about the position of bailiff? She is going to be the bailiff.

Why does she shock the locals? The fact that she is going to be bailiff.

Who becomes Gabriel's assistant? Cain Ball.

What is the news of Fanny? That she followed her lover's regiment when it left Casterbridge.

GCSE style question: how does Hardy represent Bathsheba as a powerful character in this chapter? The fact that she insists upon running the farm herself; that she will be the equal to the men in her working habits.

A Level style question: compare and contrast the representation of Bathsheba with another working woman in another text of your choice.

Creative response: write a poem/description/story about some issue connected with gender politics, e.g. a woman working in a traditionally male profession/sport etc, or vice versa.

CHAPTER XI
OUTSIDE THE BARRACKS—
SNOW—A MEETING

What is the weather and time of day when Fanny arrives at the barracks? It is snowy and dark.

What does Fanny plead with Troy for him to do? To arrange for them to get married.

What is stopping them getting married, according to Troy? He hasn't got permission from his officers.

Where does he agree to meet Fanny the next day? To meet her at her lodgings.

GCSE style question: how does Hardy present Troy and Fanny's relationship in this chapter? Fanny is very much the subservient person, pleading with Troy to get married. Troy is presented as being ambivalent about the relationship; laddish and tied to the values of the army. The weather is possibly an example of the pathetic fallacy in that the cold snowiness of the scene representing the desperation of Fanny.

A Level style question: compare and contrast this snowy scene with another snowy scene in a literary text of your choosing.

Creative response: write a poem/story/description called 'Meeting in the Snow'.

CHAPTER XII
FARMERS—A RULE—AN EXCEPTION

What makes Bathsheba stand out in the cornmarket? She is the only woman.

What is her response to the contempt and sexism of the farmers? She continues to drive a hard bargain; ignoring the stares of the men.

Who is the only person who is indifferent to Bathsheba? Boldwood.

Why is she curious about Boldwood? She has heard a rumour that he is has been 'jilted'.

GCSE style question: how does Hardy make the scene in the cornmarket such a telling and revealing scene about Bathsheba and the world of the farmers? Hardy presents Bathsheba as tough-minded, refusing to be bowed by the masculine, sexist world of the farmers, who don't really understand who she is at all.

A Level style question: compare and contrast the presentation of the male world of the farmers with another presentation of masculinity in another text of your choice.

Creative response: write a poem/story/description of a world/scene which is dominated by one gender, either male or female.

CHAPTER XIII
SORTES SANCTORUM—THE VALENTINE

What does Liddy persuade Bathsheba to do? To predict who she will marry using the Bible.

What does Bathsheba decide to do with her Valentine card, which she had bought to send to a child? To send it to Boldwood.

What does the seal on the card say? 'Marry me'.

Why does she send the card to Boldwood? To make him notice her.

GCSE style question: how does Hardy make the sending of the Valentine such an interesting scene?

A Level style question: compare and contrast the presentation of Bathsheba's interest in Boldwood with another similar relationship in another text of your choice.

Creative response: write a poem/story/description called 'The Valentine Card', or write Liddy or Bathsheba's diary for this chapter.

CHAPTER XIV
EFFECT OF THE LETTER— SUNRISE

What does Boldwood initially do with the Valentine Card? He stares at it for a long time.

How does the card haunt him? It appears in his dreams.

Who does he stare at when wakes early? Gabriel appearing over the hill near Bathsheba's farm.

GCSE style question: how does Hardy develop Boldwood's character in this scene?

A Level style question: compare and contrast the representation of Boldwood with another similar character in another text of your choice.

Creative response: write a story/poem/description called 'The Obsession' or write Boldwood's diary for this scene.

CHAPTER XV
A MORNING MEETING—THE LETTER AGAIN

What does Oak bring to the Malthouse? Four lambs.

What does Fanny's letter say? That she is very pleased that she is going to marry Troy.

Whose handwriting does Oak recognise on the Valentine? Bathsheba's.

GCSE style question: how does Hardy develop suspense in this chapter?

A Level style question: explore how Hardy and another author of your choice investigate the theme of naivety.

Creative response: write a story/poem about a naïve person.

CHAPTER XVI
ALL SAINTS' AND ALL SOULS'

Where does Troy wait for Fanny and for how long? At the church of All Souls for an hour.

What happens when he leaves? Fanny appears.

Where had Fanny been? Waiting at another church, All Saints, thinking it was the right one.

What does she plead with Troy to do and what is his response? She pleads with him to name another wedding day, but he refuses to.

GCSE style question: how does Hardy represent Troy and Fanny in this chapter? Troy is represented as easily embarrassed, and spiteful, while Fanny is represented as a victim.

A Level style question: compare and contrast Fanny with another person in a literary text who is presented as a victim.

Creative response: write a story/poem/description called 'Late' or write Troy and/or Fanny's diaries for this chapter.

CHAPTER XVII
IN THE MARKET-PLACE

What does Boldwood do and feel at Casterbridge market? Observes Bathsheba's beauty, feeling jealous when he sees her with another farmer.

What does Bathsheba think and feel about Boldwood? She notices that he seems different, but she feels indifferent towards him, except for the fact that she is sorry about sending the Valentine.

Why is Bathsheba worried about apologizing to Boldwood about the Valentine? Either it will hurt Boldwood's pride or it will make her look too 'forward'.

GCSE style question: how does Hardy represent Boldwood and Bathsheba's relationship in this scene? He represents it as very uneasy and awkward.

A Level style question: compare and contrast the presentation of the theme of jealousy in this text with another text of your choice.

Creative response: write a poem/story/description called 'Jealousy'; or write Bathsheba and/or Boldwood's diary for this chapter.

CHAPTER XVIII
BOLDWOOD IN MEDITATION –
REGRET

What does Boldwood do in his stable-yard? Paces up and down.

What has happened to his feelings? From being virtually non-existent, they have become 'extreme'.

What does Boldwood do which causes Bathsheba embarrassment? He watches her and Oak trying to make a ewe accept another lamb.

GCSE style question: how does Hardy represent nature in this chapter?

A Level style question: how does Hardy explore the theme of embarrassment in this chapter?

Creative response: write a poem/story called 'The admirer' or write Boldwood's diary for this chapter.

CHAPTER XIX
THE SHEEP-WASHING—THE
OFFER

What is Bathsheba doing when Boldwood calls? She is supervising the farm, helping with the sheep washing.

What does Boldwood do as soon as they are alone? He proposes marriage.

What does Boldwood feel gave him hope? The Valentine.

What is Bathsheba's response? She apologises for the Valentine and that she has not fallen in love.

What alarms Bathsheba about Boldwood and how does she manage to get rid of him? She is alarmed by the strength of his feelings; she gets rid of him by asking for time to consider his offer.

GCSE style question: how does Hardy make Boldwood's proposal such a tense moment in the novel? We know about the strength of Boldwood's feelings; we are aware that Bathsheba does not feel as strongly for him, and yet encouraged him with the Valentine.

A Level style question: to what extent is Bathsheba the victim of a patriarchal system in this chapter?

Creative response: write Bathsheba's diary for this chapter.

CHAPTER XX
PERPLEXITY—GRINDING THE SHEARS—A QUARREL

What is Bathsheba's decision regarding Boldwood's proposal and why does she make this decision? She decides not to accept his offer because she wants to be 'absolute mistress' of the farm.

What does she ask Gabriel to do while he is grinding sheep-shears in the barn? To deny rumours that she is getting married to Boldwood.

What is Gabriel's response? He won't do it.

What does Gabriel say about her conduct when she asks for his opinion of her? He calls Bathsheba's conduct 'unworthy'.

What does Bathsheba do when faced with Gabriel's criticism of her? She sacks him, giving him a week's notice.

What does Gabriel do? He leaves immediately.

GCSE style question: how does Hardy make the conversation between Bathsheba and Oak so compelling?

A Level style question: how does Hardy explore the "battle of the sexes" in this chapter?

Creative response: write a story/poem called 'Criticism' in which one person criticizes another person.

CHAPTER XXI
TROUBLES IN THE FOLD—A MESSAGE

What happens to Bathsheba's sheep the next day? They break a fence and get into a clover field, and as a result become bloated and may die.

What does Bathsheba do after one of the sheep die? She sends for Oak.

What is Oak's response to Bathsheba's curt message? He refuses to help her unless she asks him politely.

What does Bathsheba do after another sheep dies? She writes a desperate letter to Oak, saying 'Do not desert me, Gabriel!'

What happens when Oak returns? He skillfully saves the sheep by lancing their bloated stomachs.

What does Bathsheba ask of Oak after this? For him to stay as her shepherd.

GCSE style question: how does Hardy make the bloating of the sheep both a comic and suspenseful scene? Bathsheba's dependence upon Oak is revealed, but we don't know if they will reconcile.

A Level style question: compare and contrast Hardy's representation of the farming world with another text which depicts some aspect of farming.

Creative response: write Bathsheba's diary for this chapter, including her thoughts and feelings about the sheep, the farm workers and Oak.

CHAPTER XXII
THE GREAT BARN AND THE SHEEP-SHEARERS

What does Bathsheba admire about Oak? His speed and skill while he is working in the old barn.

What does Oak do when Boldwood enters and why? He accidentally wounds a ewe because he is worried that Boldwood will marry Bathsheba.

Why is it ironic that Oak stops the workmen gossiping about the possible marriage between Boldwood and Bathsheba? Oak is worried about the very same thing.

GCSE style question: how does Hardy create a sense of mystery in this chapter? We don't know what Bathsheba's intentions are.

Creative response: write a story/poem called 'The Gossips'.

CHAPTER XXIII
EVENTIDE—A SECOND DECLARATION

What happens at the shearing supper? Bathsheba sings accompanied with Gabriel on the flute, while Boldwood sings on bass.

What does Bathsheba sing about? A soldier with a winning tongue.

What happens after the supper? Boldwood proposes again.

What is Bathsheba's response? She will try to love him and will give her answer by harvest time.

GCSE style question: how does Hardy present the rural ways of life in this chapter? There is a strong sense of tradition in the way people eat, sing, work and socialize.

A Level style question: how does Bathsheba's song foreshadow what is to come?

Creative response: write a poem/story/description about a sociable supper. Or write Bathsheba's diary for this chapter.

CHAPTER XXIV
THE SAME NIGHT—THE FIR PLANTATION

Why does Bathsheba go out at night? To check on the farm buildings.

What happens to her skirt? It gets caught on a soldier's spur.

What does the soldier say to her as he is trying to untangle himself? That Bathsheba is beautiful.

What is Bathsheba shocked by? Troy's flirtatious manner and words.

Why does she ask Liddy for more information on Troy? Because she is intrigued and attracted by him.

GCSE style question: how does Hardy make the meeting with Troy and Bathsheba such a charged and gripping scene? It is at night, there is a sense of threat, Troy's flirtatious conversation is unlike anything we have heard in the novel.

A Level style question: compare Troy's flirtation with Bathsheba with another scene where two characters flirt from another text.

Creative response: write Bathsheba's diary for this chapter.

CHAPTER XXV
THE NEW ACQUAINTANCE DESCRIBED

What do we learn about Troy in this chapter? He is the illegitimate son of a high-born man, and is better educated than most soldiers. He is attractive and a good talker.

Why is Bathsheba more relaxed than normal? Because Boldwood is absent.

How does Troy embarrass Bathsheba? By helping with the hay making.

GCSE style question: how does Hardy present Troy in this chapter?

Creative response: write a description of a flirtatious person, exploring why he or she is like that.

CHAPTER XXVI
SCENE ON THE VERGE OF THE HAY-MEAD

What does Troy apologise for? For insulting Bathsheba.

What is the effect of Troy's flattering? She becomes 'feverish'.

What is happening with Troy's regiment? It is leaving in a month's time.

What does he say about his feelings towards Bathsheba? That he fell in love with her at first sight.

What is Bathsheba's response to this? That this is impossible.

What does Troy try and give her? His gold watch.

What does he manage to get Bathsheba's permission for? To work in the fields.

GCSE style question: how do we see Bathsheba's dignity being compromised in this chapter? Troy's flattery and flirtations make Bathsheba feel things she has never felt before; she is attracted by him, but can't admit it to herself.

A Level style question: compare the presentation of Troy's behavior with Boldwood's.

Creative response: continue writing Bathsheba's diary for this scene, exploring her complex feelings for Boldwood, Oak and Troy.

CHAPTER XXVII
HIVING THE BEES

What does Troy offer to help Bathsheba with? Hiving the bees.

What does Bathsheba ask Troy to show him? His sword-exercise.

What does he persuade her to do? To meet him alone that evening.

GCSE style question: how does Hardy make the hiving of the bees a sensual moment in the novel?

Creative response: write a description/poem/story about bees.

CHAPTER XXVIII
THE HOLLOW AMID THE FERNS

Where does Bathsheba wait for Troy? In a secluded hollow.

What does Troy show her? He shows a fast display of sword cuts.

How does Troy lie to Bathsheba? He says his sword is blunt.

What does Troy do to Bathsheba with his sword? He cuts a lock of her hair and spits a caterpillar on her breast.

What does Troy do at the end of the chapter? He kisses her.

GCSE style question: how does Hardy make the encounter in the hollow so sexually charged?

A Level style question: compare and contrast Troy's seduction of

Bathsheba with another seduction scene in a text of your choice.

Creative response: write a story/poem/description called 'The Seduction' or write Bathsheba's diary for this scene.

CHAPTER XXIX
PARTICULARS OF A TWILIGHT WALK

What does Gabriel realise about Bathsheba? That she is in love with Troy.

What does Gabriel say to Bathsheba to try and change her mind about Troy? He criticizes Troy, and reminds Bathsheba of what has happened with Boldwood.

What is Bathsheba's response? She defends Troy.

What does Bathsheba try to do again? To sack Gabriel.

What is Gabriel's response? He refuses to listen to her, and insists that she appoints a bailiff; he feels it is his duty to safeguard her concerns.

How does Gabriel realise Troy has lied to Bathsheba? Troy told Bathsheba that he had attended church by a secret door, but Gabriel finds that the door can't be opened.

GCSE style question: how does Hardy present Bathsheba in this chapter? As infatuated and naïve.

Creative response: write Gabriel's diary for this chapter, outlining his concerns for Bathsheba.

CHAPTER XXX
HOT CHEEKS AND TEARFUL EYES

What does Bathsheba write in her letter to Boldwood? She is declining his proposal of marriage.

Why is she upset by the servants talking? Because they are gossiping about Troy's womanizing.

What does Bathsheba confess to Liddy? That she loves Troy to the point of 'agony'.

Why does she become upset by Liddy? Because Liddy refuses to deny rumours about Troy's wildness.

Who apologizes and why? Bathsheba apologizes to Liddy and they make up.

GCSE style question: how does Hardy present Bathsheba's contradictory state of mind in this chapter? She calls Troy 'a steady man in a wild way'.

Creative response: write a story/poem called 'Rumours' or write Bathsheba's diary for this chapter.

CHAPTER XXXI
BLAME—FURY

Who does Bathsheba meet on Yalbury Hill and what does this person ask her to do? She meets Boldwood and he begs her to pity him, and tells her off for sending the Valentine.

What does Boldwood guess? That Troy has robbed him of Bathsheba.

What does Boldwood threaten? To kill Troy.

What is Bathsheba worried about? Troy's safety.

GCSE style question: how does Hardy represent Boldwood in this chapter? As savagely jealous; he wants to kill Troy because of the way he has taken Bathsheba from him.

A Level style: compare and contrast Hardy's representation of jealousy with another text which explores the theme of jealousy.

Creative response: write a story/poem called 'Jealousy' or write Boldwood's diary.

CHAPTER XXXII
NIGHT—HORSES TRAMPING

What does Maryann see? Someone stealing a horse and attaching it to a carriage.

What do Gabriel and Coggan do? They borrow Boldwood's horses and chase after the person.

What do they discover at Sherton turnpike? That the 'thief' is Bathsheba.

What does Bathsheba tell Oak she is going to do? To go to Bath to warn Troy about Boldwood and to give him up.

GCSE style question: how does Hardy create tension and excitement in this chapter? There is a secretive atmosphere and a sense of threat; the discovery that the thief is Bathsheba is shocking and, even more disturbing, is her confused state of mind.

A Level style question: compare and contrast the scene where Oak catches Bathsheba with another scene where someone is caught doing something which they don't want other people to know about.

Creative response: write a poem/story called 'The Thief'; or write Oak's diary for this scene.

CHAPTER XXXIII
IN THE SUN—A HARBINGER

What does the letter to Maryann from Bathsheba say? That Bathsheba is delayed on business.

What are the workers doing? They are busy with the oat-harvest.

Who is supervising the farm effectively? Oak.

What news does Cainy Ball bring? He has been in Bath and seen

Bathsheba having a long discussion with Troy.

GCSE style question: how does Hardy create humour and suspense with Cainy Ball's news? Cainy Ball is impressed by the thermal spring in Bath, while Oak is desperate to know what happened with Bathsheba.

Creative response: write Cainy Ball's diary for this chapter.

CHAPTER XXXIV
HOME AGAIN—A TRICKSTER

Who does Bathsheba refuse to see? Boldwood.

What does Boldwood confront Troy about in Weatherbury? Fanny's claims on him; how he can't be serious about Bathsheba.

What does he offer Troy if he marries Fanny? Money.

Why does Boldwood change his mind and try to bribe Troy to marry Bathsheba when he overhears Bathsheba and Troy talking? He realizes that Troy has slept with Bathsheba.

What does Troy do? He takes the money and then shows Boldwood a newspaper clipping which reveals he and Bathsheba are married.

What does Boldwood vow to do? To get his revenge against Troy.

GCSE style question: how does Hardy make the conversation between Boldwood and Troy so suspenseful? We, the reader, don't know, like Boldwood, that Troy has already married Bathsheba; we don't really know what will happen. Will Troy accept the money? Boldwood's unstable state of mind is revealed in the way he changes his mind about why he should give Troy the money.

A Level style question: explore the representation of the trickster figure in literature in this text (Troy) and another of your choice.

Creative response: write a story/poem called 'The Trickster' or write Troy or Boldwood's diary for this scene.

CHAPTER XXXV
AT AN UPPER WINDOW

Why does Troy throw down money to Coggan and Oak from the window? To drink his health.

What does Oak do with the money? He rejects it.

Who appears on horseback and what is this person's mood? Boldwood; who seems very unhappy.

GCSE style question: how does Hardy present Troy in this chapter?

Creative response: write a poem/story/description called 'Just Married'.

CHAPTER XXXVI
WEALTH IN JEOPARDY—THE REVEL

What does Oak warn Troy about on the night of the harvest supper? That there is going to be a storm.

Who is in charge of the farm now and why? Troy, because he has a discharge from the army and married Bathsheba; in those days a wife's property became the husband's upon marriage.

What does Troy order should be brought to celebrate his marriage? Strong drink.

Who does Troy send away? The women and children.

What does Oak decide to do when he leaves the party? To cover the hayricks.

What happens when he goes to the men for extra help? They are asleep from the drink.

What does Oak do? He covers the ricks with waterproof cloths and starts to thatch the barley ricks.

GCSE style question: how does Hardy present the position of women in this chapter? Bathsheba has become powerless because Troy is now in charge, being her husband.

A Level style question: compare and contrast the presentation of Troy and Oak in this chapter.

Creative response: write a poem/story/description called 'The Party' or write Oak's diary for this scene.

CHAPTER XXXVII
THE STORM—THE TWO TOGETHER

Why is Oak in danger? He is thatching the ricks when there is thunder and lightning.

How does Bathsheba help him? By carrying reeds up the ladder.

What does Bathsheba confess to Oak? She married Troy because she couldn't bear the thought of him being with another woman and because she didn't want a scandal.

GCSE style question: how does Hardy make the scene in the storm such a thrilling and vivid moment in the novel? He describes the storm in great detail, suggesting nature's power and danger.

Creative response: write a poem/story/description called 'The Storm'.

CHAPTER XXXVIII
RAIN—ONE SOLITARY MEETS ANOTHER

How long does Gabriel work? All night.

Who does Oak meet at dawn? Boldwood.

What has happened to Boldwood's ricks and why? They were all left uncovered and now are ruined. Boldwood doesn't care because he has lost Bathsheba.

What is Boldwood thinking of doing? Of committing suicide.

GCSE style question: how does Hardy make Boldwood a poignant and broken figure in this chapter? By presenting him as not caring what happened to his property or his life; this contrasts very strongly with how he used to be like.

Creative response: write a poem/story called 'Broken' in which you describe a person/thing which is broken.

CHAPTER XXXIX
COMING HOME—A CRY

What has Troy lost at the races? Over £100.

Why do Bathsheba and he quarrel? Because Troy won't give up his plans to attend another race.

Who meets them on the highway? A beggar woman who sees Troy and faints.

What does Troy say and give to Fanny? He tells her to meet him on Grey's Bridge the next morning and gives her all his money.

What is Bathsheba's response? She is suspicious and want to know who the woman is.

GCSE style question: how does Hardy make the re-appearance of Fanny such a shocking and moving moment? Fanny has been ruined and destroyed by poverty, illness and neglect; her poverty contrasts with Troy's and Bathsheba's wealth.

Creative response; write a poem/story/description of a homeless person. Or write Troy's diary for this chapter.

CHAPTER XL
ON CASTERBRIDGE HIGHWAY

How much does Fanny sleep? Only a few hours.

What does she use to help her walk? Two sticks as crutches.

What helps her walk as she nears Casterbridge? She leans on a large dog.

Where does she collapse? On the steps of the workhouse.

GCSE style question: how does Hardy present Fanny as a figure of pathos here?

A Level style question: explore the presentation of the vagrant in literature, using Fanny as a starting point and the look at other texts of your choice.

Creative response: write a description/poem/story about a difficult journey.

CHAPTER XLI
SUSPICION—FANNY IS SENT FOR

How much money does Troy get from Bathsheba? £20.

What does Bathsheba notice when Troy opens his watch? A lock of blonde hair.

What does Troy tell Bathsheba about the lock of hair? That it is the hair of a former sweetheart.

What does Bathsheba guess about the woman on the highway? That she is the woman whose lock of hair he has.

GCSE style question: how does Hardy present marriage in this chapter?

A Level style question: compare and contrast Hardy's presentation of marriage with another text which explores the theme.

Creative response: write a story/poem/description about an item which is treasured by someone because it is connected to a former love like a lock of hair etc., call it 'The Memento'.

CHAPTER XLII
JOSEPH AND HIS BURDEN—
BUCK'S HEAD

Where does Joseph collect the coffin from? The workhouse.

Where does Joseph stop and what happens to him there? He stops at the Buck's Head inn and gets very drunk and forgets the time.

Who takes the coffin back to Weatherbury? Gabriel does.

Where does Bathsheba insist the coffin is brought to? Her house.

What words does Gabriel remove from the coffin lid? 'And child'.

GCSE style question: why do you think Hardy makes both Boldwood and Oak not reveal the identity of Fanny's lover to the villagers or Bathsheba?

A Level style question: examine Hardy's portrayal of the death of Fanny, analyzing the way he juxtaposes the comic banter of the villagers with her tragic death.

Creative response: write Gabriel's diary for this chapter.

CHAPTER XLIII
FANNY'S REVENGE

What rumour does Liddy tell Bathsheba about? That Fanny had an illegitimate child.

Who does Bathsheba want advice from and why does she not seek it? She wants to ask Gabriel's advice but sees him praying through his window and leaves him alone.

What does Bathsheba realise when she opens the coffin? That Fanny was Troy's lover and that this is Troy's child.

How does she stop her jealous feelings from overwhelming her? By putting flowers around the dead bodies.

What does Troy learn about when he returns? That Fanny had his child.

What does Bathsheba beg him to do and what is his response? She begs him to kiss her, but instead he kisses Fanny.

What does Bathsheba do? She runs away.

GCSE style question: how does Hardy make the opening of the coffin such a shocking and suspenseful moment?

A Level style question: explore the role of illegitimate children in this text and another text of your choice.

Creative response: write Bathsheba's diary for this chapter, exploring her feelings for Fanny, Troy and Oak.

CHAPTER XLIV
UNDER A TREE—REACTION

Where does Bathsheba sleep? Outdoors, near a swamp.

What does Liddy tell her? That Troy has left the house.

When does Bathsheba return to the house? When Fanny's coffin has been taken away for burial.

Where do Liddy and Bathsheba stay for that day while they wait for Troy's return? In the disused attic.

What do they see happening at sunset in the churchyard? Men making an expensive headstone.

GCSE style question: how does Hardy present Bathsheba in this chapter?

Creative response: write Liddy's diary, exploring what she feels towards her mistress, Troy and the events so far.

CHAPTER XLV
TROY'S ROMANTICISM

What did Troy do when Bathsheba left? He recovered the coffin.

What happened the previous day when he was supposed to meet Fanny? He had waited but when she did not appear he went to the races, and then went home.

What does Troy insist is made for the dead Fanny? An ornate tombstone.

What does he do around Fanny's grave? Plants flowers.

Where does he stay that night? In the church porch.

GCSE style question: how does Hardy present Troy in this chapter?

A Level style question: explore the way Hardy presents Troy's 'romanticism' in this chapter.

Creative response: write Troy's diary for this chapter, exploring his feelings for Fanny and his dead child.

CHAPTER XLVI
THE GURGOYLE: ITS DOINGS

What happens to flowers on Fanny's grave? They get washed away by the rain.

What does Troy decide to do when he wakes? Leave the area.

What does Bathsheba do when she sees the ruined grave? Orders that it be repaired. She replants the flowers.

GCSE style question: how does Hardy present Bathsheba in this chapter? She ceases to be jealous and we see compassion enter her heart.

A Level style question: compare and contrast the ways in which this text and another of your choice explore the theme of compassion.

Creative response: write a poem/story/description called 'The Tombstone' or write Bathsheba's diary for this chapter.

CHAPTER XLVII
ADVENTURES BY THE SHORE

Where does Troy take a swim? In Lulwind Cove.

What happens to him while swimming? He is taken away by a strong current, but manages to hail a boat and be rescued.

GCSE style question: how does Hardy make Troy's disappearance suspenseful?

Creative response: write a poem/story about swimming.

CHAPTER XLVIII
DOUBTS ARISE—DOUBTS LINGER

What does Bathsheba think will happen when Troy returns? They will be evicted because of his debts, and ruined.

What happens when she is informed that Troy has drowned? She faints.

What does she really think has happened? She thinks somehow he is alive.

What helps convince her that he probably is dead? The eye-witness account in a newspaper and the arrival of Troy's clothes.

Who is now very hopeful things will be better for him? Boldwood.

GCSE question: how does Hardy maintain the suspense and momentum of the story in this chapter? By using dramatic irony; we know Troy is alive, while everyone else thinks he is dead. We predict, at some point, he will reappear.

Creative response: write a story called 'Missing' about a missing person. Or write Bathsheba's diary in which she reflects upon Troy's 'death'.

CHAPTER XLIX
OAK'S ADVANCEMENT—A GREAT HOPE

Who does Bathsheba appoint as bailiff? Oak.

What happens to Boldwood's crops? They rot.

Why does Oak agree to look after Boldwood's farm? Because he will be given a small share of the profits.

What do the villagers think of Gabriel? He is now a respectable, rich man.

What does Bathsheba wear and why? Black because she is in mourning for Troy.

What does Boldwood learn from Liddy? That Bathsheba may marry in six years' time if Troy fails to return.

What does Boldwood convince himself of? That if he waits, Bathsheba will marry him.

GCSE style question: how does Hardy present Boldwood in this chapter? As increasingly obsessed and deluded.

A Level style question: compare and contrast Boldwood's obsessive nature with another similar obsessive person in another text of your choice.

Creative response: write Boldwood's diary for this chapter.

CHAPTER L
THE SHEEP FAIR—TROY TOUCHES HIS WIFE'S HAND

What does Oak take to Greenhill Fair? Bathsheba and Boldwood's sheep.

What is Troy doing there? He is the star performer, playing a highwayman on a horse.

What has Troy been doing for the intervening time? Travelled to the United States, worked as a fighter and sword showman, and at circuses as a showman.

How does he avoid being recognised by Bathsheba? By disguising himself with a heavy beard.

Who recognises him? Pennyways, the bailiff that Bathsheba sacked.

What does Pennyways try to do when he realizes who is at the fair? He tries to speak to Bathsheba, who refuses to speak to him, then he tries to send her a note.

How does Troy stop Pennyways communicating with Bathsheba? He cleverly and secretly takes the note.

GCSE style question: how does Hardy present Troy in this chapter? As a risk-taker, as a showman, who works well under pressure. He has also become more unpleasant and calculating.

Creative response: write Troy's diary for this chapter, outlining his thoughts about seeing Bathsheba again.

CHAPTER LI
BATHSHEBA TALKS WITH HER OUTRIDER

What does Boldwood do when they return back to Weatherbury? He proposes to her.

How does Bathsheba try and stall him? She says that she believes Troy is still alive.

What does Boldwood argue? That if Troy does not return within six years, she is entitled to re-marry.

What does Bathsheba promise him? Not to marry anyone else, but that she will give her final word at Christmas.

What does Bathsheba confide to Oak? That she thinks Boldwood may be mad.

Why does Bathsheba take Boldwood's proposal seriously? Because she regrets sending the Valentine.

GCSE style question: how does Hardy present Oak and Bathsheba's deepening relationship in this chapter? Oak is both a father figure to Bathsheba and a potential lover.

Creative response: write Bathsheba's diary for this chapter, exploring her feelings towards Oak, Boldwood and Troy.

CHAPTER LII
CONVERGING COURSES

What clothes does Bathsheba dress in for the Christmas Party, and what does Boldwood dress in? Bathsheba dresses in mourning clothes, while Boldwood wears his best party clothes.

What does Boldwood confide in to Gabriel? That he will get married to Bathsheba.

What does Troy plan to do in Casterbridge? To gatecrash Boldwood's party and reclaim his wife.

What does Boldwood put in his pocket? His engagement ring to give to Bathsheba.

What does Gabriel repeatedly try to tell Boldwood? Not to get his hopes up.

What does Troy do? Disguises himself in an overcoat and walks to Weatherbury.

GCSE style question: how does Hardy create an impending sense of doom and disaster in this chapter? He presents Boldwood as hopelessly deluded; Oak is powerless to stop him; Bathsheba is clearly depressed and

Troy is presented as wicked and scheming.

A Level style question: compare and contrast the ways in which Hardy presents the theme of hope in this novel with another text of your choice.

Creative response: write Boldwood's diary for this chapter or write a story/poem called 'The Great Hope'.

CHAPTER LIII
CONCURRITUR—HORAE MOMENTO

What are the villagers discussing? The rumour that Troy is still alive.

What happens when the villagers see Troy outside Warren's Malthouse? Laban is sent to warn Bathsheba.

How does Bathsheba behave at the party? She refuses to dance and after an hour tries to leave.

What does Boldwood manage to extract from Bathsheba? A promise to marry him in six years' time.

Why does Bathsheba agree to wear his engagement ring? Because Boldwood is so insistent; almost violent in his insistence.

What does Troy do when he enters the party? He orders Bathsheba to come with him, and then seizes her when she won't obey.

What does Boldwood do? He shoots Troy, then tries to shoot himself and then leaves.

GCSE style question: how does Hardy make this such a thrilling and possibly melodramatic climax to the novel? The ending brings the "love triangle" together: Boldwood, Troy and Oak. Boldwood's bullying mad obsession for Bathsheba is similar to Troy's callous manipulation of her; they both want to control and possess her in different ways. Boldwood's shooting of Troy annihilates both men at once as possible suitors. The scene is very melodramatic because of the extreme confrontation in front of everyone.

A Level style question: compare and contrast this climactic moment with another climax from another text of your choice.

Creative response: write Bathsheba's diary for this chapter and/or a story/poem/description called 'The Showdown'.

CHAPTER LIV
AFTER THE SHOCK

Where does Boldwood go? To surrender himself at Casterbridge gaol.

What does Bathsheba do? Nurses Troy and tells Oak to fetch a surgeon.

What does Bathsheba ask to happen to Troy's body? To be taken to her house where it should be prepared for burial.

Why is the surgeon angry when he arrives? That the body has been moved.

What does Bathsheba do? She has a 'series of fainting fits'.

GCSE style question: how does Hardy present Bathsheba in this chapter? Hardy presents her as stoic and heroic as she deals with Troy's death, but then everything gets too much for her and she collapses from the strain.

Creative response: write Bathsheba's diary for this chapter or write a story/poem/description called 'It's All Too Much'.

CHAPTER LV
THE MARCH FOLLOWING—
"BATHSHEBA BOLDWOOD"

Why is there a plea for mercy at Boldwood's trial? People believe he was out of his mind.

What sentence does Boldwood receive? Death.

What is discovered in Boldwood's house? Clothes, items all labelled 'Bathsheba Boldwood'.

Who spends time with Boldwood as the scaffold is prepared? Oak.

GCSE style question: how does Hardy build suspense in this chapter? We worry that Boldwood will be hanged when he is clearly mad.

A Level style question: compare and contrast Boldwood's trial with another courtroom drama in another relevant text.

Creative response: write Oak's diary for this chapter, reflecting upon his feelings for Boldwood; or write a newspaper article about the trial.

CHAPTER LVI
BEAUTY IN LONELINESS—AFTER
ALL

Who does Bathsheba leave the running of the farm to? Oak.

What does Gabriel tell Bathsheba as she is going to choir practice? That he is thinking of emigrating, even though he has been offered the leasehold on Boldwood's farm.

What is Bathsheba's response? She pleads with him to stay.

Why does Oak intend to resign his position as bailiff of Bathsheba's farm? He has decided to take on the leasehold of Boldwood's farm and he has heard rumours that he intends to marry Bathsheba.

What does Bathsheba indicate he should do again? Propose to her again.

What is Gabriel's response to Bathsheba's hint? He proposes and she accepts.

GCSE style question: how is this proposal scene similar and different to the first proposal scene between Gabriel and Bathsheba? They both are lightly humorous scenes; Hardy uses dialogue to create a sense of flirtatious doubt between the two characters; but in this scene, Bathsheba seeks out Gabriel. He has become almost the more 'feminine' one.

A Level style question: compare and contrast the resolution (the happy ending) with another similar resolution in a text of your choice.

Creative response: write a story/poem/description called 'Second Chance' or write either Bathsheba or Oak's diaries for this chapter.

CHAPTER LVII
A FOGGY NIGHT AND MORNING—CONCLUSION

What is Gabriel and Bathsheba's wedding like? Quiet and secret.

Who are the witnesses? Laban and Liddy.

What happens outside their house that night? The village band plays.

What does Gabriel send to Warren's Malthouse and why? Food and drink for the locals to celebrate.

How has Bathsheba changed? She is more serious and nervous.

GCSE style question: how does the celebration of this wedding contrast with the celebrations after the 'Troy' wedding? Oak is respected and loved by the locals who affectionately mock him when he says 'my wife'. Oak does not encourage the locals to get blind drunk (like Troy had done) and is inclusive in his attitude.

A Level style question: compare and contrast this ending with another ending of a relevant text of your choice.

Creative response: write Bathsheba's diary for this chapter, outlining her feelings for Oak and the villagers.

Speaking and Listening Exercises

Work in a group and devise a **chatshow** based on the novel. Make sure that you have an interviewer (chat-show host) who questions the main characters in the novel about their thoughts and feelings regarding what has happened to them. The aim is that students need to show that they understand the storyline and characters by talking in role about the events in the novel. You can include dead characters such as Gabriel Oak, Bathsheba, Troy, Boldwood, Liddy, Cainy Ball and Joseph Poorgrass if you wish to do so. You could also invite

You could put Boldwood on **trial**, accused of murdering of Troy. Set things up so that you have a prosecuting lawyer who is accusing Boldwood of the crimes. Have a defence lawyer who argues that there is evidence that he should be treated leniently. Call witnesses for the prosecution and defence who are characters from the novel such as Oak, Bathsheba, Jan Coggan, Cainy Ball, and Liddy etc; or the author; or "made-up" characters such as a psychiatrist who has assessed Boldwood's state of mind. Use the trial to explore different views on the novel. Then possibly write it up as a script or review what you have learnt from doing it.

Put the main characters in **therapy:** Oak, Boldwood, Troy, and Bathsheba are the most obvious ones, but you could possibly put Joseph Poorgrass/Fanny Robin in therapy as well. Have them visit a therapist to discuss their problems with him/her. You could do this so that they go into therapy at various stages during the story. Write a review of what you have learnt from doing this afterwards.

Work in a group and devise a **radio drama** of the major parts of the novel. Different groups could work on different sections of the book; e.g. the opening with Oak proposing to Bathsheba; Bathesheba sending the Valentie and Boldwood's growing obsession; Troy's seduction of her and their married life; Troy's disappearance and the death of Troy. Make the drama short and punchy. This exercise will help you get to know the text in much more depth: the editing of the novel will help you summarise key points.

How to write top grade essays on the novel

In order to write a good essay about *Far From The Madding Crowd*, you need to understand it. You will need to know what the difficult vocabulary means and be aware of how the text is the product of the world it comes from: nineteenth century England. You will also need to be aware of what the examiners for your particular question are looking for. For GCSE, it appears that most questions are, at the time of writing this guide, "extract based"; you will be given a small extract and asked to consider how the author builds suspense or drama in the extract, or presents the characters or key themes in a particular way. In order to achieve highly, you will need to answer the question carefully and not simply re-tell the extract; this is something that I have seen many good students do. The A Level questions are much more like the ones posed in the **essay question section** of this study guide and the A Level style questions posed in the chapter questions. Sometimes, you might be asked to compare the novel with other literary texts, depending upon the nature of the task and/or exam board. For A Level, you need to be aware of other literary critics' views on the novel.

You should consider a few key questions with extract questions:

For extract questions, consider how has the author **built up** to this particular moment? Think carefully about what the reader already knows before they have read the extract. You will need to know the story well in order to do this.

What literary devices does the author use to make the passage interesting or to reveal a particular character in a certain light? Think very carefully about the author's use of language: Hardy's use of descriptions to create a certain atmosphere or paint a sketch of a character/event; his use of dialogue to reveal character and create drama/tension; his use of imagery (metaphors/similes/personification). You will need to pack your essay full of the relevant terminology if you want to aim for higher marks as it appears in many mark schemes as a key requirement.

You need to be aware of a number of different interpretations of the novel. The weblinks below should help you with this.

Finally, you need to provide evidence and analysis to back up your points. As a cornerstone of your essay writing technique, you should be aware of the **PEEL** method of analysing texts: making a Point, providing Evidence, Explaining how your evidence endorses your point, and Linking to a new point.

Writing about the story/narrative

I would strongly advise you to read my section on the **structure and themes of the novel here** before writing about the effects the narrative structure of the book creates. There are many, many things to say about the story of the book, but you should think about your own personal response as well: what did you find the most engaging parts of the novel and why? Look back over the notes you have made while you read the novel and use them to shape an original response. You need to avoid just re-telling the story, which is very easy to do in highly pressurised situations and you're not thinking straight!

Writing about the characterisations

There are many websites which can help you with writing about the characters in the novel, already listed earlier on in this book. What most of them don't say is a very important thing I've already mentioned; Hardy's characters are *not* real people, they are literary creations and we become interested in them because of their similarities and differences. A central technique of Hardy's is to make the reader think about how and why characters are similar and different; we are constantly being invited to compare and contrast characters in our minds. This is a central way that Hardy generates suspense and drama in the novel; the novel is full striking comparisons and contrasts. Where Oak is solid and reliable, Troy is unrealiable and not trustworthy; where Troy is flirtatious and enticing, Boldwood is not. Where Bathsheba is independent and often unpredictable, all the other women in the novel are not. Bathsheba forms a striking contrast with Fanny Robin: they are both in love with Troy, but Bathsheba is rich and free to do as she pleases, while Fanny is poor and trapped by her own situation. Thus we can see that a central technique of Hardy's is to invite the reader to make these comparisons and contrasts between characters; this is how he brings them alive.

Task

Look at some character studies online and devise a chart or **visual organiser** which illustrates the similarities and differences between the major characters, exploring the effects that these similarities and differences have upon the reader.

Writing about the settings

Hardy is famous for his detailed description of his various settings. The air, the smells, the sights and the sounds of the Dorset countryside rise up as we read the pages; we learn about living in the fields, looking after sheep, and running a farm properly. Equally, we learn about the harshness of the settings: while it is a beautiful world that Hardy describes, it is also a brutal one. This is a world where people and sheep die easily; a world fraught with accidents of nature and of man, a place of dangerous fires, life-threatening storms, death-inducing weather. It is also a harsh social world beyond the confines of the Weatherbury Farm: Fanny dies in childbirth largely because she is an unmarried, poor girl who has no family or anyone to turn to.

You can find more information about settings here:

Task

Look carefully at the use of settings in the novel; what purpose do they serve? Why does Hardy set particular scenes in particular settings? Think also about the time of day/night he sets his scenes; how does the time of day/night create certain effects?

Love and Fate

Two central themes that Hardy explores are those of love and fate. They are inextricably inter-twined. It is worth re-reading the first part of my section on **Structure and Theme** to understand how and why this is so. It is also worth looking for specific phrases and words which suggest these themes.

Task

Look back over the novel, and work out when and where the themes of love and fate arise; they inform just about every chapter. For example, we see in the very first chapter the seeds of Oak's love for Bathsheba in the way that he looks at her and we see this love develop over the whole of the book. His love manifests itself in a very different way to Boldwood and Troy. Hardy invites us to think about the nature of love in the novel: is love the equivalent of sexual attraction? Is love about fidelity? Is love about control? Equally fate plays a huge part in the novel; the reversal of Oak's fortunes leads him fatefully to take a job on Bathsheba's farm, while Bathsheba's fateful Valentine and her accidental meeting with Troy in the twilight lead to the ultimate tragedy. Devise a visual organiser which charts the moments of love and fate so that you can see clearly on one page where such moments occur, and think about the effect they have upon the reader.

Use of language

Above all, you need to analyse the effects of Hardy's language upon the reader; exploring what the language makes the reader think, feel and see.

Task

Devise a chart/visual organiser/notes on the different types of language Hardy uses in the novel, providing quotes and examples for the following types of language:

Descriptive language: language which describes people, places and situations

Imagery: language which makes comparisons

Important dialogue: important quotes that people say that make the plot move on.

Useful links

These websites contain some incisive analysis on the use of language:
http://www.shmoop.com/far-from-the-madding-crowd/literary-devices.html
http://www.sparknotes.com/lit/maddingcrowd/section12.rhtml
http://www.novelguide.com/far-from-the-madding-crowd/metaphor-analysis

Possible essay titles

To what extent is *Far From The Madding Crowd* a novel about love?

To what extent does *Far From The Madding Crowd* deploy the conventions of the pastoral?

To what extent is the novel a melodrama?

'*Far From The Madding Crowd* is primarily a feminist novel'. Discuss whether you agree with this statement or not.

To what extent is the novel about the conflict between passion and reason?

Compare and contrast the novel with another text which explores the themes of love and fate.

To what extent is *Far From The Madding Crowd* a social commentary and criticism of Victorian society?

To what extent does the novel celebrate the local life of Weatherbury and its surroundings?

Glossary

Agricultural (adj) from "agriculture" or farming, to do with farming, or "farm".

Architect someone who creates plans to be used in making something (such as buildings)

Aroma Smell, usually pleasant smell

Astute Clever

Authorial An adjective meaning 'belonging to the author or writer'

Autobiography A personal account of the author's own life, with the events usually relayed in the order in which they happened

Ballad A long song or poem that tells a story.

Contexts The worlds from which a text is created and emerges; the social, biographical and literary background to a text

Embodiment a new personification of a familiar idea; Troy is the embodiment of sexual prowess with his sword because he is so attractive and skilful; his actions with the sword reveal that his skills as a lover

Establishment A group of people in power who make the rules and decide who is in and out of favour

Dynamic Purposeful, energetic

Feminist A person who believes passionately in equal rights for women

Fetishism The practice of using an inanimate object as the focus of sexual pleasure.

Genre Type of text, e.g. horror, sci-fi, Gothic

Gentry The most powerful people in society

Gothic An adjective describing narratives which are full of supernatural happenings and extreme emotions, involving damsels in distress in haunted castles

Hero / heroine The main character (male / female) in a narrative, who exhibits truly fine qualities

Humbled Brought down low

Incarceration Imprisonment

Infatuation A sudden, uncontrollable passion for someone or something

Idyll An idyll or idyl (or) (from Greek eidyllion, little picture) is a short poem, descriptive of rustic life, written in the style of Theocritus's short pastoral poems, the Idylls.

Imagery All the poetic devices in a text, in particular the visual images created for the reader's mind to feed on and the comparisons that make a reader think and reflect upon an issue

Implicit implied though not directly expressed; inherent in the nature of something; "an implicit agreement not to raise the subject"

Immortalise To make live forever, to bring fame to

Malt-house An old fashioned drinking den or pub

Materialistic Obsessed with material things, with acquiring things, greedy

Melodrama A story with extreme emotional events and characters, e.g. suicides, threats, blackmail, mad wives, lustful husbands

Mundane Ordinary

Novel A made-up, extended story

Ostracized to be made an outsider

Pastoral A poem describing the life and manners of shepherds; a poem in which the speakers assume the character of shepherds; an idyll; a bucolic;

Phallic symbol A symbol for the penis, or male desire

Preoccupied Caught up in your own thoughts, thinking about other things

Protagonist The main character

Radical Extreme (politically or otherwise)

Realism In literature, a movement which aimed to simulate 'reality' in fiction

Saliently Relevantly

Rural Of the country

Satire A work which mocks or ridicules (usually humorously) an individual or a prevailing trend (adj. satirical)

Seductive Attractive, alluring, tempting

Sensual Attractive and engaging the senses

Serial form Producing a novel in weekly or monthly instalments

Sexual awakening Learning about sex

Sexual prowess Sexual power, being good in bed

Stability Reliability

Social position Where people are ranked in society, their position of importance relative to other people

Socialist A person who believes in socialism, who argues for social justice

Stereotype An author's method of treating a character so that the character is immediately identified with a group. A character may be associated with a group through accent, food choices, style of dress, or any readily identifiable group characteristic. For example, Troy could be considered a stereotype because many soldiers were considered to be sexually confident 'cads' or bad men. Troy is a stereotype in this sense.

Tragic in tone Extremely sad in atmosphere

Traumatized Very upset

Subdued Quiet, beaten down

Subversive Troublesome, rebellious, seeking to overthrow a current system

Symbolic Representative of a particular issue or message, e.g. Troy's sword is a symbol for his penis!

Theme An important idea in a text

Tone An atmosphere conveyed in the writing

Turbulent Stormy

Vivacious Very lively

Victorian Belonging to the UK's Victorian era (i.e. the reign of Queen Victoria, 1837–1901)

Voyeuristic Finding it pleasurable to spy on someone, often for sexual pleasure

About the Author

Francis Gilbert is a Lecturer in Education at Goldsmiths, University of London, teaching on the PGCE Secondary English programme and the MA in Children's Literature with Professor Michael Rosen. Previously, he worked for a quarter of a century in various English state schools teaching English and Media Studies to 11-18 year olds. He has also moonlighted as a journalist, novelist and social commentator both in the UK and international media. He is the author of *Teacher On The Run*, *Yob Nation*, *Parent Power*, *Working The System -- How To Get The Very Best State Education for Your Child*, and a novel about school, *The Last Day Of Term*. His first book, *I'm A Teacher, Get Me Out Of Here* was a big hit, becoming a bestseller and being serialised on Radio 4. In his role as an English teacher, he has taught many classic texts over the years and has developed a great many resources to assist readers with understanding, appreciating and responding to them both analytically and creatively. This led him to set up his own small publishing company FGI Publishing (fgipublishing.com) which has published his study guides as well as a number of books by other authors, including Roger Titcombe's *Learning Matters* and Tim Cadman's *The Changes*.

He is the co-founder, with Melissa Benn and Fiona Millar, of The Local Schools Network, **www.localschoolsnetwork.org.uk**, a blog that celebrates non-selective state schools, and also has his own website, **www.francisgilbert.co.uk** and a Mumsnet blog, **www.talesbehindtheclassroomdoor.co.uk**.

He has appeared numerous times on radio and TV, including Newsnight, the Today Programme, Woman's Hour and the Russell Brand Show. In June 2015, he was awarded a PhD in Creative Writing and Education by the University of London.

Printed in Great Britain
by Amazon